WILLIAM S. McFEELY is Dean of Faculty and Professor of History at Mt. Holyoke College. Before taking his present post, he was Associate Professor of History and American Studies at Yale University.

YANKEE STEPFATHER

GENERAL O. O. HOWARD

(Reproduced with the permission of the Library of Congress)

YANKEE STEPFATHER

General O. O. Howard
and the Freedmen

by William S. McFeely

The Norton Library

W · W · NORTON & COMPANY · INC ·
NEW YORK

BOOKS THAT LIVE

The Norton imprint on a book means that in the publisher's
estimation it is a book not for a single season but for the years.

W. W. NORTON & COMPANY, INC.

SBN 393 00537 2

PRINTED IN THE UNITED STATES OF AMERICA

1 2 3 4 5 6 7 8 9 0

FOR MARY

Preface

Many people helped me with this study and I am deeply grateful. Richard Harwell made available the O. O. Howard Papers not only in the days when they were in the attic of Bowdoin's old library, but also since their move to the excellent new building, where the college's important manuscript collections are maintained in accordance with the highest standards of research scholarship. The loan of the Howard letterbooks for the period of the Freedmen's Bureau was an unusual courtesy, but it is even more pleasant to read the General's letters on his own campus in Brunswick. Judith A. Schiff and her colleagues in the Sterling Memorial Library at Yale were always most helpful, and so too were the people at the Library of Congress.

W. Saxton Seward of New York City graciously made available the relevant volumes of his grandfather's fascinating eighty-year diary. I am delighted, too, to add my name to the long list of Reconstruction historians who owe thanks to Sara Dunlap Jackson. She is an archivist of great professional devotion and skill. Her ability to find, in the Freedmen's Bureau Records in the National Archives, exactly the document needed borders on the uncanny. And a special word of thanks is due Lottie Kemp. Meeting Washington Kemp through her reminiscences was, like meeting Willard Saxton in his diary, a strangely moving experience. Those two Reconstruction grandfathers were not great men, but they were two ordinary Americans, black and white, not at all afraid to share their land with each other.

Norman Holmes Pearson was sustaining throughout, and so too were John Morton Blum and Howard R. Lamar. Thanks of a special sort are due Sheldon Hackney for never once asking how it was going. Staughton Lynd read the study in an earlier version and his thoughtful comments were most encouraging, as were

Preface

those of Daniel T. Rodgers. Wilton B. Fowler read a later manuscript with close attention and his critical comments were invaluable. I am also much indebted to John and LaWanda Cox for their criticism. I truly wish that we could agree about the man to whom they introduced me. Anne J. Granger, with much goodwill, typed the manuscript which Mark Klugheit helped prepare for the publisher. The errors which remain are mine.

My greatest thanks are due two southern friends who dealt with this Yankee with remarkable patience. Willie Lee Rose helped me think through many troubling issues, and her charming encouragement often arrived at critical moments. I do not know how to thank C. Vann Woodward adequately. My debt to him, not only for his advice and assistance every step of the way but also for his deep human concern for the issue central to this study, is immense. I have been a burden, but I cannot say with honesty that I regret a minute of it.

W. S. M.

New Haven, Connecticut
January 1, 1968

List of Abbreviations

AHR	American Historical Review
AJ Papers	Andrew Johnson Papers (microfilm by the Library of Congress)
BRFAL	National Archives, Record Group 105, Bureau of Refugees, Freedmen and Abandoned Lands
Charles Howard Papers	Charles H. Howard Papers Bowdoin College Library Brunswick, Maine
JSH	Journal of Southern History
LC	Library of Congress
MVHR	Mississippi Valley Historical Review (Journal of American History)
OOH Papers	Oliver Otis Howard Papers Bowdoin College Library Brunswick, Maine
Saxton Diary	Manuscript Diary of S. Willard Saxton

Contents

Introduction

Black Americans did not have much of a chance on their drive to achieve equality in the First Reconstruction. At the close of the Civil War, many white Americans were happy to help them celebrate their emancipation, but the freedmen were neither invited to share a reconstructed land nor given the opportunity to build their own new Canaans on empty lands, as Englishmen had been able to do two centuries before. The experience of slavery had given the Negroes little to equip them to assert their demands on the nation, and neither they nor their white friends could make such an assertion without other white men feeling that their interests were being threatened.

As the war ended, the nation did make one attempt to build an institution that would enable Negro Americans to struggle, with some hope of success, for the social, economic, and political rewards in a community offering equal opportunities to its citizens. In May 1865 Congress created the Bureau of Refugees, Freedmen and Abandoned Lands, which everyone called the Freedmen's Bureau. This national effort preceded the experiments of Radical Reconstruction which, if nothing else, gave the American Negroes of the Second Reconstruction, a century later, a political past to reactivate. Despite the great worth of such innovations as the grant of the franchise to the freedmen, the radical program for the rebuilding of the South did represent a national responsibility shrugged off on the states. Congress was the architect of the effort but it did not hold the nation to the task of sustaining the egalitarian programs it called on the southern states to undertake. The Freedmen's Bureau, the national institution designed to bring the new black citizens into the nation, came earlier.

In 1903, in W. E. B. DuBois' *The Souls of Black Folk* was an elegant essay, "Of the Dawn of Freedom." As he described his "tale," it was "an account of that government of men called the Freedmen's Bureau—one of the most singular and interesting attempts made by a great nation to grapple with vast problems of race and social condition."[1] To DuBois the Bureau had been the freedmen's, and its purpose had been to make them truly free. It had failed. "For this much all men know: despite compromise, war and struggle, the Negro is not free."

By "black farmers are peons" and Negroes "are a segregated, servile caste" DuBois meant that the Freedmen's Bureau had not done what it should have. Its legacies were two: the still unsolved problems of the American Negroes and the striving necessary to solve them. DuBois considered that the Bureau had sought to do its task, but forces outside the agency had prevented it from succeeding. He called on his own long generation to do the work the Bureau "did not do because it could not."[2]

To DuBois, the Bureau had failed because it did too little. Making prophecy of history, he wanted the beginnings he thought had been made by the Bureau to predict the great changes necessary if the Negroes were to gain their freedom. He saw that the Bureau should have been a medium of social change and not just the agent of reconciliation between ex-slaves and their former masters. Fifty years later, when a full study of the Freedmen's Bureau was written, this view of the agency was still rejected. George R. Bentley had a different use in mind in *A History of the Freedmen's Bureau.* Judging the agency by its effect on white Southerners and their mores, as he understood them, Bentley concluded that the agency "sought too much for the Negro too soon."[3] Claiming that Negro aspirations were exploited by radical Republican outside agitators, he did not appreciate, as did DuBois, that those aspirations were no less real because they were exploitable.

1. W. E. B. DuBois, "Of the Dawn of Freedom," *The Souls of Black Folk* (Chicago, 1903), pp. 13–40. Originally entitled "The Freedmen's Bureau," the essay first appeared in 1901, *Atlantic Monthly,* 87 (March 1901), 354–65.

2. DuBois, p. 40.

3. George R. Bentley, *A History of the Freedmen's Bureau* (Philadelphia, 1955), p. 214.

Bentley would have had the Bureau feed and school the freedmen and protect their persons but otherwise retard their advance toward equality. He remained convinced, as Paul S. Peirce had been in 1904, that the Bureau was, fundamentally, a southern task force of the Republican party.[4] Bentley retained his commitment to the old claim that the white South knew best about its Negroes. The nation, he concluded, would have been better advised to leave the freedman "free to be influenced by the normal wiles of politicians representing the people of his home land."[5]

One of the theses of this study is that the Freedmen's Bureau did acquiesce to exactly what Bentley prescribed. Before 1865 was over, Andrew Johnson, with great skill and understanding of southern politics, put the freedmen under the discipline of southern politicians whom he had restored to power. The Freedmen's Bureau had not stopped the delivery of the Negro labor force into the hands of Johnson's planter and businessman allies. On the contrary, it was used by the President to accomplish this purpose.

The Freedmen's Bureau did not light DuBois' dawn and neither did it feed "the flame of race hostility," as Bentley claimed.[6] Instead, it banked the fires of the freedmen's aspirations. Only the freedmen prevented the fire from going out. By insisting that the Freedmen's Bureau was theirs, even in the face of evidence that it was not, the Negroes forced the men of the Bureau to reckon with them and attempt to reverse the national government's course. But this attempted reversal came only after enormous damage had been done. The white men of the Freedmen's Bureau had let great opportunities go by.

By staying doggedly loyal to the Freedmen's Bureau and its Commissioner, the Negroes forced the nation to recognize that they had economic, political, legal, and educational needs and that there was a national obligation to meet them. As long as the agency existed, that obligation, however dishonored, was still on the books. To remove it, the Freedmen's Bureau was destroyed.

4. Paul S. Peirce, *The Freedmen's Bureau: A Chapter in the History of Reconstruction* (Iowa City, 1904), p. 171.

5. Bentley, p. 214.

6. Ibid.

Other researchers, working at the same time that Bentley wrote, did at last heed DuBois' plea that the Bureau should be judged in terms of the opportunities it offered the freedmen. Two historians, John and LaWanda Cox, who pioneered fifty years after DuBois marked the trail, wrote an article inviting a reappraisal of the Freedmen's Bureau.[7] They suggested in this essay, as did Mrs. Cox in a later article, "The Promise of Land for the Freedmen," that the Bureau had the wherewithal to provide the freedmen with so sound a beginning in freedom that, had it been put to use, possibly no Second Reconstruction would have been needed.[8]

The "forty-acre program" required under the Act of March 3, 1865, creating the Freedmen's Bureau was, according to Mrs. Cox, "a plan that would aid the Negro without compromising his new status as free man, would safeguard him from abuse, would foil the selfish designs of northern speculators, and would transform the South from a plantation economy to an economy of small, family-owned farms." This act was "a victory . . . for that commitment to freedom and equality inherent in the American heritage."[9] Whether the men chosen to administer the Bureau had a similar understanding of the commitment and were prepared to honor it as they got down to work remained unanswered.

The Coxes did their research in the papers of Oliver Otis Howard, the Maine general who was the agency's only commissioner, and titled their seminal article "General Howard and the 'Misrepresented Bureau,' " a phrase the General himself had used. These historians, like Howard before them, called for a better understanding of what he sought to accomplish as commissioner of the Freedmen's Bureau. Such an understanding is the purpose of this study. No attempt has been made to do what Bentley and the authors of the studies of the Bureau in the various states have already done. This is neither an administrative history of the

7. John and LaWanda Cox, "General Howard and the 'Misrepresented Bureau,' " *JSH, 19* (1953), 427–56.

8. LaWanda Cox, "The Promise of Land for the Freedmen," *MVHR, 45* (1958), 413–40.

9. Ibid., p. 440.

agency nor an account of all its work; it is rather an inquiry into the purposes of the Freedmen's Bureau and its performance in pursuit of them. Regarding General Howard as the key to understanding the work that he led, the research focused on him and his leadership of the agency in Washington. The conclusion reached was that much of the work of General Howard in the Freedmen's Bureau served to preclude rather than promote Negro freedom.

Howard's biographer, John A. Carpenter, never faltered in his admiration for his subject. Assuming the worth of the Christian General's faith and finding him "ever mindful of his reliance on his avowed master, Jesus Christ," Carpenter judges Howard a hero.[10] He acknowledges "a little known fact that Howard and his subordinates often got criticism from [those] . . . concerned about the freedmen.[11] These attacks by friends of the freedmen who thought the Commissioner unmindful of the needs of the Negroes, like the complaints of those who accused Howard of favoring the freedmen, are cited by Carpenter only as an "example of what Howard was up against."[12] The Commissioner is admired for having withstood attack from both sides.

Carpenter builds a strong defense for Howard against white complaints that the Bureau's government of the Negroes was lax, but he does not explore the Commissioner's neglect of the freedmen during the tightening up process. Howard is applauded for having "bent every effort to root out [of the Bureau] the undesirables and the misfits."[13] In depicting him as a valiant foe of corruption, Carpenter does not disclose that most of the men Howard removed from the South were considered undesirable and unfit, not because of laziness or dishonesty, but because when they tried to help the freedmen, powerful white men complained. It is no accident that C. W. Buckley, who was accused by Johnson's emissaries in the South of owning a plantation while serving

10. John A. Carpenter, *Sword and Olive Branch: Oliver Otis Howard* (Pittsburgh, 1964), p. vii.

11. Ibid., p. 148

12. Ibid., p. 149.

13. Ibid., p. 152.

in the Bureau, had advocated confiscation so that Negroes, who "by patient industry" had earned the right, might be made "proprietors of the soil."[14]

Recognizing Howard's enormous task in the Bureau, Carpenter accords the General the praise for which he asked: "My glory, if I ever have any, consists in results attained; and the results in the case of the Freedmen's Bureau are, for me, more marked than those of the war."[15] The present study conforms to the General's delineation. It deals with Howard as commissioner of the Freedmen's Bureau. That post was the focus of his widespread efforts to minister to the needs of the southern freedmen.

It was not as an interested private citizen but as a government official that Howard had the power and responsibility to define his own and the nation's commitment to the ex-slaves. The story of Howard's efforts in his church, at Howard University, with the Freedman's Savings Bank, and as Superintendent at West Point, as revealing as it is of northern white attitudes toward the Negro over the span of the Reconstruction era, is auxiliary to his post in Andrew Johnson's administration. All of these other activities derived from his identification with the freedmen and their Bureau. Confident that his was a nation with a mission, Howard, as head of the Freedmen's Bureau, viewed the freedmen and their problems as a great opportunity for Christian service. He depended on "the genuine, practical spirit of the Lord Jesus Christ to make our people agree to reconstruct our Government."[16]

In this study there was every disposition to give Howard and his colleagues in the Freedmen's Bureau the benefit of the doubt in the hope of documenting the "legacy of service" which DuBois said the Bureau bequeathed to us.[17] The days of jubilee in celebra-

14. Report of James B. Steedman and J. S. Fullerton (Ala.), dated 20 July 1866, New Orleans, La., undated, unidentified news clipping, OOH Papers; C. W. Buckley to T. W. Conway, 18 June 1865, quoted in *Philadelphia Inquirer*, 17 July 1865.

15. O. O. Howard to G. W. Williams, 25 Nov. 1886, quoted in Carpenter, p. 168.

16. O. O. Howard addressing a rally in celebration of emancipation, 27 Apr. 1865, Oliver Otis Howard, *Autobiography of Oliver Otis Howard* (2 vols. New York, 1908), 2, 325.

17. DuBois, p. 41.

tion of emancipation were over when Howard began his work in the Bureau; perhaps his story revealed patterns of responsible thinking relevant to later times. This hope led to disappointment; both Howard and his faith failed the freedmen.

The failure was not the result of conspiracy or hypocrisy, although there was some of both. General Howard acknowledged a responsibility to the freedmen and, to his credit, continued to do so when he wrote his *Autobiography* forty years after his bureau experience, a time when such a commitment was even more embarrassing than in 1865. The bureau men had been subjected to intense pressures from those outside the agency who did not want it to assist the freedmen's advance, but this alone does not account for the result. The Bureau itself failed the freedmen, and the failure was that of many men, among them General Howard himself. He did not meet the responsibility to the freedmen that was his as commissioner of the Freedmen's Bureau.

In the last days of the Bureau's life, General Howard, ironically, was vilified by racists who were determined to drive from the government, and particularly from the army, a man who to them represented the intrusion of the Negro into places where he did not belong.[18] The Negro got little useful help from the General in the 1870s, but Howard's enemies, "who hate the blacks," were not entirely off the mark.[19] Howard had come to think that he did personify a faltering national moral responsibility to the freedmen despite the fact that after March 1867 he had lost the authority to implement it.[20]

Before the advent of Military Reconstruction, General Howard for two years was commissioner of a federal agency with resources for achieving much economic and social reform for the freedmen. Congress had "committed" to his Bureau "the control of all subjects relating to [the] . . . freedmen."[21] To know the true character of the nation's commitment to its new citizens just after the

18. Carpenter, pp. 200–08, 220–25; *American Missionary* (Aug. 1870), p. 178.
19. O. O. Howard to S. P. Lee, 29 Dec. 1873, OOH Papers.
20. O. O. Howard to Edgar Ketchum, 12 July 1870, OOH Papers.
21. *13 United States Statutes at Large* (*U.S. Stat.*), 507–09.

Civil War, it is important to scrutinize Howard's performance in the Freedmen's Bureau.

This is a study of those years in the Freedmen's Bureau in which Howard had the power to change the freedmen's position in the nation. It is not an exposé of a knave, but rather a record of naïveté and misunderstanding, timidity, misplaced faith, disloyalty to subordinates who were loyal to the freedmen, and an attempt to diminish the Negroes' aspirations. The sobering fact is that it is the record of the man regarded with remarkable unanimity by Americans as the best man for the job.

No historian has offered a substitute who he thinks would have been markedly better at the job than Howard. In the "dark and bloody ground" of Reconstruction history, where heroes topple daily, Howard has remained the recipient of high praise even by those critical of the Bureau.[22] James G. Randall and David Donald, students of Reconstruction who built their conclusions on a review of a wide range of scholarship of the period, call Howard a man "of the finest character."[23] Kenneth Stampp says that the Bureau was "competently and conscientiously directed by General O. O. Howard," and George Bentley, less inclined than Stampp to admire what both regarded as the radical objectives of the Bureau, says firmly that "charitable, conscientious and kind Howard surely was."[24]

Howard's contemporaries were just as complimentary. Abolitionists, workers for the freedmen's aid societies, Southerners eager to forget the war, Northerners prejudiced against Negroes but troubled by the plight of the destitute ex-slaves (and those not so troubled), members of his own bureau staff, leaders of all the large Protestant denominations, senators and congressmen, and finally the freedmen themselves concurred that he was "a

22. This literature is skillfully canvassed in Bernard Weisberger, "The Dark and Bloody Ground of Reconstruction Historiography," *JSH*, 25 (1959), 427–47.

23. James G. Randall and David Donald, *The Civil War and Reconstruction* (Boston, 1961), p. 576.

24. Kenneth M. Stampp, *The Era of Reconstruction: 1865–1877* (New York, 1965), p. 132; Bentley, p. 56.

splendid man," one in whom they could rest "entire confidence"
as he entered his "humane and difficult service."[25] The *New York
Times* saluted the "eminent fitness . . . of this Christian patriot."[26]
Even the skeptical spokesman for the well-educated and discerning bilingual Negro community in New Orleans said that General Howard "metrité les éloges de tous les vrais amis de l'abolition."[27] Few Americans disagreed with Henry Ward Beecher's
pronouncement that Howard "is of all men yet mentioned the
very one."[28]

The services of Oliver Otis Howard were what the nation was
prepared to give its freedmen. By taking measure of Howard and
his work in the Bureau, we make a troubling assessment of
America during Reconstruction.

25. W. T. Sherman to O. O. Howard, 17 May 1865, OOH Papers; Saxton
Diary, 20 July 1866; Charles Sumner to O. O. Howard, 15 July 1865, OOH
Papers.
26. *New York Times*, 15 May 1865.
27. *New Orleans Tribune* (*La Tribune de la N. Orleans*), 20 July 1865.
28. H. W. Beecher to E. M. Stanton, 3 May 1865, OOH Papers.

1. The Grand Review

Otis Howard did not enjoy his greatest day. He did not, though there was splendor to spare in Washington on May 24, 1865. The Civil War was over and won, and the capital was gaudily celebrating the victory. The people of the city turned out to hail the triumphal entry of the nation's returning armies. Light coming through bullet-shredded flags and the cool shine of rifles denied the discordant dirt and heat of recent battles, and there were choruses of great cheers which rolled on through the day.[1]

As General Howard rode beside General Sherman at the head of all the armies of the West, he had as much right to feel exultant as any man. He was treated to the exhilarating experience of hearing cheers shouted for him alone. Washingtonians called out his name; he knew they already recognized him as the commissioner of the new Freedmen's Bureau (and were, no doubt, sizing him up).[2]

He sat a horse well—that gave him confidence—and he rode with a great warrior at the head of a great army, up to the White House to be greeted by his President. But instead of feeling triumphant, this hero was out of sorts. He had wanted to step back from his new post for the day and lead his old Army of the Tennessee but deferred to Sherman's respect for the prerogatives of his successor, the flamboyant John A. Logan, and rode instead at Sherman's side.[3] As the procession began, a girl stepped out from the crowd and offered Howard a wreath of flowers for his

1. Marian Hooper to Mary Louisa Shaw, 24 May 1865, Ward Thoron, ed., *The Letters of Mrs. Henry Adams, 1865–1883* (Boston, 1936), p. 8; "The Grand Review of Washington," unpublished, undated ms., OOH Papers; Montgomery Meigs Diary, 24 May 1865, LC.

2. Washington *Evening Star*, 24 May 1865.

3. W. T. Sherman to O. O. Howard, 20 May 1865, OOH Papers; Howard, *Autobiography*, 2, 211.

horse. The battle of Fair Oaks had cost him an arm, and he could not manage his horse and the flowers too. He smiled, passed the girl by, and, doing so, reminded the crowd of the grimmer face of war.[4]

Once before, his missing arm had been read as a symbol of sacrifice by a great crowd. In January 1864 Howard had taken part in a rally for the Civil War's YMCA, the Christian Commission, at the Academy of Music in Philadelphia.[5] The beautiful hall, young then, and wearing bunting, was filled with enthusiastic people who applauded the officers and famous preachers of the Commission.[6] Howard, who was not well known (he was only a substitute for General Clinton B. Fisk), was there as a representative of the men at the front.[7] The mother of one of his close friends who had been killed in the war was in the audience and, with considerable gallantry, she wrote to Howard's wife of his triumph: "when he came forward . . . with his empty sleeve . . . the whole people rose and echoed their welcome."[8]

This assembly in Philadelphia had a common point of view which the people watching the Grand Review had not. Many Americans, Howard among them, were persuaded that a perfect faith in God would, some day, manifest itself in the creation of a perfect society in America. Not even the horror of civil war disillusioned them; on the contrary, it provided them with the most important (if most terrible) test which they must pass to demonstrate their faith. The members of the Christian Commission gathered in the Academy were anxious to hear, from a general just back from battle, how well the test was being met.

Cautiously, Howard, slight and young, began to speak. With an unimpressive voice, taken as a confirmation of his sincerity,

4. Washington *Evening Star,* 24 May 1865.

5. *Philadelphia Inquirer,* 29 Jan. 1864; G. H. Stuart to O. O. Howard, 30 Jan. 1864, OOH Papers.

6. Susan V. Greble to Mrs. O. O. Howard, 30 Jan. 1864, OOH Papers.

7. *Philadelphia Inquirer,* 29 Jan. 1864.

8. Susan V. Greble to Mrs. O. O. Howard, 30 Jan. 1864, OOH Papers; Benson J. Lossing, *Memoir of Lieut.-Col. John T. Greble* (Philadelphia, 1870), pp. 95–99.

Howard made the progress of the war a metaphor for the troubled state of the nation's soul.[9] He told his audience that the patriotic zeal of the early days of the war had not been enough to prevent the North's share of defeats. These he saw as the product of a "fearful power of evil," which brought with it "demoralizing tendencies [which] crushed out the principles of good in the soldier's heart."[10] As a purpose equal to the task of winning the war, the saving of the Union was not sufficient. As he put it later, in a letter from the front, "I fear and tremble . . . that we have not virtue enough in this country to stand the trial."[11]

To win the war, Howard was sure the nation needed a moral cause. In his address, he congratulated the Christian Commission for giving the men hope of personal religious salvation and, thereby, giving them the will to achieve victory. This was no Abolitionist exhortation. Nowhere in Howard's speech did he even hint that slavery was the cause of the nation's damnation or that emancipation would accomplish its redemption. There was no indication that a year from then Howard would ask Americans like these to support him in a moral enterprise in which the freedmen would be substituted for the soldiers' souls as the object of their enthusiasm.[12] His audience was with him. His speech met with great enthusiasm and, later, Howard could remember that these people cheered him as they did no other man who spoke at the rally.

No one overshadowed Howard that night in Philadelphia in 1864, but John Logan was a massive suggestion of those in Washington who would. The little girl did not have to turn back into the crowd with her flowers after Howard had gone by. Logan, coming along in the lead of Howard's men, leaned down from his gray stallion and, with extravagant graciousness, accepted both the wreath and the crowd's adoration.[13]

9. Susan V. Greble to Mrs. O. O. Howard, 30 Jan. 1864, OOH Papers.

10. *Philadelphia Inquirer*, 29 Jan. 1864.

11. O. O. Howard to James G. Blaine, 24 Aug. 1864, OOH Papers.

12. *Philadelphia Inquirer*, 10 June 1865.

13. *New York Times*, 25 May 1865; Washington *Evening Star*, 24 May 1865.

"Black Jack" Logan had demonstrated that there were tasks that Howard could not handle. Riding up Pennsylvania Avenue in the Grand Review, Howard already had grounds for misgivings about his new assignment in the Freedmen's Bureau. Perhaps it was an insult. He knew there were men with whom he had fought who thought working with the freedmen was no job for a man— certainly not for an army man.

During the closing winter of the war, Howard was aware that he had to construct a peacetime career which would equal his wartime major-generalship. He seemed lucky. He was one of the first generals to be given an important postwar job, but it was neither an undertaking for which West Point had prepared him nor one which many West Pointers would respect. Philadelphians had responded to his rhetorical abstraction of Christian service, but the freedmen's troubles were as solid and old as the land. Howard had high expectations of the people in the Academy of Music, but he had been around the army long enough to know what many of these parading men thought of sharing that land with Negroes.[14]

With Sherman, Howard joined President Johnson, General Grant, and Secretary Stanton in the White House reviewing stand.[15] He watched men he had led across Georgia and through the Carolinas march up Pennsylvania Avenue. His new responsibilities were not yet visible.

From antiquity to Verdi, Negroes were manacled slaves in triumphal entries. Two years after the Emancipation Proclamation, this would have been a miscasting, but the black man was not left out entirely. In the line of march were detachments of contraband laborers with shovels rather than rifles on their shoulders; Negro soldiers had been edited from the score.[16] At the end of one brigade, a half-dozen colored women walked along

14. His doubts were to be demonstrated on 9 June 1865 in a street fight between men of General W. S. Hancock's 15th Corps and Negro residents of Washington. *Philadelphia Inquirer*, 12 June 1865.

15. *New York Times*, 25 May 1865; Marian Hooper to Mary Louisa Shaw, 24 May 1865, Thoron, p. 6.

16. *New York Times*, 25 and 26 May 1865.

in bandanas and patched dresses. Behind them, male contrabands led two little mules with pickaninnies astride; hardtack boxes, their sides slatted, were piled up behind the children and game cocks stuck out their heads, as did two young 'coons. To this baggage was tied the lead of a goat who trotted along beside.[17] A salute to the President was reserved for generals as the troops passed the White House, but now one of the Negro boys turned and tipped his cap to Andrew Johnson.[18] The crowds roared their delight; they had been treated to a classic American comedy, with hardly a symbol missing.[19]

Otis Howard never did have much of a sense of humor, and these contrabands were a parody of millions of Negroes whose troubles had not seemed funny to him in Georgia, the Carolinas, or Virginia. As Howard understood his new job, he was to assume for the nation the responsibility for the freedmen, which had accrued to armies like his own as they invaded the South. The personal ambitions of the young General were invested in this commitment to assist the freedmen and its genuineness was important to him. Here, only a month after the end of the war that ended slavery, the Commissioner of the Freedmen's Bureau was mocked, as his clients were paraded before him like clowns.

The next morning O. O. Howard was back at his desk in the Bureau's office for his first meeting with his assistant commissioners. No doubt he was more eager than before to take his job with dead seriousness.[20] Doubts could not be given standing room or splendid abstractions of equality might trip over contraband pack trains. Work had to begin or the nation's commitment to do something for its freedmen might get hidden away as neatly as the Negroes had been disguised in yesterday's parade. Howard

17. Ibid., 25 May 1865.
18. Marian Hooper to Mary Louisa Shaw, 24 May 1865, Thoron, p. 8.
19. This incident is not mentioned in the brief account of the Grand Review in the General's *Autobiography*. In an unpublished manuscript he spoke of "little scenes [which] enliven the day" and mentioned the goats and gamecocks but referred to the Negroes as "families of freed slaves." Howard, *Autobiography*, 2, 212; "The Grand Review of Washington," OOH Papers.
20. *New York Times*, 26 May 1865.

counted on that commitment. If his job was not going to make him a failure and a fool, he had to make the commitment a reality. He had to state its terms to his subordinates in the Bureau and to the public.

At first glance, Howard and his colleagues did not seem much different from other army officers on more conventional peacetime military assignments. Most of them were young men who had fought hard in a terrible war and, having become accustomed to rapid promotions, felt entitled to successful peacetime careers. The war had not made them zealots either for their own cause or for that of others. They had experienced chaos and watched killings; they wanted order and security. None of them was the kind to ally himself to a cause with no hope. These organization men assumed that their postwar enterprise would succeed.

Howard's commands had been informal and his relationships with his staff members were intimate.[21] Men such as Thomas Osborn and Eliphalet Whittlesey were not merely trusted subordinates; they were close friends.[22] So too were General William E. Strong, the Bureau's inspector general, Colonel James Scott Fullerton, Howard's adjutant general, who had recently written to the General, "my relations have been so pleasant with no officer in the Army as with you," and two of his personal aides, Major Harry Stinson (after whom Howard named a son) and Lieutenant Joseph Sladen.[23]

Orlando Brown was to be the assistant commissioner for Virginia, and Howard had a specific order to give him: he had already promised Francis B. Knowlton, a young Congregationalist minister in the American Missionary Association, that he would

21. C. H. Howard to his mother, 29 Dec. 1861, Charles Howard Papers.
22. Thomas W. Osborn ms. diary, Bowdoin College Library, Brunswick, Me.
23. Howard, *Autobiography*, 2, 125; David P. Conyngham, *Sherman's March Through the South* (New York, 1865), p. 304; J. S. Fullerton to O. O. Howard, 11 Feb. 1865, OOH Papers; G. H. Balloch to O. O. Howard, 22 May 1865, OOH Papers. Stinson, Mrs. James G. Blaine's nephew, died in Florida in 1866—Harry Stinson Howard was born in 1869. Sladen was still Howard's aide when the General negotiated with Cochise in 1872.

get Brown to give him a larger building for his school.[24] Knowlton, like Howard, was from Maine and he had called on Howard not only to plead for the new school but also to meet and appraise the new Commissioner. Home-state loyalty no doubt contributed to his praise. "Howard is *the man* for this business," he told Senator Fessenden. Knowlton was glad that the Commissioner was an army man and approved of the fact that the assistant commissioners would also be army men. His conversation laid to rest any doubts that he may have shared with radicals who were dismayed by Howard's astringent first circular warning that the freedmen would not be "sustained in idleness," and he was optimistic: "I have had a free conference with Gen. Howard; his views and plans are practical & right, in my judgment. He says he will give the freedmen *protection, land & schools,* as far and as fast as he can—& his assistants he says are men whom he knows sympathize with him in this work."[25]

Although he never spelled it out, Howard considered sympathy with the freedmen's plight a requisite for service in the Freedmen's Bureau. That such a qualification for such a job is too obvious to need stating is, unfortunately, not true. One of Howard's chief duties—one which he performed with small success—was to keep the governing of the freedmen in the hands of men whose sympathies were even minimally with the Negroes. Howard worked on the premise that just being a good-hearted young army man was enough to ensure that a man would also be a good assistant commissioner—or even commissioner. He believed sympathy for the work would somehow be converted into acts helpful to the freedmen.

Howard confidently believed such a conversion would take place and would result in the construction of a society satisfactory both to the freedmen and to the white Southerners with whom they would live. It would be like the war, in which bumblings and discouragements and terrible disappointments of defeat had, in the end, brought splendid success. So it would be in the Freed-

24. E. Knowlton to W. P. Fessenden, 20 Mar. 1865, Fessenden Papers, LC.
25. Ibid., 20 May 1865.

men's Bureau. To be successful in the war, it had been necessary to find a moral purpose. For some it had been emancipation of the slaves. For Howard it had been the joint redemption of his men and his country; through the sacrifice of fighting and dying, they and the nation had been saved.[26]

Reconstruction needed a moral issue too, and from platforms across the North and South, Howard planned to articulate this moral in the way that he had spoken to the Christian Commission in Philadelphia during the war. Support for the freedmen—his new job had brought them, rather incidentally, into his moral education—would come as soon as he got his message across. Americans and America could be made better through service to those hurt by slavery and the war.

Meanwhile, with few specific programs to implement, he and his men would start to govern. At the meeting the day after the Grand Review, Howard had gathered together his generals and his staff much as he might have done on any night during the war to encourage his men to meet the challenges of the coming day. The routinely pleasant visit with the President, who greeted them as he might have greeted any new group of officials in his administration, was, similarly, not a time for the defining of duties but for giving to their undertaking an illusion of common purpose.[27]

Nothing was said to shake the optimism of these men anxious to make useful careers for themselves. But their jobs were in the Bureau of Refugees, Freedmen and Abandoned Lands, which everyone already called the Freedmen's Bureau, and freedmen had made Washington laugh just two days before. Their Commissioner knew this, and he also knew that not all those who wished the bureau men well were as sure as he was that all would work out as he hoped.

A week before the Grand Review, Otis Howard rode over into Virginia, where William Tecumseh Sherman had his headquarters. These two men, very unlike and yet loyal to each other,

26. O. O. Howard's address at Gettysburg, 4 July 1865, and *Philadelphia Inquirer,* 7 July 1865.

27. *New York Times,* 26 and 27 May 1866.

talked at length about Howard's new assignment.[28] That night, in
a letter, Sherman, with his intense, driving prose, continued the
conversation of the day. His subject was the Negro, of whom he
had a low opinion. He admonished Howard against making the
Bureau part of any "New Revolution" which would produce another war (in which the "North West may take a different side").
"I am more than usually sensitive on this point," Sherman added,
"because I have realized in our Country that one Class of Men
Makes War and leaves another to fight it out. I am tired of fighting."

Peace, Sherman thought, could be kept only if "the theorists of
New England" were not allowed "to force the Negro on the
South" as something more than a man entitled to "have his own
labor." To insist that the freedmen vote would bring on the new
revolution; to enforce, as Howard contemplated, land redistribution by the sale of confiscated rebel lands to the freedmen would
cost ten times the money received from such sales merely "to pay
the troops that will be needed . . . to maintain possession of the
purchasers." Sherman urged Howard to limit his expectations:
"[T]hough in the kindness of your heart you would alleviate all
the ills of humanity [in which Sherman specifically included
strong prejudice of race] it is not in your power. Nor is it in your
power to fulfill one tenth of the expectations of those who framed
the Bureau."[29]

Private citizens had led the call for a government agency to
aid the freedmen, and congressmen had framed the legislation
that brought it into being, but army men had been selected to
put it into operation. In one sense, these men were responding
simply to a change in military assignment, but each of them knew

28. For a striking picture of the contrast between the two generals, see
Conyngham, p. 327. "Sherman . . . passing up and down, with an unlit cigar
in his mouth, abruptly halting to speak to some of his generals around him.
. . . Above all the men I have ever met that strange face of his is the hardest
to read. . . . Sitting on log . . . was Howard, reading a newspaper and occasionally stopping to answer a question of Sherman's. . . . Howard always
looked the same—the kind, cautious general, the Christian soldier."

29. W. T. Sherman to O. O. Howard, 17 May 1865, OOH Papers.

that there were new, nonmilitary dimensions to the job. As Sherman's warning testified, not every army man thought this new service an opportunity to enhance a career. General Oliver Otis Howard was their commander and his commander, William Tecumseh Sherman, speaking of Howard's Freedmen's Bureau assignment, said to him that he had not known "whether to congratulate you or not but of one thing you may rest assured that you possess my entire confidence and I cannot imagine that, what may involve the future of four million slaves, could be put in more charitable or more conscientious hands."[30]

30. W. T. Sherman to O. O. Howard, 17 May 1865, OOH Papers.

2. O. O. Howard

"Hell, we've got enough major generals up here. What we want is hard tack."[1] This, as the story goes, was the reply of a Union sentry who challenged a coastal boat that was bringing a war secretary and still another major general to join Sherman in Savannah. Otis Howard was one of the major generals who had already been there, and nothing in the history of his service during the Civil War sets him very far apart from his twenty-six colleagues in that crowded city.[2] But another assignment put him to a unique test. Howard became the head of a federal agency charged with the job of creating a new way of life for American Negroes, most of whom lived in the South and had been slaves. It was his work with the men freed by the Civil War that tested him. The freedmen gave Howard his opportunity to be a man apart from other men: to be the hardtack that his country and its new black citizens needed.

That slaves would need assistance once they gained their freedom had been apparent from the earliest days of the war to almost anyone who encountered contraband refugees.[3] After the Emancipation Proclamation created millions of displaced persons, the need became even more obvious, and the American Freedmen's Inquiry Commission was created by executive order on March 16, 1863 to determine what form the help should take.[4] The commissioners were instructed to inspect the conditions

1. W. T. Sherman to Mrs. Sherman, in M. A. DeWolfe Howe, ed., *Home Letters of General Sherman* (New York, 1909), p. 328; Benjamin P. Thomas and Harold M. Hyman, *Stanton: The Life and Times of Lincoln's Secretary of War* (New York, 1962), p. 346.

2. W. T. Sherman, *Memoirs of General William T. Sherman* (2 vols. New York, 1886), 2, 238, 335–40.

3. C. B. Wilder's Ledger of Public Orders at Fortress Monroe, 15 Mar. 1862, Todd Family Papers, Yale University.

4. John G. Sproat, "Blueprint for Radical Reconstruction," *JSH*, 23 (1957), 25–44.

under which the Negroes were living behind Union lines and to "report what measures will best contribute to their protection and improvement" as well as "how they can be most usefully employed in the . . . suppression of the rebellion."[5]

Meeting the latter requirement first, the Inquiry Commission recommended the use of Negro troops and then called for the creation of a federal agency that would protect other ex-slaves and assist them in making a living independent of their masters. The Commission, reflecting on the close interest of Secretary Stanton on its formation, recommended that the agency be established within the War Department.

In December 1863 Congressman T. D. Eliot of Massachusetts introduced a bill to establish such an agency within the War Department. By a small majority, it passed the House of Representatives on March 1, 1864. In the Senate, Charles Sumner's Committee on Slavery and Freedom rewrote the bill and awarded the agency to the Treasury Department.[6]

These two departments had engaged in a jurisdictional dispute over the freedmen all through the war. The War Department argued that the armies met and were impeded by the slaves and therefore should decide what to do with them; the Treasury Department had on its side the logic that, like other forms of seized property, the chattel Negroes should be in its custody. Surprisingly, Charles Sumner, the champion of Negro rights in the Senate, supported the Treasury. Accurately sensing the postwar problems of the freedmen, he insisted that the department which controlled abandoned farmlands should also supervise the freedmen.[7] They should not be separated from their best source of livelihood.

Congress made no decision whether Eliot's plan or Sumner's would prevail before it adjourned in the spring of 1864.[8] When the matter reoccurred in the new session of Congress and the old

5. Willie Lee Rose. *Rehearsal for Reconstruction: The Port Royal Experiment* (Indianapolis, 1964), p. 208; *Official Records of the War of the Rebellion,* Ser. III, 3, 430–54.

6. Bentley, *Freedmen's Bureau,* pp. 36, 39–40.

7. Ibid., p. 40.

8. Ibid., p. 43.

struggle between the Treasury and War Departments resumed, Sumner had still another idea.[9] He proposed that, instead of a bureau, the new agency be made a department with its own secretary of cabinet rank, who would have jurisdiction over both the freedmen and the lands taken by Union armies. This proposal, referred out of the conference committee, passed the House of Representatives but failed in the Senate, where fourteen Republicans (including Lyman Trumbull, who would be the sponsor of a bill to enlarge the Freedmen's Bureau just a year later) joined the Democrats to defeat it.[10] Sumner's plan would have permanently institutionalized the nation's responsibility to its Negroes, and this defeat was a major one.

The task of salvaging something for the freedmen was assumed by Sumner's colleague from Massachusetts, Henry Wilson. As chairman of the Committee on Military Affairs, Wilson favored the War Department over the Treasury. He was willing to trust the freedmen to the Secretary of War, Edwin M. Stanton, a man whom Henry Ward Beecher fulsomely described as having "all the elements of old John Adams, able, staunch, patriotic, full of principle, & always unpopular."[11]

If some of his generals were notoriously antinegro, William Lloyd Garrison attested that the Secretary himself was not, and there was much to be said for the argument that the freedmen needed an army to serve as a police force to protect them.[12] Congress heeded Sumner's warning and gave Stanton's department jurisdiction over the lands as well as the freedmen. From the point of view of the Negroes' welfare, nothing was unpropitious about Wilson's bill, which, in a flurry of preadjournment activity and with little debate, passed both houses of Congress on March 3, 1865.[13]

9. Ibid., p. 46.

10. Ibid., p. 48.

11. H. W. Beecher to Robert Bonner, 20 May 1865, Beecher Family Papers, Yale University.

12. Russell B. Nye, *William Lloyd Garrison and the Humanitarian Reformers* (Boston, 1955), p. 184.

13. Bentley, p. 49.

The bill created the Bureau of Refugees, Freedmen and Abandoned Lands, an agency within the War Department to exist for a year from the end of the war. A commissioner and ten assistant commissioners were to be named by the President with the Senate's consent. This gave the White House a crucial role in determining the operations of the Bureau. The agency was to distribute food, clothing, and fuel to destitute white refugees and freedmen, under the direction of the Secretary of War, who would draw on the army commissary for the needed goods. Potentially of great permanent importance, the commissioner of the Bureau was specifically made responsible for the control of all lands in the South commandeered during the war. He was also directed unequivocally to divide these abandoned lands into forty-acre plots and to lease them to the freedmen at an annual rent of six percent of their 1860 value for a period of three years.[14]

The War Department's suitability for this job of defining and executing the government's freedmen policy had been so extensively discussed that Edwin Stanton must have wondered what kind of man should head the Bureau. There were three logical sources of candidates: the private sector, the semiofficial wartime organizations, and the army. Stanton could have looked to the private sector if he wanted to link bureau work to the Abolitionist movement of prewar days, and one of its leaders such as William Lloyd Garrison or Wendell Phillips could have been chosen. Or Stanton could have sought out an Abolitionist of the "hoe and trowel" tradition like James Miller McKim of the Freedmen's Aid movement, who had long been working with the freedmen on the Sea Islands. Another possibility would have been a minister of great popular and national appeal, such as Henry Ward Beecher. Or Stanton might have chosen a leader from one of the conservative volunteer associations—perhaps Lyman Abbott, the American Union Commission's worker with white refugees. In point of fact, no one in the private sector seems to have been considered.

The second source was the semiofficial organizations, which

14. *13 U.S. Stat.*, 507–09.

were operating in conjunction with the armies as they invaded the South. The Sanitary Commission was a private organization, which had undertaken the vast job of organizing the care of the wounded during the war. That there had been a need for a major effort to augment the medical care available in the army was attested to by the grim facts of uncared-for wounded men who lay on the battlefields after the first terrible encounters of the war. Later, as Negroes came behind the Union lines, the Sanitary Commission members came in contact with them as well as with the army's sick and wounded. George Bentley claimed that James Yeatman, who headed the Commission's western sector, was Lincoln's choice for commissioner. Yeatman had reported on the grave injustices committed by Union speculators, who had rented confiscated plantations and gotten freedmen as contract laborers in the bargain.[15] General Sherman proposed him for a postwar job, and President Lincoln did inquire about the man, but there is no evidence that it was the Freedmen's Bureau that they had in mind.[16] (It is probably just as well, as his postwar concern with the freedmen seems to have consisted of impressing a group of them to build, gratis, a monument to the Emancipator.)[17]

The other semiofficial agency which might have supplied a commissioner was the Christian Commission. A close relative of the YMCA, this agency was both humanitarian and evangelical. Either as chaplains in the army or as their auxiliaries, the agents of the Christian Commission, with tracts and prayer meetings, tried to make the war bearable and possibly meaningful for the men in the field, particularly the wounded. Because they had been sent to minister to those made miserable by the war, many of the Christian Commission members worked closely with Negro refugees, and the Commission urged that its man be named to head the Bureau when it was established. The leader of the Com-

15. Bentley, p. 51.

16. Abraham Lincoln to E. M. Stanton, 28 Mar. 1865, Stanton Papers, LC.

17. James Yeatman to O. O. Howard, 22 June 1865, 7 July 1865, OOH Papers; O. O. Howard to James Yeatman, 11 July 1865, BRFAL.

mission, the Reverend George H. Stuart of Philadelphia, urged for the post General Clinton B. Fisk, who had had experience working with the freedmen in Tennessee.[18]

Neither Fisk nor Colonel John Eaton, Jr., who had General Grant's confidence because he had directed work with the freedmen in the Mississippi Valley under him, was chosen, and it appears that neither experience nor connection with any of the established institutions, private or semipublic, engaged in work with the freedmen was an asset to the candidates.[19] The commissioner was chosen, instead, from the third source of personnel available to Stanton—the army itself.

The choice of an army man was logical for several reasons. Congress had created the Bureau in such a way that its personnel would be army officers. In addition, all the other activities of the War Department, below the secretariat itself, were conducted by army men, and it was consistent to have a general at the head of a new bureau in the department.

Fisk or, with a promotion, Colonel Eaton would have fitted that specification and so too would Rufus Saxton, the general who had led the private freedmen's aid experiments on the Sea Islands, but these men were passed by. They had all made enemies as they gained experience, but that alone probably did not doom their chances. Saxton, who had the backing of the Chief Justice of the United States for the post, knew why someone else got the job as commissioner.[20] Stanton was looking not for a man who was sympathetic with the freedmen and only secondarily an army man, but for a man whose success in the war as a general promised success in a peacetime assignment. Saxton was a West Pointer, and many thought his work on the islands a great success, but while he had fought and been wounded, he had no great battles to claim as his. Stanton's job (Lincoln and Johnson seem to have left it to him) was to find a general who could both claim

18. G. H. Stuart to O. O. Howard, 15 May 1865, OOH Papers.
19. Howard, *Autobiography*, 2, 225.
20. S. P. Chase to E. M. Stanton, 20 May 1865, Stanton Papers, LC.

such victories and who could be counted on to have concern for the welfare of the freedmen.

Oliver Otis Howard was Stanton's choice from this narrow field. From Maine, and a West Point graduate, he had fought many of the great battles of the war. Howard had commanded men in defeat at Fredericksburg, in the awful turning of the tide at Gettysburg, and in victory at Atlanta. He had risen finally to command one of the two great armies that marched with relentless success to the sea—Grant's and Sherman's old Army of the Tennessee. And Howard, during the long fighting of the war, had come to be known as the "Christian General."

"Leeds has never had a village," wrote Otis Howard of the town in Maine where he was born.[21] A pair of churches stand on high open ground, and the farms are patched out on uneven slopes and hills. In 1830, when Howard was born, it was less sparse than it is today; but then, as now, it was lean and remote. Fifty years before the boy was born, his great-grandfather had founded Leeds. His mother's father, Oliver Otis, came a few years later, and his father's father, Captain Seth Howard, who fought in the Revolution, came in 1801.[22] They were all immigrants from Massachusetts proper, who came to farm Maine lands lying well inland east of the Androscoggin River.

When the boy was three, his father, Rowland Howard, began the family's leave-taking of Leeds. He tried to establish himself in New York State, but the move was unsuccessful, and he returned to his farm, bringing with him a Negro boy who was to help with the work.[23] Decades later, as General Howard looked back on his work in the Freedmen's Bureau, he recalled his boyhood friendship with Edward Johnson and said it "relieved me

21. "Leeds Centennial," 15 Aug. 1901 (one hundred years from the town's formal organization), unpublished address, OOH Papers.

22. J. C. Stinchfield, *History of the Town of Leeds* (Lewiston, preface–1901), pp. 19, 163.

23. Eliza Otis Howard to R. B. Howard, 14 July 1833, OOH Papers.

from that feeling of prejudice which would have hindered me from doing the work for the freedmen."[24]

This was a stiff, negative summation of a relationship, which not many New England farm boys experienced. Each rare mention of Edward Johnson by Howard or his brother invites curiosity. The General related the longest account of Johnson in his *Autobiography* seven decades later. He told of the "coasting, the skating, the games with marbles and with kites" which they shared. He remembered too that "in work, such as comes to every New England farm lad, we toiled side by side, or at our respective stints in which we competed for success and finish." Howard claimed they never quarreled but added that Johnson "was never cringing or slavish."[25]

These meager details make it difficult to assess the nature of this boyhood experience. The story was undoubtedly edited by time and the General's need for an easy explanation of his racial attitudes, but it is possible that Howard's intimate boyhood experiences with Edward Johnson were just as important to his understanding of the freedmen as he says they were. This makes us miss all the more an account of the quality of those experiences.

The trouble with the story is what is left out. Howard knew Edward Johnson in the private boys' world of his family's farm, but he tells us nothing about how his friend fared as a lone black boy in the public world of Leeds. Nor does the General mention that the authority of shared farm chores was the standard citation of countless Southerners, who claimed to know the Negro best. Edward Johnson left the Howard farm after four years, but Otis Howard did not forget him.

Rowland Howard died when Otis and his two younger brothers were still children and, with a farm to manage as well, his widow, Eliza, married again within the year. She moved a short distance south of her old farm with her new husband, John Gilmore. Eliza Gilmore had not found a way to leave the farms of the

24. Howard, *Autobiography*, *1*, 13.
25. Ibid., p. 12.

Leeds country, but she was determined to see her sons advance in
the world.

She chose a superior education as their road out. She allowed
neither her own loneliness at their absence nor their homesickness
to obstruct her program.[26] Her links to her sons, and theirs to
her and to each other, were letters. Scores of these, some scratched
in haste, some stretched to fill a lonely Sunday, and all rich in the
life of nineteenth-century New England, remain as records to the
family's cooperative project in education.

Otis, the oldest, left first. He boarded in the village of Wayne
while attending school there and then went to live with his lawyer
uncle, John Otis (whose wife had inherited a magnificent library), in the handsome river town of Hallowell.[27] Later he spent
a term at Monmouth Academy, nearer Leeds, and one winter,
because a good schoolmaster lived only two and one-half miles
away, Otis was able to attend school and live at home.[28] At fifteen
he enrolled in Allan H. Weld's North Yarmouth Academy, a
preparatory school that sent its graduates to nearby Bowdoin and
to Harvard and Yale.

Dressed in a homemade suit, young Howard was driven to the
seacoast town by his stepfather.[29] The school was austere and
Howard spent many lonely winter weeks there. By spring he
wanted to return to Monmouth Academy with one of his cousins
from Leeds, where he "should be more amongst [his] equals."
He complained that nearly all the boys at Yarmouth were "lawyer's sons and thourough [sic] scholars and aristocratic a little
with all." He and the other boys "having rusticated habits" were

26. O. O. Howard to his mother, 7 July 1844; his mother to him, 7 July
1844 and 15 Mar. 1854, OOH Papers.

27. Howard, *Autobiography, 1,* 17. John Otis had married the grand-
daughter of Benjamin Vaughan, a close friend and an intellectual peer of
Benjamin Franklin and Benjamin Rush. General Howard never mentioned
this heritage which was his cousin's but not his. Emma Huntington Mason,
Old Hallowell on the Kennebec (Augusta, Me., 1909), p. 91; Robert Hallowell Gardiner, "Memoir of Dr. Vaughan," *Collections of the Maine Historical
Society, 6* (Portland, 1859), 85–92.

28. Howard, *Autobiography, 1,* 22, 23.

29. Ibid., p. 24.

"made fun of as it is termed," and he pointed to the most tangible cause of his unhappiness: his lack of "so costly a suit of broad cloth," which his more affluent peers enjoyed.[30]

During the summer of 1846 Howard studied hard to pass his examinations for entry into college. He wasted no time "in any sport" and steadfastly "resolved to remain here [at North Yarmouth on] the fourth of July, [although] most all are going to Portland."[31] Happily, Howard broke his resolution, and he went down the bay to celebrate with Lizzie Waite, whom he married eight years later. Despite his holiday, Howard passed the feared oral examinations and enrolled in Bowdoin.

Bowdoin stood well up in the front ranks of American colleges, and its teachers were distinguished exponents of a classical curriculum in which the existence of God and the continuance of the Republic were at once proved by the laws of natural science. An abridgment of Paley's *Evidences* was helpful in this process. As one of Otis' less reverent friends put it, "if Christianity is not a failure those evidences are. . . . I had much rather taken Christianity for granted than be bored by those months with Paley."[32]

A good teacher could overcome a dull text, and when Professor Calvin Stowe lectured,

> Everybody seemed to listen to him with eagerness and wonderment. I couldn't comprehend how a man in the short space of thirty years could lay in such an immense store of knowledge. He lectured on the Old Testament, reconciling the apparent geological inconsistencies—and showing these very passages were strengthened by this science. He seemed to possess a fund of humor, mingled with a bluntness of speech which was for me almost irresistible.[33]

30. Seth Howard to O. O. Howard, 16 Apr. 1846; O. O. Howard to his mother, 3 May 1846, OOH Papers.

31. O. O. Howard to his mother, 18 June 1846, OOH Papers.

32. P. S. Perley to O. O. Howard, 4 Dec. 1849, OOH Papers.

33. O. O. Howard to his mother, 19 Nov. 1851, OOH Papers. Howard suggests that Stowe, in class, was a different man from the one whose private terrors and public bravery are so brilliantly described in Edmund Wilson, *Patriotic Gore* (New York, 1962), pp. 59–72.

Although a tone of moral responsibility permeated the Bowdoin curriculum, there was not much application of that responsibility to political issues. The members of Bowdoin's class of 1850 were more inclined to agree with the college's president, Leonard Wood, who greatly admired that year's compromise, than with the new faculty wife, Harriet Beecher Stowe, who did not.[34] Back in the country, Howard's family was more intensely interested in the slavery question than was the future head of the Freedmen's Bureau. Driving through a neighboring town, Eliza Gilmore had to dissuade Howard's stepfather from stopping for a meeting protesting fugitive slave laws. She wanted to avoid a cold ride home in the evening; it was eight below zero at noon.[35] The family had been antirum Whig and became antislave Whig; Otis went along, but his Abolitionist brother, Rowland, despaired at his apathy. Otis was more interested in getting a job after college than he was in the moral questions of politics.

What job? Education was his mother's religion. Her letters to her sons were punctuated with a piety that was second nature to her, but she never found in any church a substitute for her passion for obtaining an education for her sons. Her program ended with college, however, for she was not clear about where education led. In her letters to Otis, she spoke in abstractions of attainment and usefulness but suggested no specific vocation. Sometimes, when her own unhappiness threatened her commitment to her sons' education, she came close to defining these abstractions as material acquisitions. In those (rare) bitter letters her language stopped not quite short of encouraging a commercial expression of the New England ethic. That road had many travelers, but the Howard brothers were never comfortable on it.

No prospect opened up after Bowdoin except teaching in a one-room school in a country town. Howard had taught before, between college terms, as had several of his friends, but he wanted no more of it—even temporarily until he had enough money to

34. Leonard Woods, Jr., *A Eulogy on Daniel Webster* (Brunswick, 1852), pp. 48–51.
35. Eliza Gilmore to O. O. Howard, 19 Jan. 1850, OOH Papers.

go west and get into business, as Uncle John Otis recommended.[36] His uncle, the family's successful man, was serving a single term in the House of Representatives and came up with an alternative career. His own son could not pass the physical examination for West Point, and the disappointed Congressman transferred the appointment to his nephew. Otis took it, despite his own and his mother's lack of enthusiasm for a military career.

Howard was nineteen when he crossed the Hudson River to reach West Point in September 1850. He had just visited New York City for the first time. He was on his way, by appointment of a congressman uncle, to an academy that produced "over twenty members of Congress," as Uncle John put it in a letter designed to persuade him to go to West Point.[37] Howard was ready to face military life with some assurance (more, now that he had, on advice, discarded the Bowdoin man's high silk hat). Still, he was bothered to be crossing the Hudson only because he had nowhere else to go.[38]

Howard fought a private war with West Point and, though there were occasional truces, it lasted a lifetime. He never left the army, and all his quarrels with the world were fought on battlefields he had paced out first as a cadet at the Academy. Throughout his career he had to make personal compromises to survive in the West Point world. These settlements came at considerable cost to public social values he had sought to honor.

Ironically, the Academy's initial effect was to alert him to public issues. His personal unhappiness caused him to question things that had not disturbed him in the comfortable environment of Bowdoin. In December he wrote home to his mother: "I perceive every time I get a glance at the paper that the fugitive slave law has kindled much excitement at the north. . . . What is father's opinion on this all-engrossing subject. No political excitement ever gets within this secluded prison."[39]

36. John Otis to O. O. Howard, 14 Apr. 1850, OOH Papers.
37. John Otis to O. O. Howard, 20 June 1850, OOH Papers.
38. Howard, *Autobiography*, *1*, 44.
39. O. O. Howard to his mother, 8 Dec. 1850, OOH Papers.

At the end of the first year, Howard stood at the top of his class, but he was not fond of the Academy.[40] "In many respects this [is] the best school in the union, in others the worst. The moral education that a person would receive in this place is just none at all." One matter that troubled him was the open and approved enforcement of class distinction. When Otis discovered that Warren Lothrop, an old boyhood friend from Leeds, was stationed at West Point, he went to the enlisted men's quarters to visit him.[41] For this, the cadet was punished; but, privately, Howard would not acknowledge that he was wrong. He and Warren were reduced to communicating by surreptitious notes.[42]

In his second year, Howard was attacked by an effective conspiracy, and he became the victim of a childish and cruel ostracism. Years later he tended to stress a public-policy reason for this nasty treatment which was sufficiently effective to cause his official performance (judged often by his fellows) to suffer and for him to seriously consider withdrawing. He claimed to have expressed antislavery attitudes, which were resented by future rebels. His letters at the time, however, do not identify this as the focus of his trouble; there is little evidence that Howard actually did take a strong stand on the slavery issue.

Howard himself said, "I would not have owned at that time that I was an abolitionist."[43] As an opponent of slavery, he was not sufficiently committed to suit his more crusading brother Rowland. He did, however, admit to another cadet in social conversation off the base that he favored Seward's opposition to extending slavery into the territories.[44] There were many Southerners at West Point, and in the fifties the more ardent of these used "Abolitionist" as a blanket term of derision covering any suggestion of opposition to slavery.

40. Howard, *Autobiography, 1,* 54.
41. O. O. Howard to his mother, 6 Apr. 1851, OOH Papers.
42. Howard, *Autobiography, 1,* 50, 51; "W.L.L." to O. O. Howard (?), 27 May 1852, OOH Papers.
43. Howard, *Autobiography, 1,* 48.
44. R. B. Howard to O. O. Howard, 17 Jan. 1853, OOH Papers.

Abolitionism of any sort was a forbidden loyalty at West Point in the fifties. It was logical, therefore, for the future Union general and head of the Freedman's Bureau to claim later that anti-slavery sentiments were the cause of his trouble and that the cabal that organized his ostracism was entirely composed of Southerners. But at the height of his difficulties he got into a fight, and the two men he fought were from Massachusetts and Maine.[45]

Otis Howard was cutting across a more narrow grain. Advocacy of prayer meetings and temperance[46] probably contributed as much as any indiscretions on the slavery issue and, above all, it was his manner which caused trouble. He met ostracism with self-righteousness. Howard was a slight man, with heavy dark hair which offset undistinguished eyes; rigorous workouts in the academy's gym made him a strong but not impressive man. He never overcame mannerisms such as fidgety gestures and a shrill voice; his priggishness baited the young gentlemen of West Point.[47]

A classic prescription stopped the conspiracy. The commandant of the Academy called Howard aside and advised: "[If] I were in your place I would knock some man down." Howard did, and his unpopularity and demerits, awarded by cadet officers, diminished.[48] At the start of his third year, Howard expected his troubles to increase because the father of the cadet he considered his greatest tormenter arrived as the new superintendent.[49] These expectations proved groundless. Colonel Robert E. Lee ended the competition between Howard and his son, Custis Lee. Howard was encouraged to become a debater and achieved respect in that role. At graduation, the Maine man stood fourth; the Virginian was first.

45. Howard, *Autobiography*, *1*, 49, 52; "W.L.L." to O. O. Howard (?), 27 May 1853, O. O. Howard to his mother, 20 Dec. 1852, OOH Papers.

46. O. O. Howard to his mother, 12 Sept. 1852, R. B. Howard to his brother, "election day" 1852, OOH Papers.

47. Thomas W. Osborn ms. diary, Bowdoin College Library.

48. "W.L.L." to O. O. Howard (?), 27 May 1852, O. O. Howard to his mother, 20 Dec. 1852, OOH Papers; Howard, *Autobiography*, *1*, 53.

49. Eliza Gilmore to O. O. Howard, 26 Sept. 1852, O. O. Howard to her, 9 Oct. 1852, OOH Papers.

Having gained his commission, Howard achieved his greatest desire: he got out of West Point. Even the achievement of high rank had not dispelled his doubts about the value of a military career. Time and again, as if to convince himself, he wrote his mother about the worth of a military career. He reiterated that the nonresisting martyr serves only his own soul, while the soldier, killing to defend a just country, serves his whole land and God as well. But his doubts remained: "If I believe from my heart a war to be unjust, I would have difficulty to ask the blessing of God to rest upon me in its prosecution. The army officer, even *here* in America, is not his own master. The citizen is or may be. Here on this account the position of the latter is preferable."[50] When he took charge of the Freedmen's Bureau thirteen years later, Otis Howard was still trying to reconcile his dreams of personal fulfillment and his sense of moral duty with the constraint and purpose of the army—which had so strong a hold on him.

His reluctance to leave the military reflected little faith in its worth. He hoped to resign to pursue another career but, in a moment of honesty, gave a down-to-earth reason for staying in the army:

> Had I the head of Daniel Webster a struggle with poverty might tend to develop my dormant energies, might call into action hidden talents and give power and character to an intellect filled with a heterogeneous mass of shapeless material. But however much vanity might make me swell with importance, after all I am only O. O. Howard; . . . it becomes [him] never to trust to chance . . . while he is within the haven of security."[51]

O. O. Howard never left his steady job, but, in war and in peace, it was often far from a haven.

Lieutenant Howard left West Point in June 1854 on the river

50. O. O. Howard to his mother, 20 Dec. 1852, OOH Papers.
51. Ibid.

steamer *Thomas Powell.* A more impressive passenger was General Winfield Scott, and when the young officer from Maine was introduced, the old warrior counseled against marriage. Howard was "glad enough to have the conversation turned. . . . I knew well enough the limitations of his authority, and the inalienable rights of even a brevet second lieutenant."[52] But Howard was often slow in the pursuit of happiness.

He and Lizzie (Elizabeth Ann Waite) had courted in college and endured the four trying West Point years without constant patience. Now they decorously waited still longer and were married the next winter, on February 14, 1855. Lizzie was small, cold to strangers, determined, and wise in ways that make a family endure. Public display of a wife's usefulness to a husband's career was not a dimension of the Howard marriage; theirs was a lasting private affair.

Otis Howard took his bride to the Watervliet Arsenal just outside Troy, New York. His cadet rank permitted him to choose an assignment, and he had selected ordnance, because that branch of the army provided housing for officers' wives. Soon he was transferred to the Kennebec Arsenal near Augusta, Maine, where he became a friend of James G. Blaine, editor of the *Kennebec Journal,* who was just entering the political lists. The two men were very unlike, but the dramatic politician was later a patron of the sober soldier.

In the fall of 1856, Howard was ordered to Florida, where a desultory war against the Seminoles was taking place.[53] Because his first child, Guy, was only a year old, Howard went alone and sent home letters rich in his impressions of the South. Among the passengers on the coastal steamer which took him south were three Catholic clerics and several slave-owning planters. Howard found himself compatibly allied with one of the planters in combating "the priests' sophistry."[54] The trip was "pleasant," and

52. Howard, *Autobiography, 1,* 61.
53. O. O. Howard to his wife, 28 Aug., 26 Dec. 1856, OOH Papers.
54. Ibid., 4 Jan. 1857.

the new country he entered on the St. Johns River was fascinating to him. From Palatka he crossed Florida:

> We have been traveling all day in a forest of pine trees. Occasionally we would pass a place where a man has squatted with his family miserably poor, his shelter an old log hut, with his children thin and meager little creatures, with matted hair the color of the white sand in which they play. These huts were never nearer to each other than four or five miles."[55]

By night, no squatters intruded. He borrowed the stage contractor's saddle horse and "rode . . . for seven or eight miles. While riding I saw two deer skipping along for we had a bright moon."[56]

Fort Brooke, where he was stationed, was neat and domesticated, except for the volunteers whom he found "worse behaved than the Indians, for the latter are seldom seen or heard from."[57] In fact, the Seminole War was in danger of ending by default until General W. S. Harney, driven more by rage than reason, determined to hunt down the enemy.[58] They eluded Harney, and his successor detailed Howard to find the Seminole chief to make a peace settlement. This was O. O. Howard's first assignment as a liaison between the government and a minority group and, prophetically, the mission ended without resolution.

With an Indian interpreter, two companies of men, and a captured Indian woman as guide, Howard set out to find and talk with the Seminole chief. He observed the miserable conditions in which they lived, and he offered a classic American answer to the problem: move away from it. "Our policy is to treat the prisoners with marked kindness . . . and try to get them to emigrate. I wish for their sakes they would leave this miserable country where they never will be left alone."[59] The guide did not lead them to Chief Bow Legs, but Howard believed that his offer to

55. Ibid., 10 Jan. 1856 ['57].
56. Ibid., 10 Jan. 1856 ['57], OOH Papers.
57. Ibid., 18 Feb., 15 Mar., 18 Mar., 4 Apr. 1857.
58. Ibid., 10 Jan. 1856 ['57], 4 Mar. 1857.
59. Ibid., 3 May 1857.

negotiate peace did reach the chief. After Howard left Florida, a lasting, if not just, settlement was reached.

The march to Lake Okechobee through the wild terrain of Florida and the terror of unseen Indians who shared it were high adventure, but Howard claimed that a different search surpassed the martial excitement. That spring, Otis Howard, lonely for his wife and prompted by letters from his brothers, consciously tried to find religious salvation.[60] It was a year of fervent revivalistic enterprise in the nation, and Howard's family and friends in Maine were actively seeking to succeed in it. In Florida, Howard went to work as "I have gone about any business of importance. Colonel Loomis kind good old man has assisted me with books and conversations—but it is through the Methodist protracted meeting that I have been enabled to gain . . . the assistance I needed."

He sought to share this emotional adventure with his wife and wrote long letters exploring for her, and for himself, the topography of conversion. Some days the terrain was uneven: "[Today] I was in search of 'that peace which passeth understanding' and didn't get it—I got a letter from you." The next night he went to a revival meeting. The preacher "didn't excite me or attract me," but one of the converts did; she precipitated Howard's public expression of conversion. The impetus, however, was external rather than internal, and it was not exalted. Howard was not a Becket humbled before the grandeur of an abstraction; he was impelled by an embarrassment he felt for another person. When the preacher finished his sermon he called on sinners to come to him; "some came forward, women all of them." (One was a hunchback, he recalled later.) "Some young men were laughing & making sport . . . I went forward, more in pride perhaps than in humility. I trembled like a leaf, but my head was clear & I didn't shed tears like the rest."[61]

60. C. H. Howard to O. O. Howard, 28 Oct. 1853; R. H. Gilmore to O. O. Howard, 1 June 1857, OOH Papers.

61. O. O. Howard to his wife, 31 May 1857, OOH Papers; Howard, *Autobiography*, 1, 82.

This was not all. A sympathetic response to social cruelty was, for him, insufficient evidence of religious commitment. That evening he read Hedley Vicars' *Diary Notes* and "tried for that joy which Vicars & [his brother] Rowland got" but did not find it for himself. The private struggle continued through the night, and the ecstasy (drained of vitality by language borrowed from countless revival preachers) is recorded in a letter describing his moment of salvation, of expurgation, when "the tugging & burning left me, the choking sensation was gone & for once I enjoyed happiness."

At the end of the summer, Lieutenant Howard, of Leeds, Maine, got safely away from the South and arrived home a licensed "Exhorter in the M[ethodist] E[piscopal] C[hurch] South."[62] He reported for duty in September 1857 at West Point, where he was to teach mathematics. Howard was a diligent teacher, but he wore his conversion heavily and made himself an informal chaplain at the Academy.[63] He conducted a Sunday school class and regular prayer meetings and actively campaigned for the conversion of the cadets who attended. He preached an orthodox New Light Christianity with no distractions of social concern.[64]

In 1858 he marshaled the Bowdoin commencement, and his reaction to the visiting preacher, Abolitionist Theodore Parker, was entirely free of interest in slavery: "Parker was profane—gave great offense and hurt the feelings of Christians. Called our Saviour 'the most popular God of Modern times.' "[65] That summer Howard preached at churches in Maine, and when his Bowdoin class had its tenth reunion in 1860, its program announced that Lieutenant Howard contemplated leaving the army to become a "minister of the gospel."[66]

62. D. B. Lyne [sic], Pastor (document signed), 17 Aug. 1857, OOH Papers.

63. J. E. B. Stuart to O. O. Howard, 17 June 1859, OOH Papers.

64. T. P. Tannett to O. O. Howard, 22 Dec. 1857; W. S. Graham to O. O. Howard, 27 Jan. 1858; C. C. Lee to O. O. Howard, 1 Nov. 1858, OOH Papers.

65. O. O. Howard ms. diary, Howard University Library, Washington, D.C.

66. Ibid.; R. B. Howard to O. O. Howard, 7 June 1859, OOH Papers; Tenth Reunion of the Class of 1850, pamphlet, Bowdoin College Library.

The Civil War put an end to that plan. In the spring of 1861, the West Point community finally divided on the subject they had so long tried to avoid discussing. For some, like Winfield Scott, the regular army commanded a loyalty stronger than any other, but most West Point men pledged allegiance to their own states and added their personal ambitions to the fires of disunion. The volunteer regiments needed officers, and handsome promotions were in the offing.

Howard wrote to Maine's governor, Israel Washburn, in the hope of a colonelcy, but the governor, seeing his people's army as a democracy electing its own officers from the ranks, rejected Howard's bid.[67] James G. Blaine, the speaker of the Maine House of Representatives disagreed, however, and sponsored his army friend for the command of a Maine regiment. Howard left West Point for Maine to press his candidacy, but before he reached Augusta, Blaine sent word that the regiment was his.[68]

The Third Maine regiment left Augusta on June 5, 1861. A half-century later Howard recalled the departure and painted the day with the richness of lilacs and the shadows of green maples with the sun on the water of the Kennebec River and waving picnickers lining its bank as "streams of bright uniforms rushed down the slopes to the trains."[69] The men stretching out of train windows to respond to the fluttering colored handkerchiefs were to Howard unforgettable. So was the silence with which they expressed their fear of war. The patriotic noise of the band received "no responsive cheering from the cars." And quickly a "curve in the tracks shut off the view; and thus departed this precious, typical freight of war."[70]

The Civil War took Otis Howard a long way. The lieutenant who was discontentedly teaching algebra in the spring was a brigadier general by fall.[71] For the first time since entering the

67. Howard, *Autobiography, 1*, 106.
68. J. G. Blaine to O. O. Howard, quoted in Howard, *Autobiography, 1*, 113; O. O. Howard, ms. of biographical sketch of Blaine, OOH Papers.
69. Howard, *Autobiography, 1*, 120, 121.
70. Ibid., p. 122.
71. Abraham Lincoln to Simon Cameron, in Roy Besler, ed., *The Collected Works of Abraham Lincoln* (8 vols. New Brunswick, 1953), *4*, 504–05.

army, his job equaled his ambition, and he brought to his command a businesslike zeal. He even used his recovery leave, after the amputation of his arm at Fair Oaks, to recruit across Maine and returned to a long line of battles—Antietam, Fredericksburg, Chancellorsville (his second son was born that day and named Chauncey), Gettysburg (which he refought the rest of his life, defending his command decisions of the first day), and then, joining the armies of the West, Missionary Ridge and Atlanta.

Howard was employed in some of the worst carnage of the war and, as the campaign stretched down into Georgia, his letters tell of individual experiences of death.[72] The despair of the living troubled him too. One night near Marietta, exhausted and with only a pencil handy he scrawled a note to Lizzie about a woman he had met that day on the road.[73] Tired, frightened, and alone, she had six children to care for; her husband was off in the war. Lizzie didn't need to be told that her husband, looking at the desperate Georgian family, had seen her and their children. There was no resolution of his story. "Oh how much misery and suffering grows out of this rebellion," was all he could say.[74]

Many Negroes traveled the roads of Georgia too, but Howard seldom mentioned them in his letters. He may have been oblivious to their troubles, which his own troops made worse, but it is more likely that he had trouble identifying himself with their experiences and even more difficulty making them understandable to Lizzie. He did not, for example, tell about his encounter with a Negro boy named Johnson, as did his brother Charles.

One day a soldier in Howard's regiment, sufficiently sure of his general's kindness, approached the headquarters tent holding a dirty little boy by the hand. The child, a Negro about eight years old, had wandered starving into the camp. As Charles Howard (serving on his brother's staff) told it, "Otis took him and had him stripped and washed thoroughly in an outer tent. The boy

72. Particularly, O. O. Howard to his wife, 23 and 29 July 1864, OOH Papers.

73. Ibid., 12 June 1864.

74. Ibid.

was reluctant about putting his head under water so Otis took him up and plunged him in." This ordeal over and the lice gone, the victim was presumably rewarded with some food, and he stayed at the camp for several days. Charles Howard watched him with fascination. "I often thought of 'Edward' [the Negro boy who had lived on their farm in Leeds]," wrote Charles, and he wondered whether Otis made the same connection. Coincidence contributed to such an identification (they were both named Johnson), and Charles told his mother that the camp urchin "is a funny fellow and it is very doubtful whether we will be able to make anything of him. At any rate Otis will have the satisfaction of knowing he saved one little boy from probable death."[75]

As the tubbing of the boy suggests, when great battles are not being fought, some warriors become domestic. One morning in January 1862, near Falmouth, Virginia, Howard sent his two contraband servants into town on horseback to pick up his laundry. On the way back an incident occurred; the two opposing accounts, one told by Charles Howard and the other by Otis, tell something of the General's attitude toward Negroes as well as reveal how events and responsibilities changed in Howard's memory.

Charles Howard wrote home about the incident: the two Negroes were riding back from town when they ran into some soldiers of the "Irish brigade" walking back from picket duty. The soldiers ordered the Negroes to get down from their horses. One, frightened, rode away quickly. The other, Jackson, told his challengers that his errand was for General Howard and, confident that this would ensure his safety, he refused to dismount. They shot him.[76] He was taken to the hospital, where his arm was amputated. General Howard visited the dying man. Charles took comfort that he was "a good and praying boy" and hoped that his death would be as mercifully quick as his pain was great.[77]

75. C. H. Howard to his mother, 26 Feb. 1862, Charles Howard Papers.
76. C. H. Howard to his half-brother, R. H. Gilmore, 13 Jan. 1862, Charles Howard Papers.
77. C. H. Howard to R. H. Gilmore, 13 Jan. 1862, Charles Howard Papers.

The story of this incident was told very differently by Otis Howard in his *Autobiography* forty-five years later. He disconnected himself from the event entirely. The man for whom the errand was being done was identified as an officer from Minnesota, and the Irish picketers became "enlisted men" holding "views similar to the New York rioters of 1863." Not only did the General neglect to mention that the laundry was his, but also he failed to take credit for visiting the man in the hospital.[78]

And the overtrusting Negro errand boy, who was, to Charles, an individual whom he called by name and who died in great pain, also underwent a metamorphosis in Otis Howard's memory. In his autobiography the person Charles had told about became a symbol. He was now a "mulatto" of "handsome figure, pleasant face and manners, and rather well dressed for the field," out "riding as usual." In the General's memory a Negro of a superior sort had been murdered by base and undiscoverable kinsmen of city rioters who "hated a negro except as a slave and . . . kept alive in their circle of influence an undercurrent of malice more or less active."[79]

The General gave this version of the story in the *Autobiography* to establish his own and his army's antislavery credentials. Speaking of the murder he said: "Friendly voices murmured against the crime, and with set teeth echoed the settled thought: 'Slavery must go.' "[80] The trouble was that the story did not fit such usage. The murdered man would have been safer in prewar Virginia, where doing an errand for the master was sufficient reason for a Negro to be on a horse while white men walked. And Jackson was not still a slave; technically he was a contraband, an ex-slave, but not yet free.

In his *Autobiography,* Howard sought to make Jackson's sacrifice of his life worthwhile by telling of it as a prelude to an appreciation of the Emancipation Proclamation; unfortunately, the story is more revealing of northern and military antinegro

78. Howard, *Autobiography*, 2, 182.
79. Ibid.
80. Ibid., p. 183.

attitudes. Perhaps it was because in 1908 these still were not overcome that the diversionary reference to the end of slavery, which was achieved, was chosen to close this racial murder story.

The purpose for comparing the two versions of this incident is not to indict O. O. Howard as a liar. All men lie, to some extent, as they publicly remember, and Howard's overall record for honesty is high in his *Autobiography,* which he wrote with his, not Charles', letters before him. It is relevant, however, to speculate on the reasons the General could not live with the unedited memory of a Negro boy to whom he had been kind, but who had died because working for him proved no protection at all. His telling was an unsuccessful attempt to explain the event and at the same time to extricate himself from it.

If the quietest days of the Civil War yielded this much ugliness, it must not have always been too difficult to resume the primary business of a soldier—winning the war. Howard's part in that responsibility increased when his friend, General James McPherson, was killed near Atlanta in 1864. Already a major general, Howard was chosen by William Tecumseh Sherman to lead the Army of the Tennessee in the march to the sea.[81] It was his men who severed the Confederacy by capturing Fort McAllister on the coastal waters below Savannah.[82]

Sherman and Howard stood on the roof of a shed on a rice plantation and watched the deadly pageant of the taking of the fort, which barred the approaching Union navy. Little daylight remained and Sherman was greatly impatient. The first ship arrived and stood off just below the fort. Finally Howard's men under General William B. Hazen broke out of the woods and began the attack. The firing was so heavy that smoke curtained the battle. When it rose, Sherman saw that "the parapets were blue with our men."

"This nigger will have no sleep this night!" was Sherman's

81. Grant thought John A. Logan would have been the preferable candidate. Ulysses S. Grant, *Personal Memoirs,* ed. E. B. Long (Cleveland, 1952), p. 487.

82. W. T. Sherman, *Memoirs* (2 vols. New York, 1875), 2, 231.

salute to the victory. He and Howard climbed down from the shed roof, took a skiff from some of their men who had been gathering oysters, sat down in the stern, and had themselves rowed across to the fort. "Inside . . . lay the dead as they had fallen, and they could hardly be distinguished from their living comrades, sleeping soundly side by side in the pale moonlight."[83]

After dinner Sherman and Howard were rowed out to greet the navy. Their great march to the sea was behind them, and they went aboard the gunboat *Dandelion* to send word to Washington that that part of their job was done. Sherman, in his message to Secretary of War Stanton, outlined the army's next task. Nearby Savannah he considered already gained, and in preparation for entering the city he said, "my first duty will be to clear the enemy of surplus negroes, mules and horses."[84] His brother officers were helpful in taking the horses off his hands and there is no further record of the mules, but the Negroes remained undisposed of as the conquering generals rode down Savannah's streets and appropriated suitable quarters.

Oliver Otis Howard of the Army of the Tennessee moved into the "sumptuous house—belonging to Mr. Molyneux, British consul formerly, but now in Europe."[85] On the last night of 1864, Otis Howard and his brother Charles lay in the Englishman's bedroom and talked into the New Year.[86] They spoke of private matters and personal ambitions. The road these two men so soon took in pursuit of these ambitions paralleled the trail of troubles of the refugee Negroes that Sherman complained of, but there is no evidence from Savannah that the Howards knew it.

83. Ibid., pp. 198–99.
84. Ibid., p. 201.
85. C. H. Howard to his mother, 27 Dec. 1864, Charles Howard Papers.
86. Charles Howard ms. diary, 1 Jan. 1865, Charles Howard Papers.

3. The Sea Islands

On New Year's Day, 1865, Charles Howard went north on leave, and General Howard, under new orders to prepare for an invasion of the Carolina coast, took two corps of his Army of the Tennessee and moved onto the Sea Islands which lie between Savannah and Charleston.[1]

These islands had been in Union hands since 1861. The planters who abandoned their lands abandoned their slaves as well. Extensive attempts to devise a new way of life for these freedmen were undertaken in an enterprise known as the Port Royal experiment. On lands granted to them or as wage earners on lands owned by Northerners, the freedmen grew cotton and subsistence crops with considerable success, and both children and adults attended schools run by northern teachers. Bold Negroes who escaped from mainland plantations came to the islands all through the war and, once Sherman's men had cleared the way for others to reach the coast, ex-slaves were arriving in great numbers. Howard's men competed with the refugees for the attention of the officers in charge of the islands; the Union troops had been well schooled in disregard for private property in the march across Georgia, and the freedmen were particularly sensitive to the prerogatives of property, perhaps because their hold on it was so recently acquired.[2]

Despite the troops he brought with him, General Howard was welcome. His arrival at General Rufus Saxton's Beaufort headquarters on the island of Port Royal signaled the war victory for which the islanders had been waiting.[3] That the marauding troops

1. Charles Howard ms. diary, 1 Jan. 1865, Charles Howard Papers; O. O. Howard, "Sherman's March thru the Carolinas and Savannah," undated ms., OOH Papers.

2. Rose, *Rehearsal for Reconstruction*, pp. 320–22, 324.

3. Saxton Diary, 3 Jan. 1865.

("a rough looking set") who followed Howard were a sign that not all the freedmen's troubles were over, the official family of sea-island army men and women schoolteachers chose to ignore as they turned out to greet the first of the generals of Sherman's army to visit them.[4]

As Willard Saxton, Rufus' brother and aide, reported it, the hosts at first misjudged their guest. Their "attempt at something rather grand as a dinner party . . . was a failure," but the inclusion of Howard in simpler domestic events in the house was a great success. Willard Saxton's boy reminded Howard of his own sons, and he enjoyed singing with the family around the piano. The Saxtons soon concluded that he was a "very pleasant gentleman, affable and agreeable, & an exceedingly good man."[5]

The islanders tested this goodness; they were delighted to find Howard at home in the schools with the Negro pupils. Far from being a fierce warrior embarrassed by so much innocence, Howard enjoyed himself thoroughly. He was a Sunday school teacher again, back at his favorite occupation, giving inspirational talks to young people devoutly trying to improve themselves. The Saxton ladies were indefatigable guides to the island schools; on one day they got Howard to five of them, including Laura Towne's on St. Helena's Island and Elizabeth Hyde Botume's near Beaufort on Port Royal Island.[6] The schoolteachers gave the ordered society, over which General Saxton presided, exactly the right tone and convinced Howard that there was an alternative to the chaos he had seen among the Negroes who had pursued his army.

Saxton, although older and more experienced in work with the freedmen, eagerly made Howard an ally in his effort to have the findings of the Port Royal experiment put into practice all over the South once all the slaves were freed. The day after the most ambitious of the school tours, Saxton took Howard to Savannah

4. Ibid., 4 Jan. 1865.
5. Ibid.
6. O. O. Howard, "Sherman's March thru the Carolinas and Savannah," OOH Papers.

to consult with Secretary of War Stanton, who had arrived on an inspection tour.[7] The talk undoubtedly stressed the need for some humane consideration to be given to the problem of the refugee Negroes whom Sherman found an irritating digression from the business of winning the war.[8] Stanton evidenced an attractive curiosity and sought the advice not only of the white generals, but also of the freedmen themselves. In what may have been the first time that a high official of the United States government asked the Negroes what they wanted, Stanton met with a group of twenty black men headed by Garrison Frazier, a carpenter and part-time minister. All but one were from South Carolina and Georgia, most were either freeborn or had been out of slavery for some time, and all were either preachers or active churchmen. They recommended that the freedmen of South Carolina and Georgia be given land, and fearing for the safety of their fellows, they further recommended that the lands be in areas where there would be only Negro residents.[9]

Howard and Saxton invited Stanton to visit Beaufort and tour just such a colony as Frazier had envisioned. On January 14, 1865, Stanton arrived.[10] Negro troops stood at attention, and their regimental band played as Saxton met Stanton at the dock, took his arm, and led him up the short walk to his tall, comfortable house. The Secretary of War, whose health was never good, had been feeling particularly uncomfortable in the preceding weeks, but the sea-island climate lived up to its reputation, and Stanton soon felt well and relaxed.[11]

The day after his arrival, a beautiful Sunday, General Saxton took the Secretary to see Mrs. Botume's school, and his brother

7. Saxton Diary, 10 Jan. 1865.

8. Ibid., 30 Dec. 1864.

9. Montgomery Meigs Diary, 13 Jan. 1865, LC; H. W. Beecher to E. M. Stanton, 8 Feb. 1865, Stanton Papers, LC. Stanton sent a transcript of the conference to Beecher, who read it from the pulpit in Brooklyn and released it to the *New York Daily Tribune*, 13 Feb. 1865; *Official Records of the War of the Rebellion*, Ser. I, 47, p. 2, 37–41.

10. Montgomery Meigs Diary, 14 Jan. 1865, LC.

11. Saxton Diary, 14 Jan. 1865; Thomas and Hyman, *Stanton*, p. 346.

Willard took others on Stanton's staff to visit other schools. These tours for northern wartime visitors were already a tradition of Beaufort hospitality, and this day's outings proved to be a particular success, for Stanton informed his host of his promotion to the brevet rank of major general. Saxton's brother interpreted the promotion as evidence that "the Gen's work has been recognized by the Dept. in Washington, that his past action has been approved."[12]

General Howard, whose army in the meantime had begun its invasion of the Carolina coast, briefly returned to Beaufort and was with the Saxtons the Sunday of the promotion. The following morning he wrote a letter committing himself to an alliance with both Saxton and Stanton concerning work with the freedmen. For an ambitious general, accustomed to promotions himself and concerned about his postwar career, the freedmen business may have looked promising.

Just when Congress was considering which department should be charged with the responsibility for determining the nation's policies toward the ex-slaves, Howard, with his letter, became involved in a quarrel between the War and Treasury Departments. He chose the winner. He wrote to a fellow Bowdoin alumnus, Secretary of the Treasury William Pitt Fessenden, and tactfully asked that a troublesome treasury agent be withdrawn from Port Royal. The emphasis of the letter lay not on the agent's liabilities, but on Saxton's assets. He noted that the two men had pursued similar policies "except with regard to moral & religious things." These were the things which mattered to Howard, and he went on to endorse, unequivocally, the program that Saxton had been following on the islands: "Whenever [Saxton] has been untrammeled in his work, he has introduced system and order and industry among these poor people, in such a manner as to afford a practical example of the best method of dealing with the negroes, as fast as they are freed."[13]

12. Saxton Diary, 15 Jan. 1865.

13. O. O. Howard to W. P. Fessenden, 16 Jan. 1865, Fessenden Papers, Bowdoin College.

Diplomatically, Howard went on to suggest that Stanton's men, and not members of the Treasury Department, would be better suited to work for the freedmen's future. The General added that his endorsement was written "without consultation with others and with no motive other than an earnest wish to see a work, as well begun here under the supervision of a completely practical mind, have a chance to develop and thrive, till the curse of slavery shall have been buried deep beneath the blessings of freedom."

Conversations and observations, if not consultations, had informed Howard, and his move was shrewd. Fessenden cared little for the Treasury and hoped to return soon to the Senate.[14] Howard's letter enhanced his reputation with the Secretary of War and with one of the most important postwar senators. His declaration was a political decision. Howard had not only cast his lot with the War Department as stewards of the freedmen, but he had recognized that becoming free was not going to be instantaneous and would require decision and leadership. He was also committed not to a system in which the freedmen would merely survive, but to one in which they would "thrive."

Both Stanton and Howard learned much from their stay on the islands, which, during these weeks in January 1865, provided an informal training camp for future staff members of the Freedmen's Bureau. The Sunday school to which Willard Saxton took Stanton's aide, General Edward Townsend, "another of the good men in a high place," was conducted by Alexander P. Ketchum, who was to become Howard's land officer in South Carolina.[15] A week after Townsend's visit, Eliphalet Whittlesey, the future assistant commissioner for North Carolina, spoke to Ketchum's pupils along with Howard, who "made one of his genial, Christian talks to the colored children & the grown up ones, too."[16] William E. Strong, later Howard's inspector general in the Freed-

14. Francis Fessenden, *Life and Public Services of William Pitt Fessenden* (2 vols. Boston, 1907), *1*, 365, 366; *2*, 1.

15. Saxton Diary, 15 Jan. 1865.

16. Ibid., 22 Jan. 1865.

men's Bureau, was with him on the islands and so was Lieutenant Joseph Sladen, who was to serve with Howard in the administration of the Bureau in Washington.

And the Sea Islands produced Rufus Saxton, whom Chief Justice Chase thought best qualified for the post of commissioner of the Bureau.[17] But Saxton, who immediately pledged his support when Howard, instead, received the assignment, was made assistant commissioner of South Carolina, Georgia, and Florida, whose hostile mainlands were joined to his island domain after the war. The story of Saxton's period of service in the Freedmen's Bureau is the record of the destruction of Howard's commitment to Saxton's practical answer to how the ex-slaves could best make their way as free men.

Saxton's example had promised the former slaves much and that promise was broken, but only after he struggled valiantly to keep it. Rufus Saxton fought to give substance to the freedom that the war had given the freedmen. He wanted them to have farms. "I wish every colored man, every head of a family, to acquire a freehold, a little home that he can call his own."[18] A farm was a place to begin—an economic foundation on which families could build their lives.

Rufus Saxton was the son of Jonathan Ashley Saxton of Deerfield, Massachusetts, and his wife, Miranda. The Saxtons were an old and honored family in this western Massachusetts town, and Rufus grew up not only in the security of an established family but also in the company of a remarkable man, his father. Jonathan Saxton was a rebel in that most dangerous realm, the world of the mind. Unlike Otis Howard's mother, who worshipped education but had no idea how it should be used, Jonathan Saxton insisted that ideas must be practiced.

To the conventional eye, Jonathan Saxton was careless with his children's education. There was no self-sacrificing to put his sons

17. S. P. Chase to E. M. Stanton, 20 May 1865, Stanton Papers, LC.

18. Rufus Saxton at Zion Church, Charleston *Courier*, 13 May 1865, quoted in Francis B. Simkins and Robert H. Woody, *South Carolina During Reconstruction* (Chapel Hill, 1932), p. 228.

through the best colleges in New England. Education was not achieved in an institutional way, and the children did not prove to be successful in a conventional manner. One son, Mirand, was a black sheep of the classic sort.[19] Another, Willard, whose diary tells us much about his brother Rufus and about the daily tasks of an agent and clerk in the Freedmen's Bureau, succeeded best in living itself; he died at 103. Rufus, born in 1824, died in 1903, an obscure retired army officer. But in the middle of his life, he lived five bright years, which proved what a man can do when ideas are at work.

Jonathan Saxton was a radical Unitarian (a minister, he said succinctly, should not sound like the "President of a Bank"), an Abolitionist, and a great friend of George Ripley.[20] Saxton, troubled with the way Americans had ordered their society, hoped that his son Rufus could join Ripley's Brook Farm to learn a trade and develop an awareness of how men could better form a community.[21] Rufus did not go to Brook Farm; that experience fell to his younger brother Willard, who recorded it in the first volumes of his eighty-year diary.[22]

Going about as far from Brook Farm as one could, Rufus accepted an appointment to West Point. After graduating, he led a surveying party in the Rockies. He is also credited with inventing a sounding instrument for maritime exploration, an accomplishment that won the attention of the geologist Edward Hitchcock, and an honorary M.A. from Hitchcock's Amherst College.[23]

Rufus Saxton, an artillery officer, taught military tactics at West Point until the outbreak of the Civil War, when he entered active service. Wounded in the battle at Harper's Ferry, he was

19. J. A. Saxton to S. W. Saxton, quoted in Saxton Diary, 9 Apr. 1866.

20. J. A. Saxton to his father (Rufus Saxton, the General's grandfather), 3 Mar. 1845, Saxton Family Papers in possession of W. Saxton Seward, New York City; Thomas D. Howard, Sophia W. Howard, Sally D. Howard, *Charles Howard Family Domestic History,* ed. Elizabeth H. Andrews (Cambridge, 1956), p. 169.

21. J. A. Saxton to his father, 3 Mar. 1845, Saxton Family Papers.

22. Ibid.

23. Horace W. Hewlett, secretary of Amherst College, to the writer, 20 Sept. 1965.

transferred to the Department of the South and ordered to the Sea Islands off the coast of South Carolina, Georgia, and Florida to take charge of the Negroes who had been abandoned there by the planters escaping the invading Union navy. This was no ordinary military assignment, and Saxton proved to be no ordinary army man.

Northerners interested in the antislavery movement immediately seized the opportunity to make these islands the scene of experiments in which the slaves would learn to live as free men. Teachers opened schools, ministers performed marriages and encouraged the Negroes to accept the family as the basic social unit, speculator-philanthropists taught the Negroes to work as a wage-earning labor force in raising cotton, and other (better) friends divided abandoned plantations so that the freedmen's families could have their own farms.[24]

Over all of this, Rufus Saxton presided as governor. His ability to reform derived from the war power; he represented the armed force of the nation that captured the islands, and this invested him with authority. His approach to governing, however, derived from the life of the mind in which his father lived such an active life. Through all his years on the Sea Islands, conducting his own Brook Farm, Rufus Saxton received tough-minded letters of encouragement from his father, who, in his seventies, had not abandoned the marriage of skepticism and faith which produced in him and in Rufus a belief in trying to make reform work.[25]

Reforming not only the American Negroes' way of life but also the white Americans' attitude toward them was no easy task. The freedmen were ignorant and their learning, though surprisingly quick in some areas, was, at times, discouragingly slow. But

24. Rose, *Rehearsal for Reconstruction;* the Saxton Papers corroborate the findings of Mrs. Rose's excellent study. Much rich additional detail is contained in the Saxton Diary and the recently acquired Charles Howard Papers in the Bowdoin College Library.

25. The wartime letters themselves—save bits in scrap books— have not survived but Willard Saxton quotes from them and comments on them in his diary.

worse, there were many white Americans who did not want Saxton to succeed.

Army men, anxious to win the war and also possessing a certain malice born of the feeling that they as white men were fighting the Negroes' fight, were eager to draft the sea-island farmers.[26] The methods employed by General John Foster, as Saxton bitterly complained, were close to impressment. Foster—"that miserable puppy" to Willard Saxton—undoubtedly caused hardships to individual Negro families (hardships they shared with many white families of conscripted men elsewhere in the nation).[27] The Negro troops were discriminated against in pay and in being assigned to menial tasks, but despite this, the Negro men who served in the army achieved something of great value for themselves and for the freedmen's cause then and since—the pride of proving themselves able fighting men.

The real threat to the islanders was not Foster's impressment but a more subtle enemy. The high quality sea-island cotton was valuable, and the freedmen were making money in its production. This brought others to the islands to compete for the profits. Rufus Saxton, who had long defended the freedmen against exploitation, hoped that victory in the war would also become a victory for the Port Royal experiment.[28] If he could fend off the northern predators until the war was over, the freedmen's hold on the lands that they and their forebears had worked for generations might be secured.[29]

Over those lands that mattered so much Rufus Saxton's battle for the freedmen was waged and lost. And the enemy was not long in showing itself. Through the years of the building of the Port Royal community, the mainland coast was hostile, and yet that very hostility provided the barrier that made the experiments possible. The Negroes of the islands did not have to share their

26. Rose, pp. 328–30.
27. Saxton Diary, 3 Feb. 1865.
28. Rose, p. 328.
29. Saxton Diary, 9 Jan. 1865.

lands with their former owners. But when the Union army reached the coast, it rejoined the islands to the troubled world of the mainland and ironically liberated the white planters who would soon compete for the lands held by the freedmen on the islands.

As soon as Sherman's troops had secured the coast, Saxton and his wife went over from Beaufort to Savannah to visit the mainland port so long estranged from their island capital. They went feeling a bit triumphant and came back in a melancholy mood. They found the city dirty and the people hungry, but, in meeting their problems, the victorious Northerners seemed to have turned the Saxtons' world upside down: "Charities from the North are given to rank secesh women in silks, while poor whites & destitute negroes are turned away, and told to go to work."[30]

Saxton was one of many who wrote to northern newspapers asking that food be shipped to Savannah.[31] He made no suggestion in his request that the food be given only to Negroes or to Unionist whites; his dismay was not that rebels ate, but that the poor, black and white, were elbowed out of the way by prepossessing whites. Sherman had told Stanton that "with a little judicious handling and by a little respect being paid to their prejudices, white Georgians, ready to accept the fact that slavery was over, would now support the Union."[32] The Saxtons found rebel prejudices being respected, and it troubled them. They were also disturbed by the onrush of northern businessmen to reestablish relations with the commercial leaders of Savannah. Ships stood off Hilton Head waiting to reenter Savannah as soon as the army opened the port. In New York, Abolitionists and the Chamber of Commerce quarreled over whether to send shipments of food and clothes with no quid pro quo or whether to send the supplies in exchange for cotton, thus profiting the rebel businessmen, who contested its ownership with the Union army.[33]

30. Ibid., 24 Jan. 1865.
31. *New York Tribune,* 17 Jan. 1865.
32. W. T. Sherman to E. M. Stanton, 19 Jan. 1865, Stanton Papers, LC.
33. *New York Times,* 21 Jan. 1865.

If proud enemies could so quickly reassert their authority in breadlines or in the commodities market, could they not also be expected to do so with the sea-island lands? The vanquished took quick inventory. As the wife of James Chesnut, one of the great landowners of South Carolina, put it, her husband's "bank stock, his bonds, his railroad stocks as well as his hundreds of Negroes are all given up. Nothing but land remains, and debts."[34] Because these lands were inland, they had been neither confiscated nor abandoned, but the Chesnuts held their lands as resolutely as their brother landowners sought to regain theirs from their former slaves on the Sea Islands, who were, as Edward Barnwell reported, "living in great comfort."[35]

Rufus Saxton and his wife had seen in Savannah only a hint of the power which the great Confederate families would muster later in the year. In January 1865 it appeared that Saxton had power on his side. His promotion was a symbol of this. A commander of one of the great armies of the war, General Howard, had visited the islands and had approved of what he had seen. And so had Secretary of War Stanton, the most powerful man in President Lincoln's cabinet who awarded Saxton his major generalship. But visitors such as General Sherman and Howard's troops, with their contempt for the Negroes, were a warning that all opposition to this humanitarian work would not end with the winning of the war. Nevertheless, Saxton saw his promotion as an acknowledgment of the nation's obligation to the freedmen. Secretary Stanton and General Howard, by their presence, gave him greater assurance than he had ever had that the obligation would be met. The sharp-eyed, unimpressive-looking little governor with a high vanity and a ranging temper—often employed in a worthy cause—was ready to fight for his freedmen, secure in the belief that he would be strongly supported.

Willard Saxton called the day of his brother's promotion the

34. Mary Boykin Chesnut, *A Diary from Dixie,* ed. Ben Ames Williams (Boston, 1961), p. 540.

35. Ibid., p. 540.

"dawn of a new era . . . in the history of the Freedmen."[36] One year later, the brothers read a letter from their father predicting that Andrew Johnson would succeed in bringing Reconstruction under a "disastrous eclipse."[37] Jonathan Saxton was right. The week that his letter arrived, Rufus was relieved of his duties and sent away from the Negroes on the Carolina coast to do quarter-master duty in the North.[38] And both Stanton and Howard had agreed to his removal.[39]

When Howard had been with them in January 1865, he had seemed fully converted to the Sea Islanders' ways. The Northerners there found Howard entirely sympathetic with their work of assisting the "new Southerners."[40] Unlike Howard, however, Sherman did not hide his attitude toward all this goodness, which mocked his ugly job of winning the war. The Saxton ladies pronounced him "horrid looking" and were happy when he followed Howard's looting troops over to the mainland on January 24.[41] Shortly, Howard sent his thanks to the Saxtons for their hospitality and his apologies for his soldiers, who had not respected the island Negroes' property any more than the rebels' property on the mainland.[42] After the Army of the Tennessee left, Saxton's assistants continued to receive reports from the freedmen of stolen chickens and graver indignities committed by the soldiers of liberation. "I trust the memory of us may be pleasant after the smart of roughness shall have been forgotten," wrote Howard to Saxton. "Stick to your sturdy integrity," he concluded, "and [your] unflinching faith in a righteous [sic] God and He will bless you and make you prevail in every good work."[43]

36. Saxton Diary, 9 Jan. 1865.
37. Ibid., 15 Jan. 1866.
38. Ibid., Saxton returned briefly in 1868 to the South, ironically to Atlanta, a city he had been accused of ignoring as assistant commissioner (Cornelia Hancock, *South After Gettysburg: Letters of Cornelia Hancock, 1863–1868,* ed. Henrietta Stratton Jacquette [New York, 1965], p. 228.
39. Saxton Diary, 30 Mar. 1866.
40. O. O. Howard ms., "Sherman's March thru the Carolinas and Savannah," OOH Papers.
41. Saxton Diary, 23 Jan. 1865.
42. Ibid., 21 Jan. 1865.
43. O. O. Howard to Rufus Saxton, 29 Jan. 1865, OOH Papers.

On May 9, 1865, Howard and his Army of the Tennessee were in Manchester, Virginia; the war was over. He had led his men from the Sea Islands through South Carolina, where, with sullen savageness, they had inflicted destruction at least as bad as Georgians had seen. Drunk and wild, his men had burned Columbia.[44] North Carolina fared better and, finally, the Army of the Tennessee marched north toward Virginia.

Lee had already surrendered to Grant at Appomattox, and Sherman had accepted the military surrender of his adversary, General Joseph E. Johnston, on April 17 near Durham Station, North Carolina. Sherman and Johnston, knowing (their troops and officers did not) that Lincoln had been shot and had died the day before, shared a mistaken fear that the assassination might invoke chaos more uncontrollable than the violence of the war.[45] Sherman, in order to achieve stability and peace, was willing to allow the existing governments of the southern states to reenter the Union without insisting on any political adjustments that would benefit the slaves freed by the war. The Union government, dominated in the post-assassination crisis by Secretary Stanton, revoked Sherman's agreement and insisted that it be replaced by an unconditional arrangement like Grant's and Lee's.[46]

General Grant telegrammed Howard on May 8 ordering him to Washington for an assignment in a federal effort to reconstruct the South. Otis Howard arrived the next evening and had his first interview with Secretary Stanton on the morning of May 11. Stanton gave him the text of the bill enacting the Freedmen's Bureau; after Howard read it, Stanton offered him the commissionership of the new agency.[47]

For three weeks, in the provisional capital of the freedmen

44. For a powerful description of the fire by a member of Howard's staff, see Thomas W. Osborn ms. diary, Bowdoin College Library; Conyngham, *Sherman's March*, p. 332; *Who Burnt Columbia?* (Official deposition of W. T. Sherman and O. O. Howard, Charleston, 1873); Katherine M. Jones, ed., *When Sherman Came: Southern Women and the 'Great March'* (Indianapolis, 1964), pp. 156–63, 167–70, 170–72, 202.

45. Sherman, *Memoirs*, 2, 347–51.

46. E. M. Stanton to U. S. Grant, 18 Apr. 1865, Stanton Papers, LC.

47. Howard, *Autobiography*, 2, 206–08.

movement, the talk had been that Howard would get the post. Beaufort, South Carolina, was both proud and apprehensive as it yielded its supremacy in the governing of the freedmen to Washington. The Yankee islanders had been there since 1861 trying out ways in which the slaves could adapt to being freemen. It had been part of the point of their work that it serve as a model for similar programs all over the South when the war had ended. The Freedmen's Bureau was to succeed to work they had been doing, and the islanders felt a certain proprietorship in the agency and great curiosity as to who would be named to head it.

Northerners curious about these experiments with the Negroes (and attracted to the beautiful and accessible Sea Islands rather than elsewhere, where work with the freedmen also went on behind Union lines) had been coming to the islands to have a look all through the war. Senator Lyman Trumbull had come with a party which included Senators Grimes, Ramsey, Morrill, Doolittle, Wade, and Sherman in March, but in April, at the close of the war, attention was shifting to the mainland.[48] A band of preachers, politicians, and antislavery leaders headed by Henry Ward Beecher had come to Charleston in order to celebrate the raising of the flag again over Fort Sumter (and had found the best hotel already full of northern businessmen conferring with their southern brethren).[49]

Beecher commanded this new army. He did so at the invitation of Secretary of War Stanton, and he read his commission as more than a request for a talented speaker.[50] He impressed upon members of his party that he was there not only as the chief orator of a not noticeably reticent group of notables, but also as "sort of inspector & agent of [the] Secy of War," who could not accompany the group himself because Secretary of State Seward had suffered an accident.[51]

The ceremonies at Sumter were austere in comparison with the

48. Saxton Diary, 19 Mar. 1865.

49. Ibid., 15 Apr. 1865.

50. E. M. Stanton to H. W. Beecher, 1, 5, 6, and 7 Apr. 1865, Beecher family Papers, Yale University.

51. C. H. Howard to O. O. Howard, 22 Apr. 1865, OOH Papers; E. M. Stanton to H. W. Beecher, 6 Apr. 1865, Beecher Family Papers.

events in Charleston itself. On April 16, 1865, Beecher preached to 3,000 Negroes in Charleston's Zion Church. His son-in-law said he "never saw him or heard him do better." The auditorium was crammed; a "sprinkling of white officers & ladies" were in front "near the pulpit, the rest . . . [were] negroes of every size, sex, color, age." As Beecher spoke, "emotion began to work in the audience like the rising of the wind in the forest or the sobbing of the waves upon the Beach." The men and their turbaned women in colorful plaid dresses followed Beecher intently and responsively. There were tears and there was laughter, and the sermon was even broken into with a cry: "Thank you massa, Glory to God."[52]

Some of the "hoe and trowel" Abolitionists—men and women not under the illusion that freedom alone solved the problems caused by slavery—who had been working so long on the Sea Islands were uneasy about these liberation displays, not all of which featured the freedmen. A victory ball was held in Charleston the night of the flag raising for the visitors and the army officers stationed anywhere near enough to attend. In contrast to the rather sedate "attempt at a ball" on the Sea Islands' Hilton Head, it was a splendid event. In the morning some of the young Union officers, including the Beaufort contingent, unaccustomed to "living fast," woke up on unfamiliar sofas and mattresses and were in poor condition to match the ardor of the Negroes who gathered later in the day to honor the greatest of the visitors.[53] William Lloyd Garrison was canonized at a service even more emotional in tone than the Beecher church meeting.[54] Rufus Saxton was anxious to bring things back to earth. He urged Beecher and his party, which included Abolitionist leaders Theodore Tilton and George Thompson as well as Garrison, to come out to the islands and see how the "freedmen are living on their new farms."[55]

52. Samuel Scoville to his wife, Harriet Beecher Scoville, 17 Apr. 1865, Beecher Family Papers.
53. Saxton Diary, 15 Apr. 1865.
54. Ibid.
55. Rufus Saxton to H. W. Beecher, 18 Apr. 1865 [sic], Beecher Family Papers.

Beecher's party accepted the invitation and brought along a whirlwind of gossip and conjecture about the new Freedmen's Bureau. Charles Howard, who was a member of the party, having used his acquaintance with Beecher to obtain transportation back to the islands to take up the command of a Negro regiment, wrote to his brother that there was talk of "offering you the bureau at Washington (colored)."[56] Rufus Saxton, trying as always to perfect his Port Royal experiment, and hoping for a sympathetic commander of the Department of the South, expressed a wish that Howard be named to that post, but Senator Wilson, the head of the Committee on Military Affairs, and Beecher told Saxton that Howard was being considered for the more significant post of commissioner of the Freedmen's Bureau.[57]

Beecher's party left and hurried north when word of Lincoln's death reached the islands on April 17.[58] From Brooklyn, Beecher wrote a long letter to Secretary of War Stanton giving suggestions for the Freedmen's Bureau. He was "anxious to have the bureau in operation," but the reasons for his anxiety were not those of Rufus Saxton and the antislavery men who had been working to help the ex-slaves on the islands, in New Orleans, at Newport News, on plantation colonies along the Mississippi River, and elsewhere in the South. Beecher hoped Stanton would hurry the agency into being as "we are in danger of *too much* northern management of the Negro—The black man is just like the white, in this—that he should be left, & obliged to take *care* of himself & suffer & enjoy, according as he creates the means of either." The Plymouth Church preacher would have given the "plantation slave, a small *start,* in tools, seed, etc.," but no more: "Beyond this, I think nursing will only pauperize him. I see in the movements about here a tendency to dandle the black man, or at least, to recite his suffering so as to gain sympathy & money from the public. All this will be checked by your *bureau.*"[59]

56. C. H. Howard to O. O. Howard, 22 Apr. 1865, OOH Papers.
57. C. H. Howard to O. O. Howard, 22 Apr. 1865, OOH Papers.
58. Saxton Diary, 17 Apr. 1865.
59. H. W. Beecher to E. M. Stanton, 3 May 1865, OOH Papers.

Beecher, in describing the man who should head the Bureau, wasted not a word on either experience working with the freedmen or sympathy for them. Beecher reported that he had "conversed with Saxton & others in the south & found them very clear in favor" of Howard, whom he found to be "truly Christian . . . *pleasant* to work with; a gentleman, faithful & *cooperative* . . . [That] he is, of all men, the one who would command entire confidence of [the] *Christian public,* is the point, and, I do not know who would also, to such a degree, unite the secular public."[60]

Secular was a pejorative; Beecher wanted a commissioner who would safely steal dominion over freedman policy from the philanthropists in the freedmen's aid societies who were interested in working directly with the freedmen, as they had demonstrated in the Port Royal experiment. Beecher wanted the governing of the freedmen done in a safe institution run by a conservative member of a properly evangelical church. Clearly, he knew the "secular public" on the Sea Islands and in New Orleans was trapped. The government was about to enter into an enterprise grown too large for private persons to handle alone. The freedmen's aid people of the Port Royal stripe would have to support any organization designed to aid the freedmen or be left outside the national effort. Saxton and other activist friends of the freedmen would not have accepted a man unsympathetic to the ex-slaves. If they could not have one of their own men head the Freedmen's Bureau, they would insist on a man at least as dedicated to the work as General Howard, [61] whom they trusted on the basis of his January commitment. Their liking for Howard bolstered Beecher's conviction that he was, "of all men yet mentioned, the *very one.*"[62]

Whether Stanton read Beecher's letter before dropping it in the file on freedmen's matters he was maintaining next to his desk is not known. If he did, he found support for his decision that Howard was the right man. There is little evidence that President

60. Ibid.
61. Rufus Saxton to O.O. Howard, 24 May 1865, OOH Papers.
62. H. W. Beecher to E. M. Stanton, 3 May 1865, OOH Papers.

Lincoln gave much attention to the Freedmen's Bureau and none to corroborate the claim that he chose its commissioner. It is entirely possible that Lincoln and Stanton had made no choice before the assassination in April because in May Chief Justice Chase, much interested in Reconstruction matters, left on an inspection trip to the South with the impression that no commissioner had yet been selected.[63]

Even if Stanton got no guidance from President Lincoln and asked his new chief executive, Andrew Johnson, for none, he knew that the head of the Freedmen's Bureau must be acceptable to the President. Johnson had to make the appointment, if not the choice. The fact that Howard was so conspicuously religious might not have endeared him to either President, but Stanton had in mind making the General's religiosity an asset. Howard, safely anchored in orthodox American Christianity with ties to the Baptist, Methodist, Congregational, and even Episcopalian churches, had never been an Abolitionist or belonged to any controversial group. He could be expected to appeal to leaders of American Christianity who were anxious to capture the radical enterprise of work with the freedmen as part of their conservative goal of redeeming the fallen South and mending the broken nation. They wanted government sponsorship for their essentially voluntaristic and unsecular enterprise, and Stanton was prepared to give it to them in return for assistance in the job of Negro relief.[64]

If Howard could prove Beecher wrong and get the preacher's "Christian public" to do more rather than less for the freedmen, and if he could keep the secular freedmen's aid men loyal to their present excellent work with the Negroes, the government might be relieved of much of its responsibility to the freedmen. This, Stanton might reasonably believe, would appeal to any President faced with the problems of Reconstruction.

63. Abraham Lincoln to E. M. Stanton, 25 Mar. 1865 and S. P. Chase to E. M. Stanton, 20 May 1865, Stanton Papers, LC.

64. Congress made reliance on the private agencies explicit in the legislation extending the Bureau, Act of 16 July 1866, *14 U.S. Stat.*, 173–77.

A second reason for picking Howard was a belief that he cared about the Negroes' welfare. Both Stanton and Howard, in endorsing Saxton's humanitarian work on the Sea Islands, had committed themselves to a view that a concern for the freedmen was requisite for a man working for the Freedmen's Bureau.

There was also a third reason, and probably the most important, why Howard was the man for the job. His name had been up for consideration before and had been rejected, not for lack of experience in working with the freedmen, but because Sherman needed him to help finish the war.[65] Lack of experience was an asset; Stanton had learned that those with experience acted as reminders of the dilemmas of the work with the freedmen.[66] With Howard the administration could think it was getting off to a fresh and promising start in developing a freedmen's policy.

Furthermore, with Howard, the Bureau would be in the hands of a victorious leader of a great army. That fact coupled with the fact that friends of the freedmen—true ones as well as false—trusted him made his selection a prediction that the Bureau would succeed. As Howard was leaving the Sea Islands the previous January, Willard Saxton had proclaimed: "It seems as if success would always follow the 'Christian Howard.' "[67]

When Stanton offered Howard the job, he told him that Lincoln had wanted him for this position, but the appointment was delayed because Sherman needed him in the war.[68] In the emotional wake of Lincoln's death, such talk allowed little room for a man to say no, even if he wanted to. In his *Autobiography,* Howard told of his decision:

> Naturally as the great war drew to a close, I had been pondering the subject of my future work. Should I remain in the army or not? What as a young man of thirty-four had I better do? The opportunity afforded by this offer appeared to me at once to answer my anxious inquiries. Indeed it

65. H. W. Beecher to E. M. Stanton, 3 May 1865, OOH Papers.
66. Rufus Saxton to E. M. Stanton, 7 Feb. 1865, Stanton Papers, LC.
67. Saxton Diary, 13 Jan. 1865.
68. Howard, *Autobiography,* 2, 207.

seemed providential; so in my consciousness my mind was virtually made up before I left the War Office.[69]

One night was a decent period for reflection, and he was back to see Stanton the next morning to accept the post.

Stanton was delighted to move the responsibility for the government's freedmen policy out of his office and into someone else's where he could keep a distant eye on it but not have to contend with its daily complexities. He picked up a bushel basket in which he had been filing letters received—the one from Beecher and others—advising him on what to do about the freedmen and handed it to Howard. "Here's your Bureau," he said, and the one-armed General, who had wrist enough for the task, received from the Secretary all that he was to get in the way of specific instructions on how to begin his new job.[70] The two men parted amicably, and the new Commissioner went to open a headquarters for the Freedmen's Bureau.

69. Ibid., 208.
70. Howard, *Autobiography*, 2, 208.

4. The Men of the Freedmen's Bureau

For the headquarters of the new Bureau, Howard was given a townhouse on the northeast corner of "I" and Nineteenth streets, which had been confiscated from a Congressman who defected to the Confederacy. The agency, therefore, was physically removed from the War Department and yet the link between the army and the Freedmen's Bureau was never severed. Congress had called for the nation's most advanced experiment in social welfare but had grafted it onto the most conservative of American institutions. The connection of the Bureau to the army reflected a commitment to the restoration of order and, in the absence of any clearly enunciated policy directives from Stanton, Howard proceeded with a task familiar to any general, organizing a staff.

To facilitate this, Stanton had authorized the transfer to the Bureau of officers of Howard's old Army of the Tennessee. Congress had provided for no bureau salaries other than regular army pay.[1] Unless commissions could be granted to nonmilitary men (a difficult task as Stanton began shrinking the army), Howard had no choice but to employ officers already in the army.

This suited him. He used the fact that commissions were hard to obtain more as an excuse for keeping out civilians he did not want in the Bureau, such as the radical Abolitionist James Redpath and President Lincoln's son Robert, than as an argument that he should have an appropriation to hire men from outside the service.[2] He was used to a military command and expected from it the loyalty he had learned to depend on during the war. His favorites among the assistant commissioners were always the

1. *13 U.S. Stat.*, 507–09.

2. James Redpath to O. O. Howard, 5 Sept. 1865, J. A. Sladen to James Redpath, 15 Sept. 1865, O. O. Howard to Rufus Saxton, 15 Sept. 1865, OOH Papers; O. O. Howard to R. T. Lincoln, 24 June 1865, BRFAL.

Army of the Tennessee men who had served with him during the war. From the ranks of wartime comrades came Thomas Osborn, Wager Swayne, John Wilson Sprague, Davis Tillson, R. K. Scott, Eliphalet Whittlesey, Charles Howard, Absalom Baird, and James Scott Fullerton.

Thomas Osborn was one of the Army of the Tennessee men. His diary, kept during his service on Howard's staff during the campaigns in Georgia and the Carolinas, reveals much about his commander's personality.[3] The two men were close, and Howard was determined that Osborn should have an assistant commissionership. He was announced first for Mississippi, then Alabama, and finally Florida. When an injury received while on leave delayed his taking up his post in that state, Howard resisted giving the post to any other man.[4] The planters, not the freedmen, were the beneficiaries of the Commissioner's patience, for Osborn kept Florida Negroes firmly tied to the planters who had owned them before the war's end.[5]

Wager Swayne, a "promising young lawyer and a Christian" who was sent to Alabama, John Wilson Sprague, a "distinguished general" who went to Arkansas, and Davis Tillson, who first was subassistant commissioner for West Tennessee and then sent to head the District of Georgia when it, like Florida, was divorced from South Carolina, were all officers who had commanded units in Howard's army and earned their Commander's admiration as leaders of their men.[6] Eliphalet Whittlesey, a "brave Christian gentleman" assigned to North Carolina, had been on Howard's staff throughout most of the war, as had the General's brother, Charles Howard, who entered the Bureau in South Carolina under Rufus Saxton and became its deputy chief when he was named assistant commissioner for the District of Columbia. Generals R. K. Scott and Absalom Baird, though not among the first

3. Thomas W. Osborn ms. diary.
4. T. W. Osborn to O. O. Howard, 28 June 1865, OOH Papers.
5. William W. Davis, *The Civil War and Reconstruction in Florida* (New York, 1913), pp. 381, 382.
6. Howard, *Autobiography*, 2, 217, 218.

assistant commissioners, were nevertheless trusted by Howard because they had served him well during the war: he sent them to South Carolina and Louisiana.[7]

The other original assistant commissioners, also army officers, were put in charge of freedmen in sectors where ex-slaves had congregated behind Union lines in the South. Orlando Brown, a graduate of the Yale Medical School, worked in the hospital in Newport News, Virginia, where he came into contact with many contrabands. Howard appointed him assistant commissioner for Virginia and, partly because he was near enough to Washington for Howard to observe his work closely, he, more than any of the other new officers, gained Howard's confidence.[8]

General Clinton B. Fisk, the Christian Commission's candidate for commissioner of the Freedmen's Bureau, was given Kentucky and Tennessee (and, for a time, the northern part of Alabama).[9] Perhaps the most ambitious and certainly the most frank of Howard's assistant commissioners (he once admitted he had "brevet on the brain"), Fisk tried to add other adjacent areas to his domain.[10] Another man who was spoken of for Howard's post was John Eaton, Jr., who had been in charge of freedmen's affairs for General Grant in the Mississippi Valley. On Grant's strong recommendation ("he's your man"), Eaton was made assistant commissioner for the District of Columbia, a post which was understood to carry with it the responsibility of being Howard's deputy in the administration of the Bureau as a whole.[11] On Eaton's recommendation, Samuel Thomas, who had been in charge of work with the freedmen in Mississippi and, most

7. Saxton Diary, 19 Jan., 15 Feb. 1866; Howard, *Autobiography, 1,* 478, 479, 567.

8. John Eaton, Jr., to O. O. Howard, 9 May 1865, OOH Papers.

9. *Report of the Joint Committee on Reconstruction,* 30 Apr. 1866, 39th Cong., 1st sess., no. 30 (serial 1273), pt. 3, p. 29; G. H. Stuart to O. O. Howard, 15 May 1866, OOH Papers.

10. Alphonso A. Hopkins, *The Life of Clinton Bowen Fisk* (New York, 1890); C. B. Fisk to O. O. Howard, 2 Sept. 1865, OOH Papers.

11. Howard, *Autobiography, 2,* 225.

notably, had jurisdiction over the important agricultural community managed by the freedmen at Davis Bend, was retained in his post in Vicksburg.[12]

Rufus Saxton, whom Howard had come to know and even to acknowledge as his mentor, was kept on at Beaufort as assistant commissioner of the district originally comprising South Carolina, Georgia, and Florida. Thomas Conway, "a business-like preacher" whom, like Brown and Thomas, Howard had never even met, had been Superintendent of Free Labor in the Department of the Gulf and was given the assistant commissionership of Louisiana.[13]

The last of the Confederate states to receive the attention of the Bureau was Texas, which was sent the oldest of the assistant commissioners, General Edgar Gregory, whose credentials were neither service with Howard in the army nor experience working with the freedmen. He was a radical Abolitionist, "so fearless," said Howard, "that I sent him to Texas."[14] Gregory's first task there was to spread the word to his constituents that they were no longer slaves; as late as November 1865 this came as news to many of them.[15]

Gregory had a long career in the Bureau; he was not mustered out until the end of 1867. After he left Texas he served on Howard's staff in Washington and was later made assistant commissioner for nearby Maryland. At first glance, his career and those of others who, similarly, were transferred suggests the flexibility of the Bureau in adjusting to changing circumstances

12. Vernon L. Wharton, *The Negro in Mississippi, 1865–1890* (New York, 1965), p. 58; Whitelaw Reid, *After the War: A Southern Tour, May 1, 1865, to May 1, 1866,* ed. C. Vann Woodward (New York, 1965), p. 280; John Eaton, Jr., *Grant, Lincoln, and the Freedmen* (New York, 1907), p. 1237.

13. Reid, p. 256; Howard, *Autobiography,* 2, 217.

14. *New York Times,* 8 Nov. 1871; *New Orleans Tribune,* 25 July 1865; Howard, *Autobiography,* 2, 218.

15. O. O. Howard address on occasion of 25th anniversary of Hampton Institute, 23 May 1889, *Southern Workman* (Hampton, Va., June 1889); Claude Elliott, "The Freedmen's Bureau in Texas," *Southern Historical Quarterly,* 56 (July 1952), p. 4.

and a deliberate increasing of the radical influence in the Bureau as a whole.

In fact, however, it represents an opposite trend. One after another, the assistant commissioners in the South who obstructed Andrew Johnson's restoration policy were removed, and the most tactful way of removing them without betraying a split between the White House and the Bureau was to transfer them to the head office. In Texas Edgar Gregory had to cope with incidents of extreme cruelty.[16] General William E. Strong, Howard's cautious Inspector General, who was not given to overdramatization, reported the Negroes in the state were "frequently beaten and shot down like wild beasts, without provocation, followed with hounds and maltreated in every possible way." One planter told Strong that the reason for the killings was the need "to thin out [the] niggers a little."[17] Gregory, in traveling over 700 miles to speak to more than 25,000 Negroes, told them not only that they were free but that they must contract to work with their former owners as no land would be given them.[18]

This plea for cooperation with the planters met with a response from 90 percent of the Negroes, who by January 1866 had agreed to work for $8 to $15 a month. In spite of this David G. Burnet, once President of the Republic of Texas, complained to President Johnson that Gregory was "inspiring the freedmen to hate their former masters."[19] Not all Texans who disliked the Freedmen's Bureau were as displeased with Gregory as Burnet. One newspaper man wrote: "There are men who would grumble at the Bureau no matter by whom managed, even though the Archangel Gabriel was Assistant Commissioner."[20] Gregory protested against the charges but to no avail. Johnson insisted that he be

16. P. H. Sheridan to O. O. Howard, 3 Aug. 1865, OOH Papers.

17. William E. Strong, quoted in Elliott, "The Freedmen's Bureau in Texas," p. 6.

18. Ibid., pp. 2, 4.

19. Ibid., pp. 5, 10.

20. *Flake's Bulletin* (Galveston), 19 Apr. 1866.

moved from the state. He was brought to Washington as a member of a committee to draft procedural changes in the Bureau.

Samuel Thomas, the young businessman who was the assistant commissioner in Mississippi, frequently did not heed the Negroes' "foolish" requests and often took the planter's side in arguments involving the inefficiency of freedmen workers.[21] This, however, did not prevent Thomas from championing the Negroes in their fight to be allowed to own farms. The Assistant Commissioner took great pride in the success with which the Negroes managed their own community at Davis Bend, which had been in his jurisdiction during the war. When that excellent and prosperous experiment was destroyed not a year after the war ended, Thomas was greatly disappointed. All across the state in the fall of 1865 he found a "growing feeling in the minds of the whites against this privileges [sic] of owning lands or working at any business the negro might choose."[22]

Thomas contended "that the Freedmen will never be thoroughly emancipated till they are allowed to own lands and work for themselves at any branch of industry their inclination may lead them to pursue." This line of thinking was not congenial in a state in which the legislature, a month later, prohibited Negroes from owning land outside of towns (which meant no farmland) and in which local towns placed prohibitory taxes on Negroes who sought skilled jobs.[23] In Vicksburg "negro hack drivers and draymen are charged enormous rates for licenses and required to file bonds for five hundred dollars each, signed by freeholders, for their voucher."[24]

White Mississippians complained about Thomas and were abetted by a campaign in the Cincinnati *Commercial,* which sought the rewards of sensationalism by telling of the handsome

21. Wharton, p. 78.
22. Samuel Thomas to O. O. Howard, 12 Oct. 1865, BRFAL.
23. "An Act to confer Civil Rights on Freedmen, and for Other Purposes" (approved 22 Nov. 1865), *Laws of the State of Mississippi passed at the regular session of the Mississippi Legislature, City of Jackson, October, November and December, 1865* (Jackson, 1866), pp. 82–86.
24. Samuel Thomas to O. O. Howard, 12 Oct. 1865, BRFAL.

young Assistant Commissioner riding through Vicksburg with "a sleak span of horses and carriage to correspond" as he escorted the "gay ladies" of the town.[25] On this charge, Thomas defended himself with considerable dignity and accounted, as well, for contract fees and fines levied, which, it was alleged, he had pocketed. Nevertheless, the effort was successful and Howard "was sorry to say," Thomas was removed.[26]

As Thomas Conway put it, referring to himself and to Saxton, Gregory, and Thomas, such assistant commissioners were "true to liberty" and were forced to "give way to 'conservatives.' "[27] Thomas left Mississippi and was transferred to the head office. The same pattern was followed by lesser officials of the Bureau, including Alexander P. Ketchum, the land officer on the Sea Islands who exasperated Johnson's planter friends seeking to get their plantations back, and Stuart Eldridge, Thomas' most able deputy, who repeatedly wrote embarrassing letters to Washington questioning the treatment of the Negroes in Mississippi. Both of these able young men became aides to Howard in Washington. They, along with Thomas, called "a fine man, intelligent and a right thinker" by Willard Saxton, still another radical who had been moved out of the South, formed an informal group of officers in exile at headquarters.[28] In the hours after work, these young men participated in welfare and education programs for the freedmen in the capital. They were useful there, but the freedmen in the South had lost their services.

Not all the radicals were eased out of sensitive spots in the South this way. Thomas Conway was not given the chance to leave so gracefully, and Rufus Saxton, offered a head-office inspectorship, said he "would not touch [it] with a thousand foot

25. Samuel Thomas to T. J. Wood (copy to O. O. Howard), 26 Mar. 1866, BRFAL.

26. Howard, *Autobiography*, 2, 283.

27. T. W. Conway to O. O. Howard, 14 May 1866, OOH Papers.

28. Joel Williamson, *After Slavery* (Chapel Hill, 1965), p. 81; Samuel Thomas to O. O. Howard, 24 Aug. 1865, Stuart Eldridge Papers on loan to Yale University; Samuel Eldridge to O. O. Howard, 19 Sept. 1866, Stuart Eldridge Papers; Saxton Diary, 6 July 1866.

pole."[29] He flatly refused to deprive the freedmen of the last service he could render them—the publicity attendant on his being removed for taking their part in the struggle for land in the South.

The assistant commissioners, whether associates of General Howard in the war or officers inherited from earlier attempts to work with the freedmen, were men of similar background. They came from New England, the Middle States, and the Midwest. Only Samuel Thomas, John Wilson Sprague, and Clinton B. Fisk were not college men. All except Conway, from Ireland's County Clare, were native born; all (including Conway) were Protestants belonging to the great denominations of the center who believed that man, stimulated in the emotional atmosphere of revivals, could find salvation by working to perfect his world.

When the war ended, claims Timothy L. Smith, the leaders of the Methodists, Baptists, Lutherans, Congregationalists, Presbyterians, and even the evangelically oriented among the Unitarians and Episcopalians, were "consecrated to the task of building a Christian commonwealth in America."[30] Smith's study convinced him that the perfectionist movement was mature in 1865 and to be expected to undertake a movement of social reform. This was what General Howard counted on. He was encouraged by William E. Boardman's call for a "Christian Commission for the Masses" in the postwar world.[31] He counted on the inclusion of the freedmen in the commonwealth and expected the nation to support his men who, as assistant commissioners at the Freedmen's Bureau, would also be a part of Boardman's commission.

Several of the assistant commissioners, most notably Wager Swayne, whose family left Virginia where it had long been established, were on record as opposing slavery, but only Edgar Gregory might be said to have been an Abolitionist.[32] As was true

29. Saxton Diary, 15 Jan. 1866.

30. Timothy L. Smith, *Revivalism and Social Reform in Mid-Century America* (New York, 1957), p. 236.

31. W. E. Boardman to O. O. Howard, 28 Aug. 1865, OOH Papers.

32. Report on meeting addressed by Gregory, J. C. Fremont, Michael Hahn, Frederick Douglass, William Howard Day, Horace Greeley, and John A. Andrew, *New Orleans Tribune*, 25 July 1865.

of the Abolitionists, probably not one of the officials of the Bureau thought of any one Negro as his equal—"I never advocated equality except by law & justice," wrote Howard—but the best of them were committed to the equality of man.[33] Thomas Conway, whose good friends in the Negro press were his severest critics, was a fine example of how a man could grow working with the Negro clients of the Bureau. While still Superintendent of Free Labor in the Department of the Gulf in the fall of 1864, he spoke one day in a way typical of evangelical Christians. He suggested that the Negroes' true goal was to return to Africa and Christianize their brothers there.[34] The *New Orleans Tribune* came down hard on this. Mockingly they addressed Conway: "How are you, deportation? Good morning, colonization."[35] The editors then proceeded to set him straight: "We are Americans and mean to remain such." Conway learned quickly. A little more than a year later he spoke of the Negroes as the "best loyal men in New Orleans" and referred to their leaders as "fine scholars capable of taking a stand alongside the best white men in the country."[36] Conway's sense of equality increased during his close association with the Negro community, but it is sobering to note that the Negroes regarded this man who became the most radical of all the assistant commissioners as imperfectly committed to their equality. In August 1865 a colored writer praising a position taken in behalf of the freedmen nonetheless dismissed Conway as "imbued with the common prejudice against us."[37]

The assistant commissioners are an obscure group of men. Some of the obscurity was earned, but much was caused by the changing value judgments of society. At the time they went to work for the agency, they were excited over their prospects of succeeding with it. After they left the Bureau, most of them went

33. O. O. Howard to [name omitted], Washington, D.C., 9 Mar. 1869, OOH Papers.
34. T. W. Conway to *New Orleans Tribune*, 2 Dec. 1864, quoted in Howard A. White, "The Freedmen's Bureau in Louisiana," Unpublished Ph.D. dissertation Tulane University, 1956, p. 11.
35. *New Orleans Tribune*, 8 Dec. 1864, in White, p. 12.
36. *Report of the Joint Committee on Reconstruction*, pt. 4, p. 83.
37. *New Orleans Tribune*, 31 Aug. 1865.

on to eminently respectable and substantial careers in other fields. In autobiographical sketches their service in the Freedmen's Bureau was scarcely mentioned.[38] Similarly, the turn-of-the-century biographical dictionaries judged it unflattering to stress bureau service.

The nation and, one guesses, several of the assistant commissioners themselves turned their backs on the Negro work they had done after the war. The two men who undertook to tell in detail of their work with the freedmen deserve special credit for doing so when they did. O. O. Howard published his *Autobiography* in 1908. John Eaton, Jr., who had read Howard's work in manuscript, finished his *Grant, Lincoln and the Freedmen* before he died in 1906.[39] This work, with its excellent account of the treatment of the Negroes during the Civil War, was, with Howard's account of the involvement of the Negro in the events of Reconstruction, a strong indictment of a nation which seemed determined to separate the Negro from all of its national life.

Eaton's description of his recruitment to that work is revealing of what it meant to a young officer to step across the threshold and involve himself with the Negroes. He was the chaplain of an Ohio regiment which had moved south with Grant into the cotton-producing area of Southwest Tennessee and camped for "the first time . . . in a region densely populated by the Negroes."[40] The contrabands were leaving the plantations, fleeing from the raiding parties of both armies, and coming into Grant's camps.

> The arrival among us of these hordes was like the oncoming of cities. There was no plan in this exodus, no Moses to lead it. Unlettered reason or the inarticulate decision of instinct

38. The assistant commissioners grew old in the great day of the "mug books," regional histories which were compendiums of biographical sketches for which much of the information (as well as the funds for publication) were supplied by the subscriber-subjects.

39. John Eaton, Jr. (in collaboration with Esther Osgood Mason), *Grant, Lincoln and the Freemen: Reminiscences of the Civil War with Special Reference to the Work for the Contrabands and the Freedmen of the Mississippi Valley* (New York, 1907), p. 47 n.

40. Ibid., p. 1.

brought them to us. Often the slaves met prejudice against their color more bitter than they had left behind. But their own interests were identical, they felt, with the objects of our armies: a blind terror stung them, an equally blind hope allured them, and they came to us. Their condition was appalling.[41]

Eaton, as a chaplain, "had done what I could to relieve the most urgent . . . cases of distress, and to check the . . . elements the most dangerous to the welfare of our soldiers." By this last, he means both disease and the demoralization of the Union troops exposed to "a veritable moral chaos . . . [of] deceit, theft, [and] licentiousness."[42]

No one knew what to do with these refugees. One night in camp, Eaton was sitting around the fire with his colonel, a good friend from Toledo, and others of the regimental staff. "They were in high spirits, and something of their jokes and laughter seemed to be at my expense. . . . In the midst of the merriment I caught phrases now and then which had no meaning for me, and which yet made me vaguely uneasy, for there was an undercurrent of seriousness in what was said." The colonel finally handed Eaton an order from Grant's headquarters detailing him to take charge of the Negroes—to organize the contrabands into work companies, to provide food and shelter for them, and to use guards to protect them.

> No language can describe the effect of this order upon me. Never in the entire army service, through the whole war, during imprisonment or in the midst of battles with the roar of cannon in my ears, amid the horrors of the hospital or in facing my own exposure to assassination, do I recall such a shock of surprise, amounting to consternation, as I experienced when reading this brief summons to undertake what seemed to me an enterprise beyond the possibility of human achievement. I retired to my cot and drew the

41. Ibid., p. 2.
42. Ibid., p. 3.

blankets around me,—not to sleep, but to think it out alone.[43]

Finding men who could stand up to the indignity of serving with the freedmen was not easy. Candidates were cautious. General Grant recommended to one young gentleman, Alexander Stewart Webb, that he not take a Negro regiment but accept instead a lower rank in a white one.[44] "This is better," Webb wrote with relief: "All is O.K. now."[45] Was the position of surgeon in a Negro regiment "regarded [as] a respectable position?" another man asked of General Howard. Are the officers in the freedmen's regiments "generally intelligent Christian or moral men and are there hopes of promotion for merit?" he wanted to know.[46] Rather than cope with such reluctance, Howard, quite naturally, chose first among his close associates during the war who had proved trustworthy in other difficult assignments. He knew the moral caliber of these men and assumed that it qualified them just as well for work with the freed Negroes as for the grim and trying challenges of the war.

As a field commander, Howard had enjoyed close relationships with the officers on his staff.[47] He had not been a commander who was remote from his officers or who was easily chafed by the inadequacies or lapses of subordinates.[48] He had been open and trusting in his dealings with his officers, and his relationships with these men seem to have sustained him through the war. Howard had seen much in the army, at West Point, and during the war, which seemed to him a denial of all his moral values. Drunkenness, cruelty, and greed troubled him, but he found in his own men sufficient courage and goodness to make the war endurable.

43. Ibid., p. 5.
44. U. S. Grant to A. S. Webb, 3 Oct. 1866, Alexander Stewart Webb Papers, Yale University.
45. A. S. Webb to J. W. Webb, 5 Oct. 1866, Webb Papers.
46. Andrew Morell to O. O. Howard, 15 Aug. 1865, OOH Papers.
47. Conyhgham, *Sherman's March,* p. 304
48. Thomas W. Osborn ms. diary, Bowdoin College Library.

At River's Bridge, South Carolina, Wager Swayne was severely wounded.[49] His leg, badly torn—it was amputated that day—was so twisted that the motion of the stretcher on which he was being carried from the battlefield caused him much pain. Howard stopped the bearers, straightened the leg, and cushioned it with a giant pine cone. As Howard remembered it, Swayne responded to the pain and to the apprehension of the amputation with the words: "The Lord sustains me!"[50] From that moment on, no matter what the task, Swayne's credentials were in order in Howard's eyes.

Wager Swayne was the only one of the assistant commissioners who could claim, though remotely, to be a Southerner. He was also the official of the Freedmen's Bureau who had the least problem of job security: he had a powerful father, Noah Swayne—an associate justice of the Supreme Court, appointed by Lincoln in 1862.[51] Wager Swayne knew that a comfortable legal practice was the alternative to being fired, but his father's presence on the court made such a firing unlikely. Appointed to govern the freedmen of Alabama in 1865, Swayne lasted longer in the post of assistant commissioner than any of his colleagues. However, his staying power was due only partly to his father; it was the most ardent of President Johnson's emissaries to the South, H. M. Watterson, a man who was most eager to discredit the Freedmen's Bureau when it stood in the way of Johnson's anti-freedmen policies, who found Swayne to be "altogether a gentleman."[52]

Swayne's administration of the Freedmen's Bureau in Alabama needs study.[53] There is much which suggests that Swayne was

49. Conyhgham, p. 305.

50. Howard, *Autobiography*, 2, 107.

51. Charles Warren, *The Supreme Court in United States History* (2 vols. Boston, 1926), 2, 401, 417 n. Noah Swayne, when a very young lawyer, left Virginia because he objected to slavery. His Quaker bride, Sarah Wager, freed her slaves when she followed him to Ohio. Justice Swayne's career, particularly his years on the Supreme Court, has been neglected.

52. H. C. Watterson to Andrew Johnson.

53. Swayne is not the focus of Elizabeth Bethel, "The Freedmen's Bureau in Alabama," *JSH, 14* (1948), 49–92, or of W. L. Fleming, *Civil War and Reconstruction in Alabama* (New York, 1905).

compliant with the wishes of the planters and that Negro leaders protesting assaults and murders "were always put off," but there is also some evidence that he was truly following a middle course.[54] When his papers become available we may learn whether he was merely an agent of the planters or whether he did see his job as that of a skilled lawyer seeking a working agreement between his clients and the planters.[55] Perhaps he only served the planters; he provoked few attacks from them, and he was the last of the original assistant commissioners to incur Johnson's displeasure. At the close of 1867, however, he too joined the ranks of "radicals" whom the President had pushed out of the Freedmen's Bureau.[56]

The mustering out of the Veterans Reserve Corps, the Bureau's only source of commissioners sympathetic to the freedmen, and the transfer of Swayne, the last of his own assistant commissioners, was to General Howard the final crippling blow of Andrew Johnson's attack on the Freedmen's Bureau's effectiveness. "The President . . . musters out all my officers . . . relieves Swayne and sends him to his regiment," wrote Howard. "Measures are on foot . . . which are doubtless intended to utterly defeat reconstruction." Howard was no longer sure, as on the battlefield Wager Swayne had been, that the Lord would sustain. "I have no doubt," the Commissioner wrote his good friend Edgar Ketchum, "that God is on the side of the right but I remember that he destroys nations whenever they shall have filled up the full measure of their iniquity."[57]

The man of the Lord to whom Howard most frequently turned for counsel was Eliphalet Whittlesey, the assistant commissioner

54. A pragmatist, Swayne calmly broke the law in order to use bureau funds to pay school teachers; Howard sustained him in this (O. O. Howard to Wager Swayne, 24 June 1867, BRFAL; *New Orleans Tribune,* 24 Nov. 1865). Despite unfavorable reports of the pronegro agent Stuart Eldridge, Howard urged Swayne not to resign (O. O. Howard to Wager Swayne, 28 Aug. 1866, BRFAL; Washington *Evening Star,* 11 Sept. 1866).

55. Eleanor C. Swayne to the writer, 23 Nov. 1965.

56. Bentley, *Freedmen's Bureau,* p. 196.

57. O. O. Howard to Edgar Ketchum, 30 Dec. 1867, OOH Papers.

for North Carolina.[58] Because these two men were so close, Whittlesey became the focus of one of the strongest attacks on the Bureau by its enemies. The very fact that the Commissioner trusted him so highly was used to bring the Bureau into disrepute as an untrustworthy institution. Not without some justification, the churchman from New Haven came to be a symbol of the Bureau's corruption.

Eliphalet Whittlesey was a Connecticut Yankee—as tough and dry as his name. He was small of body but strong, and his face, with its squinting eyes and fringe of wispy hair, was intense almost to the point of being comic. He looked older than his forty-four years, but he had the last laugh when it came to age. At 70, he was tramping through Alaska; he outlived all of his colleagues save two and lived more years than either of them. He died at 88 in 1909. He was the "professor" among the bureau men. Although Howard had never studied under him at Bowdoin and despite the fact that Whittlesey was subordinate to him in rank, there was almost something of the pupil-teacher relationship in the Commissioner's dealings with Whittlesey.

In 1862 Whittlesey went to war as a chaplain but was very shortly transferred to General Howard's staff as an aide rather than as a chaplain. A wiry man of great energy, he was an excellent horseman. President Lincoln, visiting Howard's troops when they were stationed at Harper's Ferry, took note of the "parson" who rode like a "cavalier."[59] During the battle of Antietam, General Howard came to think of Whittlesey as a first-rate soldier.[60] His "imperturbability" in the face of fire, his commander noted, was "wholesome."[61] General Howard also generously thanked both the parson and his brother Charles Howard for quieting him when they "detected the least lack of coolness in me."[62] After the battle of Chancellorsville Whittlesey returned to Bowdoin

58. Eliphalet Whittlesey to O. O. Howard, 24 June 1865, OOH Papers.
59. Howard, *Autobiography*, 1, 309.
60. Ibid., pp. 298, 366.
61. Ibid., p. 298.
62. Ibid., p. 298.

for a year, but in 1864 he was back on Howard's staff as judge advocate of the Army of the Tennessee.

When the Freedmen's Bureau was established, Whittlesey was curiously not assigned to Alabama, the only southern state in which he had lived. Instead, he was sent to North Carolina and established his headquarters at Raleigh, where, concurrently, he assumed the command of a regiment of Negro troops. He thoroughly enjoyed his work in the Bureau from the start, pushing across the state at breakneck speed investigating the conditions in which North Carolina freedmen were living.[63]

Whittlesey thrived on the activity which he considered necessary to an assistant commissionership. In September 1865, while on leave in Maine, he reported almost gleefully that Bowdoin, "tired of my long absence, has quietly dropped me overboard, having declared my place vacant & then filled it electing Chamberlain." Both Howard and Whittlesey were then willing to bet on the Bureau as a place to build a career and were always contemptuous of General Joshua Chamberlain, Howard's rival as Maine's chief war hero, for choosing the conservative course. Neither Whittlesey nor Howard expected to spend their lives in the Freedmen's Bureau, but Whittlesey was sufficiently fascinated by his new job not to mind that Bowdoin's action "throws me out of employment when our Bureau breaks up, or my regiment is mustered out."[64]

Whittlesey brought the same indefatigable energy to his job in the Freedmen's Bureau that he had displayed in the war and would demonstrate later as secretary of the Board of Indian Commissioners. (As they prepared for their fiftieth reunion, he enthusiastically recommended Alaska to his Yale classmates; he had found a trip among the Eskimo fascinating.)[65] He also brought to both his posts with America's two most notably disadvantaged groups a troubling lack of sensitivity. He was sure in his optimis-

63. Eliphalet Whittlesey to O. O. Howard, 20 June 1865, OOH Papers.
64. Eliphalet Whittlesey to O. O. Howard, 11 Sept. 1865, OOH Papers.
65. Eliphalet Whittlesey to Secretary of the Class of '42, Yale College, *Class Letter* (1891).

tic faith that these lesser men could advance. There were two ways by which they would do so: by learning the ways of "civilization" and by experiencing "hardship."

Whittlesey cast even the worst sufferings of the freedmen into the asset column. Only by learning and by toughening experiences could the men of inferior races become "the equal of the Anglo-Saxon."[66] He never quite faced up to the fact that the hardships the freedmen faced were the deliberate creation of men who did not want the Negroes to advance but, instead, very much wanted to stop that advance. Whittlesey, like so many other bureau men, began his job with a fundamentally wrong appraisal of his clients' situation.

But he had been willing to learn. Nothing suggests the irony of the story of the men of the Freedmen's Bureau better than the contrast between the way Whittlesey's work in North Carolina began and the way it ended. His first report to Howard was full of energy and promise.

A good beginning has been made by Capt. Beal. . . . About 500 *poor* blacks (women and children) are gathered in log huts about 2 miles from town, and doing well. They have gardens and a field of corn which will yield a part of their support. The whites are in a worse state. I have drawn more Hospital tents and will have a camp for them today.

I have not yet assumed the work of issuing rations to whites, as I have no officers to help me.

Medical attendance is much needed, and Surgeons are not to be obtained. The Medical Director seems ready to help me but says his force is reduced very much below the wants of the Army. I have however got the promise of a Hospital Steward today.

Reports from the Western part of the state represent all quiet in the country. Freedmen are at work having made some bargain with their former masters.

66. Ibid. (1888).

At Fayetteville some suffering and disorder exists. I have applied for an officer to be sent there at once.

I propose to visit Nebern, [sic], Roanoke, Beaufort and Wilmington next week, after Capt. James arrives. Under Genl Schofield's orders a large amount of supplies is being sent to poor whites—I think *four times* as much as to the blacks, tho' I cannot give the figures.[67]

Yet a year after he wrote this, Whittlesey was hounded out of North Carolina because of the death and mistreatment of Negroes at his favorite colony at New Bern and on plantations in which he shared ownership. The Captain James whom Whittlesey referred to in his report was Horace James, on whose plantation a Negro was shot.[68] This corruption of the promising start in assisting the poor in North Carolina is part of the story of the destruction of the Freedmen's Bureau as an agency helpful to the Negroes of the South. Ultimately, all of the hope and devotion of 1865 was drained away from the Bureau.

In 1870 Howard wrote a long letter to Stuart Eldridge in which he tried to defend the men on whom he had relied most heavily in running the Bureau. Eldridge, a young man who had worked in the agency both in Mississippi and Washington, was critical of the treatment of Negroes by bureau men, and was particularly critical of Eliphalet Whittlesey. "How can you have formed such a judgment?" Howard asked. The General conceded that Whittlesey was a "blunt man" but added, "having watched his career closely for eight years and never had him deviate in a single instance from uprightness . . . I cannot believe he was doing wrong in drawing forage for his private horse." Howard found it easier to defend his friend Whittlesey's personal virtue than his performance in behalf of the freedmen. In passing judgment on

67. Eliphalet Whittlesey to O. O. Howard, Raleigh, 24 June 1865, OOH Papers.

68. Horace James had originally been named assistant commissioner for North Carolina but never served in that post (*New York Times,* 27 May 1865).

the Assistant Commissioner, Eldridge was enjoined to "seek first the 'Kingdom of God.' When your heart is full of comfort and peace you will think of these and other men differently."[69] The bureau men could try to make their own peace, but none of these personal adjustments to the failure of the work with the freedmen explained, either to themselves or to the freedmen, why Eliphalet Whittlesey's "good beginning" came to so unhappy an end.

69. O. O. Howard to Stuart Eldridge, 18 Apr. 1870, OOH Papers.

5. "What shall we do with the Negro?"

The men who would do the work were chosen, but what the work would be was not yet determined. The free Negro was the new man in America as the Civil War ended, and his problems were new ones. In the Grand Review he was the clown because some Northerners knew no other way to respond to him. The men of the Freedmen's Bureau were also perplexed, but they were denied the chance to laugh off the Negro. They had to work with the freedmen in the South, and they were given few instructions as to how to go about it.

To a great extent, the assistant commissioners were left to their own devices. Despite its tag name and the fact that the needs of the Negroes were so dramatically apparent, the objectives of the Freedmen's Bureau were never made clear.

On June 14, 1865, General Howard announced his basic philosophy to the assistant commissioners. In a fatherly tone, he wrote a letter of instruction in which he paraphrased Lincoln's famous statement that the Civil War's purpose was to sustain a government "of the people." For Howard, one of the purposes of the peace was to ensure that the poor were acknowledged as being as much a part of the people as any other group.[1] His first concern was not one of race. Whoever needed relief supplies, white men or black men, was to receive them. Howard, however, when writing to his assistant commissioners, realized that most of the poor were black.[2] He instructed them to "do all that behooves the Government in answering the question—'What shall we do with the Negro?'"[3]

1. O. O. Howard to the assistant commissioners, 14 June 1865, BRFAL.
2. From March 1865 to September 1869, 15 million rations (a bit of corn or a cup of soup) had been given to Negroes by the Bureau and 5 million to white men (Peirce, *Freedmen's Bureau*, p. 98).
3. O. O. Howard to assistant commissioners, 14 June 1865, BRFAL.

Phrased as it was, this query gave pause to those who thought the nation was dedicated to the proposition that all men are created equal. A suggestion that the Negro was to be pushed aside is inescapable in Howard's choice of prepositions. Howard's question, however, did instruct the men of the Bureau. It made them realize that the freedmen's problems called for action and not just jubilee day rhetoric. In addition, it directed attention where it belonged—to the Negro. Howard was underscoring that the freedmen's problems, unlike those of the white refugees, were not immediately soluble in the readjustment period in the early days of peace.[4]

By expressing his order as he did, Howard allowed a flexible and varied program of assistance. He invited the assistant commissioners and agents to experiment with and to solve the big question of how to make the Negroes part of the postwar society.[5]

Essentially Howard saw this work as the fulfillment of a moral obligation. He viewed himself as the man who would lead the nation in meeting this obligation. He would make of America "a Nation which cares for its children."[6] At last, he would be able to merge his desire to be a preacher with the fact that he was a general. He was proud that he was known in the nation as the "Christian Soldier." The term entitled him to appeal to the churches and to the private freedmen's aid societies, and, even more important to himself, he spoke all over the nation to rally support for his cause. He sought to establish the moral necessity of what he and his men were doing for "the poor people of every description." "Russia has freed its serfs; an aristocracy has used its treasury for the people. Can the United States do less?" he asked.[7]

4. *Report of the Commissioner of the Bureau of Refugees, Freedmen and Abandoned Lands,* 1 Nov. 1866, 39th Cong., 2nd sess., House Executive Document 1 (serial 1285), p. 7.

5. One of the most impressive examples of analysis and inventiveness on the part of a bureau man in the field is D. Burt to T. D. Elliott, 7 Jan. 1868, BRFAL. Burt, the superintendent of education in Tennessee, suggested government assistance to Negro cooperative stores (see Chap. 14).

6. Howard, *Autobiography*, 2, 203.

7. O. O. Howard to T. S. Greene, 14 July 1865, BRFAL.

Anything, thought Oliver Otis Howard, could be accomplished if it had a moral purpose. America's terrible Civil War had proved this. He had told the Christian Commission, during a break from the battlefield, that only when the battles became tests of the righteousness of individual Americans were they won.[8] Howard's peacetime command did not require the same bloody sacrifice of those who served him but, quite as much as was true during the war, success depended on the existence of a moral purpose. Long before William James articulated the concept, Howard conceived of the work with the freedmen as a moral equivalent of war. As they had in war, men could prove themselves by serving in the Freedmen's Bureau. So too could the nation by supporting those who labored in the fields of the Lord across the South. Fundamentally it was not the souls of black folk but of white Americans and white America which mattered in Howard's conception of his work.

Even though Howard was a West Point general, the army was not his only model for the organization of the Freedmen's Bureau. He thought it "hard to love a Government which was a mere machine" and condemned also the army's "martinet system" as it "suggests bones and sinews which make up the form of a man without a soul."[9] Howard looked not to the army but to another wartime source. In matters of the soul, he patterned the Bureau after the Christian Commission; for institutional structure, he went to another private agency, the Sanitary Commission. The Freedmen's Bureau did not place the governing of the freedmen in the hands of a colonel for West Tennessee or a major for the County of Anderson, but in the hands of a commissioner and assistant commissioners, sub-assistant commissioners, agents and sub-agents, inspectors and superintendents. This was the terminology of the two great Civil War commissions.[10]

8. *Philadelphia Inquirer,* 10 June 1865; ms. of O. O. Howard speech at Gettysburg, 4 July 1865, OOH Papers.

9. Howard, *Autobiography, 2,* 203.

10. For a discerning discussion of the institutionalization of America's humanitarianism during the Civil War and the nondemocratic nature of

Drawing from the Christian Commission, Howard believed bureau work was missionary work; to Davis Tillson he said, "make a garden of your field."[11] Christianity among the freedmen was to be encouraged through the example of the Christian virtue of the assistant commissioners and the bureau agents. From the Sanitary Commission, which organized field hospitals, Howard took organization as well as an attitude toward work. Although he did not share the anti-perfectionist social philosophy of the Sanitary Commission's president, Henry Bellows, and its secretary, Frederick Law Olmsted, he did accept their elitist concept that once having been given the job of performing a humanitarian task by the government, one should proceed as one personally saw fit.[12] Howard considered himself free to range outside the domains established for him by the government. To Howard, his church, the YMCA, Howard University, and his temperance and missionary efforts were, with his duties in the Bureau, all part of one great work.

His contemporaries saw it this way too. Before a gathering of New York's Cooper Union, Henry Ward Beecher described the Commissioner of the Bureau of Refugees, Freedmen and Abandoned lands as "a christian minister and soldier, doing . . . a kind of military work, but who is so performing it that it is as an iron candlestick carrying a wax candle lighted and signifying the word of God and the Spirit of Love."[13] To Howard, it was not a question of justifying the vast amount of time he spent on nonofficial duties, which were indivisible from the more limited assignment that Congress had defined and the Secretary of War had given him.

It did not yet occur to him that benevolent churchmen could let the freedmen down. In the spring of 1865, he relied on the

the greatest of these institutions, the Sanitary Commission, see George M. Frederickson, *The Inner Civil War: Northern Intellectuals and the Crisis of the Union* (New York, 1965), pp. 92–112.

11. O. O. Howard to Davis Tillson, 17 July 1865, BRFAL.

12. Frederickson, pp. 100, 108.

13. H. W. Beecher, 8 May 1866, quoted in *American Missionary* (June 1866), pp. 127–30.

godly, and they seemed eager to join him. The young Congregational minister, Lyman Abbott, secretary of the American Union
Commission, called on Howard the day that the Commissioner's
appointment appeared in the newspaper.[14] He and Howard became allies in the effort to unite his private agency, which worked
with white refugees, with the various organizations working with
the freedmen.[15]

A month after Abbott's call, James Miller McKim and John
Jay of the American Freedmen's Aid Commission called on
Howard.[16] McKim, the "building-up" Abolitionist, had been
working closely with the freedmen on the Sea Islands. To the
detriment of the freedmen's cause, Abbott defeated McKim for
the secretaryship of the united agency.[17] In June 1865 McKim
urged Howard to use his position to encourage the work of the
private agencies in the South. Howard could not pay the northern
teachers in the Negro schools in the South, but he did have available funds for transportation, buildings, and rations, and what
was more, he could encourage private contributions to sustain
the work.

In May Howard wrote to his old friend, E. B. Webb, the Boston
minister: "it would be well to call a convention [of] the different
Freedmans' [sic] associations, in order that we may secure com-
pleteness and prevent encroachments of one upon the other. The
poor white people are now calling for aid, quite as much as the
negroes, and I trust our benevolent Societies will not neglect
them."[18] Abbott had stressed successfully the needs of the white
clients of his agency.

In planning the meetings that would lead to the creation of
the American Freedmen's Union Commission, Howard was in

14. Card introducing Lyman Abbott to O. O. Howard, 15 May 1865,
OOH Papers.

15. W. H. Merrick to O. O. Howard, 6 June 1865, OOH Papers.

16. *Philadelphia Inquirer,* 14 June 1865.

17. J. M. McKim to J. W. Alvord, 27 July 1869, BRFAL; Rose, *Rehearsal
for Reconstruction,* p. 375.

18. O. O. Howard to E. B. Webb, 20 May 1865, OOH Papers.

contact with the leaders of all secular and denominational organizations engaged in relief or educational work in the South.[19] He worked with Francis G. Shaw, the father of Colonel Robert Gould Shaw, who was long devoted to aiding the freedmen, and with Samuel Vaughan Merrick, a distant relative and former president of the Pennsylvania Railroad, who during the war had the good fortune of owning an iron foundry. In June Merrick's sons reported on a "pleasant visit from Lyman Abbott," who was "in a fair way of getting a good organization . . . here as father & three or four other gentlemen will probably take hold of it."[20] Respectability and money seemed assured.

Howard was convinced that he was creating a great commission of compassionate Americans—"teachers, ministers, farmers, superintendents"—who would, in their zeal to perfect society, aid and elevate the freedmen.[21] On October 11, 1865, there was a great meeting of the benevolent, and again it was held in Philadelphia's Academy of Music. This time the group was not the Christian Commission in convention (though many of the faces were the same), but the American Freedmen's Aid Commission. Episcopalian Bishop Charles P. McIlvaine and Methodist Bishop Matthew Simpson spoke as did the president of the recently disbanded Sanitary Commission, the sternly conservative minister of New York's Unitarian Church of All Souls, Henry Bellows, who gave "a powerful address." He was followed by his Congregationalist neighbor from Brooklyn, Henry Ward Beecher, who rose and gave "the great speech of the evening." Beecher called for "elevating" the Negro and, with his audience in mind, advocated giving the Negro the vote, stressing its "necessity on na-

19. O. O. Howard to G. H. Stuart, Christian Commission, 8 June 1865, OOH Papers; J. P. Thompson, president, American Union Commission, to O. O. Howard, 28 May 1865, OOH Papers; O. O. Howard to F. G. Shaw, American Freedmen's Aid Commission, 29 May 1865, BRFAL; W. E. Boardman to O. O. Howard, 21 June 1865, BRFAL; O. O. Howard to "Officers of Various Associations for Freedmen and Refugees," 17 June 1865, BRFAL.

20. W. H. Merrick to O. O. Howard, 6 June 1865, OOH Papers.

21. R. B. Howard to O. O. Howard, 20 May 1865, OOH Papers.

tional grounds."[22] When he finished, the three thousand people in the hall rose and cheered.

Oliver Otis Howard also had been invited to speak—"Every word from [your] lips will be golden"—but the General was absent when the great Christian congregation met.[23] While his letter of greetings was being read,[24] he was on the train from Petersburg, Virginia, to Raleigh, North Carolina, on the first leg of a journey through the South, where he learned at every step of the way how bitterly disappointed the freedmen were at what the Freedmen's Bureau had been able to do for them.[25] What they had hoped and even been promised would be done for them had not been.

The predecessors of the bureau men had learned during the war at Fortress Monroe, in New Orleans, on the Sea Islands, and along the Mississippi—wherever the Union army encountered ex-slaves—that the freedmen's first problem was survival.[26] In its solution, spiritual guidance did not do as well as crops, which could be raised on lands that had been seized by the invading troops. The initial thought at Fortress Monroe, a sandy enclave on the Virginia coast, was to export the refugee contrabands to Abolitionist Massachusetts, sparsely settled Florida, or black Haiti. While relocation schemes were being discussed and rejected, the Union army, moving further into Virginia, provided a more feasible solution to the Negro subsistence problem.[27] C. B. Wilder, in charge of the Fortress Monroe freedmen, asked General B. F. Butler for permission "to take possession of all Rebel abandoned plantations" and supply the Negroes, whom he would establish on this land, with "forage, seeds and subsistence stores, at cost."[28]

22. Cincinnati *Daily Gazette,* 12 Oct. 1865.
23. R. Shipherd to O. O. Howard, 20 Sept. 1865, OOH Papers.
24. Cincinnati *Daily Gazette,* 12 Oct. 1865.
25. Railroad passes, OOH Papers.
26. J. A. Wilder to Eben Loomis, 15 July 1862, Todd Family Papers, Yale University.
27. C. B. Wilder to J. A. Wilder, 4 Nov. 1862; J. A. Wilder to May Loomis, 22 Mar. 1863, Todd Family Papers.
28. C. B. Wilder to B. F. Butler, 24 Feb. 1864, Todd Family Papers.

The lands of the South taken from the enemy were the obvious asset to put at the disposal of the ex-slaves so that they could begin their lives as freedmen.

Admirers and critics alike emphasized the Freedmen's Bureau's work in educating the freedmen.[29] This one successful endeavor of the agency which had lasting importance is stressed to the point that one might guess that its full name was the Bureau of Refugees, Freedmen and Education. It was not, and, as its inclusion in the title of the agency suggests, land was, at the start, inextricably related to the freedmen's future.[30] As the Attorney General of the United States read it, the Act of Congress creating the Bureau of Refugees, Freedmen and Abandoned Lands gave that agency (and not some other) the lands taken during the war "to conserve the interests of the refugees and freedmen."[31]

Those lands were the economic base on which the freedmen would build. And there was much building to be done as those who had experience working with the freedmen knew. The bureau men, like other Americans, experimented with metaphors to explain the Negro ex-slave. To Rufus Saxton, he was a sick man who would get well quickly; "There is a great deal of recuperative vitality in the race."[32] Not every one wanted the patient to get well, and some who did warned that the convalescence would be slower than Saxton suggested. Chaplain Mansfield French, who had been working with Saxton's Sea Islanders since 1862, wrote Howard to warn that "real elevation, having anything like a symmetrical development of this people will be *slow work*."[33]

On the other hand, Senator Henry Wilson of Massachusetts was worried not that the black man would be too slow but that the white man would be too quick. "I hope you will do all that

29. Bentley, *Freedmen's Bureau,* p. 214; Carpenter, *Sword and Olive Branch,* p. 168.

30. LaWanda Cox, "The Promise of Land for the Freedmen," pp. 413–40.

31. *13 U.S. Stat.*, 507–509; James Speed to E. M. Stanton, 22 June 1865, BRFAL.

32. Rufus Saxton to O. O. Howard, 20 May 1865, OOH Papers.

33. Mansfield French to O. O. Howard, 14 June 1865, OOH Papers.

can be done for the protection of the poor negroes," wrote Wilson to Howard, for "this nation seems about to abandon them to their disloyal masters."[34]

Wilson was aware that the freedmen were being diverted from their progress toward a new way of life which some white Southerners were willing to accept as unavoidable. "The black ball is in motion," said Mary Boykin Chesnut in June 1865, and if it were not to be destructive the South Carolina aristocrat had a recommendation: "Better teach the Negroes to stand alone."[35] Soon she and other white Southerners discovered that a radically new condition for the freedmen was avoidable; Andrew Johnson had already provided a way to stop the ball with his Amnesty Proclamation of May 29. Instead of directing the Freedmen's Bureau to teach the Negroes self-reliance and to grant them land on which to practice it, the President was on his way to restoring the old masters to their former dominion over the entire way of life of the black people of the South.

The hope that Andrew Johnson would prove to be a friend of the freedmen was based on his record as wartime governor of Tennessee. His radical advocacy of Negro rights did not survive the war. For Johnson, pressing for advantages for the Negroes to the disadvantage of the rebels was a weapon in the winning of the war. It became obsolete in the first weeks of his presidency when he began to look for support in rebuilding the nation peacefully.

Andrew Johnson's range of vision extended only to white Americans, as a Tennessee Unionist veteran who happened to be black forcefully pointed out to him.[36] Joseph Noxon wrote the President: "You say you believe in democratic government . . . yet you *dare not* avow with practical effect the right of the colored

34. Henry Wilson to O. O. Howard, 15 June 1865, OOH Papers.

35. Chestnut, *Diary From Dixie*, p. 539.

36. John Eaton, Jr., found that Johnson, as governor, had as little interest in welfare programs for the white poor as the black. "When I spoke of the opportunity for establishing schools and organizing new industries for farmers and mechanics, he was obviously quite bored" (Eaton, *Grant, Lincoln, and the Freedmen.* p. 45).

man to vote—Are you honest?" The Negro who asked so rude
a question was out of the President's sight and out of his hearing
as well. Andrew Johnson did not answer Noxon's question, nor
did he honor with any practical effect Noxon's claim: "I have
some right that you hear me."[37]

The men in the nation to whom Johnson did listen and to
whom he looked for support were those Northerners and Southerners, who, despite the recent enmity, never doubted that white
men should determine the way of life that was to be led in the
southern states. On May 29, as an expression of the spirit of
malice toward none, Johnson announced his Amnesty Proclamation.[38] Former adherents of the Confederacy (the rich and the
leaders for the moment excepted) were to be pardoned and have
their lands restored, if they had been confiscated. The provision
that those excepted from automatic amnesty needed to apply to
the President personally for pardon sounded a note of sternness
toward the disloyal, but it was, in fact, a handsome system for the
dispensing of political patronage throughout the South. The Negro newspaper in New Orleans, in its full discussion of the Proclamation, wasted no time on generalizations about forgiveness.
To them it meant they had an old—and antinegro—mayor back
again: "Dr. Hugh Kennedy . . . a été réintegré dans ses fonctions
par les authorités à Washington."[39]

Johnson, by restoring the South to white Southerners beholden
to him, was once again giving them jurisdiction over the people
who lived within their borders. That many of these people were
Negroes, he knew but did not say. The Negroes, though dis-
allowed as property available for restoration, were missing from
the benevolence of the Proclamation's words. And the Amnesty
Proclamation did not merely leave the Negroes out; it deprived
them of something.

37. Joseph Noxon to Andrew Johnson, 27 May 1865, AJ Papers.

38. James D. Richardson, ed., *A Compilation of the Messages and Papers
of the Presidents, 1789–1897* (10 vols. Washington, D.C., 1896), 6, 310–14.

39. *New Orleans Tribune (La Tribune)*, 10 June 1865. For further discussion of their particular case in print, see Chap. 9, "Louisiana," below.

Before the war the books had balanced. The white men of the South, in decidedly unequal measure, had everything; the slaves had nothing politically or economically. The events that accompanied the freeing of the slaves introduced new accounts into the public ledgers. Relief was one of them; the care of the Negroes passed from the masters to the federal government, and the states, when restored to power, were reluctant to assume the function once taken care of by private citizens.[40] Land redistribution was another; on the Sea Islands, at Davis Bend, and elsewhere, the freed Negroes had established a claim on farmlands.[41] Finally, self-interested Negroes like Joseph Noxon and politicians like Salmon P. Chase had made a political claim of the Emancipation Proclamation, making it a grant to the Negroes of a right to be heard in their governing.[42] The Chief Justice called for the "restoration to the blacks of Suffrage . . . which Slavery took from them."[43] The Amnesty Proclamation, for all its tone of kindness, was an attempt to ignore these gains made by the freedmen. It sought to balance the books again on prewar lines, not by restoring slavery but by dropping the Negro—the new entry—from national calculations.

The white Southerners were quick at mental arithmetic. They did not consider the Amnesty Proclamation as an act of kindness, which required repayment in kindness to the freed slaves with whom they would have to share the South. Instead they resumed their historic role of deciding for themselves what role the Negro was to play in society. In June a committee of Richmond Negroes

40. William T. Alderson, "The Influence of Military Rule and the Freedmen's Bureau on Reconstruction in Virginia, 1865–1870," Unpublished Ph.D. dissertation (Vanderbilt University, 1952), p. 97; Peirce, *The Freedmen's Bureau,* p. 104.

41. Rose, *Rehearsal for Reconstruction,* pp. 311–12; Wharton, *The Negro in Mississippi,* pp. 39–42.

42. Joseph Noxon to Andrew Johnson, 27 May 1865, AJ Papers; Salmon P. Chase speech before 6,000 freedmen in Beaufort, S.C., 14 May 1865, Saxton Diary; S. P. Chase to the freedmen of Charleston, 15 May 1865, quoted in Reid, *After the War,* pp. 581–86.

43. S. P. Chase to E. M. Stanton, 5 May 1865, Stanton Papers, LC.

met with General Howard to complain bitterly that the white civilians ruling the city were threatening to close the Negro schools and restore whipping as a punishment for black men.[44]

It is ironic that Oliver Otis Howard ever had to combat an Amnesty Proclamation. Unlike other Northerners, he never viewed his job as the meting out of punishment to the South. He did not see the aiding of the Negroes as a discreet form of torture for the treasonous Southerners. Howard was always ready to "extend the hand of kindness" to the fallen foe both in his speeches and in acts of private charity such as his tactful assistance to the destitute widow of a Confederate officer who had been one of his closest friends at West Point.[45] Howard was as willing as Andrew Johnson to be magnanimous with the South, but the way Johnson's magnanimity worked, the ex-slaves were to be deprived so that the white man could be treated generously. The President's kindness was an unkindness to Howard's clients.

Observers as far away as London could see more clearly than some nearer at hand that the Johnson Reconstruction program would have a negative effect on freedmen. "It is whispered even here," James M. Russell wrote the President, "that you hate the negroes . . . and that in order to secure reelection, you will pardon those who by an unjust settlement, may continue to hold the colored race as serfs, though no longer slaves."[46]

The Negroes also saw clearly what was happening. A bureau agent in Union Springs, Alabama, reported that the freedmen in that town regarded the Amnesty Proclamation as a revocation of the Emancipation Proclamation. The Negroes there were "disquieted and restless" because the "planters had circulated a rumor that President Johnson had revoked the Emancipation Proclamation." C. W. Buckley thought the black farmers at Union Springs

44. J. S. Fullerton to Orlando Brown, 15 June 1865.
45. O. O. Howard speech 19 Feb. 1865 quoted in Howard *Autobiography*, 2, 315; O. O. Howard to Mrs. C. C. Lee, 27 Mar. 1867, OOH Papers; O. O. Howard to Howard Potter, 3 Apr. 1867, BRFAL.
46. James M. Russell to Andrew Johnson, 4 July 1865, AJ Papers.

had earned the right to their own farms and favored confiscation to gain it for them. He urged "amendment" of the Amnesty Proclamation.[47]

Missing these larger implications of the President's pardoning and restoration policy, Howard, for a time, saw only the budgetary problem which the Proclamation presented for his agency. He needed the rents to pay his bills. The morning after the President issued the Proclamation, Howard acted to transfer to his Bureau the lands that other governmental agencies were reluctantly turning over to his assistant commissioners under the Act of Congress of 3 March 1865.[48] He wrote to Secretary of War Stanton and made a strong request that the President personally intervene and insist the Bureau be given jurisdiction over all abandoned and confiscated lands. He sought to offset the acreage lost in restorations to ex-rebels with transfers from the other agencies, notably the Treasury Department.

In his letter Howard stressed that Congress had specifically allotted all such lands to him. To deprive his agency of these lands, to take away the income they produced in rentals, was to remove the Freedmen's Bureau's only source of funds for its relief and other programs. Congress had made no other appropriation for the agency.[49] "Here are our ways and means," Howard said to his assistant commissioner in Virginia, Orlando Brown, referring to the lands.[50]

Johnson did not disturb Howard's effort to establish the jurisdiction of the Bureau of Refugees, Freedmen and Abandoned Lands over properties held by other federal agencies. As long as the Commissioner's program of acquiring lands remained intragovernmental, there appeared to be no reason why Johnson's program of amicable Reconstruction and Howard's program of assistance for the poor of the South were incompatible. The Presi-

47. C. W. Buckley to T. W. Conway, 18 June 1885, quoted in *Philadelphia Inquirer*, 17 July 1865.

48. O. O. Howard to E. M. Stanton, 30 May 1865, BRFAL.

49. *13 U.S. Stat.*, 507–09.

50. O. O. Howard to Orlando Brown, 24 July 1865, BRFAL.

dent, in fact, gave every indication that he regarded the Freedmen's Bureau as a useful tool in the achievement of his purposes. In his eyes, the bureau's clients were the South's white men and the attention given to the freedmen was merely to keep them in check and working where their labor was needed.[51]

General Rufus Saxton, assistant commissioner of the Freedmen's Bureau in South Carolina, Georgia, and Florida, and a fellow West Point graduate, General Quincy Adams Gillmore, commander of the Department of the South embracing the same territory, had clashed before over freedmen's matters, and now Gillmore moved to deprive 40,000 of Saxton's constituents of 485,000 acres of lands, which had been theirs since January 1865.[52] Gillmore read the Amnesty Proclamation as an abrogation of General Sherman's Field Order 15.[53] This order, which Stanton had ordered Saxton to administer, set apart, for exclusive use by freedmen, a strip of land thirty miles wide running along the coast of South Carolina, Georgia, and a small portion of Florida. Gillmore now revoked Sherman's order preparatory to restoring the lands to white planters who had formerly owned them.

Secretary of War Stanton, who had lost neither his skill as a lawyer nor his eagerness to be rid of a difficult problem, referred Gillmore's order to Howard because the Commissioner was required by Act of Congress to act for the government in matters involving freedmen.[54] Gillmore's act alerted Howard. By telegram he urged Saxton to come to Washington to discuss the matter, and by messenger he sent a letter to Beaufort, in which he countermanded Gillmore's restoration order.[55] He reinstated Sherman's Field Order 15, but with a major modification.[56] He

51. W. R. Brock, *An American Crisis: Congress and Reconstruction, 1865–1867* (London, 1963), p. 38; J. S. Fullerton to O. O. Howard, 18 Aug. 1865, OOH Papers.

52. Rose, p. 329.

53. O. O. Howard to Rufus Saxton, 8 June 1865, BRFAL.

54. O. O. Howard to Rufus Saxton, 8 June 1865, BRFAL.

55. O. O. Howard to Rufus Saxton (telegram), 8 June 1865, BRFAL.

56. O. O. Howard to Rufus Saxton, 8 June 1865, BRFAL.

told Saxton that he must allow individual white men to live on these lands. Howard, characteristically, was trying to please both Negroes and whites. He stopped the wholesale dispossession of the freedmen, but by insisting that the black-only stipulation of Sherman's order be broken, he was recognizing the propriety of the pardon principle. He was thereby honoring the Amnesty Proclamation, and Saxton knew that Howard had begun to compromise the freedmen's position. The rebel planters who had owned these lands were articulate men well able to find their way to the White House.

Saxton, aroused by Gillmore's move, had already wired Howard to ask if he too should come to Washington to discuss the restoration.[57] Saxton had seen promises to the freedmen broken before and told his brother to delay issuing his Circular 1 as assistant commissioner of the Freedmen's Bureau until he had talked to Howard.[58] The pending Circular stated that "this Bureau is entrusted with the supervision of abandoned lands . . . and the location of such [refugees and freedmen] as may desire it on homes of forty (40) acres."[59]

Before Saxton arrived in Washington, General Howard did a very sensible thing. He wrote to Attorney General James Speed and asked for his opinion of the Act of March 3, 1865, with special reference to the abandoned lands and Howard's responsibilities in relation to them.[60] Speed (with a mild slap at Howard for not submitting his request through channels) spoke as counsel to the executive branch of the government and gave an "official opinion."[61]

To Speed the basic question was whether Howard headed a land bureau or a refugees' and freedmen's bureau. He decided that it was the latter, and in the conservative language of a law-

57. C. H. Howard to his mother, 12 June 1865, Charles Howard Papers.
58. Rose, p. 329; Saxton Diary, 16 July 1865.
59. Rufus Saxton, Order No. 1, 10 June 1865, quoted in Martin L. Abbott, "The Freedmen's Bureau in South Carolina," Unpublished Ph.D. dissertation (Emory University, 1954), p. 85.
60. O. O. Howard to James Speed, 19 June 1865, BRFAL.
61. James Speed to E. M. Stanton, 22 June 1865, BRFAL.

yer, James Speed gave the bill a ruling, entirely favorable to the freedmen. There were questions he did not answer, such as the troubling matter of the validity of the title to the lands once they were granted to the freedmen, but in his interpretation of the proper use of the abandoned lands, he left no doubt who the beneficiaries should be.[62]

The Bureau, according to Speed, had unqualified "control of all subjects relating to refugees and freedmen," but its control of the abandoned lands was qualified. That "qualification," Speed decreed, was that the use of lands must relate to the welfare of the refugees and freedmen: "He [the Commissioner] has the *authority,* under the direction of the President, to set apart *for the use* of loyal refugees and freedmen the lands in question." Once Howard had exercised his "authority" (the extent to which the President's "direction" limited that authority was not explained by Speed), he was *"required* to assign to every male of that class of persons not more than forty acres of such land."[63]

Since the Bureau controlled only 800,000 acres of farmland, the assistant commissioners presumably would have to establish some system for deciding which 20,000 men would receive their own farms.[64] Another problem was that the Speed ruling posed an administrative problem for the Bureau. Division of the lands into forty acres was the only disposition of them which Congress prescribed. Thus, the bureau headquarters in the various states and the hospitals and orphanages in confiscated or abandoned buildings were in jeopardy as were the already established farm communities on which helpless aged freedmen were living. Howard repeatedly tried to persuade Speed to reread the act and agree that the forty-acre provision could be waived in favor of retaining in the Bureau those welfare facilities which were certainly "set apart for the use of . . . freedmen,"[65] as the act required.

The core of Speed's opinion was his quiet statement: "It seems

62. James Speed to E. M. Stanton, 22 June 1865, BRFAL.
63. Ibid.
64. Bentley, *Freedmen's Bureau,* p. 102.
65. O. O. Howard to James Speed, 27 June 1865, BRFAL.

to me plain that Congress looked *primarily* . . . to the personal and social interests of loyal refugees and freedmen." Commissioner Howard's "authority with regard to the lands is . . . an incident of his power in regard to the persons mentioned in the act."[66] Speed had made it clear why the Bureau existed and for whose benefit. He did not, however, concern himself with the obvious conflict between the President's restoration program and the Negroes' interests in these lands. Howard was still required to exercise fortitude if he were to make his authority meaningful for the freedmen.

Armed with Speed's opinion, Howard acted to secure his hold over the land. The bureau staff in Washington had been prodding the assistant commissioners to claim the lands from the army and from the Treasury, but now Howard introduced a note of urgency.[67] On June 26 he sent telegrams to all the assistant commissioners, telling them to list, with the detail of a title-searcher, those lands they were using for the freedmen. These wires encouraged haste: "It is necessary to have this list here very soon to save the lands."[68] The enemy now was not jealous bureaucrats in the Treasury Department or even laziness in the Bureau, but the pressure of the former landowners, who were pressing the President for restoration.

The next day the Bureau in Washington acted on the list covering lands in Virginia, which Orlando Brown had already submitted. One of Howard's assistants returned a portion of the list to Brown telling him that the details were too indefinite.[69] A properly prepared listing of buildings being used for hospitals and other asylums for the destitute freedmen and of farmlands on which ex-slaves were caring for themselves by farming was sent along to Attorney General Speed.[70] Howard felt that sub-

66. James Speed to E. M. Stanton, 22 June 1865, BRFAL.
67. J. S. Fullerton to T. W. Conway, 17 June 1865, BRFAL.
68. O. O. Howard to the assistant commissioners, 26 June 1865, BRFAL; copies of Speed's order were sent out too. O. O. Howard to Rufus Saxton ("copies to Fisk, Swayne, Whittlesey and Conway and to special agents of the Treasury in various states"), 6 July 1865, BRFAL.
69. S. L. Taggart to Orlando Brown, 27 June 1865, BRFAL.
70. O. O. Howard to James Speed, 27 June 1865, BRFAL.

mitting such lists to Speed would prove to him that the use of
these lands clearly met the purpose for which the agency was
created. The same day that the letter was sent to Speed Howard
announced publicly that twenty-thousand acres, half of the abandoned lands in Virginia, were held by the Freedmen's Bureau.[71]
This same procedure was followed in the other states, for, after
much prodding, other detailed lists were compiled and sent along
to Attorney General Speed.[72] Thus Howard established a record
of lands clearly set apart for his clients.

Just before Howard left for Gettysburg to pay tribute to the
brave Union dead (and to make no explicit mention of the peacetime problems of the freedmen) in his Fourth of July address,
he wrote Speed about a case that suggests the complexity of the
confiscation-restoration conflict.[73] A Portsmouth, Virginia, minister was pressing for the return of a building that he intended to
use as a hospital for white patients—a charitable purpose; Orlando Brown's men were using it as a hospital for Negroes.
Howard urgently sought to force either Speed, Stanton, or the
President to back confiscation squarely in such instances, for despite Speed's ruling, the White House was still ordering restorations of such properties. "I deem this course essential for the
protection of the destitute freedmen and refugees," he told
Speed.[74] Prodding the Attorney General again six days later,
Howard wrote, rather plaintively, "I will be really glad to receive
an order from the President or Secretary of War."[75]

With these efforts, Howard had made only a beginning on
protecting the freedman's interests in the matter of the abandoned
lands. All that he had done was essentially temporary. These
set-apart lands were for the emergency use of refugees and freed-

71. Washington *Evening Star,* 28 June 1865.

72. O. O. Howard to James Speed, 10 and 11 July 1865, enclosing lists of
lands in North Carolina, Tennessee, and Alabama; J. S. Fullerton to Eliphalet
Whittlesey, 11 July 1865, requesting a rewritten description giving more
details on seven large holdings in North Carolina, BRFAL.

73. O. O. Howard to James Speed, 1 July 1865, BRFAL; *Philadelphia
Inquirer,* 7 July 1865.

74. O. O. Howard to James Speed, 1 July 1865, BRFAL.

75. Ibid., 7 July 1865.

men, and sometimes the motivation for so using them was not to help the freedmen advance. When the *New York Times* approved of reserving farmlands for the Negroes to prevent their crowding into the cities, it was suggesting a way of keeping the freedmen from impeding those doing the business of the world.[76] The set-apart lands were asylums, whether they were hospitals (which often drew the destitute with "no other place to go" as well as those with identifiable diseases), orphanages, or displaced-person farm camps.[77] In writing to Orlando Brown to give permission for the cutting of wood on such a camp in Virginia, Howard confided in his colleague a hope that soon a "permanent" policy with respect to all abandoned lands would be arrived at.[78] He did not say so, but the move was his.

The next step to a "permanent" land policy was the big one. It went far beyond the use of seized lands as poor-farms on which the most helpless of the freedmen might survive. Rufus Saxton had long known of a far less limited use for the lands of the South. They could be used to make independent farmers of the freedmen if the Negroes were granted the lands on which they had been living as slaves.

When Saxton arrived in Washington he reminded Howard of his enthusiasm for the life the freedmen were living in the communities on the Sea Islands with their farms and schools. Saxton tried to convince Howard that this was the answer to his question of what to do with the Negro.[79] Unlike Howard, Saxton comprehended the basic conflict between the interests of the freedmen farmers and the returning landowners. He had decided that if one side had to lose out in the struggle for the lands, it should be the rebels.

Rufus Saxton found his Washington conference with General Howard in the last week of June disappointing.[80] He did not

76. *New York Times,* 6 June 1865.

77. Howard A. White, "The Freedmen's Bureau in New Orleans," Unpublished M.A. thesis (Tulane University, 1950), p. 80.

78. O. O. Howard to Orlando Brown, 19 July 1865, BRFAL.

79. S. W. Saxton to W. Eaton, 24 June 1865, Saxton Papers, Yale University.

80. Saxton Diary, 22 June, 16 July 1865.

think that he had convinced Howard of the necessity to move boldly and not depend on the reservoir of Christian goodwill which the Commissioner was so sure would soon be tapped. Saxton knew that the powerful articulate planters of South Carolina were determined in their effort to get their lands back; Howard's trust in the eventual cooperation of the "thinking men" of the South was misplaced.[81] Saxton left the capital and went north to Saratoga on holiday with his wife. From there he wrote to his brother and instructed him to wait no longer for direction from Washington but to issue Circular 1 informing the freedmen that they would be awarded forty-acre farms on the abandoned lands.[82] Willard Saxton signed two hundred copies of the order and sent them out to be posted in the three states of his district.[83]

Rufus Saxton had taken the bull by the horns and apparently, without knowing it, he had also encouraged General Howard to do so. The Commissioner wrote sternly to a fellow brevet major general, John E. Smith, the district commander in Western Tennessee:

> I understand that you have . . . restored . . . property . . . to former owners . . . regardless of the control given this Bureau by the Acts of Congress and orders of the President. Believing you are mistaken in your interpretation of the law . . . I have to request that you will not . . . restore without the consent of the Agent of this Bureau, any property that has been or may be now under the control of the Military.

General Howard told General Smith that he had "prepared a Circular upon the Subject . . . which is now awaiting the approval of the President."[84]

The next day, Commissioner Howard boldly issued his Circular 13, which called for a most important change in bureau practice. And he did so without waiting for the President's approval.

81. O. O. Howard to T. S. Greene, 14 July 1865, BRFAL.
82. Saxton Diary, 16 July 1865.
83. Ibid., 17 July 1865.
84. O. O. Howard to John E. Smith, 27 July 1865, BRFAL.

Now, rather than merely consolidating abandoned lands under the agency's jurisdiction so that the agency could use the income from them for temporary relief, Howard adhering to Speed's interpretation of the Act of March 3, 1865, instructed the bureau staff to "set apart" the lands for the freedmen by actually distributing the land to the Negroes in forty-acre plots.[85] The General at last used the authority Congress had given him to put farmlands in the hands of the Negroes of the South.

Whether the title which the government could convey would withstand the challenge of pardoned planters in civil courts was raised by Treasury Secretary Hugh McCulloch and others, but this dark shadow over the matter notwithstanding, Howard's order was a major step forward for the freedmen.[86] There was nothing ambiguous in the document. The General quoted directly from the Act of Congress of March 3, 1865, to the effect that the confiscated and abandoned lands would be divided into forty-acre pieces and leased to a male head of a family for a period of three years at an annual rental not greater than 6 percent of the 1860 appraisal value of the land. During the three years the farmer had the right to purchase the land at the 1860 value.[87]

The assistant commissioners got their orders in the Circular:

> They will, with as little delay as possible, select and set apart such confiscated and abandoned lands and property as may be deemed necessary for the immediate use of Refugees and Freedmen, the specific division of which into lots, and rental or sale thereof according to the law establishing the Bureau, will be completed as soon as practicable and reported to the Commissioner.

85. James Speed to E. M. Stanton, 22 June 1865, BRFAL; *13 U.S. Stat.*, 507–09.

86. O. O. Howard to William Whaley, 8 July 1865, cited in Bentley, *Freedmen's Bureau*, p. 92; Hugh McCulloch to O. O. Howard, 31 July 1865, BRFAL.

87. O. O. Howard Circular 13, 28 July 1865, BRFAL.

And at last the Amnesty Proclamation was squarely faced: "The pardon of the President will not be understood to extend to the surrender of abandoned or confiscated property."[88]

Later in 1865, and on down the years since, it has been alleged that the ignorant ex-slaves wasted time in pursuit of the myth of "forty acres and a mule."[89] The unfortunate omission of the mule notwithstanding, there was nothing mythical about Circular 13 or about the Act of Congress of March 3, 1865, on which it was based. That Howard and his men, unable to sustain their stated policy, spent the fall trying to make the Negroes believe that forty acres was just "à la mode Santa Claus" was, in reality, just an admission that a group of white generals had failed their job and not proof that the freedmen were foolish or superstitious.[90]

From July 28, 1865, until the circular order was rescinded in September, region-wide redistribution of abandoned and confiscated lands in the South was the stated policy of an agency of the United States government. It was so understood (if not put into practice) by army officers in the South.[91] Had it been implemented, every freedman would not have gotten forty acres of land, but 20,000 Negro families in all sections of the South would have gotten a start on their own farms.

It had been Otis Howard's habit when issuing a major set of instructions to his assistant commissioners to get the President's endorsement.[92] As a member of the President's administration

88. O. O. Howard Circular 13, 28 July 1865, BRFAL.

89. As authentic a teller of the myth as any is the author of Circular 13: "Naturally enough, where exaggerated stories were always rife, a rumor circulated that they would finally get somehow all the land of disloyal owners" (Howard, *Autobiography*, 2, 247).

90. Memphis *Argus*, 1 Dec. 1865; O. O. Howard Circular issued in Jackson, Mississippi, called on the assistant commissioners to kill the "rumor" that land would be made available at Christmas on the grounds that it raised "false hopes" and destroyed confidence in the Bureau (11 Nov. 1865, BRFAL).

91. W. H. Whittin to A. S. Webb, 4 Sept. 1865, Webb Papers, Yale University.

92. For example, O. O. Howard's order of 30 May 1865 was endorsed "approved 2 June 1865, Andrew Johnson, President of the United States," BRFAL.

this was logical, but he must have realized how unlikely a presidential endorsement was in this instance. He had to make the command decision himself and could not even risk a request for an endorsement from the President for fear of an outright rebuff. Howard took the matter wholly into his own hands under the general authority granted him by Congress and asserted his authority in the matter of lands for the freedmen.

Howard signed Circular 13 on Friday, July 28, and, having made the most important command decision of his career—one which would require strong leadership if it were to be sustained —he left over the weekend for a month's holiday in Maine.[93]

93. Washington *Evening Star,* 31 July 1865.

6. The Absent Commissioner

Circular 13 had a curious history. Some of the bureau men moved firmly to implement it, but it arrived at the assistant commissioners' headquarters with a cover letter which stripped it of a good deal of its authority. General Howard was not in the capital to enforce it, and James Scott Fullerton, who took the reins in the General's absence, worked actively, and successfully, to have it abrogated.[1]

Fullerton, Howard's adjutant general, was in mid-summer 1865, the Commissioner's closest confidant. His duties exceeded issuing orders under Howard's direction. Before he assumed command of the Army of the Tennessee, Howard had Fullerton on his staff and, as soon as he could, arranged that he be transferred to his new staff. Charles Howard thought Fullerton an ideal man for his brother's service: "I do hope he will get Fullerton as he suits Otis precisely—diligent, respectful, attentive, accurate and always gentlemanly in his deportment. Fullerton never tastes of liquor."[2]

Fullerton acted with the same diligence and energy in the Freedmen's Bureau. In June and July when the agency was starting its operations, he was at the center of all its activities. He was particularly ardent in pressing the assistant commissioners to arrange the transfer of lands from the Treasury agents and from field commanders to the jurisdiction of the Freedmen's Bureau. When pleading with Eliphalet Whittlesey to submit lists of lands to which the Bureau should lay claim in North Carolina, Fuller-

1. White, "Freedmen's Bureau in New Orleans," p. 138; F. H. Whittin to A. S. Webb, 4 Sept. 1865, Webb Papers, Yale University; Washington *Evening Star,* 31 July 1865; William Fowler to C. B. Fisk (copies to other assistant commissioners), 1 Aug. 1865, BRFAL.

2. C. H. Howard to his mother, 27 Dec. 1865, Charles Howard Papers.

ton lined out for the professor the fact that he would have no money to spend if he lacked land to produce rents.[3] Whittlesey might have been preoccupied with other freedmen matters, but Fullerton never forgot that he wanted to work for a solvent organization.

In July 1865 Howard sent Fullerton on an inspection trip to South Carolina and Georgia. From Hilton Head, after being in the South only twenty-four hours, Fullerton wrote Howard, strongly attacking General Saxton's administration. This predicted the kind of criticism that would characterize his more famous trip with General Steedman in 1866, except in one crucial particular. Fullerton was not, in July 1865, trying to discredit the Bureau, but instead, he was trying to build up the Bureau and drive out the men he disliked. His letter was written with the tone of one confident that the Commissioner would approve its contents.[4]

We do not know what Howard thought of Fullerton's reports. Once Howard was estranged from someone, as later he was from Fullerton, his attitude became one of gentlemanly silence. Even in letters to his closest correspondents he did not discuss his relationship with Fullerton, and his *Autobiography* has no assessment of his aide's performance in the Bureau other than Howard's own reply to the Fullerton-Steedman report of 1866, which is published verbatim.[5] Whatever else his first inspection trip in July 1865 accomplished, it kept Fullerton out of Washington while Howard was writing Circular 13.

Why Howard left on a holiday at such a crucial point in the affairs of the freedmen is perplexing. If he issued the Circular only to force the President to make a decision either to support land redistribution or halt it altogether—a decision which Howard did not care to make himself—he would hardly have been as vehement on July 27, when he ordered General Smith not to restore lands which Circular 13 would shortly effect. It appears that George Bentley is correct; Howard wanted to con-

3. J. S. Fullerton to Eliphalet Whittlesey, 8 July 1865, BRFAL.
4. J. S. Fullerton to O. O. Howard, 20 July 1865, OOH Papers.
5. O .O. Howard, *Autobiography*, 1, 522, 530; 2, 216, 241, 297–308.

front the President with a completed action which, done, the President would not undo.[6]

It does not seem altogether improbable that Howard was not fully aware of the implication of his Circular. As happened more than once during Reconstruction, the compelling needs of the Negroes drew radical moves from conservative hands. That the Commissioner was asking the President of the United States to acquiesce to the revolutionary principle of dividing large holdings of land and distributing them to the poor either escaped Howard or the battle it dimly suggested seemed worth escaping.

Howard's vacation was, as he saw it, anything but an avoidance of responsibility. He did spend some time with his family in Maine (whom he had not seen since early in the war), but essentially August 1865 was not a holiday for Howard but a search for a mandate from the American people. Properly seen, Circular 13 was but one (particularly bold) product of Otis Howard's general, vaguely defined, but overriding commitment to find a viable way of life for the freedmen within the restored Union; he saw no need to give the Circular priority and return to Washington to battle for it.

It was a personal triumph for Howard to share the commencement platform at Bowdoin on August 4 with General Grant.[7] His empty sleeve was a badge of sacrifice familiar throughout the land; his proud record in the war was known to all who came to Brunswick to salute the first postwar generation of graduates. To stand honored with the greatest of the Union heroes was surely a sign of visible election. At such a ceremony one did not have to hear about the freedmen; one could tell that the commander of the Freedmen's Bureau was, in war or in peace, destined to succeed against the greatest of adversities. (And Howard was not so impractical as to settle for a symbolic allegiance alone. His already overworked men in the field were told that the "Bureau has been promised by Gen. Grant a sufficient number of officers to assign one to every County throughout the South."[8])

6. Bentley, *Freedmen's Bureau*, p. 93.
7. *New York Times*, 9 Aug. 1865.
8. S. L. Taggart to T. W. Conway, 7 Aug. 1865, BRFAL.

When he spoke elsewhere in Maine, Howard groped for a way to convince the public that the freedmen could be accommodated to white American hopes for national fulfillment. In a speech in Portland on August 6, he disagreed with General Jacob Dolson Cox's contention (Cox was campaigning for the governorship of Ohio) that blacks and whites could not live together. As proof he told of a Washington, D.C., Negro businessman who had white clerks. Then, checking himself before he had gone too far in stating the freedmen's case, he said categorically that "social equality is an absurdity."

He spoke of his Bureau giving just a temporary start to the freedmen, who would soon be contentedly working as wage laborers for their old masters. He also noted the needs of the displaced Negroes and paid tribute to the freedmen's advances at Davis Bend and on the Sea Islands. Ignoring inconsistencies, he tried to mesh the freedmen into the ongoing work of the nation. His final appeal to his audience was to ask them to see that the "Negroes were freed by God for a purpose."[9] Somehow God's purpose for the nation and for the freedmen, as hard as each was to articulate, would prove to be compatible if only the people would join Howard and his followers in a great national movement to make it so. The Freedmen's Bureau was to be the agent of that effort.

As far as Fullerton was concerned, the agency might just as well have been a bureau of fisheries or weights and measures. His letters hardly reveal that the word "freedmen" was in the title of the agency he worked so hard to strengthen. He had contributed much to amassing considerable assets for the Bureau, and now, with Speed's ruling and Circular 13, he saw that they were to be dispersed—wasted. The agency's power in relation to others in the government would wane and, what was worse, the assets were to be distributed in a way directly contrary to the President's wishes. To Fullerton Howard had jeopardized his agency, and he was determined not to fail with it. His object was to try to turn Howard back, make him abandon the land program, and put the Bureau fully at the service of the President.

9. *New York Times,* 20 Aug. 1865.

John Eaton, as assistant commissioner for Washington, D.C., was the deputy head of the Freedmen's Bureau, and when Howard left for Maine, he was summoned back from his vacation. Somewhat disgruntled, he arrived in the capital a week later.[10] Eaton, the protégé of General Grant who was never greatly interested in the Freedmen's Bureau perhaps because he had not been chosen to run it, was nominally in charge of the agency, but it was Fullerton who took charge. Eaton wrote to Maine of the problems facing the agency, made few recommendations as to their solution, and left decisions to Howard. Not so Fullerton who was called back from leave in Ohio by a harried associate in the Bureau who was not only overworked but also felt the absence of authority; he quickly supplied the latter.[11] When Fullerton wrote to his chief in Maine, his letters were filled with advice given in a tone which suggested that it would be taken; on one important occasion, he did not offer advice but reported an accomplished fact: an action of the President destroying Circular 13.

On the Monday after Howard left Washington—and ten days before Fullerton returned to the capital—Orlando Brown submitted a number of requests for the restoration of lands in Virginia. William Fowler, in charge of the land desk, sent them back with instructions that they be refused in accordance with an enclosed copy of Circular 13. He explained to Brown that President Johnson had not yet given the new Circular his blessing, but added that "General Howard desires you to act in accordance with it, however, as the expression of his own views, until its actual approval or disapproval."[12]

The next day Fowler distributed to the assistant commissioners copies of the Circular and his cover letter, which significantly altered the effect of the order itself: "I am directed by Maj. Genl. Howard to transmit a copy of Circular No. 13 . . . and to inform

10. Washington *Evening Star*, 31 July 1865; Eaton, *Grant, Lincoln, and the Freedmen*, p. 306.

11. S. L. Taggart to J. S. Fullerton (telegram), 31 July 1865; J. S. Fullerton to S. L. Taggart (telegram), 7 Aug. 1865, BRFAL.

12. William Fowler to Orlando Brown, 31 July 1865, BRFAL.

you that although this circular has not yet received the approval of the President, still you are to be guided by it, as the expression of General Howard's views, pending submission to the President."[13]

Knowing that the President's support for the land distribution program had not yet been given—and able to guess that it would not be—the more timid or disinclined assistant commissioners did not move ahead boldly. Fowler sternly urged them at least to retain those lands already under the Bureau's control: "The control of abandoned and confiscated lands needed for the use of the Freedmen etc. is placed by law in this Bureau and military commanders have no authority to restore it to former owners without the consent of the Commissioner," who, Fowler added, "has decided, until further orders are issued, that the pardon of the President . . . does not extend to the restoration of abandoned property, set apart" for the use of the Bureau's clients.[14] Thomas Conway, who was in no way timid, released Circular 13 to the press in New Orleans and proceeded, as did Rufus Saxton in South Carolina, to implement the redistribution of lands by advertising how freedmen could apply for an allotment.[15]

Andrew Johnson did not demand immediately the rescission of Circular 13. It was a month before he had a final showdown with Howard over the order, but in August he no longer saw the Freedmen's Bureau's acquisition of lands as a mere transfer from one governmental department to another. He realized now that the Bureau could with these lands thwart his restoration policy, and this he would not countenance. Hostilities broke out between the White House and the Bureau, and, not surprisingly, the scene of battle was Andrew Johnson's home state of Tennessee.

On July 27, the day before Howard issued Circular 13, Andrew Johnson pardoned a Nashville Confederate named B. B. Leake.

13. William Fowler to C. B. Fisk, 1 Aug. 1865, BRFAL (copies to Saxton, Sprague, Swayne, Gregory, Whittlesey, Thomas, Eaton, and Conway).

14. William Fowler to Samuel Thomas, 4 Aug. 1865; William Fowler to Thomas Conway, 8 Aug. 1865, BRFAL.

15. *New Orleans Tribune,* 23 Aug. 1865.

Leake then sought restoration of land he had owned on Nash-ville's Capitol Hill, but the bureau office in Tennessee refused him. Failing to convince the Bureau to return this land, Leake followed the course that many southern families found effective in seeking to regain their prerogatives and properties; he sent a woman to plead his cause. Leake's aunt, C. Clara Cole, called at the White House and spoke directly to the President. She also left a letter at the White House:

> I have the honor to represent that General Fisk commanding Freedmen's Bureau at Nashville, Tennessee so interprets the pardon which your excellency granted to my nephew B. B. Leake as to justify him [Fisk] in retaining possession of his [Leake's] property. I beg your excellency to deliver the property at once to B. B. Leake, as he has no pecuniary means whatever, and his health is I fear permanently in-jured by his long imprisonment, and I have not sufficient to support me in comfort, much less both of us; by granting this request your Excellency will much relieve and confer a lasting favor on your truly grateful friend.[16]

President Johnson sent this letter to the Bureau on August 16 for an immediate report on this case. William Fowler, aware of Leake's able emissary and correctly guessing that the showdown over Circular 13 was near, had already wired Nashville hoping that Fisk would recommend restoration for this particular prop-erty, thus making it unnecessary for the President to act.[17] Unex-plained is why Fowler did not also alert General Howard of the danger to his land policy; perhaps the explanation is that Fuller-ton had arrived in Washington and, on his own authority, was drafting a new circular drastically modifying the firm line against restoration.[18]

Fisk responded to the telegram immediately, and Fowler re-turned the Cole letter to the White House with the information

16. C. Clara Cole to Andrew Johnson, 15 Aug. 1865, BRFAL.
17. William Fowler to C. B. Fisk, 14 Aug. 1865, BRFAL.
18. William Fowler to O. O. Howard, 16 Aug. 1865, BRFAL.

that "Genl Fisk telegraphs that he will send a full statement in a few days but cannot recommend any especial favor in this case." This did not satisfy the Tennessean in the White House; on August 16 the letter made still another trip to the Bureau. This time it bore an endorsement of the President himself, which noted that Leake had been pardoned "and thereby restored to all his rights of property, except as to slaves."[19] With a note on the back of a letter, Andrew Johnson interpreted the presidential power to pardon granted by the Constitution so broadly as to supersede congressional authority to determine the use of lands taken in the war. "Notwithstanding this [the pardon]," Johnson continued, "It is understood that the possession of his property is withheld from him. I have therefore to order that Genl Fisk . . . be instructed by the . . . Com[missioner] of the Bureau of Freedmen etc. to relinquish possession of the property to Mr. Leake." To this succinct order, the President added: "The same action will be had in all similar cases."[20] With this single sentence, Andrew Johnson had abrogated the congressional grant of jurisdiction over such lands to the Freedmen's Bureau.

The men in charge of the Bureau in Washington had no difficulty understanding the President. The day the Leake letter and endorsement arrived at their office, Assistant Adjutant General Samuel Taggart, the chief clerk at the Bureau, wrote General Fisk, quoting Johnson's endorsement and instructing immediate restoration of the land to Leake "By order of Maj. Gen. O. O. Howard."[21] This time Fisk complied and eagerly sought to assure the White House that nothing disparaging to the President would transpire in Tennessee.[22]

General Howard was not told what he had ordered. Making no mention of the Leake affair at all, Fowler—previously so staunch in his advocacy of the policy of holding the lands for the

19. S. L. Taggart to C. B. Fisk (quoting President Johnson's endorsement of 16 Aug. 1865 on the Leake request), 16 Aug. 1865, BRFAL.

20. Ibid.

21. Ibid.

22. C. B. Fisk to O. O. Howard, 26 Aug. 1865, BRFAL.

benefit of the freedmen—wrote to the Commissioner on August 16, but only to say: "The wording of Circular No. 13 seems to have caused some misunderstanding."[23] He enclosed a draft of proposed modifications written by Fullerton, who also wrote to Howard on the 16th. His was a long letter making personnel recommendations but including no reference to Fisk and the Leake case or to the destruction of Circular 13. "I wish you to enjoy your trip as much as possible," said Fullerton, "and therefore will not write to you any more than I can possibly help on business matters."[24]

On August 17 President Johnson summoned John Eaton, Jr., to the White House and gave him a dressing down that General Howard escaped by being away. Johnson objected to the behavior of those whom he regarded as pronegro bureau agents in Georgia, Louisiana, and particularly in Tennessee and told Eaton that he wanted no bureau agents in his native territory, Unionist East Tennessee.[25] To Howard, the President wrote a letter saying that he had reviewed the legal aspects of the land seizures and of his pardoning power and was "more fully convinced than ever of the justice" of restoration.[26]

Fullerton also wrote to Howard, enclosing a copy of the Leake order and the presidential endorsement, and, making no comment on them, merely said they "are self explaining."[27] With no regard for the possibility that Howard might object, Fullerton had already moved to halt Circular 13 on a broad front. The day he wrote to the Commissioner he also instructed J. W. Sprague, the assistant commissioner for Arkansas, to assist actively in the restoration of the lands.[28]

The next day (before Howard could have received news of the presidential decision), Fullerton personally intervened in Tennessee. He ordered Fisk not to establish a bureau agent in East

23. William Fowler to O. O. Howard, 16 Aug. 1865, BRFAL.
24. J. S. Fullerton to O. O. Howard, 16 Aug. 1865, BRFAL.
25. J. S. Fullerton to O. O. Howard, 18 Aug. 1865, OOH Papers.
26. Andrew Johnson to O. O. Howard, 17 Aug. 1865, AJ Papers.
27. J. S. Fullerton to O. O. Howard, 16 Aug. 1865, OOH Papers.
28. J. S. Fullerton to J. W. Sprague, 18 Aug. 1865, BRFAL.

Tennessee and to investigate reports of *"outrages and improper conduct on the part of the officers* in Pulaski." Using smear techniques, which he was to perfect on his own investigatory trip the following year, Fullerton hurled the allegations at the agents with no thought of loyalty to his bureau colleagues and no mention of how the Negroes might feel about the behavior of the officers that white men found outrageous.

These matters out of the way, Fullerton added, "Circular No. 13 . . . which you received some days ago, will not be issued."[29] Semantically, Fullerton sought to undo something that had been done. Fisk was told to return abandoned property to loyal or pardoned "owners thereof." Fullerton closed his letter: "By order of Major General O. O. Howard."[30]

If General Howard, in Maine, was alarmed by Fullerton's letter enclosing Johnson's edict destroying a formal policy of a bureau in his administration which had undertaken to carry out the express intent of the Congress, there is no evidence of it. Howard sent no telegram from Augusta ordering a stall; no defense of Circular 13 appeared in the press over the General's name.[31] And even if they had, the Commissioner would have found that both the President and Fullerton had made it a little late for any action.

Fullerton's letter had not the slightest suggestion that he expected Howard to do anything but comply with the President's decision. His insistent recommendations that men Johnson disliked be removed from office probably warned Howard not to cross Johnson. Previously, Fullerton urged that Conway be removed for want of "capacity"; now he wrote: "I fear Conway will bring us into trouble. He is working, it appears, against the President's policy in the restoration of Civil Government."[32] (Howard, in his reply, said curtly of Conway: "He should con-

29. J. S. Fullerton to C. B. Fisk, 19 Aug. 1865, BRFAL; this bureaucratic way of pretending that something done and then undone had never happened at all is repeated by historians: "it [Circular 13] was never issued" (Carpenter, *Sword and Olive Branch*, p. 108).

30. J. S. Fullerton to C. B. Fisk, 19 Aug. 1865, BRFAL.

31. O. O. Howard to J. S. Fullerton (telegram), 21 Aug. 1865, BRFAL.

32. J. S. Fullerton to O. O. Howard, 16 and 18 Aug, 1865, OOH Papers.

fine himself to his own business."[33]) Emphatically, Fullerton gave Howard some pointed advice: "Mr. Johnson is very kindly disposed towards you & the Bureau, but if we attempt to work against him or oppose his policy, then 'look out for the breakers!' "[34]

In this and a later letter, Fullerton hinted that it would be wise if General Howard were to curtail his vacation and return to Washington.[35] Fullerton did not urge this return because he wanted the Commissioner to defend the freedmen who were losing their lands, but rather he hoped the Commissioner would be able to convince the President that the Bureau would brook no opposition from the assistant commissioners in the field to the restoration program.

Howard did not shorten his trip either to oppose or to appease the President, and, in Tennessee, Clinton Fisk had no alternative but to dismantle the Bureau in East Tennessee and to restore all lands there. Not only could there be no redistribution of lands, but Fisk also had to disperse the Negroes already living in contraband camps in that part of the state. This troubled him. On August 26 Fisk informed Howard that the Negroes, who were being dispersed with instructions to find jobs, were being persecuted and that, despite cruel treatment in East Tennessee, they were refusing to return to the plantations from which they fled in North Carolina. Fisk saw no prospect for jobs and expected them to gravitate to the military posts as they had during the war.

Despite this, he told the Commissioner that he was proceeding with the dispersal of the refugees and had assigned the task to one of his best men, Colonel James Frazier Jaquess, a Methodist chaplain turned soldier in the war, who, in 1864, infiltrated southern lines to attempt to arrange peace between Davis and Lincoln.[36] Now his negotiating skill was again severely tested.

33. O. O. Howard to J. S. Fullerton (telegram), 21 Aug. 1865, BRFAL.

34. J. S. Fullerton to O. O. Howard, 18 Aug. 1865.

35. Ibid., 18 and 19 Aug. 1865.

36. James R. Gilmore, *Personal Reminiscences of Abraham Lincoln and the Civil War* (Boston, 1898), pp. 233–93.

He got little cooperation as he sought to ameliorate the condition of those dispersed: "The worst of it is," said Fisk, "the worst persecutors are the Unionists of East Tennessee."[37]

One refugee camp, where the inmates were raising crops with which to feed themselves in the coming winter, was located on property belonging to a Donelson, a name of commanding worth in Tennessee politics.[38] Mrs. Margaret Donelson, making good use of this asset, wrote directly to the President at every step of her stormy attempt to regain her entire plantation. Fisk returned her house, but the camp remained intact; soon, however, she complained bitterly to the President that she wanted back all her land, including the crops standing on it.[39]

The very least that bureau men insisted on in the whole process of taking lands from the freedmen was that standing crops should belong to the growers. Fisk explained this to the President and insisted that Mrs. Donelson had "cause to be grateful rather than censorious."[40] Johnson did not let the matter rest there; less than a month later, in answer to still more complaints, he ordered Fisk to investigate personally Margaret Donelson's charges. The Assistant Commissioner replied:

> In obedience with your order I proceeded immediately to Mrs. Donelson's plantation . . . . I found that no colored soldier had entered her house. Neither her own [n]or the lives of her family had been threatened. Her daughter had *not* been cursed. Her dog had not been shot in her dwelling. No violence had been threatened . . . . Her dog was shot & slightly wounded in her yard. The dog was a vicious negro dog & was undoubtedly set upon by the guard.

37. C. B. Fisk to O. O. Howard, 26 Aug. 1865, AJ Papers; this verdict was confirmed by a Negro teacher in Greenville. Amos Beman to George Whipple, 25 Feb. 1867, Beman Papers, Yale University.

38. Andrew Jackson Donelson was the adopted son of the President admired so much by Andrew Johnson, and even without that association the family name commanded the attention of any Tennessee politician.

39. C. B. Fisk to Ándrew Johnson, 1 Sept. 1865, AJ Papers.

40. C. B. Fisk to Mrs. Margaret Donelson, 1 Sept. 1865, AJ Papers.

In conclusion Fisk added, "She has made me more trouble than all other returned prodigals in Tenn."[41]

Mrs. Donelson was a widow, but so too were many of the black refugees with whom she was sharing this one corner of Tennessee. Unlike the others, however, she could command the attention of the President of the United States. In meeting her needs, Johnson offered no assistance to the others who were forced to leave. Not only was there no chance for distribution of land to the Negroes, but also it was clear, in Tennessee at least, that Johnson would not allow even the relief function of the Bureau, so desperately needed, to take priority over land restoration.[42]

Fisk was not sustained by Howard in his efforts to carry out established bureau policy; his fellow assistant commissioners frequently suffered similarly. In matters both small and large, they were often treated shabbily by the Washington headquarters. Orlando Brown could not have gained confidence from a one-sentence letter: "In reply to your letter of the 6th inst. marked 'personal' Genl Howard directs me to say . . . ."[43] In more important matters, the undercutting of the assistant commissioners' authority was far from accidental.

Fullerton made himself the bureau expert on personnel. In reports he had written when in the South and in letters to Howard during August, he constantly talked about the relative merits of the assistant commissioners and those in key positions under them. He always discussed these men in terms of their efficiency and their willingness to cooperate with the President and seldom in terms of their differing views on what should be done with the Negro. Some of the criticisms of Saxton's administration may have been valid, but it is not coincidental that every paragon of efficiency was a Johnsonian committed to keeping the Negroes on their old plantations, working hard for the old

41. C. B. Fisk to Andrew Johnson, 3 Oct. 1865, AJ Papers.

42. Thomas B. Alexander, *Political Reconstruction in Tennessee* (Nashville, 1950), p. 54.

43. J. S. Fullerton to Orlando Brown, 10 July 1865, BRFAL.

masters; every reference to Thomas Conway and Rufus Saxton intimated that they were incompetents. As mentioned, after twenty-four hours in South Carolina, Fullerton wrote to Howard harshly attacking Saxton's administration: "I will not make a definite report of Genl Saxton's official conduct until after I have seen him or examined thoroughly into the workings of his system—if he has any."[44] Fullerton could, with no fear of rebuke, send such a report to Howard who, seven months before, had saluted Saxton's work as a model of how to deal best with the freedmen.

Why was this so? Part of the answer lay in Howard's relationship with Johnson as his commander in chief. During the war Howard was a good general but only when he served a great one. Despite his public stance of leading the nation in freedmen's affairs, Howard looked to the President to lead him as Sherman had. When Johnson's leadership took him into areas that he saw (with conspicuous lack of clarity) to be disastrous to the freedmen, the dependable soldier did not become insubordinate.

Another probable cause of the change in Howard's view (for which there is no direct evidence) was the changed perspective from which he regarded the freedmen. Standing on Port Royal Island in January 1865, he saw the freedmen living orderly lives. Their way of life he contrasted sharply with the sickening disorder of the miserable refugees who followed his army, and he recommended that the government adopt Saxton's way of handling the problems of the displaced mainland Negroes. In postwar Washington, Howard's view was different. The southern white men, previously the enemy, were once again articulate Americans in the middle of the discussion on freedmen's affairs, as they had not been on the Sea Islands during the war. Saxton's few thousand freedmen conducting experiments-in-living under the tutelage of Northerners whom Howard admired were one thing;[45] four million black men in the land were another.

44. J. S. Fullerton to O. O. Howard, 20 July 1865, OOH Papers.

45. The most troubling sentence in Howard's *Autobiography*, "After years of thinking and observation I am inclined to believe that the restoration of

Howard regarded it of great consequence that "the freedmen were largely at work" when the Bureau opened in May.[46] That this was so meant that, for the most part, they were working for their old masters just as they had under slavery, albeit being chattels no longer. Dire threats that the freedmen would not work "unless under compulsion" proved, to Howard's relief, untrue.[47] Just as he had sought an orderly life for the Georgia refugees who followed the Army of the Tennessee, so now he sought to maintain the orderly existence of the Negroes who were not refugees but were at work.

To proclaim Saxton's way to be the way for all freedmen now would be to create disorder. One might admire the Sea Islanders and even hope that one day more Negroes could live as they did, but to invite Saxton to extend his Sea-Island land system into the mainland areas of his district would endanger the established order, which had resumed with the coming of peace. When Howard spoke of "vigilance and effort" on the part of the bureau men, he was complimenting them on their maintenance of this order.[48]

Davis Tillson was a man so complimented; he was also much admired in Tennessee. The conservative Memphis *Argus* regarded "the organization of the Freedmen's Bureau as one of the best measures that has been applied to the South. . . . [It] has accomplished much through the efficiency of the agents employed to carry out the design. The chaotic condition of the labor system is being reduced to order. It gives the employer the means of compelling the fulfillment of engagements on the part of the employee."[49] Late in the summer, Tillson was transferred from

---

their lands to the planters proved for all their future better for the negroes" (2, 244), may represent less of a change of mind by an old and more conservative man than a reiteration of a young conservative's thinking.

46. Howard, *Autobiography*, 2, 221.

47. Ibid., p. 246.

48. Ibid., p. 248.

49. Memphis *Argus*, 9 Aug. 1865, quoted Alrutheus Ambush Taylor, *The Negro in Tennessee, 1865–1880* (Washington, D.C., 1941), p. 14. Tennesseans hoped to get Tillson back with a larger jurisdiction extending "to

his post in West Tennessee and given a chance to bring a similar order to Georgia. As Howard recalled it, Tillson "explained" the purpose of the Bureau to the Johnsonian Constitutional Convention in Georgia "and corrected false impressions" which the delegates had harbored from their experience with Rufus Saxton.[50] The exemplary bureau man, as Howard remembered him, was one who sought to extract kindness from the planters—but none of their authority over their labor.

Saxton's clashes with the keepers of that order, the Union army, and the restored civil government had been, to James Scott Fullerton, inefficiency. Fullerton had been tireless (and successful) in his efforts to replace Saxton in Georgia by one who would cooperate with both the army and the civil government. To speak in terms of who was the "best organizer" or which assistant commissioner had the greater "capacity" was to avoid Howard's question about what should be done with the Negro. Fullerton found it desirable to do just that, while Howard's worries about his clients were private ones. In early September he wrote his wife about Johnson's restoration of the Sea-Island laws: "I begin to tremble with anxiety for the freedmen. This is *entre nous*."[51]

Howard was as undiscerning about the men who served under him as he was about the quality of the programs that they were attempting to enforce. The following spring, after his break with Johnson and after he had recognized that Thomas Conway, whom he had fired, had been right, he tried to defend himself against Conway's accusation that he replaced good men with poor ones by insisting that "Gen Baird . . . is equally radical with yourself. Gen Scott as much as Gen Saxton."[52] Absalom Baird

New Orleans, including Eastern Ark., West Tennessee and North Miss.—with the power of adding to Genl Howard's present policy—the appointing of a Superintendent upon each plantation whose services are agreed upon and paid by the Planter 'and to be selected equally by the Planter and the Commanding officer of the Freedmen's Bureau." D. M. Seatheman to Andrew Johnson, 8 Sept. 1865, AJ Papers.

50. Howard, *Autobiography*, 2, 249.
51. O. O. Howard to his wife, 9 Sept. 1865, quoted in Carpenter, p. 109.
52. O. O. Howard to T. W. Conway, 25 May 1866, OOH Papers.

and Robert K. Scott were as different in personality and purpose from each other as they were from Conway and Saxton, whom they replaced, and Howard betrayed his own obtuseness more than he satisfied Conway with such an answer.

In this as in other Reconstruction contexts, "radical" meant looking out for the interests of the Negroes in the South. Howard always thought he kept the Freedmen's Bureau on a radical course. He did not appreciate how finely shaded were the definitions that some of his subordinates gave to the word; he did not seem to grasp how cynically the term could be used by those whose concern for the freedmen went no further than protecting them from physical violence by the most efficient method at hand—discipline of the blacks to the satisfaction of the native whites. James Fullerton, writing about General J. Q. A. Gillmore as a man whose services he much preferred to General Saxton, reported that "Gillmore is radical enough to suit any person, except on the suffrage question."[53] Saxton's espousal of Negro suffrage, on the other hand, was rabble-rousing and sure to disturb white South Carolinians. Referring to a trip he took to a meeting of the freedmen in Charleston with Chief Justice Chase, where Chase advocated the enfranchisement of the freedmen, Fullerton concluded that "General Saxton pays more attention to such matters than to his legitimate duties as Asst. Commr. of the Bureau." What Saxton's legitimate responsibilities were Fullerton does not say, although advocacy of "imaginary 'rights'" obviously was not one of them.[54]

The "northern philanthropists" were outside agitators to Fullerton, who held them responsible for the numerous murders on the grounds that they had incited the hatred of the native white men.[55] He objected to nonmilitary citizen agents of the philanthropist stripe, like Gilbert Pillsbury, but worse was Major Martin Delany, the Negro leader who was a sub-assistant commissioner of the Bureau in South Carolina. "Whenever an order has been issued by military authorities that he does not like

53. J. S. Fullerton to O. O. Howard, 20 July 1865, OOH Papers.
54. Ibid.
55. Ibid.

he calls a meeting of colored citizens to consider it and he is the chief orator at such. He has told the negroes in public speeches that the lands that they have been working upon belong to them and they should have it."[56] Some of the agency staff in Charleston, including Willard Saxton, thought Delany's speeches well worth an evening's time, but Fullerton had no patience with bureau men acting as representatives of and spokesmen for the interests of the freedmen.[57] "This irritates and discontents the negro," he said, with some understatement, referring to Delany's position on the land question.[58]

Fullerton's campaign against Negro agents was subtly mounted. In August he wrote about the high death rate among the Negroes and, in the same letter, spoke of "local agents, and traveling agents, and clerks etc. which have been hired on account of their *peculiar* fitness for duty [by Saxton] and paid out of the cotton fund, when good suitable men could have been just as well detailed from the military service. Yet not *a single detail had been asked* for until after my [July] visit. Why could not a few physicians have been hired in place of such agents[?]"[59] Fullerton's artful circumvention of the Negro agents' real sin— that they were Negro—was surpassed by a bureau spokesman in September, who explained to William Howard Day the reason two of these agents had been shunted off to educational work. Absurdly and too well, he said they were too "thoroughly identified with the Blacks."[60]

Fullerton had some justification in criticizing Saxton for having failed to send enough men to cover Georgia adequately. Carl Schurz appealed to Johnson to send more agents to the Atlanta area, where the Negroes were unsafe without protection.[61] But it was inaccurate to suggest that Saxton was merely neglectful. Saxton appointed his agents because of their qualities and

56. Ibid.
57. Saxton Diary, 24 July 1865.
58. J. S. Fullerton to O. O. Howard, 20 July 1865, OOH Papers.
59. J. S. Fullerton to O. O. Howard, 19 Aug. 1865, OOH Papers.
60. Max Woodhull to William Howard Day, 20 Sept. 1865, BRFAL.
61. Carl Schurz to Andrew Johnson, 18 Aug. 1865, AJ Papers.

capabilities, his criteria differing strongly from Fullerton's. As he succinctly expressed himself in a letter to Howard urging that C. H. Van Wyck be kept in the freedmen's work: "I am so impressed with the necessity of securing agents for this work who are in sympathy with it."[62] Such men were scarce. Those men Saxton did send to up-country towns found the occupying army officers "not very cordial in their cooperation." The regular army men, Charles Howard reported, "seem in a measure to have resigned themselves to be 'nosed about' . . . by the native planters."[63]

It did not take long for the word to get around that the army officers who cooperated with the white Southerners were in the ascendancy over those who insisted on assisting the freedmen. If he did not know this already, Rufus Saxton had it demonstrated for him on his way back to Beaufort at the end of July. General Foster, who, as commander of the Department of the South, had impressed Negroes into the army to Saxton's dismay, now showed his contempt for the Negroes once more by insulting their friend. Foster's steamer was scheduled to pick up Saxton at Fortress Monroe where he was observing the freedmen's programs, but Foster pointedly neglected to stop. Saxton, who had to wait for another steamer, was a proud man and, in the first week of August, a very angry one. He spent the first evening after he reached Beaufort in a long discussion of his position with regard to the freedmen.[64] As he had done during the war, he projected his worries about the freedmen into doubts of the progress of his own career.

The men with whom he took counsel were Reuben Tomlinson, the Bureau's superintendent of freedmen's schools in South Carolina, John Alvord, "financial officer to the freedmen" (President of the Freedman's Savings Bank), Willard Saxton, Rufus' brother, who was a local bureau agent, and Charles Howard, now the colonel of a Negro regiment stationed on the Sea

62. Rufus Saxton to O. O. Howard, 2 Sept. 1865, OOH Papers.
63. C. H. Howard to O. O. Howard, 11 July 1865, OOH Papers.
64. Saxton Diary, 6 Aug. 1865.

Islands.[65] Charles Howard was Saxton's best source for General Howard's support; one of the few successes of Saxton's Washington trip was receiving instruction to make Charles Howard his inspector general with orders to tour his district.[66] Charles was more radical in his commitment to the Negroes than his brother, and Saxton counted on his sympathy for the freedmen. Together Rufus Saxton and Charles Howard undertook to push the reluctant Commissioner into saving the freedmen from the President's policies.

The day was growing late for the conversion of Otis Howard into a realistic leader of the freedmen's cause. Trying to launch a confused moral crusade, he not only left his men perplexed but also nearly abandoned the freedmen. He tried to pretend that racial prejudice was unreal, that Americans would gain compassion for the freedmen in the wake of the war, and that Andrew Johnson was the freedmen's friend just as he was the white men's friend. While Johnson was undercutting the unsteady authority of the young Bureau, Howard was enjoying a personal triumph, speaking to crowds across the North and ironically claiming the leadership of the freedmen's cause that his brother and other friends of the Negro in the Bureau wished he would make genuine.

Rufus Saxton interpreted Circular 13 as confirmation of his policy of not restoring lands "set apart" on the Sea Islands since 1861 for the freedmen. He immediately set about implementing the order; on Edisto Island, where the Negroes would later make so determined a stand to hold Howard to his word, he awarded 367 forty-acre parcels to the residents farming there.[67] If Captain F. H. Whittin, a local army officer, had not taken it upon himself to be disobedient, "about half the plantations" in the area around Sumter, South Carolina, would have been won by

65. Ibid.
66. Ibid.
67. H. E. Tremain to D. E. Sickles in Henry Edwin Tremain, *Two Days of War: A Gettysburg Narrative and Other Excursions* (New York, 1905), p. 279.

the freedmen. Whittin was proud to have prevented the catastrophe (in his eyes) which would have resulted "[if] the land was taken in obedience to Cir. 13 . . . War Dept dated July 28/ '65."[68]

Saxton was furious when he discovered that Circular 13 was neither deterring white planters from calling on Johnson nor restraining the army and the President from defying it. He wrote Howard and pleaded with him to be steadfast in behalf of his order; he complained bitterly of the injustice to the freedmen. On August 22, he sought to substantiate the claim of his clients: "On this soil have they [the Negroes] and their ancestors passed two hundred years of unremitting toil. Could a just government drive out these loyal men who have been firm and loyal in her cause in all her darkest days?"[69] Saxton continued distributing land, disallowing restorations, and finding his orders to follow Circular 13 blocked by the army men.[70]

In Louisiana, Thomas Conway also took Circular 13 to mean what it said. On August 28, he issued simple and clear instructions on how the freedmen were to apply for lands.[71] One contemporary report stated that "many hundreds of applications for land had come in."[72] A modern scholar reported that in Orleans Parish (city of New Orleans), fifty of the sixty applications filed were being entered by one man, Frank Glover, representing an association of freedmen that had 47 mules, 2,000 barrels of corn and $2,500 in cash ready to take to the land, when they got it.[73]

In Mississippi, an intelligent and diligent bureau agent, Stuart Eldridge, who was later on Howard's Washington staff, was troubled by the lack of direction from bureau headquarters. He became so concerned about the freedmen's condition in this

68. F. H. Whittin to A. S. Webb, 4 Sept. 1865, Webb Papers, Yale University.

69. Rufus Saxton to O. O. Howard, 22 Aug. 1865, BRFAL.

70. Abbott, "Freedmen's Bureau in South Carolina," pp. 85, 86, 93.

71. *New Orleans Tribune,* 30 Aug. 1865.

72. Ibid., 19 Nov. 1865.

73. White, "Freedmen's Bureau in New Orleans," p. 138.

period of indecision that he risked being charged with disloyalty by the Commissioner and wrote a letter to his superior officer, who forwarded it past Howard to the White House. Eldridge complained that it "is impossible to gather from Genl. Howard's [instructions] what he wants us to do, or form any rules by which we can be governed. It is not believed that he is sustained by the President in his determination to take land and houses for the use of the Bureau." (The particular house Eldridge had in mind was used for a hospital.) To Eldridge it "appears much as if the President was opposed to the Bureau and was in favor of State action on the negro question."[74]

At the end of August Fullerton again urged General Howard to return to the capital as soon as possible to assure the President that the Bureau would support fully his policies.[75] The President was anxious to see him too. When Howard finally returned, he found a curt note saying that Johnson "desired an early conference." Further, Johnson complained that there were still too many men in the Freedmen's Bureau who were frustrating his orderly return of the lands to white men. He referred to Mississippi: "Reliable information has been received here that the officers of your Bureau are converting to the use of the Bureau in that state the property of all men worth over $20,000."[76]

Try as he might, even O. O. Howard would find it difficult to be moderate enough to placate all sides now. Johnson had ordered Howard's departmental commander in Georgia, General George Meade (who was revered by Howard), to prevent Saxton from distributing any land under Howard's Circular.[77] A close student of the Bureau in South Carolina, Martin L. Abbott, concluded that the "most damaging of all the handicaps under which Saxton had to labor was the manner in which army officials actively opposed the Bureau's work."[78] On September 8, Saxton

74. Stuart Eldridge to R. S. Donaldson, 11 Sept. 1865, AJ Papers.

75. J. S. Fullerton to O. O. Howard, 21 Aug. 1865, OOH Papers.

76. Andrew Johnson to O. O. Howard, 24 Aug. 1865, AJ Papers.

77. G. C. Meade to A. S. Webb, 29 Aug. 1865; Rufus Saxton to A. S. Webb, 29 Aug. 1865, Webb Papers, Yale University.

78. Abbott, "Freedmen's Bureau in South Carolina," p. 15.

wrote to Howard. Although he was furious, his logic did not desert him. In language that should have been clear to Howard, Saxton said that the Union army was treating the bureau agents as if they, and not the rebels, were the ".enemies of the United States Government." The United States Army was preventing the Freedmen's Bureau from doing its job, as defined by Congress. Succinctly Saxton added: "It is well to forgive our enemies but it is not well to be unjust to those [the freedmen] who are loyal and faithful to their duty."[79]

79. Rufus Saxton to O. O. Howard, 8 Sept. 1865, quoted in Abbott, p. 87.

7. Edisto

Howard arrived in Washington at the start of September with an idea that he hoped would please everybody. He planned a replacement for Circular 13. In a report sent to Secretary of War Stanton, but clearly designed for the attention of the President, Howard proposed that both the freedmen working the lands and the former white owners, who wanted the lands back, yield part of their demands. Restoration was to be made conditional upon the planter's granting small plots to the freedmen who were presently working the main acreage of the plantations.[1]

Speaking of plantations that were part of the assets of planters of a net worth larger than $20,000, Howard urged that "the pardons of those whose lands are being tilled by freedmen be conditional upon the grant of 5/10 (five to ten) acres in fee simple for the life of the Grantee."[2] The Negro grantees, he suggested, should be heads of families. The land grants would be determined by three referees: one from the planters, the second from the freedmen, and the third chosen by the first two. Howard expected a bureau man would be the third.

Howard always made a proposal sound like a true and equal alternative to the discarded one. If one plan did not work, another certainly would, was his approach. His new compromise, however, was not as evenly balanced as he suggested. Under Circular 13, the grantor of the lands to the freedmen was the

1. The endorsement on this document suggests that Stanton did not deliver it to the President until 9 Oct. 1865. However, Howard saw Johnson several times in the days succeeding September 4 and undoubtedly discussed the plan with the President. O. O. Howard to E. M. Stanton, 4 Sept. 1865, AJ Papers.
2. Ibid.

United States government. The Negroes would get the lands, and the white planters, excluded from the transaction, would not be on the premises to assert their old dominance.

Now, restoration was to have priority over granting lands to the freedmen. The primacy of "the personal and social interests of loyal refugees and freedmen" that Attorney General Speed had established in his reading of the bill establishing the Bureau was surrendered.[3] Under Howard's new plan, the white planters would do the granting. They would do so as the cost of having their plantations restored, but the dependency of the freedmen would have been established in the process. The lot (not necessarily the one now occupied by the Negro family, but very likely an inferior one) would be on the old master's plantation. The garden plot would provide for the family's survival, but any additional income would come, in all likelihood, from working for the planter.

The conditional restoration plan interestingly represented a policy decision favoring the father-centered family. The plots were to be awarded to male heads of households. The Bureau's predecessors and the bureau staff from its earliest days stressed the regularizing of the informal family arrangements which were all that had been allowed in American slavery. While Rufus Saxton gave a dinner party for Chief Justice Chase and his daughter at Beaufort, his brother Willard, next door, was host to a Negro couple who came there to be married.[4] It would not be an overstatement to say that the bureau men in the field saw marriage and the formation of stable family groups as the most important thing they should accomplish for the freedmen in their charge.[5] Belonging themselves to a culture in which families were of enormous importance, the encouragement of that institution among the freedmen was the natural thing to do.

3. James Speed to E. M. Stanton, 22 June 1865, BRFAL.
4. Saxton Diary, 13 May 1865.
5. S. L. Taggart to Samuel Thomas, 10 Aug. 1865, BRFAL; H. W. Stinson to O. O. Howard, 10 Aug. 1865, OOH Papers.

As Howard tried to win the President's support for making restoration lands conditional on the grant of plots to the freedmen residing on them, General Townsend, the army adjutant general and Stanton's closest aide, assisted him in maintaining his delicate relations with the White House. Townsend felt that Howard should obtain the President's concurrence in the pending transfer of General Tillson from Tennessee to Georgia. Tillson was sympathetic to the white citizens of Johnson's home state of Tennessee. It would be wise, Townsend suggested, for Howard "to step over" to the White House for this diplomatic purpose;[6] Howard, who met with Johnson the day before at the President's direction, was finding it exceedingly difficult to avoid irritating the chief executive.[7]

The Commissioner's tactic was to keep matters as quiet as possible. James Redpath, the English Abolitionist who was controversial even among other Abolitionists, was pressing both Saxton and Howard for the post of Superintendent of Education in South Carolina at this time. Howard wrote to Saxton, "From the difficulties we are now contending with, and from what I know of him, I think him the very worst man to put in." Saxton agreed with this judgment, and Redpath was removed as a source of irritation to the President.[8]

Howard was eager to have others sponsor his conditional-restoration land plan, and one of his closest friends in the Congress, Senator S. C. Pomeroy of Kansas, came to his aid. Pomeroy, having left the capital, wrote to Secretary of the Interior James Harlan asking him to show the letter to the President; Harlan did. Pomeroy's version of the plan was more specific in detail and broad in scope. Pardon was to be given to each planter only when he granted ten acres to each Negro family living on the land at the time of the Emancipation Proclamation, and the

6. E. D. Townsend to O. O. Howard, 9 Sept. 1865, OOH Papers.

7. Secretary to the President to O. O. Howard, 7 Sept. 1865, OOH Papers.

8. James Redpath to O. O. Howard, 5 Sept. 1865, OOH Papers; J. A. Sladen to James Redpath, 15 Sept. 1865, OOH Papers; O. O. Howard to Rufus Saxton, 15 Sept. 1865, OOH Papers.

title was not only for the lifetime of the head of the Negro family but was to descend in perpetuity. Pomeroy, once an active colonizationist, sought to tie another popular tag to the plan: "I need not argue to you the advantage of a *Homestead* to the family and to the laborer."[9]

To gain the President's support for these limited grants of benevolence by the old masters, Howard was willing to make concessions to the President in other fields. Johnson accepted them all, including the gift of the useful services of the right kind of bureau workers who kept the Negroes quiet and aided in the restoration of lands. Johnson indebted Howard to him by adroit small moves such as acquiescing to moving Tillson to Georgia, while yielding nothing at all on the major matters in which Howard hoped to engage his compassion.

In a quiet passage of his autobiography, Howard relates his interview with the President to press for his compromise land program, and the single word "amused," used to describe Johnson's reactions, speaks volumes about the seventeenth President's interest in giving the Negroes the asset they most needed to make their way in our society:

> It was . . . strongly recommended by me to the President
> that all men of property to whom he was offering pardon
> should be conditioned to provide a small homestead or
> something equivalent to each head of family of his former
> slaves; but President Johnson was amused and gave no
> heed to this recommendation.[10]

On September 12, Howard wrote to Saxton in reply to his friend's anxious plea for support for the freedmen. Howard's defeat at Johnson's hand speaks through every line of the letter, and yet, as always, he went resolutely ahead, urging his subordinate to shift course as willingly as he had. He told Saxton that Georgia was to be removed from his district and given to Tillson. "I wish to keep the States separated as far as practicable that we

9. S. C. Pomeroy to James Harlan, 6 Sept. 1865, AJ Papers.
10. Howard, *Autobiography*, 2, 236.

may do as the President wishes, that is, work with the Provisional Governors."[11] He urged Saxton to cooperate with Governor Benjamin F. Perry as the regular army men were doing. Concerning lands for the freedmen, he resigned himself to the President's victory: "I do not feel secure in the possession of either confiscated or abandoned property and hence wish to stimulate the purchase of land by freedmen and securing good titles from private owners just as far as possible."[12] Already Howard was looking to the private sector to assist the freedmen where the government had failed them.

He took cognizance of Saxton's deep concern for the sea-island Negroes, but he could offer little hope: "However badly you may feel about the surrender of property . . . you can be assured it is the best that can be done." The Negroes still owned standing crops, and he told Saxton that "written obligations" for labor for the next season would "protect the interests" of the freedmen.[13] This bland statement hardly consoled the disappointed farmers who would have to abandon their own places to work for others again, and it was all the solace Howard gave Saxton, who had labored so long to hold these lands for the freedmen. Howard did add that he would visit Saxton just as soon as his office duties permitted, and in the meantime Charles Howard, returning to Beaufort, would explain the President's views to Saxton.

That same day Howard issued Circular 15, written in the White House, which defined as confiscated only those few lands sold during the war under court decree and ordered restoration by the Bureau of all other lands whose prior owners had been pardoned.[14] Circular 13, marked "not promulgated" in the bureau records, had now been officially rescinded.[15] On September 27, Fullerton, now reporting directly to the President, as-

11. O. O. Howard to Rufus Saxton, 12 Sept. 1865, BRFAL.
12. Ibid.
13. Ibid.
14. Howard, *Autobiography*, 2, 234; Bentley, *Freedmen's Bureau*, p. 95.
15. Notation at O. O. Howard Circular 13, 28 July 1865, BRFAL.

sured Johnson that he had wired all assistant commissioners that the new Circular 15 was to be "strictly observed."[16]

But the land question did not die this easily. The men in the field were still troubled by the sad scenes of Negroes being removed from lands they so hopefully had been cultivating as their own. Samuel Thomas in Mississippi relayed to both the President and Howard charges of cruelty to the freedmen and of the federal government's breach of faith; he coupled this with a prediction. The restoration policy would, he said, "drive them [the freedmen] to working for low wages or to immigration to the west." He expected Negroes "to leave in a body when the federal troops are withdrawn" if the planters did not follow an "enlightened and liberal policy."[17]

In the privacy of his diary, Willard Saxton in South Carolina expressed similar discouragements:

> The crowd of dusky faces greet my eye standing around the trees as I go to my office after breakfast. All manner of cases & requests came up & it requires patience sometimes. I feel at times like damning the whole Southern white race, as they act so like brutes & villains towards the freedmen. We need not expect justice from them, except at the point of the bayonet. I send letters & orders up on the main by the score, to try to get some sort of justice for the much abused people, but it needs a rod of iron & a fist of steel. But I suppose I may feel that it is the Lord's work & feel courage & strength to fight still harder.[18]

Howard, too, despite his defeat and his return to other official duties, could not forget that dispossession seemed the worst of the Negroes' problems. On a short inspection trip in Virginia, he wrote the President: "What troubles me most is the difficulty of making provision for the freedmen in the vicinity of Norfolk

16. J. S. Fullerton to Andrew Johnson, 27 Sept. 1865, BRFAL.
17. Samuel Thomas to O. O. Howard, 19 Sept. 1865, AJ Papers.
18. Saxton Diary, 16 Sept. 1865.

& Fortress Monroe who will soon be dispossed [sic] of their houses."[19] But Andrew Johnson did not relent.

When Charles Howard reached Beaufort to explain the President's restoration policy, he found Saxton prepared to leave to establish his headquarters in Charleston. The Sea Islands were losing one of their staunchest defenders, and the clients Saxton found waiting at the door of his Charleston office were different from those he had known at Beaufort. "Rufus is overrun with visitors, gentlemen wishing to get their property restored. They are fast getting it back & it will all be restored, according to recent orders," Willard Saxton noted bitterly. "Thus is treason punished," he added.[20]

Carolina gentlemen were active in Washington too. On October 5, Barnwell Rhett, the fire-eater secessionist's son, after stopping at the White House to offer his advice on freedmen's matters, entered General Howard's office and asked to have, as the *New York Times* put it, "the family's negroes—several hundred—transported at government expense from Alabama where they had been taken to get away from Sherman" (and Howard). Howard had coped with a lot in the last month, but this was too much. His voice went shrill with anger, and the *Times* reported that he had a guard escort Rhett from the office.[21]

There was no such satisfaction open to the Commissioner in handling the President of the United States. Although he was sarcastic in his letter of instruction to Saxton prior to his trip South—"I am directed by his Excellency"—he was submissive and did Johnson's bidding, reiterating to Saxton that only titles that had actually passed from the government to a third party by legal transfer would hold.[22] This did not pertain to the Negroes, except those few who had bought their lands in the wartime tax sales. Not only did Howard submit to the President, but he also accepted an assignment to travel through the South as

19. O. O. Howard to Andrew Johnson, 21 Sept. 1865, BRFAL.
20. Saxton Diary, 30 Sept. 1865.
21. *New York Times*, 7 Oct. 1865; *New Orleans Times*, 22 Oct. 1865.
22. O. O. Howard to Rufus Saxton, 8 Oct. 1865, BRFAL.

part of Johnson's effort to convince the white Southerners that support of the President carried with it no risks of the Negroes getting out of control.

The rescinding of Circular 13 and the alleviation of white planters fears of land redistribution was directly related to the building of confidence in the Johnsonian governments in the southern states.[23] To dispatch the head of the Freedmen's Bureau with promises of cooperation was the best way for the President to prove to the South that under his plan of Reconstruction white men would still discipline the black labor force. Land would not be granted the Negroes, and in return for hiring the unpropertied freedmen the planters were assured that work contracts would be enforced against the black workers.

By sending Howard south, Johnson masterfully exploited Howard's determination to befriend the freedmen. To the Commissioner, the embassy to the freedmen and to their former masters was another chance for him to persuade Americans to live together in Christian brotherhood. Instead of feeling that he was being sent to ratify his own defeat, he simply took the President's order to go south and to preach compliance with restoration as a new campaign of the same war he had been engaged in when he issued Circulars 13 and 15.

Johnson planned Howard's trip carefully. The Commissioner was in Raleigh, North Carolina, when that state's Constitutional Convention assembled. Johnson expected North Carolina to accept the Thirteenth Amendment and to repudiate the Confederate debt if the men convening were convinced that the governing of the Negroes in the state would be left to them. Howard told Eliphalet Whittlesey that it "is a good thing for the Bureau to be dispensed with in N.C. the moment that N.C. is prepared to do simple justice to all the people."[24] The Commissioner, calling for kind treatment of the freedmen when he spoke in Raleigh, had ceased governing the freedmen and was

23. Lillian Adele Kibler, *Benjamin F. Perry, South Carolina Unionist* (Durham, N.C., 1946), pp. 415–19.
24. O. O. Howard to Eliphalet Whittlesey, 5 Oct. 1865, BRFAL.

simply imploring the local white men who would be doing so to be kind.[25]

After North Carolina Howard went to Charleston, South Carolina. He was welcomed there by many of the sea-island veterans, who remembered how important his wartime visit to the islands had been to them. He was a symbol of success to them then, and there was still that quality in his bearing now; "Gen. H. looks natural & good as ever."[26] As apprehensive as these men were that all they had worked for in the freedmen's behalf was failing, they still had hope that, as the President's viceroy, General Howard would infuse the President's program with some of the concern for the freedmen that he had shown the previous January.

When Howard arrived at the Meeting Street headquarters, he greeted his old friends first and then received the white leaders of Charleston, who pressed views on Reconstruction very different from those which Howard had recently advocated.[27] The clerks in the Bureau eavesdropped, hoping to hear the General reprove the aristocratic South Carolinians. But the bureau men were disappointed. Howard represented national authority, but the local lords of South Carolina also derived their power from Washington.

Far from being submissive captives, Colonel William Whaley, former Governor William Aiken, and their associates came at Howard's invitation. They were secure knowing that Andrew Johnson intended the South Carolinians do any rebuilding which was needed.[28] Howard could plead for justice for the Negroes but could not demand it. The local men could promise it but were not pressed to prove that the promises would be kept. It was an open exchange between gentlemen, and O. O. Howard put more faith in it than was justified.

25. *New Orleans Tribune,* 20 Oct. 1865; *New Orleans Times,* 12 Oct. 1865.
26. Saxton Diary, 17 Oct. 1865.
27. *Ibid.,* 18 Oct. 1865.
28. Kibler, p. 418; Saxton Diary, 18 Oct. 1865.

That evening Howard carried this spirit of cooperation and open discussion into a public meeting of the Mayor and aldermen of Charleston.[29] The bureau staff, which local white Charlestonians had previously ignored, now enjoyed the sense of importance with which the General invested them. But the price for the good regard of official Carolina was high, and Willard Saxton was skeptical:

> 'Tis the policy of the President to conciliate; & Gen. H. is carrying out his orders [. I]f all would go as smooth & fair as they talked, there would be no difficulty in the State & the Bureau & troops might be removed. But the majority of them look upon the freedmen as 'niggers' & they are not to be trusted yet.[30]

It was a pleasant meeting in which General Howard urged that violence stop and Negroes be given equality under the law and advocated a board to supervise contracts between the planters and resident freedmen as lands were restored.

Representatives of the planters, the Negroes, and the Bureau would constitute the three-man commission similar to the one Howard had first proposed for settling labor disputes in Virginia. In that state he had sought to gain the white planters' acceptance through the principle of arbitration by such a board, telling them: "In nine out of ten cases the freedmen will choose [as their man on the board] an intelligent white man who has always seemed to be their friend."[31] Howard was embarrassed by the bureau men in South Carolina, who thought the boards were a good idea but agreed with the freedmen that it was more logical for the workers to put one of themselves on the board rather than a seemingly friendly white man.[32]

Perhaps the best testimony to the potential usefulness of the

29. Saxton Diary, 18 Oct. 1865.

30. Ibid.

31. Howard, *Autobiography*, 2, 252.

32. Report of H. E. Tremain to D. E. Sickles, 19 Dec. 1865, in Tremain, *Two Days of War*, pp. 249, 263.

boards in developing a harmonious interracial society in the South was the vehement objection whenever a Negro member was appointed.[33] Howard had to convince or force his men to replace the Negro members of the boards; he did so claiming that the dismissal would show the Bureau's good faith in the planters and thereby win their cooperation in treating kindly their Negro workers.[34] That Christian white men of the South had a responsibility to the freedmen was the theme of the Commissioner's talk to the aldermen in Charleston. If the Carolinians accepted this responsibility, Howard predicted that South Carolina would become the Reconstruction model for the South.[35] Despite his misgivings about the audience, Willard Saxton was impressed with Howard's presentation and said that some "wrong impressions were corrected in relation to the Bureau & we all felt we had decidedly the best of the argument."[36]

Had he been only well-meaning and not also conscientious, General Howard might have restricted his talks in South Carolina to aldermanic meetings and conversations with planters. Instead, he felt it his duty to advocate the President's program not only to those who already accepted it, but also to the freedmen. Specifically, he must visit the Sea Islands to tell Negro farmers there that they must surrender the farms the government helped them get and encouraged them to farm; they must give them back to men who had recently fought against the soldiers (including some of these farmers) of that government. On a Thursday morning in October, General Howard and his brother, Charles, a general now himself, Colonel John Alvord, president of the Freedman's Savings Bank, and Colonel William Whaley, representing the planters, took the steamer down the coast to Edisto Island. Rufus Saxton, lacking perhaps the courage

33. W. H. Trescott [sic] to Andrew Johnson, endorsed by B. F. Perry and J. L. Orr, 1 Dec. 1865, typescript, Saxton Papers, Yale University.

34. Abbott, "Freedmen's Bureau in South Carolina," p. 92; Max Woodhull to A. P. Ketchum, 4 Dec. 1865, BRFAL; O. O. Howard to C. H. Howard, 5 Dec. 1865, OOH Papers.

35. Open letter of O. O. Howard to W. H. Trescot, 23 Oct. 1865, BRFAL; *Washington Daily Morning Chronicle*, 26 Oct. 1865.

36. Saxton Diary, 18 Oct. 1865.

and certainly the heart, did not accompany Howard as he went to perform an "unwelcome task."[37]

In Washington, Whaley, a lawyer who represented the group of planters, including sixty-six from Edisto, had convinced President Johnson to block Howard's plan for Edisto, making the planters' pardons and land restorations conditional on their granting, selling, or leasing some part of these lands to the 5,300 freedmen who had always lived on them and were presently farming them.[38] Whaley's interest in Edisto was personal: it was the site of his family's plantation, and he sought tirelessly to regain it. His quest was accompanied but not altered by a kindly attitude toward the freedmen.[39] His compassion impressed General Howard more than it did his former slaves. Four months after the trip to Edisto, Howard interceded with his own land officer requesting that an exception be made and the restoration of Colonel Whaley's plantation be effected.[40]

Rumor spread over the island that Howard was coming and that he was going to take the freedmen's lands away from them.[41] Howard's difficult task was to make the freedmen leave their farms but not the island; emigration would deprive the returning planters of a labor force. The freedmen of Edisto, having organized resistance to being deprived of their farms, claimed that no one could force them to work for their old masters. The freedmen held regular weekly meetings, and when they heard about Howard's approach, they gathered in a large church on the island to tell the Commissioner that they would not be put off their lands.[42] The room was crowded and noisy when the four white men walked in.

All four knew the islands and the islanders, but now they were seeing the Negroes—the freedmen—as they had not seen them before. Alvord, the old Abolitionist, was proud of the

37. C. H. Howard to his mother, 23 Oct. 1865, Charles Howard Papers; Rose, *Rehearsal for Reconstruction,* p. 352; Saxton Diary, 19 Oct. 1865.

38. Tremain, pp. 268, 278.

39. Ibid., p. 272.

40. O. O. Howard to A. P. Ketchum, 27 Jan. 1866, BRFAL.

41. Howard, *Autobiography, 2,* 238.

42. Tremain, p. 270; Howard, *Autobiography, 2,* 238.

freed slaves' thrift; he saw their growing deposits in the Beaufort bank as a mark of their progress as free men. Charles Howard, whose Negro regiment was stationed there, saw his friend Robert Smalls, the enterprising Negro pilot of the coastal steamer that brought them to Edisto, as an example of how a free man could capitalize on his native abilities. Whaley had known Negroes in the peculiarly intimate and interdependent relationship of master and slave. General Howard could remember his triumphant stay on the islands the previous January and his pleasant visits to the Sunday schools for the freedmen run by sympathetic northern white men and women. Now all four were in a foreign land.

The Edisto farmers were menacing to them: "their eyes flashed unpleasantly." Howard noticed "one very black man, thickset and strong," who denounced him with great power.[43] The four visitors had no authority over this Negro meeting until it was given them by a Negro woman, who, in a corruption of religion, silenced the black protest. "In the noise and confusion, no progress was had till a sweet-voiced Negro woman began the hymn 'Nobody knows the trouble I feel—Nobody knows but Jesus.' "[44]

When there was quiet, Howard spoke. His tone was the one he had used at the meeting of the Charleston Board of Aldermen: reason with reasonable men and all will be well. He found the freedmen did not regard dispossession as reasonable; they argued rather than blandly accept his assertion that they must give up their lands. Repeatedly they said they would not work for their old masters and would leave the islands rather than do so.[45] They wanted to purchase the lands with the proceeds of the sale of their crops.

Howard gave ground to their argument, and by his "kind, truthful manner won their confidence and respect."[46] He com-

43. Howard, *Autobiography*, 2, 238, 239.

44. Ibid., p. 238.

45. Eyewitness account quoted in *Congressional Globe*, 39th Cong., 1st sess., pt. 1, p. 517.

46. Ibid.

mitted himself to renew his fight for them, and he predicted the course the fight would take. "Congress must meet," he told them, "before any public lands can be had and before I can buy any for you."[47] Not only was this a commitment to the Edisto farmers but also Howard's first open break with Johnson, his first appeal to Congress rather than to the executive branch for support, and his first assertion that the government ought to buy lands for the freedmen if the confiscation policy was to be abandoned.

The four visitors, after a short stay on Edisto Island, returned to Charleston "before dark after rather a hard & sad day's work."[48] General Howard wired Secretary Stanton about the meeting with the freedmen of Edisto and his efforts to do the "utmost to reconcile them to the surrender of their lands to the former owners." He reported that their "greatest aversion" is making contracts, and he told the Secretary that he was "convinced that something must be done to give these people and others the prospect of homesteads."[49]

Four days after the meeting on Edisto, Howard wrote to the farmers to confirm his understanding of what had been decided. In his letter to the Committee of the Colored People of Edisto Island, Howard hedged, as he so often did, and spoke of alternatives.[50] He knew what the freedmen wanted. They reiterated it in regular public meetings of their committee through the fall— they sought to "establish a home on their own lands."[51] At least 547 families on Edisto and small adjacent islands had learned from experience how preferable being one's own master was to working for another man.[52] The freedmen regarded giving up

47. O. O. Howard to Committee of the Colored People of Edisto Island, 22 Oct. 1865, BRFAL.

48. Saxton Diary, 19 Oct. 1865.

49. Howard, *Autobiography*, 2, 240.

50. O. O. Howard to Committee of the Colored People of Edisto Island, 22 Oct. 1865, BRFAL.

51. Edisto Negroes quoted at a December meeting, in Tremain, p. 273.

52. Tremain says there may have been 1,000 families. Ninety-two freedmen held wartime certificates from Rufus Saxton, 88 freedmen farmers had title to their farms, and 367 held Circular 13 grants. Sixty-six plantations had been carved up to create these farms. H. E. Tremain to D. E. Sickles, 27 Dec. 1865, in Tremain, pp. 27, 278, 279.

their farms and being forced to contract to work for their former owners a "practical return to slavery."[53] While Howard had stressed at the meeting his hope that he could get money from Congress to buy them land, he now put the emphasis on the far less permanent idea of their leasing lands from the returning planters.

With considerable optimism he said: "I don't think the planters will object to leasing you land."[54] Hedging against the high probability that the planters would not agree to any such thing once they got possession of the lands, Howard told the farmers that a lease was a contract in the same way that an agreement to work for the old master was. His object was to try to cast the latter contracts in the best possible light. He seemed to be trying to say that to own one's farm, to rent land one farmed, or to contract to work on someone else's were all equally desirable ways to live on Edisto. "Some can lease, some can buy and some can work for wages," he told them.[55] The farmers knew, if Howard did not, that these were not equal slices from the same pie.

Howard urged that the Negroes petition Congress, a more hopeful addressee than Andrew Johnson. Then, hoping to make a lie a truth by saying it as if it were a moral commitment, this emissary of the American mission to the poor tried to make the Edisto islanders believe that President Johnson cared about them. "The President himself will urge something in your behalf," he told them.[56]

It is hard to know how real Howard's Edisto promises seemed to him. His wire to Stanton was an acknowledgment of them, but his letter to the farmers was equivocal, and he knew that Colonel Whaley and his powerful friends would not let the President think that any concessions to the freedmen had been

53. Ibid., p. 267.
54. O. O. Howard to Committee of the Colored People of Edisto Island, 22 Oct. 1865, BRFAL.
55. Ibid.
56. Ibid.

made. Charles Howard, who had been with his brother, thought of the matter as water over the dam:

> It was a pity to disappoint the negroes about the Sea Islands as they were to have possession [for] three years & and then be allowed to buy the land. But the President having pardoned all the Rebels feels bound to restore their property. General Saxton will probably be removed as he is not satisfactory to the President nor the old citizens of South Carolina i.e. the whites. The Negroes think him their best friend.[57]

On the other hand, the *New York Times* printed a report on October 30 that General Howard wanted the government to reconsider its sea-island restoration policy. He was quoted as saying that his job was to "investigate" and not just announce the President's program.[58]

Two days before he wrote to the Edisto farmers, Otis Howard, cheerful and well, went to Columbia to call on Benjamin Franklin Perry, governor of South Carolina.[59] Perry, appointed to this post on June 30 by President Johnson, had warned the delegates to the South Carolina Constitutional Convention a month before that they must accept the end of slavery: "Until that is done, we shall be kept under military rule, and the negroes will be protected as 'freedmen' by the whole military force of the United States." The delegates accepted his warning and placed the Governor under mandate to draw "a code for the regulation of labor and the protection and government of the colored population of the state."[60]

Perry had to assure the legislature, meeting within a week to adopt his black code, that the federal army would not impede South Carolinians' enforcement of the legislation designed "to

57. C. H. Howard to his mother, 23 Oct. 1865, Charles Howard Papers.
58. *New York Times*, 30 Oct. 1865.
59. Saxton Diary, 20 Oct. 1865.
60. Kibler, *Benjamin F. Perry*, p. 407.

regulate the relative duties of employer and employee."[61] With such regulation, Perry hoped for "just and humane" treatment of the freedmen. General Howard, anxious for Governor Perry's cooperation, pledged bureau support in seeing that contracts fixing the conditions of labor, as required by the code, were met.

The Governor accepted the Bureau in this role but in no other; when efforts were made to extend its functions, he regarded them designed "to support the vicious and vagrant Southern negro."[62] Significantly, Rufus Saxton did not accompany Howard on his trip to Columbia but did, on his return, introduce him to a rally of freedmen in Charleston's Zion Church. Howard, unlike his Assistant Commissioner, desired not to side with either the blacks or the whites. His purpose was to "create a harmonious feeling throughout the state & ease the shock as much as possible, of depriving the freedmen of the ownership of the lands."[63]

Despite his promises at Edisto, Howard blandly moved to implement restoration. He could only hope to stall further restoration and exact promises from white planters to treat kindly the Negroes left residing on lands already restored. By appointing Alexander P. Ketchum, an able young lawyer and friend of the freedmen, to handle restoration matters, Howard relieved Saxton of "the duty that would have been repulsive to him."[64] Ketchum was to get the planters to sign liberal work contracts with those freedmen yielding the land.

Saxton neither retracted his view that it was "an act of gross injustice to deprive the freedmen of these lands now," nor did he desert his public statement made the previous May, "I wish every colored man, every head of a family in this department to acquire a freehold, a little home that he can call his own."[65]

61. Ibid.

62. LaWanda Cox and John H. Cox, *Politics, Principle, and Prejudice, 1865–1866* (New York, 1963), p. 178.

63. Saxton Diary, 22 Oct. 1865.

64. Ibid., 23 Oct. 1865.

65. Rufus Saxton at Zion Church, Charleston *Courier*, 13 May 1865, quoted in Simkins and Woody, *South Carolina During Reconstruction*, p. 228.

Hearing that eighty freedmen left their household goods and standing crops behind and left the islands for Savannah rather than work for their old masters must have dismayed but not surprised Saxton.[66]

Saxton knew the "high toned chivalry" was exerting pressure on the President to have him removed. William Henry Trescot, South Carolina's brilliant agent in Washington, had indeed done his work well; Johnson even asked who he would suggest as a replacement for Saxton.[67] Howard also knew about this effort to remove Saxton before he left Washington, and while he was in Charleston the War Department inquired of him by wire if he had a substitute in mind. It was suggested that it "would be a relief to the President if he [Saxton] would ask to be relieved."

This Saxton would not do, "choosing to let the responsibility of removing him rest with the President." He believed a promotion to the permanent rank of brigadier general in the regular army would be his reward for compliance, but even this did not induce him to resign. He believed he was sustained in his resolution to remain by Stanton, Howard, "& plenty in the Republican party."[68] Before Howard left Charleston, Saxton made it clear to his colleagues in the Bureau that he would stay on until, as many expected, Johnson ordered him fired.[69] Howard knew what was coming and, to the extent of writing to Secretary Stanton to urge that Saxton be retained, did try to stop it.[70]

On October 25, Stanton, having received Howard's account of Edisto, sent the Commissioner a telegram that was hardly a model of clarity and probably was not meant to be. He said: "I do not understand that your orders require you to disturb the freedmen in possession at present, but only ascertain whether a just mutual agreement can be made between the pardoned owners and the freedmen; and if we can, carry it into effect."[71]

66. *New Orleans Times,* 20 Nov. 1865.
67. Kibler, p. 418.
68. Saxton Diary, 23 Oct. 1865.
69. Ibid.
70. O. O. Howard to E. M. Stanton, 30 Oct. 1865, BRFAL.
71. E. M. Stanton to O. O. Howard, quoted in Howard, *Autobiography,* 2, 240.

A. P. Ketchum wrote contracts which were as liberal as planters would allow, but few of these satisfied the freedmen. He and Howard and Stanton probably knew that a "just mutual agreement" would result only in rare cases, if any.[72] Ketchum saw Stanton's wire in Charleston, before it was relayed to Howard, and he correctly interpreted Stanton as recommending that he go as slowly as possible in restoring lands.

The Secretary of War would hardly have issued a clear public order contradicting his President, but this wire was certainly an invitation from a very high source to stall on the return of the lands. Charles Howard and Rufus Saxton had urged Howard to do just that, and Charles, as early as September, had directed his brother's attention from the President to the Congress as the alternative source of authority on freedmen's affairs.[73] And Otis Howard had listened, as his letter to the Edisto Committee proved. Now only Congress could save these lands for the freedmen.

72. Charles Howard to O. O. Howard, 27 Sept. 1865, OOH Papers.
73. Ibid.

8. "In the Usual Way": The Contract System

Edwin Stanton's phrase "a just mutual agreement . . . made between pardoned owners and the freedmen" referred specifically to a compromise disappointing to the few hundred farmers on Edisto.[1] It referred as well to the major activity of the Freedmen's Bureau affecting hundreds of thousands of ex-slaves never directly touched by the controversy over the ownership of abandoned lands. Stanton, a lawyer, was speaking of a contractual relationship which, all over the South, was replacing the ancient legal institution of chattel slavery. The contract labor system was enforced by bureau agents, who refereed agreements between planters and former slaves.

With a nineteenth-century faith in the mutuality implicit in a contractual obligation, Stanton and Howard directed their men to bring together the southern planters and workers for the benefit of both. W. W. Davis, a twentieth-century scholar who applauded the contracts for their usefulness in disciplining the blacks, thought that the Northerners had deluded themselves. The contracts, "in the magnified vision of the black's new masters, the Bureau agents, became personal Magna Cartas . . . for the liberated race," wrote Davis, who recognized that the agreements were charters for an involuntary labor system dressed in liberty of contract.[2] The arrangement satisfied General Howard; in his autobiography it was his view that "wholesome compulsion eventuated in larger independence."[3]

As early as spring 1865, even before the Freedmen's Bureau was organized, contracts were agreed upon. On June 6, 1865,

1. E. M. Stanton to O. O. Howard, quoted in Howard, *Autobiography, 2,* 240.

2. Davis, *Civil War and Reconstruction in Florida,* p. 394.

3. Howard, *Autobiography, 2,* 221.

two Mississippians executed a document, drawn up in pencil by a Union army officer on a piece of scrap paper. It read:

> State of Mississippi
> Attalla [sic] County
> This is to certify that we were present and this day wit-
> nessed a contract between J. W. Simmons and the negroes
> (Calvin R. & Febe) which he lately owned—and that the
> substance of Col. Young's order was told to them informing
> them of their freedom and that they could hire themselves
> to whom ever they chose but that said freedmen agreed to
> remain and work for said Simmons during the present year
> for their rations and clothing in the usual way before the
> war.

The paper was witnessed by the officer after the planter signed for himself and his illiterate former slave as well. "Calvin" appears below "J. W. Simmons" in the same hand. Listed on the bottom of the document are the names of other interested parties:

> Dependants [sic]
> George   9 years
> Joe   5 years
> Tomas   4 years[4]

One can interpret the fact that J. W. Simmons signed for Calvin R. either as an act of coercion or as a symbol of a resumption of the whole complex of relationships that had drawn the planters and slaves together. For generations white southern slave owners had borne the responsibilities that slavery imposed. It was a labor system that carried with it an obligation to provide subsistence not only for the worker but also his dependents. To be sure, it provided latitude for the most cruel misuse of the power of ownership—physical abuse and displacement by sale—but the pressures of society and personal decisions favoring human decency operated to impose standards of compassion on

4. Contract executed 6 June 1865, on file BRFAL.

many slave owners. There was an intimacy with which the black people and the white people lived together as masters and slaves; it was natural for Simmons, in a fatherly way, to sign for Calvin.

Yankees misunderstood the relationship between former masters and ex-slaves. But when Otis Howard recalled his service in the Freedmen's Bureau, he saw the spring of 1865 as a much more hopeful moment in the freedmen's history than the fall of that year—or perhaps any other year of his long life. Like other optimists, Howard saw much to hope for with such contractual arrangements being made all over the South. Both black and white Southerners would eat if the crops were planted and harvested in the usual way. In the process, civil order (which had never broken down except where the war was actually being fought) would be maintained.

With each renewal of this social contract, the rise of the Negro would be accomplished. Soon the terms would include financial compensation for labor. Howard always insisted that only wages paid could mark the true end of slavery. Further, he thought that wages should not be fixed, despite the urging of many planters and others interested in the stability of the economy and the security of the freedmen. Free men should find their worth honored in the free competition of the labor marketplace, thought Howard.

In practice, there was little to suggest that more than the form of a free labor system was operating. Contract supervision by a Union officer, provost marshal of freedmen, began in the Mississippi Valley before the Freedmen's Bureau was organized. Printed contracts to be enforced by the provost's successor, the bureau agent (often the same man), were used in spring 1865. Elsewhere in Mississippi's Attala County, W. L. Wynn of Wallis Plantation entered into an agreement with "Freedmen of the same place" (the move of former slaves was not contemplated by officialdom). Wynn agreed to provide "said laborers and those rightfully dependent upon them, free of charge, clothing and food of good quality and sufficient quantity; good and sufficient quarters; medical attendance when necessary, and kind and humane treatment; to allot from the lands of said plantation, for garden purposes, one acre to each family; such allotment to include a reasonable use of tools and animals for the cultivation of same; to exact only one half day's labor on Saturdays, and none whatever on Sundays." To this, "Wiate, 27, male" and "Biday, 24, female" signified their agreement each with an X, their mark. Their "rightful dependents" were listed in a space allotted for them on the form: "Pompey, 80, male; Toboy, 7, male; Monday, 6, female; Elor, 5, female; Wadon, 3, male; Tom, 3, male."[5]

The entire printed contract form was utilized, save the final clause which was crossed out in pen. It read:

> It is further agreed, That the wages or share of profits due the said laborers under this agreement shall constitute a first lien upon all crops or parts of crops produced upon said plantation, or tract of land by their labor. And no shipments of products shall be made until the Provost Marshal of Freedmen shall certify that all dues to said laborers are paid or satisfactorily arranged.[6]

Wynn agreed to meet obligations that had been his under slavery —and no more. Many other contracts on file at bureau headquarters in Washington were similarly amended in the planter's favor.

Howard failed to see that neither Simmons and Wynn nor Calvin R. and Wiate considered the contract a promising and progressive business arrangement. Neither of these parties saw in it the beginning of something new. For them, it was the resumption of things "in the usual way." For the planters specifically, it was the restoration of something old and valuable. This policy of the Freedmen's Bureau restored to the southern white men something of perhaps even greater worth than the political rights that President Johnson gave back to them. Having their ancient prerogative of determining the rules by which they and

5. Contract executed 1 June 1865, on file BRFAL.
6. Ibid.

their Negroes were to live, the white men were rescued, in the first spring of their defeat, from the psychological dilemma that might have been their legacy from the war. Despite their defeat, they now did not have to feel impotent in a world that had for so long acknowledged their intimate power over everyone living with them on their plantation.

To speak for their former slaves, to shoulder responsibility for their welfare, to discipline them, in short, to determine how Negroes should live in America were ancient prerogatives now returned to the planters. Governor Benjamin F. Perry said to his fellow South Carolinians: "By a wise, just and humane treatment of your 'freedmen' and women, you may attach them to you as strongly in their new condition as they were whilst your slaves."[7] The southern planter's word prevailed until his cause was lost in the Civil War. Now in 1865 it would prevail again.

There is little wonder that when the southern white men drafted new constitutions in the summer and fall of 1865 and once again began to legislate public policy for their states, they enacted black codes.[8] When bureau men sympathetic to the freedmen referred to the codes as "slave laws," they too were recognizing the continuum.[9] The use of the government to reinforce the decisions which the master class of the South made about the Negroes was standard practice before the war. To put governmental authority to similar use in 1865 was a public extension of private decisions to continue life in the South "in the usual way."

The Freedmen's Bureau's orders were often an expression of such governmental authority. In February 1866 Texas could draft a "more liberal" black code than those enacted in some other cotton states, because the Bureau in Texas had already established strict vagrancy rules.[10] Assistant Commissioner Edgar

7. Kibler, *Benjamin F. Perry*, p. 407.
8. Davis, p. 394.
9. T. W. Conway to O. O. Howard, 18 Aug. 1865, BRFAL.
10. Charles William Ramsdell, *Reconstruction in Texas* (New York, 1901), p. 101.

Gregory's circular requiring the signing of contracts did state that the agreements were to be protected by liens against the crops, but he went further:

> as many persons have not learned the binding force of a contract . . . it is further ordered that when any employer . . . shall make oath before a Justice of the Peace acting as agent of this Bureau, that one of his employees has been absent from his employ for a longer period than one day without just cause, or for an aggregate term of more than five days in one month the authorities shall proceed against such person as a Vagrant. Freedmen convicted may be set to work on roads or at any other labor . . . or he [sic] may be turned over to an agent of this Bureau.[11]

There was no equivalent punishment for planters who might violate the contracts.

Not all of Calvin's or Wiate's brothers were happy with the restoration of the white planters' discipline even before it was institutionalized with codes or bureau field orders. Nonetheless, the slaves, seldom eager for vengeance, were acutely aware that the Yankees brought with them the end of slavery. What exactly this freedom meant to the four million Negroes living in the South is a question to which history has not provided a satisfactory answer. And it seems likely that we have been searching in the wrong places for the answer. Rather than measuring the decibels of Jubilee Day rhetoric, reckoning of simpler matters might better be taken. One simple, even obvious, answer was that freedom for most of the freedmen was change. And logically, they looked for evidence of this change in the everyday events of their lives. They wanted no more of a system in which their masters could "exact" their labor.

There is little evidence to support the ancient and still popular concept that the freed Negroes, in a burst of irresponsibility, rushed off from their places to taste the clean air of freedom and test their new status. The possibility that slaves may have left

11. E. M. Gregory, circular order, 17 Oct. 1865, BRFAL.

to reunite a family and to accept responsibility for its betterment contradicts the continuing legend of the freedmen as wastrels on a drunken spree.[12] False too is the ending of these odysseys, which saw the "darkies" soon back on their old plantations, sadder, wiser, and happy to go back to work for "old massa."

White Southerners, who had been proud of their slaves' loyalty, were often both embittered and chagrined when one of the freed Negroes on their plantation did leave. They took some comfort in describing the exodus as a kind of mindless caprice. Yankees, used to the lexicon of antislavery, expected just this kind of bursting forth once the shackles of slavery were undone. Interestingly, a northern observer who reported such wanderings often set the scene where he himself had not been. But even these reports make clear the hard fact that when Negroes did travel they did so for a very specific reason.

When James Scott Fullerton wrote to Howard from Beaufort, South Carolina, in July 1865 that many "freedmen in the interior take advantage of their freedom to cease work, to travel around to see the cities and towns and their 'Kin Folks,' " he suggested that one motive for the move was a compelling sense of loyalty among the freedmen toward their own families. (And simultaneously, he demeaned the emotion by stating it in the vernacular.) What Fullerton was recounting was neither unusual nor irresponsible on the Negroes' part. The *New Orleans Tribune,* a Negro newspaper, gave poignant evidence of other searches for lost relatives by freedmen. It ran long lists of letters (often without surnames: "Miss Eliza," for example) that laid unclaimed in the Freedmen's Bureau's office.[13]

Fullerton's report to Howard also acknowledged that where the alternative to working for the old master existed many freedmen sought to change their way of life and find a new job or a farm. Only the closing off of that alternative convinced many of the freedmen that they must work for the old master. "[M]ost

12. Henderson H. Donald, *The Negro Freedman* (New York, 1952), passim.

13. *New Orleans Tribune,* 9 July 1865.

of them . . . when hunger pinches, and they find that they cannot get work, and cannot live without it, soon return to their old homes, and make contracts with the planters and . . . work better than ever before."[14]

White consciences (northern and southern) were made comfortable with a vision of the freedmen as prodigal sons. Measure of the disappointment that burdened their return was not made. And it seems likely, too, that to them return meant not the forgiving arms of their old master or mistress, but the slave huts that were their "old homes." Conservatives in the main, the Negroes in the South had a "peculiarly strong attachment for their cabins." General Fullerton cites this as a fact which would enable the freedmen to accept gratefully the discipline of the contract system and accommodate themselves to a stable and prosperous restoration of the southern way of life. It is unlikely that many freedmen agreed with him.

The bureau agent was committed to seeing that the contracts were made and met. The freedman who returned or, like Calvin R. and Wiate, stayed found that not only was he still the child of an ancient paternalism, but he also had acquired a Yankee stepfather in the bargain. Fullerton wrote that the "contract system is working well. To be sure there are some freedmen who for frivolous reasons break their contracts and leave, but a little wholesome instruction by the Agents of the Bureau on the subject of living up to the contracts will in a very great extent prevent such an action. Many planters have told me they get more work out of the freedmen . . . than they ever did before."[15] Fullerton was not troubled by the thought that a version of the old way of life, more extractive than slavery had been, might be intolerable.

On Ossabaw and St. Catherine Islands (near Edisto), Negroes had known an alternative to the "usual way." They had been farming independently of the authority of their former owners since early in the war when the planters fled Union gunboats.

14. J. S. Fullerton to O. O. Howard, 28 July 1865, BRFAL.
15. Ibid.

But when the planters regained the lands after the war, eighty Negroes—men, women, and children—"left household goods and crops because the island had been surrendered to the old owners" and rowed themselves to Savannah to begin life again in a strange city rather than contract to work for their old masters.[16] Freedmen's Bureau agents, loyal to Rufus Saxton's belief that every freedman should have a farm of his own, raised this hope in the minds of many Negroes in Charleston at public rallies during the summer of 1865. These were the agents whom Fullerton deplored so vigorously in his letters to General Howard.[17]

Fullerton's campaign against Negro agents and those who favored the freedmen and his efforts to restaff the Bureau with regular army men went successfully ahead. Those agents recruited from Gideon's Band—some military and some civilian, but all dedicated to assisting the freedmen—were driven from the agency they had helped to shape. General Howard had acknowledged the worth of the northern volunteers who had helped the ex-slaves get started as freedmen; now he acquiesced to their dismissal on grounds of inefficiency. Rufus Saxton insisted that only men "sympathetic to the work" should serve as agents, but when he left the service himself in January 1866 it was a mark of the abandonment of this criterion.[18] Laura Towne, a teacher most loyal to the freedmen, told about her brother William, an agent and friend of the Negroes, willing to serve even without pay, who had to yield his post "for the military must have all such, and how they fill them! They are more pro-slavery than the rebels themselves, and only care to make the blacks work—being quite unconcerned about making the employers pay. Doing justice seems to mean . . . seeing that the blacks don't break contract and compelling them to submit cheerfully if the whites do."[19]

16. *New Orleans Times,* 20 Nov. 1865.

17. J. S. Fullerton to O. O. Howard, 20 July 1865, OOH Papers.

18. Rufus Saxton to O. O. Howard, 2 Sept. 1865, OOH Papers.

19. Laura Towne to Rosabel Towne, 23 Feb. 1866, Towne mss., Southern Historical Collection, Chapel Hill, N.C.

Harper's Weekly carried a picture of a Freedmen's Bureau agent in 1868. He stood calmly, quietly, and courageously between two evenly matched groups of bellicose Southerners—the whites with guns and knives and the Negroes with guns and sticks. He is squarely in the middle, but he stands with the freedmen facing the white men. The American flag flying from his office window waves freely over the black people.[20] There are stories of racial confrontations which called for and received just such cool courage, and there were bureau men who bravely acted and even died serving the freedmen.[21] But they were rare. As the artist of *Harper's Weekly* knew when he drew the figure that there is no such thing as impartiality, so Laura Towne knew that the bureau agent in reality more often stood with the other side.

It is not necessary to paint a Simon Legree in order to explain why this was so. A young Union officer, sent to a remote town in an unfamiliar section of the country with the task of mediating between the races, did not have an easy job. White men recently the enemy in war resented his presence; the freedmen—his clients—were black and strange. Often he could not even understand what they were saying when they came to him with complaints. The urge to overcome his loneliness at the end of a day when the bureau office was closed, did not overcome the strange feeling that he experienced when thinking of engaging socially with the Negro community. Even the most dedicated school teachers (so much assisted by having their role in an otherwise alien society defined by their recognized profession) spent their leisure hours with other white people. The male army officer serving as bureau agent was a new man in a new job, yet his only recognizable status was that of an officer in an occupying army; as such he was shunned.

Townspeople could, and often did, use the retraction of such social ostracism against a bureau agent to their advantage. With a nod or a brief conversation about discovered common cousins in Cincinnati, the white planters could soon discuss the Negroes

20. *Harper's Weekly*, *12* (25 July 1868), 473.
21. T. J. Wood to O. O. Howard, 4 May 1866, BRFAL.

with the bureau men. The advice was expert; the planters had always known them and, therefore, knew them best. If a freedman complained of a whipping, he often discovered that the agent already knew the other side of the story; he had heard about the broken hoe or the untended rows of cotton and about the frustration of the planter, whose only course was to teach the freedman a lesson. Instead of punishing the planter who administered the whipping, the bureau agent delivered a sermon to the Negro on the virtue of diligence. The disappointed freedman would then find himself working under discipline perhaps more severe for his having complained.

The freedmen had to find an escape. It seemed to them that land of their own was the only way. Charles Howard noted their "strong desire, amounting almost to a passion . . . to obtain land."[22] Seventy-five years later an Alabama Negro, the Scottsboro boy, was still in its hold: "Its what a man needs, what my people need, Land. The land they live on, have worked so much and owned so little."[23] In 1865 H. E. Tremain, another Union officer who spoke to the Negroes on Edisto, told of their "desire . . . to secure for themselves *a home.* They wished to own *lands"* and to have something more than a verbal promise that they would be enabled to do so before they would agree to "working again for their old masters." Only land he could call his, around his own house, gave the freedman security. The available alternative did not: "All concurred in the opposition to the contract system."[24]

When the Edisto Negroes were forced to negotiate, they said that "if the planters would sell them *even one acre,* they would then make agreements for service."[25] The Edisto planters resisted even this small loss of their land, fearing that it would diminish their control over the labor needed to make the lands productive.

22. *Report of the Joint Committee on Reconstruction,* pt. 3, p. 36.

23. Heywood Patterson and Earl Conrad, *Scottsboro Boy* (New York, 1950), p. 245.

24. Tremain, *Two Days of War,* p. 273.

25. Ibid., p. 276.

Ironically, freedmen with less of a bargaining base than the independent Edisto farmers (who could compel the attention of General Howard) succeeded in getting and keeping a kind of farm of their own. Washington failed to grant them land, and Mississippi went so far as to prohibit them from buying farms, but still the freedmen persisted. With only poverty on their side, they gained—after a fashion—that degree of independence which made freedom tolerable. The freedmen became sharecroppers.

Planters and workers alike were swept into this new labor system by the difficulties that confronted them in the wake of slavery's collapse. For the landowners, it was a way to get some freedmen to return to the land without yielding ownership; for the freedmen, it was a rescue from working in a field gang, which they had done in slavery and were continuing to do under the contract system. The road to sharecropping was an evolutionary one.

Initially, a "portion of the crop" suggested an arrangement like that agreed to by planter Wynn and laborer Wiate in Attala County, Mississippi. The Negroes, working in field gangs, were paid not wages but supplies bought from the proceeds of the crop plus a share in its worth in cash, if the season were a profitable one. Mississippi's Assistant Commissioner Samuel Thomas reported in the fall of 1865 that such arrangements were the rule in "a large portion of the state."[26]

Payment in shares was accepted by the Freedmen's Bureau, whose agents knew that often the alternative was no pay at all. This was particularly true in Texas, where many Negroes did not know that slavery was over until Edgar Gregory, touring the state in the fall of 1865, told them. Gregory urged that freedmen who agreed to continue working on the plantations where they lived should be rewarded with "a Fair Compensation in money or a portion of the crop."[27] Such a choice was on the printed form; the "wage" column of the contract blanks provided for either cash or a share of the crop.

26. Samuel Thomas to O. O. Howard, 12 Oct. 1865, BRFAL.
27. E. M. Gregory to O. O. Howard, 9 Dec. 1865, BRFAL.

As mentioned, General Howard was optimistic that cash wages would help the Negroes' rise. The freedmen, however, were skeptical. Few of them had known wages of any kind, and many learned at the end of a poor crop year that promises to pay were not always kept. Land was the only asset they trusted, and they found a way to turn the payment in crop shares into the acquisition of land.

Their strategy was to convince the planters to increase the "patch" customarily granted in the contracts for "garden purposes" so that a significant portion of the cash crop could be raised there. When F. M. Simson executed a bureau contract with his workers on January 1, 1867, in Grenada, Mississippi, the first three Negroes listed were over eighteen. For them, entered under the caption "Monthly rate of wages or interest in crop," were the words: "To have a third of crop raised." The next contractors were "Sam his X mark his wife Mary & daughter Sally," and below other freedmen families were similarly inscribed. They too were to get one-third of the crop that they raised, but in the "Remarks" column it was noted that "Dependant [sic] children are fed & clothed by parents."

In the body of the contract, the usual "patch" was filled in as the allotment "for garden purposes," but it is clear that the cash crop was not (or at least not entirely) raised by the freedmen working in field gangs. In pen, a provision had been added: "The parties of the second part are to take good care of all stock & tools intrusted [sic] to them."[28]

Unlike the contract system with its provisions centrally determined by the Freedmen's Bureau, sharecropping was an informal affair allowing an almost infinite variety of arrangements. Personal negotiations between landowners and croppers were amended in pen to the businesslike Yankee forms. Regularly, the arrangements called for the freedmen families to raise on a segment of land a part of the total cash crop regularly raised by the owner. The freedmen kept a share of the proceeds of the sale of the crop—two-thirds, perhaps, if some of the equip-

28. Contract executed 1 Jan. 1867, on file BRFAL.

ment belonged to them; one-half if, as was likely, the mule and plow belonged to the planter. The makeshift quality of the agreements was encouraged by the severe lack of working capital attendant on the disastrous crop failures of 1866 and 1867.[29] The only aspect of the old contract system which was beneficial to the freedman was the care that it promised to his dependents. But when the crop failed to produce enough cash to provide for those unable to work, the Negroes found the planters willing to trade off the care of the dependents in return for the use of a part of the planter's land.

In time the freedmen learned that the price of freedom from direct control by their old masters was engagement in a static arrangement in which very little chance for change existed. Although sharecropping was a way out of laboring in field gangs, it did not provide an escape from economic bondage. The credit system that grew up in the Reconstruction South provided the binding. If the cropper—or tenant, if the farmer had made his arrangement with the landlord a formal one with rents—borrowed seed and supplies from the planter or a supply merchant, a lien was placed on the crop to ensure that the debt was paid. Even if the cropper were fortunate enough to discharge current debts with the return on a crop, he usually had to borrow supplies to get through the winter. Repeatedly he pledged future crops to subsist. The concept of a lien on the crop, which had been written into the bureau contracts to protect the freedman, became, under sharecropping, a device which imprisoned the Negroes on their patch, which proved to be a highly inefficient farm unit.[30]

Like white men similarly bound to the land by poverty, the freedmen and generations of their descendants entered into an agricultural system not entirely free of involuntary servitude. It was, however, a way to avoid working under the immediate supervision of the planters, which was what made the earlier

29. Wharton, *The Negro in Mississippi*, p. 69.

30. C. Vann Woodward, *Origins of the New South: 1877–1913* (Baton Rouge, 1950), pp. 180–84.

substitute for slavery, the contract system, intolerable.[31] Still, it was not possessing a farm of one's own. Roger Shugg, who has studied Louisiana closely, writes: "Fields once cultivated by gangs of slaves came to be worked by families who shared the produce with landlords, but subdivision of these estates did not change their ownership. There was less discipline or labor and consequently less profit for capital than under the black code of slavery."[32]

The freedmen became sharecroppers to be able to assert some independence and to survive in conditions that produced actual starvation in parts of the South. Perhaps it was not the way to freedom, but the freedmen hoped they would someday have enough to buy a farm and make it truly their own. The freedmen to whom General Howard spoke as he continued his trip through the South in 1865 were unaware of the coming generations of grinding poverty that this alternative to working for "old massa" entailed. They still thought they could convince Howard that they must have an alternative to going back to work in the usual way.

Leaving Charleston, General Howard continued his trip through the deep South, stopping first at Savannah and then Fernandina—the Florida town at the southern reach of the coastal area promised by General Sherman to the freedmen. Like the Negroes already farming their own lands on Edisto, the Florida freedmen pressed the General for word that farms of their own would be a reality. At Jacksonville there was the same "erroneous impression among the negroes that the lands will be divided among them." Charles Howard reported to his mother that this "has to be met and counteracted all through this country and it is . . . quite a super human task." Charles watched his brother climb on a carpenter's bench, where he stood for a long hot hour in the center of the town talking to the Negroes and to white

31. Paul W. Gates, *Agriculture and the Civil War* (New York, 1965), p. 373.

32. Roger Shugg, *Origins of Class Struggle in Louisiana* (Baton Rouge, 1939), p. 236.

townspeople. He pleaded with the freedmen "to go quietly and steadily to work for wages." Charles, loyal to his brother, reported quietly: "They are very reluctant to engage in any way to their former masters and yet this is the most desirable course for them at present."[33]

Something of the best in Howard emerged when he met these freedmen on their home ground and when he and his party, riding into the Florida countryside, stopped to eat in a "Negro establishment." His preacher brother, Rowland, "amused" by the place, passed up the food, but the General did not. He also took the opportunity to talk to the people in the neighborhood. With these conversations and with his informal talks as he traveled, General Howard's compassion for the freedmen grew. He almost betrayed his awareness of how dirty the work he had been sent to do was, and on occasion his speeches outlining the President's position were tinged with subversion. True to instructions, he urged that contracting with their old masters was the most desirable course for the freedmen, but he qualified his statement by adding "at present."[34] In one sentence, Howard both crushed and buoyed their hopes. In a sense this response to their hopes was more cruel than kind, but it reflected a new and accurate understanding by Howard of the freedmen themselves. On these too rare trips away from the ceremonial occasions in the big cities, Howard shared experiences that some of his agents participated in every day. He learned from the freedmen rather than learning about them from others.

These face-to-face contacts with his clients did not, however, make Howard a defiant radical. He still strove to quiet the freedmen rather than stir them to demonstrate for what they wanted. At Edisto he recommended that the freedmen follow the conservative and polite course and send a petition to Congress. Most reluctantly they agreed to entrust to him the pressing of their case. In retrospect, one sees that this interpreting function of Howard and the others in the Bureau, this speaking the freed-

33. C. H. Howard to his mother, 31 Oct. 1865, Charles Howard Papers.
34. Ibid.

men's piece for them, may have been the most detrimental service that the Bureau performed. Even when he was executing Johnson's plan for Reconstruction, which called for the disciplines of slavery without the name, Howard insisted that he was expressing the nation's commitment to make freedom worthwhile for its Negroes. And he was not only the voice of that commitment, but also the interpreter of the freedmen's protest within his own frame of compromise and reconciliation.

9. Louisiana

New Orleans was the last major stop on General Howard's trip, and he showed so little comprehension of the political views of the Negroes of Louisiana that it might easily be assumed that he was ignorant of them. This was not true, however, because the leaders of the colored community in that state had taken great care to see that he was fully informed of their position. Since July he had been receiving complimentary copies of the *New Orleans Tribune,* an excellent Negro newspaper, and there is every evidence that he read it.[1] He kept clippings from many southern Negro newspapers, but those from the *Tribune* were the best written and the most thorough. His intellectual curiosity alone must have drawn him to the paper; his college French was sound enough for him to do translations for publication in later life, and the *Tribune's* alternate printings in French must have intrigued him.[2]

The Negroes in New Orleans were intensely involved in the politics of their state, and even the Commissioner, never perceptive politically, must have known this. Further, he should have realized that two high officials of the Freedmen's Bureau were deeply involved in the great struggle over the political future of the Negroes: one, Thomas Conway, stood on the side of the Negroes and the other, James Scott Fullerton, opposed them.

On July 13, 1865, Assistant Commissioner Conway wrote to

1. C. J. Dalloz to O. O. Howard, 24 July 1865, OOH Papers.
2. The *New Orleans Tribune* was published daily except Mondays. The edition in one language was not a translation of the other. Both were thoughtful, but the French edition (*La Tribune*) contained more analytical pieces directed at the intellectuals of the community; the English edition spoke both to the nation and to the English-speaking ex-slaves of Louisiana, for which the class to which the publishers belonged acknowledged a responsibility by 1865.

the mayor of New Orleans, Hugh Kennedy, protesting the arrest and sentencing to six months in jail of one John Martin.

> "What right had he [the policeman] to make the arrest? None whatsoever except that it is right to arrest as vagrants all who are poorly dressed, or who may be found carrying chickens . . . along the streets. But the trouble was not that John was poorly dressed or that he carried chickens that he raised from the hour that they came from the shell, but that he was black."[3]

Conway refused to absolve the Mayor of his responsibility in this matter merely because he followed routine procedure in certifying the recorder's judgment against Martin. Conway notified the Mayor that he was going to demand that General Canby release Martin from the workhouse. On his own behalf, John Martin made a statement and signed it with his mark, saying that his employer, Tobias Gibson, gave him permission to move to New Orleans because the floods in Terrebonne Parish had made Martin's labor impossible on the Live Oak plantation.[4]

Although the Negroes of Louisiana commended Conway's energetic defense of his clients, they expected more.[5] Freedom in New Orleans was an old tradition among the Negroes, many of whom were freeborn and members of a middle class that made its living in all the trades and skilled labor pursuits followed by white men. There was also a highly educated group of intellectuals, who had assumed responsibility for the strong drive for equality. The *New Orleans Tribune* was the voice for this group. Class distinctions favoring the freeborn were discarded as "sheer aristocracy"; freedom for the field hands as well as the gentlemen was the paper's editorial goal.[6] It would be difficult to find a single publication of the Second Reconstruction as clear in stat-

3. T. W. Conway to Hugh Kennedy, 13 July 1865, AJ Papers; *New Orleans Tribune,* 26 July 1865.

4. Deposition by John Martin, 21 July 1865, BRFAL.

5. *New Orleans Tribune,* 6 Aug. 1865.

6. Ibid., 14 Sept. 1865.

ing Negro aims for complete equality in America or as optimistic about its accomplishment.

The readers of the *Tribune* knew their enemies were powerful, but they would not allow that to deter them, nor were they prepared to hand over the battle to others. When the Freedmen's Bureau began to operate actively in Louisiana, the newspaper exercised prudent caution in its endorsement: "Pour le moment, bornons-nous à donner notre approbation cordiale à la politique du général Howard. La manière dont Mr. Conway l'applique à la Louisiana est energique et franche. Mais l'avenir dépendra de la sanction des mesures d'execution, c'est-à-dire du zèle et de l'appui des forces militaires."[7] It watched Conway with a hawk's eye as he began to utilize General Canby's military power to protect the rights of the Negroes.

John Martin's case was not unique; "The Bureau will have thousands of such cases," one official observed.[8] Negroes were unsafe on the streets. One day, eleven employed stevedores—the *Tribune* listed their names; no nameless derelicts these—were arrested on a "hypocritical charge of vagrancy."[9] The week before a servant girl on an errand was sentenced to thirty days in the workhouse for vagrancy, "with the prospect of being released to the Assistant Commissioner of Freedmen 'and being sent on the plantations.' "[10] The Negroes were anxious to see if the local authorities could count on the Freedmen's Bureau to assist or at least acquiesce to a forced labor scheme. And it was not merely on the vagrancy question that the Negroes wanted a test of strength between the city and the Bureau. When a policeman broke up a revival meeting at the Infant Jesus Society with "language too disrespectful to be printed," he threatened to arrest the sisters the next time they conducted a noisy meeting. "Let him do so," said the *Tribune,* "and let us see which is the highest power, the city police or the Commissioner of Freedmen."[11]

7. Ibid. (*La Tribune*), 20 July 1865.
8. S. L. Taggart to T. W. Conway, 10 Aug. 1865, BRFAL.
9. *New Orleans Tribune,* 6 Aug. 1865.
10. Ibid., 26 July 1865.
11. Ibid., 30 July 1865.

Conway's letter of July 13 to Mayor Kennedy made it clear that the battle was joined.

Conway, by turning to General Canby, invoked a tradition of authority in the state which stretched back to 1862. That early in the war New Orleans and several country parishes were recaptured, and Louisiana was rejoined to the Union with the army taking responsibility for governing the state.[12] This responsibility required maintaining the ancient position of the freeborn Negroes of New Orleans and placing slave refugees from the Confederate areas of the state who sought shelter and opportunity in the city.[13] How ex-slaves were to live in the society was an old question in New Orleans.

The army commanders were perplexed by the freedmen. White conservatives, who complained that the Negroes were favored under General Benjamin F. Butler, were troubled less by a more moderate general from Massachusetts, Nathaniel Banks, who replaced him. Banks left a mixed legacy to the Louisiana freedmen. By decree, he established a sound school system which was flourishing when the Freedmen's Bureau was created.[14] Also during the Banks administration, the Negroes got an important start in politics. Negro leaders asked for the vote, first for the freeborn and later for the freedmen.[15] Lincoln had recommended limited suffrage when the Louisianians met in a Constitutional Convention in 1864.[16] It was not granted, but the legislature was empowered to consider it, an action that the freedmen and their radical supporters, including Thomas Conway, took as an invitation to keep the subject very much alive.[17]

The *Tribune* criticized Conway severely for not having forced

12. Willie M. Caskey, *Secession and Restoration of Louisiana* (Baton Rouge, 1938), p. 45.

13. Donald E. Everett, "Demands of the New Orleans Free Colored Population for Political Equality, 1862–65," *Louisiana Historical Quarterly*, 38 (1955), 43–64.

14. Louis R. Harlan, "Desegregation in the New Orleans Public Schools During Reconstruction," *AHR*, 67 (1962), 663–75.

15. Everett, "Demands"; *Louisiana Constitutional Convention, 1864, Debates in the Convention* (New Orleans, 1864).

16. Caskey, p. 130.

17. Ibid.

Banks to act in 1864 when an edict of Negro suffrage by the army could have achieved what was so agonizingly sought in 1865. Conway, however, made amends for this earlier delinquency by later serving as an active member of the executive committee of the integrated Friends of Universal Suffrage.[18]

In addition to starting schools and taking an ambiguous stance on suffrage, General Banks, faced with genuine problems of mass destitution, initiated a system of forced labor, which anticipated the worst aspects of the black codes—including the vagrancy principle of discipline which Mayor Kennedy adopted and Conway protested.[19] "Louisiana, which was the best prepared state, which was ripe for the most thorough reform, reaped the worst systems of 'negro labor' devised in the conquered States."[20] Negroes who had neither homes nor jobs were sent to plantations where they worked for fixed wages, experienced slave-days discipline, and were denied the option of leaving their jobs until the crops were in.[21]

Those Negroes who got to the city and did not find employment were sent to four "Home Farms" maintained by the Bureau of Free Labor of which Thomas Conway was the superintendent. In his report of July 1, 1865—his last as superintendent before becoming assistant commissioner of the Freedmen's Bureau—Conway said that "in these establishments labor is forced, and none can avoid it, unless they are physically unable to perform it."[22] Many were physically unfit and were at least fed and sheltered in these Home Farms, which Conway regarded "as a most successful feature in the government and care of freedmen."[23]

Harsh as Conway sounded, he did understand the word "vagrant" in what we would call its sociological sense. When he used

18. *New Orleans Tribune* (*La Tribune*), 5 Oct. 1865.

19. *New Orleans Tribune*, 1, 17 and 28 Sept. 1865.

20. T. W. Conway, *Report of the Condition of the Freedmen of the Department of the Gulf* (New Orleans, 1864), pp. 7–9.

21. *New Orleans Tribune*, 10 June 1865.

22. T. W. Conway, *Final Report of the Bureau of Free Labor Department of the Gulf* (New Orleans, 1865), p. 5.

23. Ibid.

the word he had drifters in mind. He claimed that there were only 400 Negro vagrants in the state: "I find the colored people are not apt to be vagrant," and he found more white homeless unemployed men than black.[24] None of the white men were sent to the Home Farms, however.[25]

In his new post in the Freedmen's Bureau, Conway discovered that the suppression of vagrancy, for which he had personally provided so stern a model, could be achieved in crueler ways. There was a labor shortage in Louisiana in the summer of 1865 and the local government's drive on vagrants—of which John Martin was a victim—was directly related to it.[26]

The government whose actions Conway was protesting in the matter of John Martin was the civil government of the city. At President Lincoln's direction, General Banks supervised an election in 1864 and an able ex-Whig, Michael Hahn, became governor of the federally held parishes of Louisiana. Hahn's constituents were Unionists, but in 1865 the Amnesty Proclamation made the construction of a new constituency possible. Former rebels were in the ascendancy in Louisiana politics by the summer of 1865.[27] A maverick Unionist, J. Madison Wells, was governor, and rebel Hugh Kennedy was mayor of the city of New Orleans.

The Mayor was restored to his job because of a pardon from the President, and when Thomas Conway went to General Canby to get John Martin released from the workhouse, Mayor Kennedy promptly appealed to Andrew Johnson, complaining that the Assistant Commissioner's interference in civil affairs was illegitimate.[28] Kennedy did not say so, but it is likely that he enclosed Conway's letter to him about John Martin, because there is no other logical way for Conway's complaint to have gotten, as it did, into the President's hands. If this is so, it can only mean that Kennedy was confident that the account of a Negro

24. Ibid., pp. 5, 6.
25. Ibid., p. 4.
26. Washington *Evening Star,* 29 Nov. 1865.
27. Caskey, pp. 160–64.
28. Ibid., p. 167; *New Orleans Tribune (La Tribune),* 10 June 1865; Hugh Kennedy to Andrew Johnson, 21 July 1865, AJ Papers.

chicken thief would only confirm to the President that Conway's interference in local New Orleans' affairs was wrong and foolish.

Governor Wells also reported to Johnson regularly. On July 29, he wrote: "So long as the order requiring the negroes to remain and work on the plantations under the rules and regulations prescribed [by Banks] remained in force the system was working as well as could be expected. This," he continued, "has been changed however by a recent order promulgated by the Deputy Superintendent [sic] here, the Revd. Mr. T. W. Conway allowing the negroes to go where they please and to work for whom they please. The effect of this order will be to utterly demoralize the negroes, besides the ruin brought on the planters in withdrawing the labor necessary to the gathering of crops now in the ground."[29]

The Governor had reason to be alarmed. Conway's first official circulars telling the Negroes he would resist forced labor seizures were strongly worded, and the Assistant Commissioner soon put his words into practice.[30] Conway's provost marshal released the eleven stevedores arrested by Kennedy's police.[31] In his letter to President Johnson, Governor Wells also raised the familiar threat of racial disorder. He mentioned fears of Negro marauders in the interior of the state and contended that the Negroes should be disciplined rather than agitated by Conway's speeches advocating "negro suffrage and equality." Wells claimed that "Inoculatd [sic] . . . with these ideas, he [Conway] cannot perform the part of an impartial agent."[32]

The President sent complaints about Conway to the Bureau, and Fullerton, on August 20, wrote to General Howard reprehending Louisiana's assistant commissioner: "I fear Conway will bring us into trouble," he wrote. "He is working, it appears, against the President's policy in the restoration of Civil Government in Louisiana."[33]

29. J. M. Wells to Andrew Johnson, 29 July 1865, AJ Papers.

30. T. W. Conway's Circular Orders 1 and 2, in *New Orleans Tribune,* 18 and 20 July 1865.

31. *New Orleans Tribune,* 6 Aug. 1865.

32. J. M. Wells to Andrew Johnson, 29 July 1865, AJ Papers.

33. J. S. Fullerton to O. O. Howard, 20 Aug. 1865, OOH Papers.

Andrew Johnson did not want civil government in the abstract; he wanted the reelection of Madison Wells. The Governor's opponents were white Unionists of differing prewar persuasions, freeborn Negroes who, through a society called the Friends of Universal Suffrage, sought to establish black political strength, and adamant ex-rebels, whose leader, Henry Watkins Allen, the governor of Confederate Louisiana, was in exile in Mexico. Johnson judged this last group his greatest threat at the polls and recognized that their resumption of power would be too reactionary for the nation to accept.

To offset the possibility of Allen's victory, Johnson enabled Wells to offer planters an alternative as beneficial to them as a return of the Confederate leader would have yielded. The President made it clear that the Freedmen's Bureau would cooperate in providing field labor for the plantations and labor for the repair of the Mississippi levees.[34]

The various reports on Andrew Johnson's South resulted in a famous and conflicting Reconstruction literature, but the man whose reports were probably most welcomed by the President was Harvey M. Watterson. On October 14, he wrote from New Orleans that Wells was an excellent man and that the five Negro regiments in the city should be removed because they encouraged the Negroes to acts of "insolence." He also recommended that Conway be dismissed, saying that the agents of the Bureau "have encouraged the negroes to leave the plantations, and have filled them with prejudices and ill feelings against their former owners and present proprietors." No labeling could better describe the Johnsonian view of the Negro's proper relationship to his employer or more keenly justify the Negro's misgivings than "present proprietors."[35]

Watterson's justification for redelivering the freedmen to the planters was the charge, used again in the Steedman-Fullerton

34. O. O. Howard, "To whom it may concern," invoking the assistance of all in Louisiana in a levee restoration program, 2 Oct. 1865; J. M. Wells to Andrew Johnson, 29 July 1865, AJ Papers; E. M. Stanton to O. O. Howard, 11 Dec. 1865. Letters Sent Secretary of War, Military Affairs, 1800–1889 (microfilm), National Archives (Record Group 107).

35. H. M. Watterson to Andrew Johnson, 14 Oct. 1865, AJ Papers.

reports, that death and disease were rampant in the Freedmen's Bureau compounds.[36] All of Watterson's charges seriously indicted Conway and the Bureau. Conway had anticipated such attacks in July when he wrote: "Much surprise may be manifested by the apparently large number of sick . . . but it must be borne in mind that the main object . . . of these colonies . . . was to provide a place of refuge and a *home* for the aged and helpless freedmen thrown on the Bureau for support."[37] The state did not provide any alternative to these rural asylums, and Conway, knowing of no other way to give even minimum care to these people, supported these institutions. Suggestions of disorder and of maltreatment of the Negroes were, however, ammunition to support the attack on Conway.

Although Watterson's charges discredited Conway, they were not the cause of his firing. That had long been in the making. During the summer of 1865, Howard sent his inspector general, William E. Strong, to investigate the Conway administration.[38] In Howard's defense, it must be noted that Conway was less careful to give the Commissioner reports on the full range of the freedmen's troubles in Louisiana than he was to report on other freedmen workers whom he disliked. For example, in July, at the height of the vagrancy crisis, he wrote Howard in detail about the all-night visits of R. Bush Plumley, a member of the Board of Education, to restaurants and "other places which have even a worse name."[39]

This, however, would hardly have turned a temperate man like Howard against Conway, and he had other reports that Conway was diligently serving the interests of the freedmen against those of the planters.[40] Howard chose, instead, to heed warnings from General Fullerton that Conway had irritated the President with his "harangue" favoring universal Negro suffrage, which

36. H. M. Watterson to Andrew Johnson, 14 Oct. 1865, AJ Papers.
37. Conway, *Final Report of the Bureau of Free Labor,* p. 5.
38. J. S. Fullerton to O. O. Howard, 16 Aug. 1865, OOH Papers.
39. T. W. Conway to O. O. Howard, 29 July 1865, OOH Papers. There is considerable evidence to suggest that Conway's judgment in the important battle to save the Negro schools was faulty.
40. Nathanial Page to O. O. Howard, 21 Aug. 1865, OOH Papers.

will "stir up quite an excitement" among the Negroes of Louisiana.[41] By September Conway was being eased out on the grounds that his service at $200 a month was too great a financial sacrifice for him to make. Replacement, not a raise, was prescribed.[42]

Conway tried to draw from Howard an expression of "entire satisfaction" with his "course of action so far," in order to strengthen his position. He pleaded for an endorsement—and for his job.[43] During Howard's absence in August, he received in reply only an equivocal and general statement from an aide at bureau headquarters that by "untiring and unremitting attention and exertion . . . and earnest cooperation with the military . . . we shall make good headway despite the many vexatious cause[s] of delay in the work of making men free."[44] This was the closest Conway got to an endorsement from Howard until after he was fired. Then Howard's praise of the Assistant Commissioner was of little benefit to the freedmen of Louisiana.

Louisianians learned of Conway's removal in the first week of October. They did not know what it signified and had no knowledge of the man who was to replace him. The *Times* thought it was "Brent"; the Tribune, correcting its rival, said is was "Bierd."[45] Howard had selected his friend from Army of the Tennessee days, Absalom Baird, to succeed Conway but first, on an interim basis, James Scott Fullerton was named assistant commissioner for Louisiana. Howard did not even afford Conway a post in the Washington office, the usual refuge for bureau personnel who incurred the displeasure of the President. From the South the Commissioner relayed orders that the men sent to replace Conway could "employ [him in a lesser position] if they wish, otherwise I have no need of him."[46]

41. J. S. Fullerton to O. O. Howard, 20 July, 18 Aug. 1865, OOH Papers.
42. T. W. Conway to O. O. Howard, 31 Aug. 1865; O. O. Howard to E. M. Stanton, 13 Sept. 1865; T. W. Conway to O. O. Howard, 4 Oct. 1865, BRFAL.
43. T. W. Conway to O. O. Howard, 19 Aug. 1865, BRFAL.
44. S. L. Taggart to T. W. Conway, 7 Aug. 1865, in *New Orleans Tribune*, 23 Aug. 1865.
45. *New Orleans Tribune*, 4 Oct, 1865.
46. J. S. Fullerton to Max Woodhull, 17 Oct. 1865; Max Woodhull to J. S. Fullerton, 23 Oct. 1866, BRFAL.

Conway had been anxious to stay on in his post and there was no need to send Fullerton to Louisiana at this precise time as an interim appointee if there had not been a special reason to reverse what Conway had been doing. It is clear that Conway was removed from Louisiana and Fullerton sent there at the request of President Johnson. (How fully Howard knew why Johnson would want a close ally in the Bureau in New Orleans is not known; despite his residence in Washington, D.C., Howard had a tin ear for politics.) Just as Howard had been sent south so that he could be at Raleigh in time for the North Carolina Constitutional Convention, Fullerton left Washington about the same time Howard did in order to arrive in New Orleans in the crucial weeks before that state's important gubernatorial election.

Andrew Johnson was determined to demonstrate, with the reelection of incumbent Unionist Governor J. Madison Wells, that the presidential program of Reconstruction had worked. Louisianians would have told the nation that they were ready to resume their quest for prosperity within the Union and without slaves. And, in the bargain, Johnson would have formed a political alliance with the faction in control of a state soon to be restored to its full powers—including that of voting for presidents of the United States.

Johnson would be thwarted if the Confederate Governor of Louisiana, who was also a candidate, overthrew Wells. This would tell the North that Louisiana was still rebellious. On the other hand, if Wells were repudiated by friends of the Negroes or, somehow, by the Negroes themselves, the President would be unable to claim successfully that his plan of Reconstruction was a solution for the racial problem posed by the freedmen.

The Negroes of New Orleans, also intensely aware of the significance of the election, did not at first understand that Fullerton was to play an important role in its outcome. They regarded the open advocacy of Negro enfranchisement by a representative of the national government, Assistant Commissioner Thomas Conway, a political asset. But this was merely what they thought any official of the Freedmen's Bureau ought to advocate; they would expect the same from Fullerton or any other replacement for Conway.

On October 13 the *New Orleans Tribune* carried a routine dispatch about Fullerton's departure from Washington "for a few months sojourn in the southern states for the purpose of an extended and careful scrutiny into the affairs of the negroes."[47] Three days later the Louisianians learned that they were to receive his exclusive scrutiny; he arrived in New Orleans with orders stating that he, and not Absalom Baird, would be assistant commissioner. The *Tribune,* with more hope than conviction, stated: "Gen. Fullerton is in full sympathy with the cause of liberty, and from all we can learn of him, we feel that the cause of liberty will not suffer in his hands."[48]

Such optimism soon faded. One of Fullerton's first acts was to insult influential Negro and white Unionist leaders by refusing to attend a meeting at the Orleans Theater in honor of the departing Thomas Conway. Fullerton, underscoring his statement that things would now be different, announced that bureau policy prohibited its officials from participating in public meetings.[49]

Conway, the Baptist preacher, was treated to a fashionable farewell. Women were invited and, beautifully dressed, many were there in the integrated audience of lawyers, judges, ministers, and members of the flourishing Negro urban society. Even the opponents of the Negro movement came to evaluate its strength.[50] The tribute paid Conway was gracious, and he replied in kind, declaring that he would not consider the meeting as just a personal testimonial to him but as a symbol of the Negroes' aspirations including those which were political.[51]

Fullerton may have affected political neutrality by not attending mass meetings, but his acts in office belied it. Prior to the election scheduled for November 6, he engaged in four schemes,

47. *New Orleans Tribune,* 13 Oct. 1865.
48. Ibid., 17 Oct. 1865.
49. J. S. Fullerton to Richard C. Taylor, 27 Oct. 1865, AJ Papers.
50. *New Orleans Tribune (La Tribune),* 27 and 28 Oct. 1865.
51. Ibid., 28 Oct. 1865.

all of which were related to the outcome of the voting. First, he closed the bureau courts on the grounds that the Negroes, having entrance to civil courts, did not need the federal agency to obtain justice.[52] A few days later, on November 1, he received a telegram directly from the President (not relayed via the Bureau or even the War Department), instructing him not to collect the school tax that supported the Negro schools and that was unpopular with the white voters on whom Johnson counted to support his slate.[53]

Even before announcing the tax cut and the restoration of local white jurisdiction over Negro delinquents, Fullerton started his third project—granting property to voters at the expense of nonvoters.[54] While Thomas Conway was still cleaning out his desk, Fullerton began a massive restoration of lands.[55] Conway quoted Fullerton as telling him at the time that this restoration had been specifically ordered by the President in private conversation.[56]

"The property given up in the course of about a week covered half a million dollars; in fact each property-holder seemed to have priority almost in proportion to his wealth."[57] Even houses that were being used as Negro schools and asylums were forfeited. But Fullerton's cruelty is most immediately apparent in its effect on the children in the city's two large Negro orphanages. He sent information to the white newspapers (only) telling readers how they might apply for the services of these children who were to be bound out. Francis G. Shaw's New York Freedmen's Aid Society ran one of these homes, and Madame Louise de Mortié, a remarkable woman, directed the other in Pierre Soulé's mansion.[58] She protested so vehemently the dispersal of

52. Ibid.

53. Andrew Johnson to J. S. Fullerton, 1 Nov. 1865, AJ Papers.

54. *New Orleans Times,* 21 Oct. 1865.

55. A long list of these properties was in the *New Orleans Times* of 1 Nov. 1865.

56. *Report of the Joint Committee on Reconstruction,* pt. 4, p. 85.

57. T. W. Conway testimony, *Report of the Joint Committee,* pt. 4, p. 85.

58. *New Orleans Tribune,* 25 and 27 Oct. 1865.

her sixty children (it was hardly a "crowded pest house") that even Fullerton temporarily rescinded his order restoring that property.[59]

Of even greater damage to the Negro cause than such cavalier treatment of the orphans was the return of the vast farmland holdings Conway had hoped would one day be divided among the Negroes. One of the ironies of the story of the Freedmen's Bureau in Louisiana is that at the very time Fullerton was restoring the lands, the *Tribune* continued to print Conway's official order instructing the freedmen how, before January 1, 1866, they might apply to the Bureau for lands.[60]

Fullerton's fourth act, like the others, was calculated to meet with the approval of conservatives, who did not want Louisiana's social problems to be visible on their streets. His October 21, 1865 open letter to the freedmen called for the enforcement of an anti-vagrancy policy which recalled "the worst days of General Banks' administration" and was like the one Conway had so vigorously protested in John Martin's case.[61] Fullerton informed the chief of police of the large number of freedmen in the city "without any means of support, who are in fact vagrants." They were to be arrested and turned over to bureau officials, who would "secure for them employment." Full cooperation from Mayor Kennedy's police was instantaneous.[62] In fact, the cooperation was so great that the courts and workhouses were overtaxed and the services offered by the Bureau availed of.[63] The alternative to spending time in the workhouse for a Negro convicted of vagrancy was contracting to work as a field hand on the plan-

59. Ibid., 24 Oct. 1865; Ibid. (*La Tribune*), 27 Oct. 1865; Soulé's pardon by President Johnson was noted in the *New Orleans Tribune* (*La Tribune*), 3 Nov. 1865.

60. *New Orleans Tribune*, 19 Oct. 1865.

61. Fullerton based his order on Howard's of 4 Oct. 1865, which said that where local vagrancy law did not distinguish between black and white violators it could be enforced against the Negroes. *New Orleans Times*, 2 Nov. 1865; *New Orleans Tribune*, 28 Oct. 1865.

62. W. T. Hire to Andrew Johnson, 13 July 1865, AJ Papers; T. W. Conway to Hugh Kennedy, 17 July 1865, AJ Papers.

63. *New Orleans Tribune*, 3 Nov. 1865.

tations, which were reporting difficulty in getting enough workers.[64] The Freedmen's Bureau always tried to veil its enforcement of the contract system with talk of mutually beneficial arrangements freely entered, but the basic assumption that the worker entered into his contract voluntarily was clearly violated in Louisiana. Assistant Commissioner Fullerton, however, remained faithful to the rhetoric: "This thing you must learn above all other," he told the freedmen, "a contract must be sacredly observed."[65]

Fullerton took measures to insure that his work was appreciated. Two days before the election he wrote a fellow Missourian, Frank Blair, on whom he could rely to show his letter to President Johnson. He praised Johnson for thwarting any extension of the move of Confederates to Mexico by creating confidence in the minds of planters, who had "thought that their property would never be restored." Fullerton also told Blair that all white men, except a certain "clique" and their *"very few* black followers," supported his policies.[66] Johnson and Fullerton made certain that the Louisiana voters, whose votes counted, went to the polls feeling secure in the possession of their lands and confident that laborers to farm them would be available. The only remaining uncertainty was whether the Negroes of Louisiana would accept this state of affairs. The Negroes were organized and articulate, and anything that dampened their ardor would help the Johnsonian party gain the confidence of the white voters.

The day before the election an unexpected visitor came to New Orleans. "News of the arrival of General O. O. Howard, head of the Freedmen's Bureau, spread yesterday like wild fire throughout the city."[67] The Negroes there were intensely excited because they had worked out an extraordinary way to demonstrate that they wanted to vote, knew how to vote, and would vote. They had scheduled a mock election to be run exactly as the

---

64. Washington *Evening Star*, 29 Nov. 1865.

65. J. S. Fullerton's open letter to the freedmen, *New Orleans Times*, 21 Oct. 1865.

66. J. S. Fullerton to Francis P. Blair, 4 Nov. 1865, AJ Papers.

67. *New Orleans Tribune*, 6 Nov. 1865.

official balloting was conducted. The complicated ritual of registration had been followed, and polls were established in the city and on those plantations where they were permitted. Clearly and persistently the *New Orleans Tribune* told its readers how the election would work.[68] The Negroes were running a candidate for "delegate to Congress," who, when "elected," would take their case for the franchise to Washington for them.

When Howard's presence in the city became known, a meeting was called hastily in the New Orleans Theater so that the General could be heard. An hour before the meeting began the theater was already crowded, mainly by black people. "It is strange with what telegraphic rapidity news travels just among the Negroes," commented the conservative *New Orleans Times* uneasily.[69] On the stage with Howard were leaders of Creole de couleur society, such as J. B. Roudanez, whose family owned the *New Orleans Tribune.* Sitting with them were other Unionist politicians, including the young flamboyant carpetbag candidate for delegate to Congress, Henry Clay Warmoth, who was hoping for an endorsement. Also on the committee for the meeting were several white radicals, one of whom was killed for his political views within the year, as well as several Negro politicians.[70] As Howard noted in his speech, the crowd was there to hear him talk politics.

Howard began his talk by asking why he was on his southern trip. He ignored Johnson's having sent him on a specific and publicly announced errand to Charleston to accomplish land restoration and, generally, to bolster the restored Johnsonian governments in the southern states by spreading the news that there would be no land distribution to the Negroes at Christmas. He claimed, instead, that he had come to investigate and to return to Washington with a report on the "precise condition of the freedmen."[71] He then sought to establish his credentials as a friend

68. See particularly *New Orleans Tribune,* 12 Sept. 1865.

69. *New Orleans Times,* 16 Nov. 1865.

70. Ibid., 6 Nov. 1865.

71. Howard's speech, carefully outlined, was the lead article on election day under the heading, "Good Advice to the Freedmen," *New Orleans Times,* 6 Nov. 1865. The full text was printed 7 Nov. 1865.

of the freedmen and spoke of his experience during the war with the 8,500 refugees who had followed his army, had been cared for, and had gained their freedom. Howard told his New Orleans audience that the Emancipation Proclamation had effectively ended the white supremacy of slavery days and sought to link President Johnson to the Proclamation by noting that he was Lincoln's successor. Explaining Johnson's apparently antinegro actions, he said that the President had to be the white man's President as well as the black man's. Rhetorically, at least, Howard had established equality.

Howard also asserted that, with legal restriction against the Negro being lifted, acts of restriction would also be eliminated. Since Negroes had legal admittance to the courts, he claimed they had obtained equal justice and, after putting to rest any hope for a distribution of lands and making reference to the evil of idleness, he extolled the benefits of wage labor in agriculture. He used himself as an example, telling his listeners that he had been a farm boy who rose in the world through hard work. The analogy between the Leeds farm boy who did chores on his family farm when he was not in good schools to which his family (by scraping) could send him, and the Negro who came to the city to make his way but was forced to go back and contract with a former slave owner to work as a field hand under the planter's discipline, in return for wages, was slight. But Howard was undaunted. He stressed that a reconciliation between old masters and ex-slaves should be a first objective of the freedmen, praised the wages they would receive, and told them about the coming branch of the Freedman's Savings Bank in which their wages could be saved.

Finally he discussed what the Negroes had come to hear. The *New Orleans Times* printed a verbatim account of the speech:

> I have not touched on any political topic. I deprecate it now. Let us be satisfied with what we have, and improve upon it. Let us put down the pins and hold onto what we have and be sure we have got it before we push ahead any

further. [cries of no] I want to say this, that in . . . the
French islands . . . where good wholesome rules were introduced, where labor was undisturbed, that education com-
menced and prosperity was uniform. On the others, where
the people got divided up, pro and con [,] by political agita-
tions before labor was settled, there became anarchy and
everything went backwards.[72]

Howard no doubt hoped that his flattering reference to the
French islands in contrast to the bloody uprisings on English
Jamaica would be convincing to the large portion of his audience, which was still closely tied by name, education, and
language to the French Caribbean.

Hearing of the General's arrival, the *New Orleans Tribune*
scheduled an "extra" for election morning, but Howard's speech
proved a disappointment to Roudanez and the Negroes' cause.
He did not make a statement in favor of even the principle of
Negro suffrage, much less give an endorsement of Warmoth's
candidacy. The *Tribune* reporter, impressed by Howard's "strik-
ingly modest manner," said that his speech was not an oration
but "an unpretending effusion from an honest heart mingled
with kind advices, the wisdom of some of which we may perhaps
dispute; but whose complete sincerity was undeniable."[73]

The conservative *New Orleans Times* was less concerned with
Howard's tone than with the speech's contents, with which it was
delighted. On November 6 the paper carried three editorials entitled "What Shall We Do with Him," a loose paraphrase of
the question Howard had been asking his assistant commissioners
about the Negro; "Gen. Howard's Address"; and "The Election
To-Day." In the first editorial the *Times* rejected what it considered the two extremes. Colonization was unchristian and
impractical (and, the paper might have noted, labor was in short
supply). Universal suffrage and equality were at the other
extreme of the spectrum and should also be resisted. Concerning

72. *New Orleans Times,* 7 Nov. 1865.
73. *New Orleans Tribune,* 6 Nov. 1865.

Howard's speech, the paper noted that on the question of politics the Negroes had been "disappointed," and it called the speech a wise one.[74] On the election, the paper claimed to be nonpartisan but patriotically urged "every registered voter" to "sustain the President." They did, four to one.

Wells was reelected with 22,312 votes. His closest rival, the expatriate Confederate Governor Allen, received 5,497 votes.[75] But the victory had its shadows. The mock election, which the *New Orleans Times* branded as "treason" and tried to minimize by not printing the returns, produced astonishing results.[76]

Henry Clay Warmoth, with 16,512 votes in New Orleans' parishes, had "run far ahead" of Wells in that city.[77] He got 2,300 white votes in the regular balloting, and in all his supporters claimed that he got 21,405 votes in the entire state, including the 2,500 votes cast by sympathetic white voters in this voluntary poll in which the Negroes demonstrated so dramatically their desire to vote.[78]

President Johnson received several congratulatory messages for the outcome of the official election. Cuthburt Bullitt, Governor Wells' emissary to Washington, telegraphed from New Orleans that the victory was due to Johnson's "perfect administration of the government."[79] A few weeks later, Mayor Kennedy confirmed that Wells' election was directly attributable to the President and suggested that those parishes that voted for Allen (Wells' own was one) should be punished by having Negro troops stationed in them. Kennedy promised to continue to keep the President informed on the progress of their program. Of the present assistant commissioner in New Orleans, he said, "The

74. The *New Orleans Times* had also printed a speech by another Northerner which they thought relevant to the election—Henry Ward Beecher's celebrated endorsement of Andrew Johnson. *New Orleans Times,* 31 Oct. 1865, quoting *New York Times,* 23 Oct. 1865.

75. Caskey, *Secession and Restoration,* p. 178.

76. *New Orleans Times,* 6 and 15 Nov. 1865.

77. Caskey, p. 181.

78. Ibid.

79. Cuthburt Bullitt to Andrew Johnson, 9 Nov. 1865, AJ Papers.

happiest effects have followed the brief official visit of Gen'l Fullerton and all parties interested in the welfare of the State now breathe more fully. He did all that was desirable."[80]

Perhaps a little uneasy about the desirability of all that he had done, Fullerton wired the President "direct as requested" shortly after the election.[81] He reported his conversations with newly elected legislators quickly assembled to enact a black code. They promised him that the school tax, already collected from the Negroes before Fullerton suspended collections, would go to the Negro schools (a promise not kept). With the dispersed vagrants in mind, he expressed his hope that the prosperity attendant on Johnson's policies would bring the Negroes good wages. If he needed reassurance that what he had done was right, he got it quickly. President Johnson telegraphed back that he was "highly gratified" by Fullerton's dispatch and the course of events in which he had participated in New Orleans.[82] Fullerton had done the job he had been sent to do; on November 8, two days after the election, he proceeded north for a holiday. The *Tribune* announced the pending arrival of the permanent Assistant Commissioner Absalom Baird.[83]

The Negroes of New Orleans had learned from their experience with the Freedmen's Bureau and the men who ran it. They had always been skeptical of Thomas Conway and watched him closely, applauding him only when they felt sure he deserved it. Once he made a study of conditions in the state in order to bolster his case against the local vagrancy policy and issued a letter sharply critical of the forced labor practices of the city and state governments. To suggest the relationship between the vagrancy principle and forced labor, he unmasked the fact that the arrests were made for a reason other than to control a massive problem with drifters: "[T]here are not five hundred negro vagrants in Louisiana." Sensitive to the possibility that even their few white

80. Hugh Kennedy to Andrew Johnson, 23 Nov. 1865, AJ Papers.
81. J. S. Fullerton to Andrew Johnson, 9 Nov. 1865, AJ Papers.
82. Andrew Johnson to J. S. Fullerton, 10 Nov. 1865, AJ Papers.
83. *New Orleans Tribune,* 8 Nov. 1865.

allies might be condescending, the *Tribune* editors asked: "Why did Mr. Conway not expect so small amount of 'negro vagrancy'? There is only one answer. The newspaper then gave its stern explanation, "because he was imbued with the common prejudice against us." The paper went on to philosophize on the matter. "Philanthropists are sometimes a strange class of people; they love their fellowmen, but . . . these . . . to be worthy of their assistance, must be of an inferior kind. We were and still are oppressed; we are not demoralized criminals."[84]

Thomas Conway had no easy task earning the respect of such critics. When he was fired, the *Tribune* both praised and criticized him: "M. Conway, qui tombe aujour d'hui, victime de la réaction, est . . . une victime de ses propres fautes." If he had gotten the Negroes the vote during Banks' regime, as the *Tribune* contended he should have, "il serait aujourd-hui le plus grande homme du Sud." Conway was ten years too young, but that did not trouble the *Tribune* as it pressed its criticism of the Assistant Commissioner. Had he done what the Negroes had advised, he would have been, it conjectured, reconstructed Louisiana's "premier senateur."[85]

By the time Fullerton arrived, the *New Orleans Tribune* reflected deep disillusionment among the Negroes in Louisiana. When the new Assistant Commissioner issued his first order telling the freedmen to eschew idleness and contract to work for the planters, the newspaper expressed no rage—just resignation. Referring to the Freedmen's Bureau and its predecessor in the state, the Bureau of Free Labor, it said that "nearly two years of experience have taught the freedmen what a contract is and what the Freedmen's Bureau is for."[86] "Idleness" and "vagrancy" were words of a white myth which suggested that the blacks lacked discipline.[87] "The necessity of working is per-

84. Ibid., 31 Aug. 1865.
85. Ibid. (*La Tribune*), 5 Oct. 1865.
86. *New Orleans Tribune,* 22 Oct. 1865.
87. For a modern rendition of the myth, see Donald, *Negro Freedmen;* ibid.

fectly understood by men who have worked all their lives."
The *Tribune* was also realistic about the Bureau's rhetoric of
thrift as guarantor of a bright future: "Let us suppose [the ex-
slave] goes naked and lays by the whole of his wages. Then he
will have 'capital' of only one hundred and twenty dollars, if
paid faithfully, at the end of the year. It is not enough to buy *one*
mule, and therefore a very impotent means of buying land and
establishing himself in business even as a partner in association
with his peers."[88]

Before General Howard reached New Orleans, the Negroes
abandoned their hope that the Freedmen's Bureau would serve
as their agent in the search for an escape from oppression:

> Nous comprenons que nous sommes abandonnés à nos
> propres forces et qu'il nous faut désormés combattre dans
> une position politique inégale. Mais soit. Et si le Bureau des
> Affranchis devient l'Agence des planteurs, le drapeau des
> Etats Unis flotte encore audessus de nos têtes, et les injus-
> tices ne s'accompliront pas impunément à l'ombre de dra-
> peau, en presence des braves militaires qui ont combattu
> sous ses plis.[89]

The *Tribune* was wrong in the prediction of the extent of injustice that Negroes would experience under that flag; it was
right in its fear that the Freedmen's Bureau might become the
planters' bureau. And nothing in Howard's speech gave the
paper grounds to desert its disillusioned view of the agency.
Yet somehow the Negroes' confidence was partially restored.
There was a resumption of trust, not in the Bureau but in its
Commissioner. The General's words belied this trust, but his
"sincerity of manner" suggested to the audience in the Orleans
Theater that he not only wanted to help them but also could.[90]

No doubt some of this new optimism that diluted the *Tribune's* earlier skepticism was due to the mock election and the

88. *New Orleans Tribune,* 22 Oct. 1865.
89. Ibid. (*La Tribune*), 28 Oct. 1865.
90. *New Orleans Tribune,* 22 Sept., 6 Nov. 1865.

moral victory that it gave the Negro cause. The *Tribune*, disappointed in Howard's failure to endorse political equality, was pleased that at least he had not branded the demonstration of Negro political ability as "subversive" as others had done.[91]

On election day Howard received Negro leaders at the headquarters of the Bureau des Affranchis (for the bilingual Negro Louisianans so intent on gaining the franchise as well as being freed from forced labor practices, there was double irony in the agency's name.) The callers found themselves as welcome at the office on Carondolet Street as they had been in Conway's administration, and the General's willingness to talk with them suggested a repudiation of Assistant Commissioner Fullerton which Howard never formally stated. The conversations were cordial and "the visitors were thoroughly satisfied by the sincerity and good intentions of General Howard,"[92] who, they believed, would take to Congress a report, on which all their hopes now centered, of the grievances they experienced under the state government that President Johnson had restored.[93]

Two days later Howard sat on the deck of a river boat taking him to Vicksburg to meet Absalom Baird, who was on his way to assume his duties as assistant commissioner of the Freedmen's Bureau in Louisiana. As the boat moved up the river he fell to talking with another passenger, Edward Tinchant, a New Orleans Negro of means. The General told Tinchant that if he were a private citizen he would support the Negroes of Louisiana. He approved of their having elected a delegate to Congress, although he doubted that young Warmoth was the man for the job.[94]

Howard told Tinchant that Warmoth got the Negroes to the polls by buying their votes. Unbelieving, Tinchant pressed the General to learn the "influential source" of this rumor. Howard reportedly admitted that his informant was one of Governor

91. Ibid., 6 Nov. 1865.
92. Ibid., 7 Nov. 1865.
93. Ibid., 5, 9, and 30 Dec. 1865.
94. Edward Tinchant to the editor, 8 Nov. 1865, *New Orleans Tribune*, 11 Nov. 1865.

Wells' servants. (The cook told the white man what she thought he wanted to hear.) In rebuttal, Tinchant argued that the election had been first carefully planned and then well advertised. The interest was great; it was not cash that stimulated such broad participation.[95]

Howard was on his way back to Washington. Perhaps the farmers of Edisto and Jacksonville and the editors and merchants of New Orleans were sending north a wiser Commissioner of the Freedmen's Bureau. Howard had at least ceased referring to his trip as a carrying out of the orders "of his Excellency," and he had convinced hopeful Negro leaders that it was an investigation into the condition of the freedmen. Surely his report would reflect their great hope for land and for the vote. Howard protested that if he were a private citizen he would support the Negroes; why he did not have an even greater obligation to do so as the Commissioner of the Freedmen's Bureau he did not explain. He had encouraged the freedmen of both Edisto and Louisiana to press their case with Congress. The *New Orleans Tribune,* concurring with Frederick Douglass that "Johnson has sold us," put its faith in the National Congress, hoping that it would grant the freedmen what the President had made impossible for them to attain in their states.[96]

95. Ibid.
96. Frederick Douglass to J. B. Roudanez in *New Orleans Tribune,* 27, Oct. 1865.

10. Allies in Congress

At bureau headquarters in Washington the staff was anxious to know what their chief proposed to do about some of the problems that developed during the month that he was away. They sent a telegram requesting his itinerary and recommending that he attend to one matter before returning to the capital. "Col. Eaton," who had much experience in the region that Howard was visiting, "suggests that before you leave the Mississippi Valley, the Assistant Commissioners should be instructed in regard to the regulation of labor for the next year."[1]

The Commissioner would have to turn his attention from the heady talk with New Orleans gentlemen about political equality and consider again how difficult it would be to get the Negroes who worked in the fields to accept the bitter fact that they were not going to receive the land Congress had promised them. The year in which slavery came to an end (1865) was nearly over, and the freedmen were not very far along in their pursuit of happiness. As General Howard himself wrote in his *Autobiography,* referring to Presidential Reconstruction in the period just before Congress reconvened in December 1865, "the freedmen were left outside of all proper citizenship. They had no voice directly or indirectly in the new governments over them, and soon, worse than that, vicious laws were passed that made their actual condition deplorable. They were, indeed, but for military protection, which still lingered in the South, worse off than under slavery."[2] Although expressing such views years later, Howard probably felt this way as he returned to Washington in November 1865, but then he expressed his grave misgivings

1. Max Woodhull to O. O. Howard, 12 Nov. 1865, BRFAL.
2. Howard, *Autobiography,* 2, 277.

only in private.[3] When he reached the capital, a reporter from the Washington *Evening Star* interviewed him and then wrote that Howard "speaks encouragingly of affairs in the South."[4] Despite the usual brave front, the trip had sobered him. He had "worked hard for what seemed the best interest of the freedmen," but in Edisto, Jacksonville, Mobile—wherever he had gone—he had seen evidence and heard from the Negroes much that made him doubt that the presidential program was in their interest at all.[5]

Howard had participated in depriving the Negroes of a good deal on his trip. He had been engaged in dispossessing some freedmen of the land on which they had farms, in depriving others of the hope that they would be granted land to farm, and generally in advising the freedmen to settle down and make their old masters love them again. And yet, as he did these things and undercut the agents and assistant commissioners most concerned about the freedmen, he also made the Negroes feel that he was personally involved in the freedmen's future. Even in his disappointing speech in New Orleans, he repeatedly referred to himself and his predominantly Negro audience as "we" and spoke of what "we" should try to achieve.[6]

The man in command of the freedmen's cause seemed to be riding two horses which he could not head in the same direction. All of the rhetoric of his commission of Christian common purpose had proved hollow as he confronted the reality of the problems men faced in the South. The freedmen's goals and those of the white men with whom President Johnson was working were in direct conflict. Much as he had submerged his doubts about the army at West Point and remained under its discipline, he had accepted the command of the President in September

3. *New Orleans Tribune,* 7 Nov. 1865; O. O. Howard to Henry Wilson, 25 Nov. 1865, OOH Papers.

4. Washington *Evening Star,* 2 Nov. 1865.

5. O. O. Howard to Henry Wilson, 25 Nov. 1865, OOH Papers; O. O. Howard to E. M. Stanton, 5 Nov. 1865, BRFAL.

6. *New Orleans Times,* 7 Nov. 1865.

and gone south to dutifully discharge the order given him, but this had not removed his doubts.

Not only had the trip troubled his conscience but the sophisticated Negroes of New Orleans may have convinced him of the danger of losing his leadership of freedmen affairs. They were aware of the Freedmen's Bureau's shortcomings and, while still hopeful about Howard himself, they were skeptical. When, from Jackson, he issued his order telling the assistant commissioners to dispel the "rumors" of the grant of forty acres by Christmas, the *New Orleans Tribune,* disillusioned, said they always knew the "intended measure would fall to the ground" and pointedly noted that granting land to the Negroes was Congress' intention and not the Bureau's.[7]

If the freedmen were in grave trouble, would not the Bureau —and Howard—be judged to have failed? His command position was shaky. If Howard declared the President's program to be so disastrous as to invite Congress to overturn it (as the Negroes of New Orleans confidently expected), it would be imprudent of him to remain too fully committed to the White House. On the other hand, to declare the situation in the South hopeless might invite Congress to bypass the Bureau and provide a new reconstruction program. When Howard arrived in Washington, he regrouped his forces and looked for new allies. His object was to convince both the President and the Congress that "the Freedmen's Bureau, or," he added with winning modesty, "some substitute having the same purpose, would have to be continued at least a year longer."[8]

A confident statement to the press was Howard's first move in his offensive. His second was to enlist Edwin Stanton in the effort, for the war secretary too had much at stake in the performance of any agency in his department. Howard and Stanton were not close, but they could always talk to each other; when Howard began to sound more like a preacher than a general,

7. O. O. Howard, circular order, 11 Nov. 1865, BRFAL; *New Orleans Tribune,* 19 Nov. 1865.

8. O. O. Howard to E. M. Stanton, 25 Nov. 1865, OOH Papers.

Stanton would bring him down to earth sharply without incurring Howard's resentment.[9] There was much loyalty in their relationship as evidenced when Howard later stood by in the Secretary's office during the days of the removal crisis.[10]

When Howard had returned to Charleston from Edisto and wired Stanton how sad it made him to have to order the bureau men to restore the lands, Stanton replied, "I do not understand that your orders require you to disturb the freedmen in possession at present." Stanton spoke both as a lawyer (reminding the Commissioner that by act of Congress he was in charge of freedmen's affairs and the possessors of those lands were freedmen) and as a tough-minded friend.[11] His telegram might have read: if you feel so strongly about restoration, why don't you do something about it?

On November 21, General Howard, along with Secretary Stanton, went to the White House to persuade Johnson to protect the freedmen from those men who were economically and politically controlling the South. The Massachusetts senator, Charles Sumner, still spoke to the President as "a faithful friend and supporter of your administration" when he requested Johnson to cease the return of the freedmen to the control of the states. Undoubtedly, Howard's tone was much the same.[12] Howard, as a commissioner of a bureau in the Johnson Administration, had considerably more to lose from a break with Johnson than did the troubled but powerful Senator from Massachusetts.

In the interview Howard spoke of Edisto and of Saxton's work in South Carolina; he told Johnson of such things as the six hundred Negro children in Mobile who were about to lose their school because of the restoration of a medical school building.[13] As the Commissioner no doubt pointed out, restoration is fine

9. Howard, *Autobiography, 2,* 390.

10. Washington *Evening Star,* 22 and 24 Feb. 1868.

11. E. M. Stanton to O. O. Howard, 25 Oct. 1865, quoted in Howard, *Autobiography, 2,* 240.

12. Charles Sumner to Andrew Johnson, 11 Nov. 1865, AJ Papers.

13. O. O. Howard to E. M. Stanton, 5 Nov. 1865, BRFAL; O. O. Howard to Rufus Saxton, 22 Nov. 1865.

(and doctors needed), but what about the freedmen? Such conversations between Howard and Johnson were hardly new, but this one differed from the humiliating talks in September, when the President was merely amused by Howard's pleadings in behalf of the Negroes, because Secretary Stanton was present. Now, too, Howard had seen the South for himself, and Congress was soon to meet. In the days following his meeting with the President, Howard sent the White House letters to reinforce his oral argument that the freedmen were not safe without the protection of the Freedmen's Bureau.[14]

Edwin Stanton was an important ally. In subsequent days, Howard pointedly mentioned that the Secretary accompanied him on his visit to the President. He wrote to A. P. Ketchum to authorize him to stall on the restoration of lands. The freedmen were to be "suitably provided for" before any more lands were returned."[15] Howard had his new adjutant general, Max Woodhull, write to Absalom Baird to suggest, rather gently, that he discontinue the harshest of Fullerton's antinegro activities and that he try to have the education tax collected to save the Negro schools.[16] (He also had Woodhull write Fullerton in Ohio to deny that the Bureau had issued any attack on him.)[17]

Fullerton returned to Washington and, on December 4, 1865, replaced John Eaton, Jr., as assistant commissioner for the District of Columbia when Howard's first deputy returned to Tennessee to edit the *Memphis Post.* For the first time Fullerton had an official position equal to the power he had so long exercised in the agency, but ironically his chance to direct the course of bureau policy was gone. He had put his faith in the White House and with great success had urged his chief to do so too, but when Howard began to work with Congress, Fullerton lost his

14. R. S. Donaldson to J. H. Weber, contending that the Negroes would need continued army protection if they were not to be allowed to testify in courts or to own property, 17 Nov. 1865, forwarded to Howard by Assistant Commissioner Samuel Thomas with the endorsement, "Col. Donaldson's letter is but a repetition of those of all other officers," AJ Papers.

15. O. O. Howard to A. P. Ketchum, 21 Nov. 1865, BRFAL.

16. Max Woodhull to Absalom Baird, 24 Nov. 1865, BRFAL.

17. Max Woodhull to J. S. Fullerton, 24 Nov. 1865, BRFAL.

influence. Howard never again depended on him as he had during the summer and fall, but the promotion hardly indicated that Fullerton had been repudiated. By dismissing him because of many of his own acts, Howard would be admitting failure, and what was more it would almost certainly antagonize the President. Not until February 1866 when Fullerton crossed Howard again, this time in an effort to destroy the Bureau, did Howard remove him and put Charles Howard in his place.[18]

Having made peace momentarily with the President's ally in the Bureau, Howard turned his attention to Rufus Saxton, who was opposing Johnson's restoration program the most. The Commissioner wrote to Saxton to report that he had discussed his tenuous hold on his assistant commissionership in South Carolina with Stanton and Johnson and again with Stanton privately. Stanton wanted Saxton to stay on but cautioned that if he did a promotion might be forfeited. Howard also warned Saxton to curb the "extremes" (the pronegro positions) of some of his agents.[19]

The Commissioner also had an aide write to his old friend Thomas Osborn to silence a rumor that the Bureau was to be dissolved.[20] In his written report to the Secretary of War, Howard dissassociated himself from some of the odious things he had done in the South. He laid the responsibility for his acts on "the Executive under whose express orders I was acting."[21] He reopened the question of obtaining land for the freedmen and closed by saying: "I would recommend that the attention of Congress be called to the subject of this report at as early a day as possible, and that these lands or a part of them, be purchased by the U.S. with a view to the rental and subsequent sale to the Freedmen."[22]

18. Howard recorded the day of Fullerton's leave-taking as 7 Feb. 1866, but Fullerton wrote to the President on bureau stationery on 9 Feb. 1866, *Report of the Commissioner,* 1 Nov. 1866, p. 21; J. S. Fullerton to Andrew Johnson, 9 Feb. 1866, AJ Papers.
19. O. O. Howard to Rufus Saxton, 22 Nov. 1865, BRFAL.
20. Max Woodhull to T. W. Osborn, 24 Nov. 1865, BRFAL.
21. O. O. Howard to E. M. Stanton, 24 Nov. 1865, BRFAL.
22. Ibid.

Stanton's previous wire to Howard about the Edisto lands was the first suggestion from a superior that an alternative to Johnson's Reconstruction plans existed. But his brother Charles and others had been urging him to seek Congress' help for the freedmen. "Let the matter [of the sea-island lands] be deferred till Congress meets & I am sure a permanent title will be given to the actual settlers," wrote Charles in September.[23]

Congress was scheduled to meet in the first week in December for its first session since the Freedmen's Bureau had begun its work, and, over the preceeding weekend, Howard set out to achieve a major new alliance. He wrote a long letter to Senator Henry Wilson who was in Massachusetts preparing to leave for the capital. Wilson was less famous as an advocate of Negro rights than his august colleague, Charles Sumner, but he was known to be interested in the welfare of the Negroes in the South; as chairman of the Senate's Committee on Military Affairs, he could be expected to manage any bill dealing with the Department of War.

In his letter to Wilson, Howard expressed his full confidence that Wilson would be sympathetic to whatever he had to say. He told Wilson that he wanted to confer with him as soon as he arrived in Washington. In the meantime, he stated that his trip South had convinced him that the federal government should not relinquish its authority in freedmen matters to the states. He was "sorry for the policy adopted of restoring lands . . . without affixing conditions," and he conceded that Fullerton had been "wrong" in New Orleans. He argued that the Bureau must be "continued at least a year longer for the settlement of questions of national importance as touching labor, relief of the helpless, justice and privileges such as the ownership of lands, or its rental, of asylums, schools, &&."[24] Here was the whole business of the Freedmen's Bureau and a request to a leading member of Congress that the Bureau be empowered to continue.

In this private letter Howard told one member of Congress what he planned to tell all of them in his first annual report. If

23. C. H. Howard to O. O. Howard, 27 Sept. 1865, OOH Papers.
24. O. O. Howard to Henry Wilson, 25 Nov. 1865, OOH Papers.

there is a successful example of that strange literary form, it is the report that goes beyond justifying the past and predicts a future. This is just what Howard did. He juggled all the inconsistencies of the previous months to make the Bureau seem strong and necessary. Normally such a document would seem a vapid weapon for a military counteroffensive, but the General made it work.

In the opening sentences of the report, Howard quoted the language of the Act of March 3, 1865, in order to remind his readers just what it was that Congress had ordered him to do. His job was "the supervision and management of all subjects relating to refugees and freedmen from the rebel states, or from any district . . . embraced within the operation of the army."[25] Not only was Howard suggesting how huge and difficult was his task but also how clear it was that his territory had been invaded by the President's restoration policy. If Howard clearly had jurisdiction over all abandoned lands and over all matters pertaining to the freedmen, then the President was a usurper.

Howard's object was not, however, to divide himself from the President. He diligently pursued his familiar course of appeasement on personal matters. He spoke favorably of all the changes Johnson had insisted on, including the Fullerton interlude in Louisiana. When he explained his technical violation of the law—naming more than ten assistant commissioners and sending Davis Tillson to Georgia—he went out of his way to criticize Rufus Saxton for being unable to handle his job. Speaking of Saxton, whom he had once acknowledged as his mentor in freedmen's affairs, Howard used, as explanation for diminishing his authority, the familiar euphemism for incompetence, "poor health." An unadorned reference to the difficulties of administering the double territory of South Carolina and Georgia would have been sufficient had Howard not felt the need to prove his loyalty to President Johnson.

Howard's moral cowardice in the Saxton matter was inexcusable but understandable. Howard viewed the whole of the Bureau as more important than even the best of his assistant

25. *Report of the Commissioner*, 1 Nov. 1865, p. 1.

commissioners. He still considered his work to be a moral crusade, more essential than any of its individual components. He knew now how keen and effective was Johnson's opposition to all but the conservatives in the Bureau, and he judged winning the President's support again worth the cruelty to Saxton.

Even more important to him now was Congress. He wanted it to restate the instructions of the March 3 Act of Congress, which created the agency. Congress' job must be to continue the Freedmen's Bureau to ensure "the actual and continuous protection of life and property of the freedmen." He supported this by citing Negro opinion: "[Every] colored man I met [on my trip South] of any considerable intelligence pleaded earnestly for the continuance of the bureau." This he balanced with an undocumented threat that there would be "universal disturbance among the freedmen as a consequence of [the Bureau's] removal." He insisted that his agency must be retained until "society [became] more settled and state action more liberal than at present."[26]

As Howard hoped, Congress began making Reconstruction decisions of its own. The Commissioner had a conference with Charles Sumner at which the Massachusetts Senator showed Howard Carl Schurz' report on his trip South; this famous attack on Johnson's Reconstruction policies reinforced Howard's resolve to work with those who sought to change them. He was reported "enchanted" by the Schurz report and, no doubt, flattered that its author intended to call on him.[27] The radicals were proving as anxious to have Howard's support as he was to win theirs.

The Congressmen, "sharp and decisive," halted Johnsonian Reconstruction by refusing to seat the representatives of the southern states that the President considered to be once again part of the Union.[28] And on the first day of congressional deliberations, the subject that Johnson most wanted Congress to

26. Ibid., p. 33.

27. Carl Schurz to his wife, 5 Dec. 1865, in Joseph Schafter, ed., *Intimate Letters of Carl Schurz* (Madison, Wis., 1928), p. 354.

28. Ibid.

ignore was most clearly highlighted: The Negroes and their troubles were, from the first bill offered in the Senate, the business of the Thirty-ninth Congress.

Senator Benjamin Wade, long a pilot of Reconstruction waters, was anxious to consider the business of the Freedmen's Bureau. On December 19, exercised at the delay in receiving Howard's report, he requested and obtained a formal resolution requiring the President to send it immediately.[29] The same day, the senior senator from Illinois, Lyman Trumbull, who had seen the report, rose to introduce "a bill to enlarge the powers of the Bureau." The details would be worked out in his Judiciary Committee, which had wrested jurisdiction for the legislation from Wilson's Military Affairs Committee. He assured the Senate that he would waste no time in drawing up legislation "for the purpose of quieting apprehensions in the minds of many friends of freedom, lest by local legislation or by prevailing public sentiment in several of the states persons of the African race should continue to be oppressed and in fact deprived of their freedom."[30] Congress, as he saw it, was "bound to see that freedom is in fact secured to every person throughout the land."

Howard's language was similar. In his annual report he contended that "the government has set the slave free and bound itself to make that freedom an undisputed fact."[31] The similarity was no accident; the two men worked together in Howard's office writing the bill, as the Commissioner was proud to remember.[32] Their statements of purpose, so much longer in range than those in subsequent bureau legislation, suggested an expansion of the meaning of the Thirteenth amendment and a long period of service for the Bureau.

The man with whom Howard undertook to write national peacetime responsibility for the nation's Negroes into law had sponsored the Thirteenth Amendment in the previous session of

29. *Cong. Globe,* 19 Dec. 1865, p. 77.
30. Ibid.
31. *Report of Commissioner* 1 Nov. 1865, p. 32.
32. Howard, *Autobiography, 2,* 280.

Congress. But this did not in itself define the quality of Trumbull's interest in the men he freed. The total of his views on the Negro remains untallied, but if there is a constant in the confused mathematics of his career, it is his concern for the individual done wrong either by those whom the government did not control or by the forces of government itself. From Elijah Lovejoy to Eugene Debs, Trumbull championed individuals who were under attack, and in 1865 the man who needed his help was black.[33]

Private acts of cruelty have been neglected in historical explanations of Reconstruction politics, but they were very much in the minds of politicians at the time.[34] Charles Sumner, for one, had no intention of keeping the details of these acts out of the senatorial debate and, in a speech on December 20, 1865, quoted letter after letter telling of attacks by private citizens on individual Negroes.[35] No man in Congress had much chance not to know what was going on in the South.[36] The newspapers reported fully the atrocities that were being committed. For further documentation, Henry Wilson, in January 1866, urged his colleagues to ask Brown in Virginia, Whittlesey in North Carolina, Saxton ("who has been called away and is not compelled to see with his own eyes the bitter tears that are being shed over the violated promises that this nation made to the freed men on the coast of the Carolinas"), Tillson in Georgia,

33. Horace White, *The Life of Lyman Trumbull* (Boston, 1913), pp. 8–10, 413–14; Mark M. Krug, *Lyman Trumbull Conservative Radical* (New York, 1965); Howard, *Autobiography*, 2, 280.

34. Valuable for focusing our attention on private crimes is Laurent B. Frantz, "Congressional Power to Enforce the Fourteenth Amendment Against Private Acts," *Yale Law Journal*, 73 (1964), 1353–84. Frantz, undertaking to overturn the reading of history that has so long held that the Fourteenth Amendment can reach only state action and not private acts, has read the briefs of Reconstruction lawyers and the debates of the 39th Cong. and concludes that the authors of the Fourteenth Amendment were primarily troubled by the large number of well-documented stories of private violence. Frantz omits consideration of the black codes, which were unmistakably state action and demonstrably in the minds of the 39th Cong.

35. *Cong. Globe,* 20 Dec. 1865, pp. 91–95.

36. R. King Cutler to Lyman Trumbull, 6 Dec. 1865, Trumbull Papers, LC.

Swayne in Alabama, Baird in Louisiana, and Fisk in Tennessee.[37] Howard was quick to supply reports from his men; he had required that such acts be reported to him by his agents under the caption, "Outrages."

These reports of "great atrocities and cruelties" were compiled by the bureau headquarters with thoroughness. Indeed the cold official tabular form makes the stories somehow more telling than when the same incidents are told in lurid sensational narratives. Henry Wilson, deeply troubled by such cruelty, cited the bureau accounts often.[38] He was concerned not only about unpunished acts by private persons but also about state action as well:

> They have enacted a law in the state of Mississippi that will not allow a black man to lease lands or buy lands outside of the cities. Where in God's name is he to go? Into the public highway? Then he is a vagrant . . . [and] under the vagrancy laws sold into bondage.[39]

This discriminatory restrictiveness angered Wilson, and he forcefully stated that there "is not a freed man treading the soil of a rebel state to-day who is not [as] entitled to the protection of just, humane, and equal laws as I am."[40]

Howard, too, was troubled by the Mississippi black codes; reinforced by Senator Wilson's strong statements, he had an aide write to Samuel Thomas to "use all the power of the Bureau to see that the freedmen are protected from enforcement of such clauses." Further, Thomas was instructed to ask the "military force to assist" him and the letter closed with a ringing assertion that "the whole power of the Govt. has been pledged to sustain the actual freedom of the negro."[41]

The repuganance over the acts of violence and the repression

37. *Cong. Globe,* 22 Jan. 1866, p. 340.

38. Ibid., 21 Dec. 1865, p. 111.

39. Ibid.

40. Ibid.; Senate 9, a bill to outlaw the black codes was dropped as it was considered to have been made unnecessary by Senates 60 and 61.

41. Assistant Adjutant General (unsigned) to Samuel Thomas, 27 Dec. 1865, BRFAL.

of the freedmen under the black codes was deeply felt and the compassion of many of the congressmen was genuine. But assisting the freedmen in the elementary business of staying alive or permitting them to move about freely did not mean the purpose was to grant them equality. After Trumbull's bill was vetoed, Amos Nourse, former senator from Maine, wrote him to say that he had counted on Senate 60 to be a "panacea" that would "secure to the freedmen protection and a reasonable enjoyment of rights of a freeman."[42] That was what Trumbull had sought to accomplish—to guarantee to the freedmen a minimum of common-law liberties due any freeman under the Anglo-American legal tradition. That and no more.[43]

There were also limits to what General Howard would tolerate in the way of protest against bureau practices. Interference with the smooth operation of the contract labor system breached them and was not permitted. As Howard worked with diligence to convince Congress of the Bureau's usefulness, he knew that both contracting parties must appear satisfied with the system. He also knew from past experience that the white planters would complain to the President if their interests were not protected by the contracts and would be sustained in their objections. The Georgia planters were particularly fortunate to have as their assistant commissioner Davis Tillson, with his well-established reputation for insisting on contracts satisfactory to them.[44]

On December 7, 1865, two telegrams were sent to Washington from Georgia: one, addressed to the President of the United States, was from the principal of a Negro school, Aaron A. Bradley, who came right to the point: "My private school . . . was ordered discontinued . . . because I spoke against your reconstruction. Sir, will you please open my school."[45] The other telegram came from Assistant Commissioner Tillson:

42. Amos Nourse to Lyman Trumbull, 22 Feb. 1866, Trumbull Papers, LC.
43. Krug, p. 238.
44. J. S. Fullerton to O. O. Howard, 16 Aug. 1865, OOH Papers.
45. A. A. Bradley to Andrew Johnson, 7 Dec. 1865, AJ Papers.

A man named Bradley has been making speeches at
S[avannah] to the colored people criticising [sic] President's policy, advising Negroes not to make contracts except at point of bayonet, and to disobey your orders; have
arrested him, he does not deny charges, proof conclusive.
Genl Steedmen [the district commander] has ordered him
to be tried by Military Commission.[46]

The next day Howard, having read both telegrams, answered
Tillson: "Telegram of 7th just received. All right about
Bradley."[47] Strikes by the freedmen would not be allowed to mar
the record of bureau efficiency in providing a stable labor force
in the South; those who would instigate them were swiftly
stopped.

After Howard pacified the President in the Bradley matter,
he turned to the other side to assist some Louisiana Negroes who
were harvesting a peculiar fruit of freedom. These freedmen,
who had leased abandoned lands from the federal government
and farmed them, were being sued in civil court by the pardoned planters who had removed the Negroes from the land
and now were charging them with damage to the property.
Other restored planters sought "back rents" from the Negroes
for the period during which they had already paid rent to the
government. Howard wrote to Charles Sumner recommending
legislation that would protect these lessees and, in doing so,
confirmed his awareness of his clients' distress.[48]

Bureau men were also at work searching for lost Negro children. At the request of Thaddeus Stevens, Howard ordered
Orlando Brown in Richmond to help locate three children taken
from Stevens' part of Pennsylvania when Lee's army invaded in
the Gettysburg campaign.[49] Their mother, found in Savannah,
was on her way home. Here Howard was at his finest; he could

46. Davis Tillson to O. O. Howard, received 8 Dec. 1865, AJ Papers.
47. O. O. Howard to Davis Tillson, 8 Dec. 1865, AJ Papers.
48. Max Woodhull to Orlando Brown, 18 Dec. 1865, BRFAL.
49. O. O. Howard to Thaddeus Stevens, 20 Dec. 1865, BRFAL.

not have rendered a more humane service, and he richly earned the gratitude of Stevens, whose concern for the Negroes as people—whether as friends in his district or as an oppressed minority in the nation—was unique in Congress. Howard's assistance in reuniting this family earned him the confidence of the powerful radical Congressman.[50]

Howard's position was now strong. His relations with the radical leaders of the Negro cause were in good order, and he had the satisfaction of having been consulted by the powerful moderate Lyman Trumbull in the drafting of the Freedmen's Bureau bill. Trumbull's earlier Thirteenth Amendment became effective on December 18, 1865, but far from viewing it as just a ratification of emancipation already accomplished, the Illinois Senator contended that it was already being violated and, therefore, its enforcement clause needed implementation by the Bureau.

Trumbull was pessimistic about the freedmen's ability to provide for themselves. Like so many of his colleagues, he had visited the Sea Islands in the spring of 1865, but unlike most of them, he was not inspired by what he saw. When he talked with Howard in December, he declared the freedmen to be an "abject, forlorn, helpless and hopeless people."[51] In August, C. E. Lippincott, an army officer stationed in Meridian, Mississippi, had written to Trumbull to report on that state's convention, which had closed after passing an ordinance of emancipation. The convention, he wrote, "was as strongly pro-slavery in feeling as that which passed the ordinance of secession. It is their hope, and intention, under the guise of vagrancy laws et cetera, to restore all of slavery but its name." Lippincott, questioning Congress' constitutional right to enact Negro suffrage, also wondered whether the freedmen, armed only with the ballot, could effectively combat the black codes: "it seems to me very doubtful if all the danger can be averted by permitting negroes to vote."[52]

50. Lottie Kemp to the writer, 5 Feb. 1965.

51. Howard, *Autobiography*, 2, 280.

52. C. E. Lippincott to Lyman Trumbull, 29 Aug. 1865, Trumbull Papers, LC.

Lippincott claimed that there was still another thing working against the freedmen. He was disappointed by the Negroes' lack of "pluck." He did not see in them the determination to fight their way out of feudalism as Europeans had done. Without such determination, the freedmen, even if they had the right to vote, would be unable to exercise it with sufficient skill to stop the white men of Mississippi, and elsewhere across the South, who "having once regained admission to Congress . . . will be able, with what assistance may be procured from Northern Allies . . . [to] control the government in the interest of the South, quite as much as they did before the war."[53] Should this happen, Lippincott contended that the freedmen's basic liberties could not be enforced against either the southern states or the individuals living in them. They would not be safe.

Trumbull was convinced that the black codes reestablished the disciplines of slavery and violated his Amendment, and his bill, Senate 60, reported out of the Judiciary Committee on January 12, 1866, was designed to continue the Freedmen's Bureau as the means of enforcing the Thirteenth Amendment and making freedom for the Negroes inviolate all over the land. In the proposed legislation the Bureau gained dimension. The temporariness of the agency was gone and, though the word "permanent" was not used, there was neither a terminal date nor any talk of merely meeting a short-term emergency. The Bureau would continue until Congress decided to dissolve it.

The Bureau was to operate nationally wherever the freedmen (and refugees) needed it.[54] Howard's agency would no longer just express the federal government's war power directed at secessionists. If the bill passed, all freedmen, whether in Illinois, Maine, or Alabama, would be equally the concern of the federal government. Howard's responsibilities were to "extend to refugees and freedmen in all parts of the United States."[55] In debate, Trumbull acceded to bureau agents serving Negroes

53. C. E. Lippincott to Lyman Trumbull, 29 Aug. 1865, Trumbull Papers, LC.

54. *Cong. Globe,* 20 Jan. 1866, p. 334.

55. Ibid., 22 Jan. 1866, p. 339.

living in downstate Illinois, and John Cresswell said they were essential for the protection of Negroes in his state, Maryland. Their opponents, Senators Hendricks and Cowan, were as adamantly opposed to having bureau agents in Indiana and Pennsylvania as they were to having Negroes cross their borders from neighboring states.[56]

By providing for northern Negroes, Trumbull gave significant recognition that they too needed help. He may also have been giving subtle warning to his colleagues that these destitute black men in their states might soon be joined by others if Senate 60 were not passed and the freedmen tranquilized and contained in the South. But whatever their motivation, the proponents of the bill clearly knew that it was in the South that millions of Negroes lived and most needed assistance.

To respond to the magnitude of a responsibility involving 4,000,000 people, the bill specified that agents be named in each county in which Negroes lived in any number. Army men presently assigned to such duty were being mustered out of the service rapidly, and, to replace them, Howard was authorized to engage disabled veterans of the Veterans Reserve Corps. Their pensions would become bureau salaries at no new cost to the taxpayer.

Howard also received permission to hire civilians at $1,500 a year. His hopes for competent agents lay here. The agents were expected to serve the interests of both white and black men in the county to which they were assigned. One of Howard's inspectors described once the kind of man Howard was looking for: he was a local white citizen, "an educated man, a lawyer, & has clear views as to what is best for the prosperity of the District & State. He is a good friend of the freedmen, they all speak well of him, & go to him to settle their difficulties, & get his advice."[57]

Other bureau men were dubious about the civilian agents. Samuel Thomas, unable to cover Mississippi adequately due to the removal of soldier-agents, had only twenty-five agents left

56. Ibid., 20 Jan. 1866, p. 334.
57. Saxton Diary, 14 May 1866.

in April 1866. Twenty-two of them were still members of the Union army receiving service pay; the other three, veterans, "were paid by those planters who are anxious to retain an officer of the Bureau for their influence among the Freedmen." Thomas had received several petitions requesting more such civilian agents from citizens who offered to pay their salaries because they were so useful "keeping the Freedmen quietly at work."[58]

In May 1866, Assistant Commissioner J. B. Kiddoo, who had replaced Edgar Gregory in Texas, asked for twenty more men to assist him in covering the vast region under his jurisdiction. He stressed to General Howard that he wanted army men and not antinegro civilians. By July the labor shortage in Texas was so great that contractors who could supply a gang of field laborers were getting one-third or one-half of the crop. Kiddoo urged that surplus labor in other parts of the South be sent to Texas to relieve the shortage, but in August he was distressed to find the newcomers, who had contracted to work in these gangs, doing so under extremely poor conditions. He complained that the civilian agents, who by then had been authorized by Congress, were so cruel toward the freedmen that he would rather have had no agents at all.[59]

Despite such reports, Howard never gave up the hope he held when Senate 60 was drawn up—that good men in the South would volunteer to help the freedmen rather than oppress them. In the bill was a provision authorizing him to hire local civilian agents at a salary of $1,500 per annum. But this salary was only enough to supplement another income, and conflict of interests were bound to arise and vitiate the noblesse oblige on which Howard counted. How the Negroes felt about this reestablishment of the kind-old-massa principle within the Freedmen's Bureau is not clear. Their enthusiasm for the whole of Senate 60 suggests that they either overlooked this provision or thought such benevolent local men better than those who preferred violence or peonage as treatment for the freedmen's problems.

58. Samuel Thomas to O. O. Howard, 12 Apr. 1866, BRFAL.
59. J. B. Kiddoo to O. O. Howard, 8 Aug. 1866, BRFAL.

Their lack of stated objection also serves as a reminder that the freedmen were not reluctant to receive help. This does not mean that subservience was a group characteristic; the reluctance of many freedmen to work for their ex-masters is evidence to the contrary. It does suggest that assistance was sufficiently necessary that the freedmen did not damn the whole race of bureau agents. Just as men like Howard had not gotten ahead without help, the Negroes knew they needed it. Their problems were great and were not diminishing as the war receded in time.

The most immediate threat that freedmen faced in the winter of 1865–66 was starvation.[60] Destitution was present in Georgia and Alabama; the congressmen did not have to look beyond Washington to see Negroes without enough food. Senate 60 provided for government supplies of food and specifically gave Secretary of War Stanton the responsibility for its distribution.[61] Whether this reflected needless congressional worries that Howard would prove too free with handouts or whether it was simply a device to reach commissary supplies available elsewhere in the War Department, the congressional debate does not reveal, but the Bureau did participate actively in the distribution of relief goods. Stanton was authorized to issue food, clothes, fuel, medicine, and transportation "and afford such aid, medical or otherwise, as may be needful for the immediate and temporary shelter of destitute and suffering refugees and freedmen."[62] The term "refugees" was loosely defined and needy whites of all political persuasions were helped.

Senator Garret Davis of Kentucky saw in the relief section of the bill the creation of a "great system of poor-houses for the support of lazy negroes all over the Southern states." The many freedmen in the galleries were evidence to both Senators Davis and Willard Saulsbury of Delaware that they would go any-

60. An official of one of the voluntary freedmen's aid societies warned that in the winter ahead "thirty thousand negroes would perish in Georgia alone and forty thousand in Alabama." Peoria *National Democrat,* 29 Nov. 1865, clipping in Trumbull Papers, LC.

61. *Cong. Globe,* 12 Jan. 1866, p. 209.

62. Ibid., 24 Jan. 1866, p. 396.

where to loaf. In fact, Senator Davis told his less knowledgeable colleagues that a "negro will never work when he can keep soul and body together without work."[63] Further, he warned his fellow senators not to drive good white yeomen down into vassalage by building up a huge debt to help lazy Negroes.

When Senator Trumbull's friend C. E. Lippincott, serving with the army in Mississippi, heard accusations that Negroes were inevitably candidates for relief, he wrote: "I am not a very rabid negrophile but I can assert that while in command at Meridian . . . there were few cases of able-bodied negroes *applying* for rations, and it took the work of five or six hours *daily* for a Staff officer to examine the applications of white people."[64]

By the terms of the bill, the latitude to assist the poor was to be great, and those who were to be assisted need not be black. The exercise of this power established an important precedent (if not an altogether enlightened pattern) for federal action. The soup kitchen relief that was granted would have been attractive only to the starving. Certainly such assistance provisions of the bill were important, but of even greater long-range significance was the more permanent and, its opponents thought, more revolutionary sections of the bill concerned with lands for the freedmen. Even in that difficult area, the freedmen continued to have hope.

As 1865 ended and the new year began with Congress discussing the Bureau's future, Otis Howard felt secure. He had every reason to be confident that he would be sustained in his work. Congress was in the process of granting him a new mandate. The Negroes of the South had not risen in protest at the treatment they received; they still counted on the Freedmen's Bureau to assist them in the alleviation of their oppression. Local rebels were directing the repressive acts the Negroes were experiencing, but Congress would suppress this.

The Howards announced their position in Washington in the

63. Ibid., 24 Jan. 1866, p. 396.
64. C. E. Lippincott to Lyman Trumbull, 25 Jan. 1866, Trumbull Papers, LC.

traditional manner, by opening their house for a New Year's Day reception: nonalcoholic, of course, but graced with oranges sent from Nassau for the occasion by Epes Sargent, the playwright, and an old friend. The reception was pleasant. General Howard and his wife announced to the capital that they were there to stay.[65]

65. O. O. Howard to Epes Sargent, 4 Jan. 1866, OOH Papers.

The aborted revolution of which Senate 60 was a part honored values as conservative as any in our history. To provide land for the freedmen on which they could support themselves, Trumbull and Howard called for a return to the family farm.

Lyman Trumbull was from Connecticut (and Georgia and Illinois). Otis Howard was from Maine. Teaching in country schools, each went as far from his own family farm as he could get, taking with him the names of families deeply rooted in the New England soil. In 1866 the senator and the soldier paid homage to a great American institution they had rejected and prescribed the family farm for the freedmen. They wished for the Negro those gifts that the land might give them—basic things, protective and sustaining.

Trumbull and Howard felt that the freedman needed a farm of his own, even if it was only to serve as a step toward other pursuits. Other New Englanders, and the freedmen, agreed. Charles Stearns, who moved from Massachusetts to Georgia in 1866 and farmed with hired labor, wrote six years later: "Far be it from me to decry other efforts for the elevation of this long injured race, but . . . [other] necessities cannot be effectually provided for, without making him . . . the industrious owner of the land he cultivates."[1]

Privately, Otis and Charles Howard were conducting a test of the family farm prescription though neither thought of it as a controlled social experiment. The General had a servant during the war named Washington Kemp, whose wife and two daughters were still slaves and, at the end of the war, unaccounted for. The Howard brothers undertook to assist Kemp in beginning a

1. Charles Stearns, *The Black Man of the South and the Rebels* (New York, 1872), p. 15.

new life for himself in a way which both depicts the best spirit of the Freedmen's Bureau and betrays the Commissioner's naïve make-everybody-happy attitude, which characterized so many of his private and public approaches to responsibility.

The Howard brothers' mother was again a widow. Alone she had moved back to their father's old farm and was trying to manage it with the help of hired hands. She was exhausted by the effort and still unhappy at being confined to Leeds. Otis, whose career had carried him so far away from her that they had little to say and seldom wrote to each other, sent Kemp to Leeds in the spring of 1865.[2] He was to learn to manage the farm, and Mrs. Gilmore would, in time, move from Leeds to be with one of her sons. Charles arranged for the mortgage on the farm to be amended so that the farm could be rented to "Wash,"[3] who, once he learned how to manage the farm, would begin buying it over a long period of time. If all worked out, a freedman would own the Howard homestead.

Meanwhile, the Commissioner ordered the Bureau to locate Kemp's wife and daughters; this was successfully accomplished only after months of search.[4] Mrs. Kemp and the girls joined Wash in Leeds, and while they were living with Mrs. Gilmore, the Kemps' third child was born.[5] But Eliza Gilmore neither shared Otis' desire to see Kemp become a freeholder nor understood the symbolic worth of his succeeding in the opportunity Howard had given him. She did not treat Wash as a prospective equal of an Otis or a Howard or a Lothrop. She complained of his incompetence and rudeness and wanted him to leave.[6] She deprived Howard of the chance to point to his own family and Washington Kemp as a New England example to follow. And she also deprived Charles of a chance to help a man of whom he was genuinely fond. "I was in hopes to keep Wash with us

2. C. H. Howard to his mother, 12 June 1865, Charles Howard Papers.
3. Ibid., 23 Oct. 1865.
4. Ibid.
5. Lottie Kemp to the writer, 5 Feb. 1965.
6. C. H. Howard to his mother, 26 June 1866, 5 July 1867, Charles Howard Papers.

always and to help him to own a piece of land and a home of his own one of these days."[7]

The Kemps, who to some extent refute the thesis that freedmen lived in matriarchal families, left the Howard farm, but they did not leave Leeds; they remain its only Negro family.[8] Kemp bought a much simpler farm (possibly with the General's help) and kept a cow, a horse, and some chickens.[9] He became a subsistence farmer, but it was as a minstrel, not as a farmer and landowner, that Washington Kemp made his name. For years Kemp and his daughters toured country fairs in Maine as "The Kemp Family from the Old Sunny South."[10]

The adoption of Washington Kemp by Leeds did not work out as Howard planned it—at least, not in Wash's own generation. But his descendants have a claim on Leeds that the Howards have lost, and Washington Kemp made Leeds his home in a way that even the General cannot share.[11] He lies buried there.

For every Washington Kemp who ventured north, there were hundred of thousands of freedmen left in the South, and Lyman Trumbull shared the wish of Rufus Saxton, who said in May 1865 that his goal was to see every Negro family on its own freehold. Trumbull stated his belief:

> a homestead is worth more to these people than almost anything else: and if you will make the Negro an independent man, he must have a home; that so long as the relation of employer and employee exists, he will necessarily have a dependent population. I think that if it were in our power to secure a homestead to every family that has been made free by the constitutional amendment, we would do more for the colored race than by any other act we could do.[12]

7. Ibid.
8. Lottie Kemp to the writer, 5 Feb. 1965.
9. Ibid.
10. Ibid.
11. Edith Labbie to the writer, 25 Feb. 1965.
12. *Cong. Globe,* 18 Jan. 1866, p. 299.

To give a man of the nineteenth century a farm of his own was to give him equality.

As Howard often did, Trumbull used the word "homestead" as a synonym for family farm. They imagined such a farm on land already cultivated with buildings already built. Such lands almost always belonged to someone, and as soon as Trumbull realized that his family farm suggested confiscation, he discarded his dream. Howard did not and looked for an alternative way to achieve it.

One way of giving the freedmen farms (of which Otis Howard was rightly skeptical) was homesteading. Here his picture of neatly tilled plots yielded to uncleared forest tracts. It was accurate. In the five public land states of the South, much of the available 47,000,000 acres was covered with yellow pine and cypress and "looked upon as worthless."[13] The first of three land provisions in Senate 60 would have granted the freedmen access to this acreage from homesteading. The President would be authorized to release a total of 3,000,000 acres of land in Florida, Mississippi, and Arkansas under Howard's supervision.[14] (The day after the bill was introduced Howard wrote Trumbull to inform him that Louisiana and Alabama had public lands, which should also be included, and they were.)[15]

Howard doubted that homesteading would be the wonder weapon of his war on poverty. Perhaps his prewar trip across Florida past squatters' huts scattered over the sandy pine lands made him doubt the worth of the lands the government had available. Certainly he knew that in the South, as in Leeds, a farm was more than some acres of sand or rock. Tools and farm animals and seed as well as land were needed to make a farm productive. Howard was not impractical in agricultural matters. He told the secretary of the American Missionary Association,

13. Paul W. Gates, "Federal Land Policy in the South, 1866–1888," *JSH*, 6 (August 1940), 303–30.

14. *Cong. Globe*, 18 Jan. 1866.

15. O. O. Howard to Lyman Trumbull, 13 Jan. 1866, BRFAL; *Cong. Globe*, 22 Jan. 1866, p. 349.

George Whipple, that there were a few square miles of home-stead land in Florida which might be used, "but we cannot send the freedmen thither without some available means to give them support. If your association, or any other, will move in with shelter and implements for husbanding, and with intelligent supervision," he would be willing to provide transportation for totally indigent families. No others, Howard was sure, would be willing to go to such lands. He told Whipple that he would "put the homestead matter before Congress," but he stressed again that "Government cultivable lands are not very extensive.[16] Howard's pessimism proved accurate. Although 67,609 applications were filed for homestead lands in the South during Reconstruction, and 23,609 homesteaders remained determined and obtained patents for their holdings, only 4,000 of these were freedmen families, according to the General's estimate of 1870.[17]

Howard's realism about the homesteading problems was frustrating a remnant of the ancient theme to colonize America's Negroes out of the society. Max Woodhull, his adjutant general since Fullerton's promotion, strongly advocated not homesteading colonies but exportation. He claimed to have the support of old friends of the freedmen such as Mansfield French, who was very concerned about the continuing destitution of the Negroes.[18]

This destitution prompted the Bureau to agree to some alarming enterprises. In November Woodhull wrote to a man who wanted to export 500 workers to Peru and to a firm on the Sandwich Islands interested in gaining laborers that, although the Bureau did not pay for the transportation of freedmen leaving the United States, it could pay for the transportation of those Negroes dependent on the government to the ports from which they were to be "shipped."[19]

16. O. O. Howard to George Whipple, 25 Nov. 1865, BRFAL.

17. Paul W. Gates, *Agriculture and the Civil War* (New York, 1965), p. 361.

18. Max Woodhull to O. O. Howard, 24 Oct. 1865, BRFAL; *New York Tribune,* 30 Oct. 1865.

19. Max Woodhull to S. U. Niles, 27 Nov. 1865, and to Messrs. Britton, Gay, & Van Arman, 29 Nov. 1865, BRFAL.

The "Negroes actually dependent on the government" were, the American Colonization Society discovered, often the "sick and wounded in military hospitals" and were "not the type of settlers desired."[20] This old conservative organization had been trying for decades to settle America's race problem by relocating the Negroes in Liberia. In the postwar period it did attract some freedmen who, it was claimed, "were tired of starvation and freedom," but not many.[21] Only 2,494 moved to Liberia between 1865 and 1870.[22] This clearly indicated that the southern Negroes had little faith that conditions would be better elsewhere.

The officials of the Colonization Society "could not understand why . . . Howard had not been able to do more for colonization."[23] The answer was he had not tried. The Commissioner had always been skeptical of resettlement schemes even in this country, fearing that lack of experience, credit, tools, and benevolent supervision made such enterprises risky.[24] Giving little support to emigration, Howard was far more anxious to see European capital invested in southern farmlands rather than American cash spent in the old world. This would provide the Negroes with steady pay.[25] One spokesman for the Colonization Society charged in 1867 that "[Freedmen's] Bureau officials . . . were making it part of their business to counsel and influence the colored people not to emigrate."[26]

Another enterprise of those who opposed the dispersal of Negroes was the partitioning of Florida. In January Woodhull thanked Thomas Osborn for sending detailed plans which showed how the lands in the southern half of that state might be opened exclusively to Negro homesteaders.[27] This sparsely populated

20. Willis Boyd, "Negro Colonization in the National Crisis, 1860–1870," Unpublished Ph.D. dissertation (University of California, Los Angeles, 1953), p. 309.
21. Ibid., p. 324.
22. Ibid., p. 340.
23. Ibid., p. 309.
24. O. O. Howard to H. B. Cadbury, 26 Mar. 1866, OOH Papers.
25. Ibid.
26. Boyd, p. 309.
27. Max Woodhull to T. W. Osborn, 14 Jan. 1865, BRFAL.

area had long had the attention of those who thought it wise to separate some of the freed Negroes from society, but this solution also got little support from the Commissioner.[28]

Homesteading to most Americans meant moving west. But senators from the West had constituents who had no desire to invite Negroes to their section of the country. In fact, the fear that Negroes might become homesteaders on white yeoman lands in the West, which had been kept free and white, provided the greatest threat to passage of the bill.

Howard tried to prevent this issue from becoming so inflamed that it would endanger the legislation. He sought to assure one critic that such an exodus was not his idea of what should happen. He said that to "remove all the freedmen from the South, would in my opinion be a great mistake. The feeling of hostility now existing between the two races, I do not regard as permanent. The interests of both tend to decrease it. . . . I think it preferable that they remain where they are, rather than attempt to colonize in large numbers."[29] The settling of individual Negro families on homesteads was never debated at the Bureau; group settlements were the topic of homesteading discussions there.

Some of the opponents of Senate 60 sought to make the threat of Negro homesteaders defeat the whole bill. On January 23, Garret Davis of Kentucky, who called himself an "old line Whig" and stated that "the questions and measures which separated the Democracy and me have passed," offered as one last "obstacle . . . to throw in the way of [Senate 60's] passage" an amendment deleting the words Florida, Mississippi, Arkansas, Louisiana, and Alabama from the homesteading section of the bill. In other words, he moved to invite the freedmen to take advantage of the homesteading opportunities in the West and to move as well "to Indiana, Illinois, Ohio, and the states in that degree of latitude." Davis speculated that probably half of the freed Negroes of the United States, if they were allowed to select

28. C. B. Wilder to J. A. Wilder, 4 Nov. 1862, Todd Family Papers, Yale University.

29. O. O. Howard to G. W. Nichols, 29 Dec. 1865, OOH Papers.

their homes, "would choose the salubrious climate" and "fertile soil" of that line of states and even those "a little north of that line."[30] Kentucky's Governor Thomas E. Bramleth initiated a similar scheme with the purpose of dissolving Howard's agency. He proposed a law to be passed in his state that would prohibit citizens of Kentucky from hiring Negroes or leasing land to them. In this way, he could remove "the 'Bureau' by emptying its contents up on Ohio and other states north and west."[31] When Davis' proposal was made on the Senate floor, the negatives muttered by proponents of the bill were audible.[32]

Lyman Trumbull called the Kentucky Senator's bluff and agreed to support the amendment.[33] Davis, who enjoyed seeing the Midwesterners squirm at the idea of Negroes moving into their part of the country, did not have enough votes to make his strategy work. He could not even rely on northern opponents of the bill to support him; Thomas A. Hendricks of Indiana, for example, was determined to be consistently antinegro.

There was no racial clause in the Homestead Act, but Hendricks simply assumed that the freedmen would not settle on individual sites and that special tracts of land would have to be opened for them if they were encouraged to move west as Davis suggested.[34] The western homesteads were in demand by white settlers, he claimed, and since "there is not likely to be a great demand for homesteads for white settlers" in the South, "there will be no injury resulting from a withdrawal of three million acres" in that section of the country for the use of the Negroes.[35] Senator Saulsbury of Delaware, as anxious as Davis or Hendricks to kill Senate 60, raised another point calculated to make his colleagues of the North and West nervous: he reminded them that the "negroes . . . are to be located [on the homestead lands] at government expense." Howard had the authority to provide

30. *Cong. Globe,* 23 Jan. 1866, p. 371.
31. T. E. Bramleth to Andrew Johnson, 12 Feb. 1866, AJ Papers.
32. *Cong. Globe,* 23 Jan. 1866, p. 371.
33. Ibid., p. 372.
34. *12 U.S. Stat.,* 392–93; *Agriculture and the Civil War,* p. 285.
35. *Cong. Globe,* 23 Jan. 1866, p. 372.

transportation for freedmen and refugees, and in 1865 and 1866 he enabled 30,000 Negroes to move.[36] If it were the sense of Congress that the whole West and not merely the five southern states was the proper destination for the Negroes who might want to move and start homesteads, then Howard could pay the freedmen's way west.

When Trumbull saw his opposition split he was clearly delighted; making a derisive crack about the ineffectiveness of the old compromise alliance of "old Whigs and old Democrats," he withdrew his support for the amendment and called for a vote. The Republicans spared themselves the embarrassment of a roll call and, by voice vote, defeated the amendment. Homesteading for Negroes was to be kept in the South.[37]

The second of the three sections of the bill dealing with land was to be a redemption of Howard's pledge to the freedmen at Edisto. The Sea Islanders and the coastal farmers on lands granted to them by General Sherman's Field Order 15 of January 1865 would be assured of these grants as long as the head of each freedman's family lived. This would have brought to a reasonably successful end Rufus Saxton's long fight to hold back restoration of the experimental farms on the Sea Islands.

As the Edisto farmers made clear to Howard, these lands meant a great deal to the Negroes living on them. Their sense of these farms being theirs was as deep as that of any American farmer anywhere. To have left the farms in the freedmen's hands would have confirmed the wisdom of the members of Gideon's Band, who contended that land of their own was the asset of greatest value to the freedmen. Two years after the nation's opportunity to make this investment was lost, Cornelia Hancock wrote from Mount Pleasant, South Carolina, about the freedmen she knew: "Their chief anxiety is to get possession of land. . . . How I wish the Government had apportioned them some confiscated land at the end of the war."[38]

36. *Report of the Commissioner*, 20 Oct. 1869, p. 21.
37. *Cong. Globe*, 23 Jan. 1866, p. 372.
38. Hancock, *South After Gettysburg*, p. 285.

Opponents of establishing Negroes on their own lands naturally pointed to the injustice of giving land to fifty or sixty thousand freedmen and not to millions of others in the South;
Howard himself wondered if it were wise to "discriminate, etc."[39]
But if rigid consistency were the requisite for all reform, little
would change. The proponents were as aware as the opponents
that confirming titles of these particular lands to the Negroes
and depriving white men of them would be an enormously important precedent. But before Senate 60 got to the floor of the
Senate for debate, the provision which would have provided
congressional validation of these grants which meant so much
to the future of the Negroes in America was destroyed by a
compromise.

The white planters of South Carolina worked diligently to
make restoration a fait accompli before such validation could be
passed by Congress. In October, when in Charleston, General
Howard told them that their island lands would be restored.[40] In
exchange they acknowledged only that they had been admonished
to be kind to their workers and, when contracting with the farmers who would revert to the ancient role of field hands, to submit
to the supervision of a board which would arrange the contracts.[41]
But William Whaley had accompanied Howard to Edisto where
he heard the General, when pressed hard by the Negro farmers,
give them the hope that restoration would not come. The Commissioner urged the freedmen to wait to see what Congress
would do for them. With the threat of what the legislators in
Washington might do, the planters pushed hard in November
to get their lands back.

Their chief obstacle was Rufus Saxton. They chose to ignore
Howard's pledge to the Edisto Negroes and remembered only
his pledge to assist them in restoration and in contracting with

39. O. O. Howard to Henry Wilson, 25 Nov. 1865, OOH Papers.

40. O. O. Howard to Rufus Saxton, 8 Oct. 1865, BRFAL; Howard, *Autobiography*, 2, 238.

41. W. H. Trescott [sic] to Andrew Johnson, 1 Dec. 1865, typescript,
Saxton Papers, Yale University.

the resident freedmen if they would agree to having A. P. Ketchum supervise the execution of the contracts. The white Carolinians were furious at Saxton's stubborn subversion of Howard's restoration order. Saxton believed that if the freedmen were to lose their farms in restoration (and he was never ready to concede that they should), the very least they needed to protect their interests was representation. One of their own men, a Negro, should be on the board supervising the fixing of conditions under which they would work. Saxton, along with the freedmen, felt that to have the third member of these boards be someone other than a Negro was to invalidate the whole concept of representation for which Howard argued when he first advocated such arbitration bodies.

Howard's friend William Whaley thought differently. Seldom so "unguarded in his comments," he marched into bureau headquarters in Charleston on November 21 and announced to the Saxtons that "he would rather his lands . . . sink to perdition than that a black man should compose one of the board."[42]

Rufus Saxton was resolved to hold the lands for the freedmen until Congress formally confirmed his wisdom in doing so. During the week after Whaley called, Saxton received one planter after another asking for the return of their lands, and, on November 29, R. I. Middleton called with a slightly different plea. He claimed that his family had been Unionist, a proposition that he had successfully maintained in earlier conversations in Washington with General Howard and the President. Saxton saw this as no more a reason for restoring the lands Middleton had abandoned when the Union navy took the Sea Islands than if Middleton had been the most fiery of rebels. Their conversation was a failure: "The Gen. quietly informed the 'h.t.' that if he did not leave the office he would kick him out. The 'high toned' was very mad and the Gen. cooler than usual."[43]

The satisfaction of bettering the aristocratic Middleton was of brief duration. The Bureau in Charleston knew that wartime

42. Saxton Diary, 21 Nov. 1865.
43. Ibid., 29 Nov. 1865.

Unionist sentiment or lack of it had little to do with restoration; the planters, all Johnson men now, had a very powerful ally. The Saxtons expected the President to force Howard to "yield to the pressure of the blatant and lying rebels."[44] That they were afraid Howard would indeed yield was indicated by Willard Saxton, who was disgusted with the result of Howard's very generous and gentlemanly treatment of the planters both in Washington and in Charleston. It would serve them all right, Saxton snorted, if "we had Ben. Butler at the head of the Bureau."[45]

The planters thought they had a Butler as they bristled at the treatment they were receiving at General Saxton's office. On December 1, 1865, they formally said so. William Henry Trescot, as South Carolina's executive agent, wrote a letter to President Johnson, which bore the endorsement of both Provisional Governor B. F. Perry and Governor James L. Orr. The letter began: "Gen. Howard, in pursuance of your instructions, ordered the restoration of the Island lands where the owners consented to make contracts with the freedmen." It continued with an accusation that Rufus Saxton and A. P. Ketchum, the land officer appointed by Howard to oversee the drawing of contracts, were subverting the restoration program. As Trescot detailed it,

> [Howard's] representative, Capt. Ketchum decided that a negro should be one of the board. Gen. Howard, while I was in Washington, telegraphed that he meant the board to be composed of whites—one selected by the freedmen. In defiance of this instruction, a negro has been placed upon the board. He [the black man that the Negro farmers insisted must represent them] has declared that no contracts will be made, that nothing but the ownership of the lands will satisfy the freemen.

Trescot was enraged that Saxton—through Ketchum and the Negro representative—was encouraging the farmers by suggesting that they be sounded out to see whether they "will buy the

44. Ibid., 22 Nov. 1866, 9 Dec. 1865.
45. Ibid., 9 Dec. 1865.

lands of the former owners, if assisted by the United States. . . . I earnestly urge," continued Trescot, "the removal of Gen. Saxton. Here is proof of the utter impossibility of doing anything as long as he controls this department of the Bureau." To clinch his argument, Trescot alluded to the rebellious spirit of the farmers: "I have just received reliable intelligence that Gen. Sickle [sic] has been obliged to order a company to Edisto. I again most earnestly appeal for the immediate removal of Gen. Saxton."[46]

When the letter reached the White House (very likely delivered by William Whaley, who arrived in the capital the first week of December), Commissioner Howard faced the embarrassment of having his ambiguous stand on restoration revealed. Genuinely troubled by the Edisto farmer's protests of injustice and probably hopeful that Saxton could stall until Congress enacted the bill (which he had helped draft) that would validate the Negroes' titles to their farms, he was nevertheless aware of his commitments to the planters. On December 4, Howard conversed at length with Carl Schurz, whose report on his famous trip to the South in August 1865 despaired of the freedmen's condition under the state governments restored by President Johnson. On the day after the Congress broke with the President and failed to seat the representatives from the South, the two generals talked of the "remarkable" mood of Congress, which boded well for Senate 60, and of the President who, they concluded, "has become timid but fails to bear his defeat with good humor." Schurz reported to his wife that the head of the Freedmen's Bureau "agrees with me in all the impressions I brought away from the South."[47]

Schurz' acknowledgment that white men in the South were exploiting the freedmen did not, however, deter Howard from trying again to sail between the black and white conflict without

46. W. H. Trescott [sic] to Andrew Johnson, endorsed by B. F. Perry and J. L. Orr, typescript, Saxton Papers, Yale University.

47. Carl Schurz to his wife, 4 Dec. 1865, in Schafter, *Intimate Letters,* p. 354.

taking sides in the contest on Edisto Island, where freedmen were actively resisting exploitation. The day after his conversation with Schurz, Howard, bypassing Saxton, wrote his brother Charles and sought his assistance in getting him through this difficult passage. He maintained that for the freedmen supervised contracts were a satisfactory alternative to land titles and sought only to have the vexing question of the black representative on the board supervising the contracts considered in any way that would not further rock the boat. "My action in South Carolina has received the verbal approval of the President and the Secretary," he wrote; he then turned abruptly to the treatment being given the planters: "I feel very sorry to find that Mr. R. I. Middleton had [sic] been received in the manner he was for I assured him that Genl Saxton would treat him kindly and hear him patiently and listen to the proofs of his uncle's loyalty." He recommended that the restoration of that family's lands "go to a board: Saxton appointing one, Middleton one & both appting a third man." Howard seemed unperturbed that this foreclosed the possibility of Negro representation. Hoping he had heard the last of this particular matter, Howard implored his brother "to have this matter arranged and not refer it to me if it can be helped."[48]

Further revealing the awkwardness of his position, he told Charles: "I yield to General Sickles and Genl Saxton's judgement as to the colored man on the Edisto board, yet it would have relieved me from being misunderstood and misrepresented if the people had been requested to choose a white man." General Howard was chafing at what seemed perilously like insubordination by Saxton: "Mr. Whaley, Mr. Trescot and others knew my intention," he added, referring to the South Carolinian's letter of Dec. 1, "and believed that I had been overridden."

The planters had no intention of allowing Howard to evade the Edisto dilemma; they were determined to achieve full restoration. "Col. Whaley has been here," Howard wrote Ketchum on December 12, "and we have seen the President together."

48. O. O. Howard to C. H. Howard, 5 Dec. 1865, OOH Papers.

Whaley contended that much of his former land holdings on Edisto were unworked, and perhaps he suggested that those in cultivation were not efficiently cared for. After the two men left the White House, Howard issued a vague order to Ketchum: "I think where there are few or no freedmen at all, there will be no harm in restoring the lands. . . . The President seems very much in favor of cultivating these lands, as far as possible, and I think leans very much towards restoring, according to Circular 15, provided always that the freedmen are provided for properly."[49]

This order with its specific reference to the general restoration circular was a strange one to be made by the co-author of a bill, then being considered, under the terms of which Circular 15 was to be overridden and the titles of the Negro farmers validated. Though Howard must have known of the peculiar stance he had taken, he suggested once again that there was nothing lost by risking appeasement of the planters, but in his attempt he admitted that he was now powerless to guarantee the worth of the risk. Referring to the bill, he wrote to Ketchum in what must have seemed less than reassuring words: if "Congress should confirm their titles, my act of restoration would then be overruled."[50]

The chance that Congress would redeem Howard's promise to the Edisto farmers was waning. Any lawyer, and certainly one as skillful as Lyman Trumbull, would have had to agree with Andrew Johnson that the wartime grants of land on the Sea Islands would have had difficulty withstanding challenges in the civil courts by prewar title-holders.[51] A congressional confirmation of the titles would make such challenges more difficult, but such legal action might also throw into question the constitutionality of Senate 60 and the continuation of the Freedmen's Bureau, in which General Howard had such a stake.

A feeble alternative to the lifetime grants was put forward in

49. O. O. Howard to A. P. Ketchum, 12 Dec. 1865, OOH Papers.
50. Ibid.
51. O. O. Howard to William Whaley, 8 July 1865, in Bentley, *Freedmen's Bureau*, p. 92.

the hope that it would meet Johnson's objections to depriving his planter friends of their lands. An amendment to Senate 60 was worked out and offered by Trumbull himself. The freedmen were to be given "possessory" titles to the lands for three years, during which time Howard and the bureau men could try to get voluntary grants or sales of lands to the freedmen from the planters, who were about to get their lands back.[52] Realists in the Bureau knew that Howard was counting on a false hope. Rufus Saxton had long contended that it was nonsense to expect the South Carolina planters to give, sell, or rent lands to the freedmen voluntarily. The planters admitted it. Trescot was on record in Washington as believing that to give some Negroes the advantage of their own lands would make others, the laborers, unwilling to work as hired hands.[53] There was, however, one chance of at least a semblance of concessions being made to the freedmen. Under the amendment the agreements with the freedmen could be abrogated and the lands restored before expiration of the three-year titles if the bureau men approved an "amicable" new agreement between the freedmen and the planters.[54] Howard, trusting his contract system, accepted the change rather than risk Johnson's displeasure and the probability that the three years was more than he would have gained in an out-and-out fight for the lands.

The one remaining obstacle to this amendment, which would save face for Commissioner Howard and possibly a kitchen garden or two for a few freedmen, was Rufus Saxton. Months before, the South Carolina Assistant Commissioner made it known that he would have to be removed from office if the government was going to get away with either breaking its promise to the island freedmen or offering them a substitute as flimsy as the one being proposed. Otis Howard had his brother sound out Saxton on the possibility of a transfer, but Saxton would not hear of it.[55] The

52. *Cong. Globe,* 18 Jan. 1866, p. 298.
53. W. H. Trescot to Andrew Johnson, 12 Mar. 1866, BRFAL.
54. *Cong. Globe,* 18 Jan. 1866, p. 298.
55. Saxton Diary, 29 Nov. 1865.

President, wanting Saxton to ask for a transfer, offered "any position he wanted, & . . . another brevet promotion (Brig Gen) in
the regular army," but "very wisely R[ufus] will not do that as
he has the interests of this work too much at heart." All the
bureau men in Charleston knew "it would be a relief to the
President if he would . . . be relieved."[56] On January 9, 1866, he
was. He received a curt note from Howard removing him from
his post.

The freedmen, the bureau men, and the schoolteachers in
South Carolina were shaken by the news. "We have talked about
this a good deal, but it has taken us unexpectedly at last. It rather
unsettles all things," wrote Willard Saxton. "It is a triumph for
the rebels, which they have long labored to attain—in one of
the 'compromises' which have been the bane of the nation for
years past. It is a 'conservative' gain."[57] As was usual in nineteenth-century American political compromises, large or small,
the Negro lost.

Saxton would make no compromise at all. Howard tried to
make amends for his treatment of his earliest friend in the freedmen's work by offering him the position of inspector general
of the Bureau with an office in Washington.[58] Saxton refused
this exile at headquarters, which, as mentioned, was the standard
fate of radical field officers removed from duty. Saxton still assumed that Howard had been overruled in another attempt to
keep him at his post. Had he known then, as he was to learn
later, that Howard had been instrumental in his removal, the
dejection of his last days in Charleston would have been even
greater than it was.[59] At a huge rally (one of several held by the

56. Ibid., 23 Oct. 1865.
57. Ibid., 9 Jan. 1866.
58. O. O. Howard to Rufus Saxton, 8 Jan. 1866, BRFAL.
59. The letter of W. H. Trescot to Andrew Johnson, 1 Dec. 1865, claiming that Saxton would not yield, as Howard was commended for having done,
not only to restoration of the lands but also to removal of the Negro members
of the contract supervision board was marked by Willard Saxton. "The following letter shows why Gen. Saxton was removed," Saxton Papers, Yale
University; Mrs. Rufus Saxton to Willard Saxton, quoted in Saxton Diary,
30 Mar. 1866.

freedmen in his honor), the freedmen said goodbye with much affection, but Rufus Saxton could not bring himself to attend.[60] At the end of his stay in the South, Saxton walked down to the city docks alone feeling "defeated & disgraced."[61] He had nothing more to give to the Carolinians who loved him. The freedmen presented him with an impressive sword as a tribute to a warrior in their cause; the nation deprived him of promotions that routinely should have been his.[62] Johnson's animosity was persistent.[63]

The junior bureau agents, in a "delightful state of uncertainty," eager to learn whether the pending bill to enlarge the agency would mean more important assignments for them, and anxious to know what a change in assistant commissioners would mean for their careers, forgot their old chief quickly. When Rufus Saxton boarded a steamer on January 23, 1866, there was "not a person at the wharf to see him off" for the North and an assignment in the Quartermaster's Corps.[64] From the *Freedmen's Record* there came "a wail of sorrow."[65]

Saxton had been removed, and on January 18 Trumbull introduced the three-year plan as an amendment to his own bill and thereby removed from Senate 60 any effective means of holding the sea-island farms for the Negroes. Only two senators, Charles Sumner and Jacob Howard (no relation to the Commissioner), noted how large a loss the freedmen had sustained. Trumbull insisted that the life-tenure titles would not withstand court test, and with no further discussion the amendment was accepted.[66]

The third section of Senate 60 does greater service both to

60. Saxton Diary, 14 and 17 Jan. 1866.

61. Ibid., 23 Jan. 1866.

62. Ibid., 18 Jan. 1866.

63. In a letter marked personal and confidential, Howard told Saxton that both Senators Wilson and Sumner agreed that it was the "President himself who changed the order of recommendation" which resulted in a Saxton promotion being bypassed. O. O. Howard to Rufus Saxton, 2 Mar. 1867, OOH Papers.

64. Saxton Diary, 22 and 23 Jan. 1866.

65. *Freedmen's Record,* February 1866, p. 2.

66. *Cong. Globe,* 18 Jan. 1866, pp. 298–99.

O. O. Howard's memory as a friend of the freedmen and to his reputation as an imaginative social innovator. He advocated that the government buy land for the freedmen and sell it to them on time. Others, most notably Rufus Saxton in his annual report of December 8, 1865, had spoken of such plans.[67] Howard seems to have adopted the idea without ideological overtones as the only practical answer to a seemingly insoluble problem. It came out of Howard's long and vexing struggle to solve the land title controversy on the Sea Islands. In November Howard, who was very patient, told Henry Wilson that the only sure way that he could see to solve the dilemma was for the government to buy the Sea Islands from the rebel planters and resell them to the freedmen.[68] This idea had a respectability that confiscation had lost since the end of the war, but like so many of Howard's ideas, it ignored the crucial fact that there were many white men in the nation who did not want to give the Negroes the introduction into the society that a freehold would provide.

Howard's idea was incorporated in Senate 60, and it was extended to include the whole South, although on a very limited scale. The bill stated that Howard could, under the President's direction, buy "such tracts of land in the several districts as may be necessary to provide for the indigent refugees and freedmen dependent on the government for support." He was also authorized to sell these lands for "not less than the cost . . . to the United States."[69] Howard was further instructed to make no commitments until Congress made specific appropriations for the purchase or rental of lands. Howard, never hesitant to use bureau funds for the freedmen programs he approved of, had already authorized Samuel Thomas in Mississippi to use these funds to buy lands in that state, where he knew a Negro farmer was ready to begin a lease-purchase transaction.[70]

67. The sale of lands seized for taxes during Lincoln's administration was cited as precedent by Charles Howard. C. H. Howard to O. O. Howard, 2 Nov. 1865, OOH Papers; Abbott, "Freedmen's Bureau in South Carolina," p. 103.

68. O. O. Howard to Henry Wilson, 25 Nov. 1865, OOH Papers.

69. *Cong. Globe,* 12 Jan. 1866, p. 210.

70. Max Woodhull to Samuel Thomas, 27 Dec. 1865, BRFAL.

There were no other stipulations. Howard was free (within the tight collar of appropriated or acquired funds) to provide poor Negroes with lands at either government expense, if authorized by congressional appropriation, or at Confederate expense, from the proceeds of confiscated lands sold or rented. If a permanent flow of income from either source were made available to him, Howard could involve the federal government permanently in the process of land redistribution. The government's earning ability was to be substituted for the poor man's inability so that he might be equipped with a sufficient asset to rid himself of his poverty.

This section of Senate 60 was the closest that Howard ever came to getting enacted a plan under which Negroes could buy their own farms. He presented the idea imprecisely and hesitantly many times in his years at the Bureau. It was his most practical idea and perhaps the one that would have been the most useful form of assistance the federal government could have extended to the Negro. Realizing the freedmen's lack of capital Howard called for "the government . . . to purchase [the lands] and allot them for rental and subsequent purchase by Negroes."[71]

The very government that Howard hoped would sell the freedmen the asset they most needed for economic "takeoff" granted the railroads of the nation 67,336,000 acres of land in the three years of the Freedmen's Bureau's life.[72] The railroad lands could have provided the freedmen families of the South (assuming three in the family, a man, his wife, and one child) with their forty acres (with land enough left over to exchange for a good many mules). Congress, which enthusiastically used the capital assets of the country to encourage one form of development, did not take the opportunity to develop a viable economic base for the freedmen even on the sensible lease-purchase arrangement Howard suggested.

71. O. O. Howard to Henry Wilson, 25 Nov. 1865, OOH Papers.

72. Series J 44–48, "Public Land Grants by United States to Aid in Construction of Railroads," *The Statistical History of the United States from Colonial Times to the Present* (Stamford, Conn., 1965), p. 239.

Lease-purchase would be our present-day equivalent of Howard's non-down-payment mortgage and would have utilized the freedmen's income potential. Howard's references to "rental and subsequent purchase" and similar phrases called for the government, out of the sale of government bonds, such as those that financed the war, to buy farmland from large (and often cash-poor) planters in the South.[73] (As governmental interest in the Bureau waned, Howard urged his friends to establish private philanthropic corporations to carry out similar programs.)[74] The lands would be leased to Negroes and to whites (poor rather than speculative) for low rents on a one-to-a-customer basis. When the rents, payable after the crop was in, had accumulated to equal the cost of the land at the time of governmental purchase, the title to the land would then go to the farmer, and the proceeds of the rents would extinguish the debt to the bondholder. In this way more of the nation's Negroes could own land and possess the liberty that land ownership carried with it in the nineteenth century.

There was a note of revolutionary change in this land proposal in Senate 60, and the court system included in the bill was as subversive of the traditional state-nation relations as any proposal contained in other Reconstruction legislation. Ambitious lawyers recognized quickly the expected addition to the jurisdiction of the federal courts and began writing their congressmen about district court appointments, envisioning an increase in those courts.[75]

Senate 60 called for the transfer of jurisdiction of civil rights cases—of legal actions to protect individuals because they belonged to a hated group—from state to federal courts. This procedure was to exist until the state courts in the South were ready to grant equal rights to the Negroes. The Negro was not to be denied by state or local ordinance, by the police, "or other

73. For a similar proposal six years later, see Stearn, *Black Man of the South,* pp. 531–35.

74. O. O. Howard to Jay Cooke, 14 Oct. 1868, OOH Papers.

75. C. M. Hawley to Lyman Trumbull, 3 Jan. 1866, Trumbull Papers, LC.

regulation . . . any of the civil rights or immunities belonging to white persons." The Negroes, however, could not expect to do everything white men could. The rights granted were limited but valuable common law liberties, which Trumbull went on to list: the right to "make and enforce contracts, to sue, be parties and give evidence, to inherit, purchase, lease, sell, hold, and convey real and personal property, and to have full and equal benefit of all laws and proceedings for the security of person and estate."[76]

Howard was to extend military protection to Negroes whose rights were threatened. The bureau agent's job in enforcing the protection of rights was made more specific in the second of the two bills Trumbull reported out of the Judiciary Committee on January 12—the Civil Rights Bill of 1866. In that bill, Senate 61, still available for enforcement today, bureau agents, along with United States attorneys, marshals, and commissioners (the last appointed by the district courts), were instructed to "institute proceedings" in federal courts against civil rights violators.[77]

Approval of some kind of Freedmen's Bureau bill had been expected since the congressional session began. The chief argument for supporting passage was the appeal that could be made to the need for the Bureau in the slow process of healing the broken Union. This argument incorporated a conservative assumption which proved false. When Senator Fessenden of Maine, favoring the bill, said, "Time is necessary to over-come prejudice," he was intimating that time *would* overcome it.[78] He misunderstood which way time was working. The nation did not need the Bureau to give its prejudices time to change. It needed to give the Bureau time and a mandate to enforce an assistance program for the freedmen despite the continuance of prejudice.

In the House of Representatives, Congressman Samuel S. Marshall of Illinois had no intention of abandoning his prejudice. His statements in opposition to the bill were as classically

76. *Cong. Globe,* 12 Jan. 1866, p. 209.
77. Ibid., p. 211.
78. Ibid., 23 Jan. 1866, p. 367.

conservative as Fessenden's in support of it. Marshall contended that the Bureau and the freedmen would deter the advance of the nation. "Although we have the finest country on earth, our people are now borne down almost to the verge of poverty by a system of class legislation." General Howard, he said, was "a gallant and excellent officer," but, looking up in the galleries, Marshall commented that the Commissioner should not have the power to coddle "the children of Ham, who are to be fatted out of the Treasury of the country."[79]

John H. Hubbard of Connecticut disagreed. "I feel proud of my country" (prouder of it than of his state, perhaps; Connecticut had recently rejected Negro enfranchisement) "when I behold it stretching out its strong arm of power to protect the poor, the ignorant, the weak and the oppressed." He contended that this peacetime effort would bring the nation "a richer revenue of honor than all the . . . glory of her battlefields." In his view, our country "is and must be cosmopolitan. The [founding] fathers invited the oppressed of all nations to come here and find a happy home."[80] To Hubbard, the freedmen were African immigrants in need of help.

Congressman Samuel W. Moulton of Illinois suggested a different reason for supporting Senate 60 and thus increasing the Bureau's services. Beyond quieting midwestern fears, the bill could even solve problems in foreign relations: "Wherever the colored man is completely and fully protected in the southern states he will never visit Illinois, and he will never visit Indiana, and every northern State will be depopulated of colored people, as will be Canada."[81]

Whatever the motives, Trumbull and thirty-six of his Senate colleagues voted for Senate 60 and passed it.[82] Five of the ten opponents were from the Union slave states of Kentucky, Maryland, and Delaware. Four other votes opposing the bill came

79. Ibid., 3 Feb., 1866, p. 630.
80. Ibid.
81. Ibid., p. 631.
82. Ibid., 25 Jan. 1866, p. 421.

from senators from Indiana, Pennsylvania, and New Jersey, all of which bordered on states with large and potentially mobile Negro populations. The tenth opponent was James A. McDougall of California; his vote had been clearly forecast the day before when he paid tribute to the Negroes' ability to "mimic like monkeys and sing like birds."[83]

The House of Representatives considered Senate 60 early in February. The bill had been charged to the Select Committee on the Freedmen, chaired by T. D. Eliot of Massachusetts, a man much trusted by O. O. Howard.[84] His group redrafted the bill making an important change to which the House and Senate agreed.[85] Howard could now provide not more than forty acres of public land or land bought with public funds to any Negro granted land under Sherman's Field Order 15 who faced dispossession because of restoration.[86]

The House, which passed the bill as a whole by a vote of 136 to 33, made one other major change.[87] It restricted the Bureau to those states in which the writ of habeas corpus was suspended at the time of the bill's passage. This would have limited the Bureau to the Confederate states plus Kentucky, but the Senate refused to accede to this change and the national jurisdiction of Howard's agency was restored.[88] On February 13, 1866, the bill was formally enrolled in both houses of Congress and sent to the President for approval.[89] Black men were jubilant.

Did the Negroes, who followed the progress of the bill every step of the way, have much to cheer about? They watched white men, some of whom wished even the cheerers were down

83. Ibid., 24 Jan. 1866, p. 401.

84. Howard, *Autobiography, 2,* 198.

85. The bill was now titled, "A Bill to amend an act to establish a Bureau of Freedmen and Refugees." The original number, Senate 60, was retained. *Cong. Globe,* 13 Feb. 1866, p. 807.

86. *Cong. Globe,* 6 Feb. 1866, p. 634.

87. Ibid.

88. Ibid., 5 Feb. 1866, p. 654; 6 Feb. 1866, p. 688; 8 Feb. 1866, p. 747.

89. Ibid., 13 Feb. 1866, pp. 806, 812.

South, approve a piece of legislation that might enable a few Negroes in South Carolina, Georgia, and Florida to keep their lands a little longer, make available some barren acres for a few more, and, if the money could be found, establish still fewer on good purchased farmlands. A cynic might have thought this less than adequate to stay the restlessness of 4,000,000 people and keep them contentedly in the South.

The freedmen had good reason to be cynical about the Freedmen's Bureau, because some of its agents served planters and not freedmen, but cynicism did not seem to have been a dominant characteristic of the southern Negroes. Neither did restlessness. One of the most commented-on phenomenon of the freedmen's first years in freedom is their mobility. Whether as irresponsible looters or as nature's noblemen, they are pictured as taking a walk into freedom. Otis Howard had seen enough in Georgia and in the Carolinas to know why they were on the roads, following the armies. They were looking for help. Howard, from his own experience, realized that people who do need help often will accept it disregarding its source. An uncle whom Howard disliked sent him to West Point; a stranger whom he met on a train helped him pass the embarrassments of entering the Academy; a brassy politician got him his colonelcy. He did not choose to inquire into the motivations of those who helped him, and neither did the Negroes in the galleries watching Congress at work.

Howard was much more willing than he should have been to sacrifice the character of the assistance to be rendered the freedmen in order to assure the continuation of the nation's commitment to give them help of some kind. The only justification possible for his abandonment of Saxton and Conway was his relentless drive to save the Freedmen's Bureau and to keep the President and the nation in the business of helping the freedmen. Howard and Trumbull addressed idealists when they said in Senate 60 that freedom required governmental action. Mere emancipation was not enough; opportunity could come only to landed farmers protected by county agents and justices of the peace responsible to the federal government. Heads of families should have farms of their own, "bare subsistence" is not enough for a free man, said Howard to a leader of the agency for South Carolina, who indefatigably sought restoration.[90] Senate 60, which could have been a great beginning for the freedmen, went to the President for signature on 13 February 1866.

Negroes had crowded the galleries of the Senate chamber each winter day for the debate of Senator Trumbull's bill.[91] Indeed, the Negro spectators, who followed the debate so intently, considered it theirs. The President's restoration of white rule in the South had presented a peacetime emergency which the Negroes looked to the Congress to meet. They hoped to see the conversion of the Bureau, built to meet emergencies occasioned by war, into an agency of permanent change in southern society. They cheered when it was passed. They were distressed and noisy about it when the President's veto of the bill was read, and their angry talk interrupted the debate and the vote the day the veto was sustained. Senate 60 never became the law of the land.

Historians have looked back at the bill and the veto and seen it as no more than an early stop in the course of presidential and congressional conflict that progressed to the Fourteenth Amendment and on to the congressional Reconstruction acts.[92] In this historical view, the radicals, sparked by the veto of Senate 60, replaced moderates and pushed forward on their own. Eric McKitrick, in analyzing the deterioration of President Johnson's relations with Congress, sees Senate 60 as a moderate bill. A

90. O. O. Howard to W. H. Trescot, 14 Jan. 1866, BRFAL.

91. In the *Congressional Globe* are frequent references to Negroes in the galleries of both houses of Congress. For example, see the complaint of Congressman Samuel S. Marshall of Illinois: "From the commencement of this session . . . [the] galleries [have been] crowded with the children of Ham . . . that come here day after day to darken these legislative halls." *Cong. Globe,* 3 Feb. 1866, p. 630.

92. "[Congressional] expressions of principle were started toward statutory fruition by Senator Trumbull's Bill," *Brief for Appellants in the case of Oliver Brown, et al., in the Supreme Court of the United States,* October term, 1953, pt. 2, p. 81; for a similar statement more recently, see Stampp, *The Era of Reconstruction,* p. 85.

wise President, he suggests, would have made common cause with the congressional moderates and supported it.[93] To many observers, the veto was Johnson's first mistake because it forced Congress into radicalism.

This legislative progression is, of course, chronologically accurate but, in terms of achieving basic change in the social structure of the South, Congress was engaged in regressive process. Senate 60 was not equalitarian and did not invite Negroes to move north or west, but it was, for all its failings, radical. It called for changes in restored institutions in the South favoring the southern Negro, and it put the national government squarely in the business of programming and enforcing those changes.

The motive of some of the bill's supporters may have been to keep the Negroes happy in the South so they would not come north, but the bill would have at least invested the freedmen with assets they desperately needed. The bill was addressed to the fundamental needs of a deprived class frankly viewed as such. When Garret Davis of Kentucky sought to attack the bill by mockingly renaming it, he described its contents with remarkable accuracy:

> I move to amend the title by substituting this for it: a bill to appropriate a portion of the public land in some of the southern states and to authorize the United States Government to purchase lands to supply farms and build houses upon them for the freed negroes; to promote strife and conflict between the white and black races; and to invest the Freedmen's Bureau with unconstitutional powers to aid and assist the blacks, and to introduce military power to prevent the Commissioner and other officers of said bureau from being restrained or held responsible to civil courts for their illegal acts in rendering such aid and assistance to the blacks; and for other purposes.[94]

93. Eric McKitrick, *Andrew Johnson and Reconstruction* (Chicago, 1964), p. 277.

94. *Cong. Globe,* 25 Jan. 1866, p. 421.

While the Negroes in the gallery would have said that strife between the races needed no promotion, they would not have dissented from the rest of Davis' outline of the Bureau's expanded responsibilities. For Davis' fellow southern neighbor, Andrew Johnson, even the abstractions of Negro rights in the Fourteenth Amendment might have been less hard to live with than a bill empowering men to give Negroes the nuts and bolts of freedom. Andrew Johnson's veto was not an awkward error of a maladroit politician. It was a response to real danger.

Heretofore Johnson shrewdly waged war on the Bureau by quietly subverting it, while saying as little as possible about either the agency or the freedmen. That preoccupation with the Negro was unhealthy for the nation was the subtle theme of many letters Johnson received from respectable Northerners who supported his position. They saw Johnson's program as bringing business prosperity to the South and applauded this. These Americans much preferred to have the nation's problems stated once again in monetary metaphors where values could be securely established.

The freedmen, encouraged by developments on Capitol Hill, carried their advocacy to the White House as well. It was there, on February 7, that Andrew Johnson finally lost patience with the whole freedmen business. Frederick Douglass called on him to present a petition requesting Negro suffrage; Johnson, who was quoted privately as saying "the white race was superior to black," had always been curtly polite in receiving Negro delegations, but this day he spoke harshly.[95] The President approached "very near to Mr. Douglass" and said that the poor whites and the Negroes in the South were natural enemies and the Negroes pressing for the vote would cause a race war.[96] Then, somewhat irrelevantly, the President accused the freedmen of preferring to work for their old masters rather than for the good yeomen of the South, who were the ones who had suffered

95. R. R. French to Andrew Johnson, 8 Feb. 1866, AJ Papers.
96. Philip S. Foner, *The Life and Writings of Frederick Douglass* (4 vols. New York, 1950–55), 4, 22.

during the war, being forced to fight the planters' battles for them.[97] A friend of Johnson's, hearing about this line of argument, understood it (as Douglass must have) as a reiteration of the President's previously private view that the superiority of the white race was natural and, contradictorily, must be maintained artificially by keeping the lower classes of white men progressing faster than the freedmen.[98]

Douglass was angry too. He indicated that what worried Johnson was for whom the Negroes would or would not vote, if enfranchised.[99] Moving to the realm of the rights of man, the eloquent Negro leader had the better of the verbal exchange.[100] He made the President of the United States a cracker again, and Andrew Johnson hated him for it.

It might be postulated that Johnson's angry reply to Douglass' request for the vote would ensure a presidential signature on Senate 60. This line of reasoning proceeded from a recognition of the Negroes' need for protection and a desire to refute the claim of equalitarians that the freedmen needed the vote for their protection. If protection could be had in some other way, the vote need not be given them. If Senate 60 promised such protection (and if the Civil Rights Bill gave them rights enough for any black man), then the freedmen would have no need to ask for the vote. Trumbull knew as well as Johnson did that Negro votes would be votes for radical Republicans.

But the signature was not to come, and Henry Asbury, a friend of Trumbull's, writing to the Senator about the Douglass-Johnson exchange, came close to predicting the presidential veto of Senate 60. Asbury noted that Johnson's talk with Douglass was "humiliating" to the President.[101] Johnson had been humiliated by a Negro; he had been forced to drop his fatherly tone and

97. Washington *Evening Star,* 7 Feb. 1866; J. H. Embrey to Andrew Johnson, 9 Feb. 1865, AJ Papers.

98. R. R. French to Andrew Johnson, 8 Feb. 1866, AJ Papers.

99. Foner, *4,* 22.

100. Henry Asbury to Lyman Trumbull, 11 Feb. 1866, Trumbull Papers, LC.

101. Ibid.

rail out at Douglass. Douglass, for his part, had shown no signs of agreeing to lead his people back to work for their old masters, even under the protection of the Freedmen's Bureau. He would go right on working for the vote that Johnson had told him would produce a "collision of the races."[102] If this happened, whatever in Senate 60 was valuable to the President would be lost. The freedmen would not be kept quiet.

The conservative Republicans led by Lyman Trumbull intended to keep Johnson in their camp despite their view that he "was not big enough for the place he occupies."[103] Perhaps he would be replaced at the next election.[104] They feared that Johnson's outbursts would play into the hands of the radical minority. "Good Senator—for God's sake keep our President from so much talking," continued Asbury in his letter to Trumbull. The Senator had hoped that Senate 60 would do just that, but Douglass had proved him wrong. The conservative Republicans wanted to hold their dominance of the Republican party, and, while they feared defections to the left, they also feared that men like Wisconsin's James R. Doolittle might go from "Conservative Republican to just plain Conservative."[105]

Johnson, with no intention of leaving the White House, intended to build a majority party of his own with men like Doolittle and southern conservatives to whom he had given power through the restored state governments.[106] He wanted these men back in Congress, and he wanted them available for presidential balloting. Senate 60 was not going to silence the Negro question. Douglass promised him that. Instead, it represented a fusion of conservative and radical Republican aims and contributed to strengthening the Republican party enough so

102. Ibid.

103. Henry Asbury to Andrew Johnson, 11 Feb. 1866, Trumbull Papers, LC.

104. Horace White to Lyman Trumbull, 21 Feb. 1866, Trumbull Papers, LC.

105. Henry Asbury to Andrew Johnson, 11 Feb. 1866, Trumbull Papers, L.C.

106. Support for the establishment of such a new party came in the flood of letters to Johnson supporting the veto. See particularly R. W. Sanders, mayor of Niles, Mich., to Andrew Johnson, 26 Feb. 1866, AJ Papers.

that it could continue to thwart Johnson's attempt to build a new North-South conservative party of his own.

After the President decided to veto Senate 60, he had his ally in the Bureau, James Fullerton, draw up, in his own hand on bureau stationery, a twenty-page letter giving his objections to the agency he worked for. In addition to stressing the cost of the Bureau (which he underscored in a second report), Fullerton skillfully played up to the President's personal attitudes.[107] He saw the Bureau as functioning for the freedmen at the expense of poor whites, and he charged the Bureau with exerting the same kind of tainted paternalism that the planters had been accused of under slavery. Charging that some bureau personnel were corrupt and cruel to the Negroes, he argued that the freedmen would fare better under the authority of the restored state governments in the South. Fullerton endorsed Grant's plan of December 1865, which suggested that regular army men in the South be given bureau duties in place of the special bureau personnel. The military could augment the state governments and protect the employers' labor supply.[108]

Fullerton articulated the President's objections better than Johnson himself. In the semiprivacy of his cabinet room, Johnson spoke his opposition in subjective terms. He saw the bill as a result of a conspiracy against him and spoke of "intrigues."[109] His friend James Embrey, speaking with disgust about a "half black and half white" meeting in Philadelphia, where the Negro leader Douglass attacked Johnson as "no Lincoln," connected Douglass with Stevens and Sumner and told the President that he would gain votes in New York State if he "stands up to the Negro."[110] A few days later, in a curious way, Johnson did. At a rally celebrating his veto of Senate 60, he delivered his famous denunciation of Wendell Philips, Charles Sumner, and Thaddeus Stevens.

107. J. S. Fullerton to Andrew Johnson, 9 and 12 Feb. 1866, AJ Papers.
108. Ibid.
109. Gideon Welles, *The Diary of Gideon Welles* (3 vols. Boston, 1911), 2, 432.
110. J. H. Embrey to Andrew Johnson, 9 Feb. 1866, AJ Papers.

That strange speech was full of talk of secret cabals and treasonous intrigues. Its images were drawn from the first feverish days of his Presidency, and the nation was caught up in the excitement of assassination plots, both fantastic and real. All of these illusions bear little relevance to the facts of congressional action and the content of Senate 60. Johnson seems almost to have created a fantasy of imagined horrors, which disguise the true subject of his dislike for the bill, the Negroes, and men like Sumner and Stevens, who would betray their race to help them. Johnson, in his formal veto message, in his explanation of it to his cabinet, and in his speech to the Washington's birthday crowd, avoided any description of the Freedmen's Bureau which suggested that agency was responsible for the welfare of the freedmen. He did not even use Fullerton's relevant attack on the antinegro attitudes of many of the bureau agents.[111]

President Johnson profoundly misunderstood the northern nation which he led. As an English writer put it, he had "forgotten that he was President of these United States, and remembered only that he was Andrew Johnson, a white man of Tennessee," who did not understand "the principles of the second revolution."[112] He was a Southerner among Northerners, and he did not share their sense of insulation from the Negroes. It must have been a source of wonder to him, as it was to an eccentric correspondent from Massachusetts, that Charles Sumner could speak of the Negro as "equal before the law," when any Negro knew that although "Massachusetts has been intensely antislavery for the past ten or twelve years, the colored people of this state are as much ignored as ever . . . are debarred the hospitalities of the dominant race at their firesides . . . and at the ballot box can only choose between two men of a different color from their own!"[113]

Since Johnson had become President, he had received a great many letters from Northerners who sought to change the social

111. Washington *Daily National Intelligencer,* 23 Feb. 1866.
112. *Pall Mall Gazette,* 22 Feb. 1866.
113. Anonymous [D. W. Lothrop] to Andrew Johnson, 17 Feb. 1866, AJ Papers.

and economic structure in the South and who assumed, from Johnson's Jacksonian talk of assisting the common man, that he would apply his sympathy equally to both the black man and the white. This must have sounded totally unreal to him, and he may have come to think, when Thaddeus Stevens talked of leveling to the benefit of poor blacks and whites in the South, that the Congressman was just mocking him. Such men who supported Negro equality Johnson took to be malicious; they were jeering the democracy that meant so much to him.

On February 19, the President's son, Robert Johnson, walked into the Senate chamber with his father's veto. Debate was interrupted and the clerk read the accompanying message.[114] The authorship of this document has been investigated by John and LaWanda Cox, who have concluded that six of Johnson's advisers, including James Fullerton, had a hand in it. They find Seward's contribution to be the most significant and deplore the fact that his statement—that the federal government did have a responsibility for the freedmen—was discarded. They credit the President himself with two crucial ideas: an insistence that the southern states should not be legislated for while they were not represented in Congress, and an appeal to race prejudice through extolling the ability of white men to care for themselves through honest toil while the freedmen needed help.[115]

The message was quiet in tone. It carried in it none of Andrew Johnson's anger, but the Negroes in the gallery shouted with anger when the reading came to an end. Their demonstration was long, and senators asked for quiet and quarreled over how to achieve it. Trumbull wanted those making the noise removed; Senator Sumner wanted all of the spectators removed if any of them were to be ordered out. White men sat in the ladies' gallery; Negroes were seated in the gentlemen's gallery on the west side of the chamber. When the noise did not stop, the "western gallery" was ordered cleared.[116]

114. *Cong. Globe,* 19 Feb. 1866, pp. 915–17.
115. John H. and LaWanda Cox, "Andrew Johnson and the Ghost Writers," *MVHR, 48* (December 1961), 460–79.
116. *Cong. Globe,* 19 Feb. 1866, pp. 917–18.

The next day Lyman Trumbull tried to get sufficient votes to override the veto, but he failed. Eighteen senators voted to sustain the President's action; thirty (two less than two-thirds) were counted in the bill's favor. The original opponents of Senate 60 were joined by Senators Dixon of Connecticut, Doolittle of Wisconsin, Morgan of New York, Norton of Minnesota, Stewart of Nevada, and VanWinkle of West Virginia, all of whom had favored Senate 60 when the legislation cleared Congress. Also voting to uphold the veto were Senators Cowan of Pennsylvania, Nesmith of Oregon, and Willey of West Virginia, who were absent when the vote on the bill was taken. Senator Wright of New Jersey, who opposed the Bureau, and Senator Foote of Vermont, who favored it, were absent for the veto tally.[117]

Senate 60 was dead and the spectators made no secret that they mourned their loss. The noise was so great that the western gallery was again cleared and the Negroes left the hall.[118] They walked away from Capitol Hill without the help they had come to get.

117. Ibid., 20 Feb. 1866, p. 943.
118. Ibid.

12. "keep good faith"

General Howard, who had been on a two-week lecture tour of
New England, returned to Washington the day the veto message
was read in Congress.[1] It might have been expected that the
President's public withdrawal of support for the Bureau, so
damaging to Howard's dream of a great national effort, would
have unsettled the Commissioner. On the contrary, he conducted
his business as usual and even called on the President a few days
later to try again to stall the restoration of the sea-island lands.[2]
Although Howard helped to restore the Edisto plantation of his
companion William Whaley, when visiting the island, he still
resisted returning lands to planters he did not know.[3] He refused
to accept the argument that the veto made immediate restoration
of all lands of pardoned owners mandatory.[4]

The Joint Committee on Reconstruction, which had also
contributed to the President's dislike of Senate 60, continued to
inquire about conditions in the South. The assistant commissioners thought this an excellent opportunity to document the
need to continue the Bureau. Orlando Brown and Charles
Howard, who had succeeded Fullerton as assistant commissioner
for the District of Columbia, actively recruited witnesses to support this contention.[5] They both testified, as did Wager Swayne,
Clinton Fisk, and Eliphalet Whittlesey. Former Assistant Commissioners Rufus Saxton and Thomas Conway were heard too,

1. Washington *Evening Star,* 19 Feb. 1866.
2. Ibid., 28 Feb. 1866.
3. O. O. Howard to A. P. Ketchum, 27 Jan. 1866, BRFAL.
4. W. H. Trescot to Andrew Johnson, 22 Feb. 1866; O. O. Howard to
Andrew Johnson, 21 and 22 Feb. 1866, AJ Papers; W. H. Trescot to Andrew
Johnson, 12 Mar. 1866, BRFAL.
5. C. H. Howard to J. M. Howard, 26 Feb. 1866; Orlando Brown to
J. M. Howard, 15 and 24 Mar. 1866, Justin Morrill Papers, LC.

as were Alexander P. Ketchum, the South Carolina land officer, John W. Alvord, the Bureau's superintendent of education, and William E. Strong, General Howard's inspector general.[6]

The Committee interrogators, systematically building a case against Presidential Reconstruction, drew from the assistant commissioners statements supporting continuance of the Bureau on the grounds that it was needed to keep the peace, and substantiating the contention that the pardoned rebels of the South were generally to be distrusted. Essentially the members of the Committee, from the tone and direction of their questioning, did not seem to be interested in the daily work of the bureau staff. When the Bureau failed to improve the Johnsonian governments' treatment of the freedmen with the power that Congress granted it in 1866, the radicals were no more inclined to put the power of reconstructing the South into the Bureau's hands than Johnson had been.

In April Congress, prodded by Thaddeus Stevens, gave the Bureau an appropriation to meet the needs of the destitute during the spring starving time.[7] It also passed the Act of July 16, 1866, extending the life of the Bureau.[8] This bill survived Johnson's veto, and, with an appropriation of $6,940,450 for the fiscal year ending June 30, 1867, which more than compensated for the lack of income from the restoration of most of its rentable lands, the Bureau had the substance with which to proceed as long as sympathetic men were available.[9] Congress appeared to have restored the mandate that the President had withdrawn with his first veto.

The President, as usual, went on with his war on the Bureau. After the first veto, Johnson did not court the wrath of Congress by giving his support to a bill designed to end the Bureau forth-

6. *Report of the Joint Committee on Reconstruction,* pt. 1, pp. 111-15; pt. 2, pp. 123-28, 181-91, 231-42, 243-61; pt. 3, pp. 29-32, 33-48, 100-02, 138-41; pt. 4, pp. 35-39, 78-86.

7. O. O. Howard to Thaddeus Stevens, 6 Jan. 1866, OOH Papers; Howard, *Autobiography,* 2, 294.

8. *14 U.S. Stat.,* 173-86.

9. Howard, *Autobiography,* 2, 331; *14 U.S. Stat.,* 173-76.

with. Gideon Welles wrote, "I prefer nonaction" to Senator Doolittle's frontal assault. "And I think the President does too."[10] But instead of nonaction, Johnson pursued a more subtle strategy of subversion—his favorite tactic against the agency. This failed in New Orleans because the Negroes remained loyal to the Commissioner even though Assistant Commissioner James Scott Fullerton had persecuted them. But with Congress resisting his wish to dissolve the Freedmen's Bureau altogether, Johnson realized he would have to render the Bureau impotent by discrediting it in the eyes of its constituents and their friends. If, as was feared in Mississippi, the bureau offices became points where Negroes could gather to learn how to negotiate with the planters and to organize for their own advantage, Johnson's smooth running governments in the South might encounter trouble.[11]

Johnson chose to investigate the Bureau and to expose the members who reportedly mistreated Negroes in order to convince the nation that there were justifiable reasons for terminating the agency. The President intended to demonstrate that the freedmen would fare better if left free of guidance from the Bureau and required to make their own way with their white employers. For this assault on the Bureau, Johnson again used the talents of Fullerton; he sent him on an investigatory tour with John B. Steedman, a genial Democratic general who, while in charge of Union troops in Georgia, proved himself no friend of the Negro.[12] Friendly reporters followed them across the South; the newspapers that favored the President's Reconstruction policies gave their tour much coverage.

During the agency's first year, no bureau member was safe if Johnson decided he was obstructing his conservative friends in the South. When the Senate, on April 9, 1866, overrode

10. Welles, *Diary*, 21 Feb. 1866, 2, 437.

11. Wharton, *The Negro in Mississippi*, p. 78.

12. James E. Sefton, "The United States Army and Reconstruction, 1865–1877," Unpublished Ph.D. dissertation (University of California, Los Angeles, 1963), p. 35; Saxton Diary, 26 May 1866.

Johnson's veto of Trumbull's Civil Rights Bill—Senate 61—the bureau agents felt more secure. A. P. Ketchum, now removed from his unhappy job as land officer on the Sea Islands and assigned to duty at Washington headquarters, wrote confidently that it was no longer safe for "the Executive to undertake the chopping off of the official heads of men who have the confidence & support of the great Radical Loyal party."[13]

But Ketchum's colleagues knew Johnson had other means of dispatching them, and with Fullerton and Steedman on their way South, they braced for what was to come. Willard Saxton, still in Charleston, noted that they had begun their descent on the South and gave his prejudgment of the tour: "A large sized cocoa-nut the milk of which will be developed in due time."[14] General Howard, who could guess from the private reports he received in 1865 what Fullerton's tone would be, sought to close the ranks to meet the expected assault, which would certainly strike Fullerton's favorite target, New Orleans. The Commissioner telegraphed Absalom Baird, whom Fullerton had sponsored for the Louisiana post, and asked him to stay there until after the inspection was over.[15] Baird did, to his enormous regret, for nothing pleasant lay ahead for him in the Bureau.

The freedmen knew Steedman and Fullerton's motive. In Augusta, Georgia, where Steedman had once been stationed, the *Loyal Georgian* flatly asserted that the Negroes thought the generals had been sent to find an excuse to end the Bureau.[16] Steedman had been quoted in South Carolina as saying his object was "to break up the Bureau."[17]

The Augusta Negroes had been feuding with their assistant commissioner, Davis Tillson. They wanted to decorate the graves of the Union dead who were buried in the city. Tillson, who had himself led federal troops across Georgia, disapproved,

13. Quoted in Saxton Diary, 13 Apr. 1866.
14. Ibid., 16 Apr. 1866.
15. O. O. Howard to Absalom Baird, 15 May 1866, BRFAL.
16. *Loyal Georgian* (Augusta, Ga.), 9 June 1866, clipping in OOH Papers.
17. Saxton Diary, 26 May 1861.

saying that it would be disruptive and distressing to the planters, with whom he got on so well. When Steedman and Fullerton got to Augusta, Tillson treated them to a display of how cooperative his constituents were. He summoned the freedmen to an open-air meeting, and, with Fullerton and Steedman seated beside him, he asked the Negroes to raise their hands if they agreed not to decorate the graves. None did. Again he asked for hands; again no response. Red with embarrassment, Tillson implored the freedmen to demonstrate their loyalty to him, and finally a few reluctant hands went up. Not overwhelmed by this display of acquiescence to the leadership of the Bureau, Steedman selected five men and, pointing to each in turn, asked if they liked the Freedmen's Bureau. Each immediately answered yes.[18] They wanted the Bureau, but they wanted it to take their side, not the planters'.

The investigators chose not to try to understand the Georgian freedmen. In Charleston, Willard Saxton, hearing about Tillson's position on decorating the graves, understood. In disgust, he wrote: "This tells well for the reconstructed & better still for our own apostate officers. . . . Shame on them, the dough faces."[19]

The apostates were praised in the Steedman-Fullerton reports.[20] As if defying the reaction of the Augustans, Steedman and Fullerton concluded by damning the Bureau as an institution and by praising Davis Tillson as the most capable assistant commissioner they had encountered. Not surprisingly, Thomas Conway was singled out and scorned, and Louisiana was labeled the state most in need of improvement, due to his lax administration.[21] But it was North Carolina to which Steedman and Fullerton pointed with the most telling effect in their accusation of the Freedmen's Bureau. Eliphalet Whittlesey, the restless and tireless assistant commissioner in that state, was made to stand trial for

18. *Loyal Georgian,* 9 June 1866.

19. Saxton Diary, 20 May 1866.

20. Official transcripts of Steedman-Fullerton Reports (news clippings), OOH Papers.

21. Ibid.

the whole concept of the Freedmen's Bureau as the carrier of a new order to the South.

Eliphalet Whittlesey and Otis Howard, both teachers, were determined to see both the freedmen and their former masters learn to live a new and better life. They actively recruited among capitalists hoping to engage other enterprising Northerners (and Englishmen) to teach along with them. Plantations operated with businesslike efficiency were to be the lyceums of this education in principle and practice. Each was to be a new community with school, church, and—to complete the trinity— work. The Negro here could accrue the prerogatives of a free working man; through virtue the planter would receive his reward in this new southern city on a hill.

The bureau men, some with undoubted moral energy and capable of much hard and unselfish labor, built the model. It crumbled, however, and ran to waste in the Tar River the day— March 25, 1866—the body of Alsbury Keel was pulled out of the weeds downstream from Yankee Hall, the plantation of the Reverend Horace James of Massachusetts.[22] James, a chaplain with the Massachusetts Regiment stationed at Fortress Monroe, was drawn into such work by the freedmen who sought sanctuary there. In 1863, as the region that the Union forces occupied increased, district responsibilities were established: Orlando Brown and Charles B. Wilder were given the areas that lay in Virginia, and James was assigned to North Carolina. Originally James was to continue that assignment as an assistant commissioner of the Bureau, but the post was given instead to Whittlesey. Despite this change, the chaplain did not leave the region; he continued as a bureau official in the northeastern corner of North Carolina, with which he was familiar.

By January 1866, Horace James had been mustered out of the army but was retained in his bureau post as superintendent for the Eastern District [of North Carolina], although he was later to claim: "I have not given an average of five minutes a

22. All details from unpaged manuscript record of General Court Martial (#00–1682) of Brevet Brigadier General Eliphalet Whittlesey, 1866, National Archives.

day to duties of the Bureau." He was too busy managing his investments. James was the master of Yankee Hall (and two other adjacent plantations), which he owned in partnership with Eliphalet Whittlesey and Winthrop Tappan, a neighbor of Whittlesey's in Brunswick, Maine.

One hundred and fifty freedmen workers along with one hundred and fifty children and aged Negroes lived on the plantations. The object of James' experiment was both to counter the argument that Negroes would not work as free men and to make a profit. There were no written contracts, but James, the only partner in residence, agreed orally to pay wages ranging from five dollars plus rations per month for boy workers to fifteen dollars plus rations for male adult laborers. The pay was given in cash or, more frequently, in credit at Horace James' "company store."

The wares available in the store included army surplus clothes, which the Bureau had allotted to James for distribution to destitute freedmen. Justifying his whole plantation community as an attack on destitution, James was proud of his generosity—"We have let them have land [in some] instances for a rent of one third of what they produce, but the gardens and all the other things [huts and tools] are entirely free"—and content that the freedmen got the clothes, although they had to pay for them. Out of the stock, Alsbury Keel stole eight pairs of shoes and forty pairs of pants.

Keel was caught and called before James, who sentenced him to dig a ditch on another James' plantation across the river from Yankee Hall. It was "honorable" work; the ex-chaplain claimed that Keel was ordered to join one "of his best hands," who was already at work on the project. But through a later investigation, it was learned that the other man's task was somewhat different. He (a Negro) was an armed guard ordered to watch Keel, but he did not fire when Keel ran from the ditch and escaped into the swamp.

That night Keel came back to the plantation to ask other Negroes for help in crossing the river. Two of those he approached, Sam Grimes and Stephen Wilson, reported his return to David Boyden, a white man who worked for James. Boyden went down to the riverbank and spotted Keel by his campfire. Keel ran for the river. Boyden yelled to him to stop. Keel kept running and plunged into the river. Boyden shot at him. The swimmer's splashing stopped; Keel disappeared in the dark water.

James reported this event of March 10 to the nearest active Bureau agent, F. A. Seely, saying that Boyden shot a fugitive from justice—"a negro name unknown." When Seely investigated, James wrote: "I justify Mr. Boyden's course of action and gave orders to the guard to shoot him when put at work in the ditch should he attempt to escape. The hands upon the place generally feel that Alsbury received nothing more than he deserved. I certainly think so myself and trust that we may be sustained in this opinion by our superior officers."[23]

Two of these superiors, Generals Fullerton and Steedman, arrived in North Carolina at the time of the incident. Precisely, they were in Raleigh when the report of finding Keel's body reached bureau headquarters. A better incident with which to embarrass General Howard and the bureau agents who viewed the agency as charged with the duty of defining a new way of life for the freedmen could hardly have been devised. On May 15, 1866, Whittlesey, James, and nine other bureau officials, accused of crimes ranging from theft of quartermaster stores to torturing Negroes, were arrested.

General Howard was notified of the action; he acknowledged to Whittlesey his awareness that the legal action had begun and ordered him to reply to the Fullerton-Steedman charges.[24] Whittlesey was removed from his assistant commissionership and replaced by General Thomas Ruger, the district military commander, who immediately appointed as his assistant for freedmen's affairs Major C. A. Cilley, the only bureau member in

23. Horace James to F. A. Seely, 15 Mar. 1866 (copy of the letter in the record of the Court Martial).

24. O. O. Howard to Adjutant General of the United States (E. D. Townsend), 15 May 1866; O. O. Howard to Eliphalet Whittlesey, 16 May 1865, BRFAL.

North Carolina of whom Steedman and Fullerton approved. Howard wrote a calm but strong letter to Edwin Stanton urging that the military investigation of the charges against his old friend Whittlesey be "fair & complete."[25] Privately he defended Whittlesey. He wrote to Davis Tillson: "I do not agree with you, with regard to Steedman and Fullerton. . . . I know some agents are corrupt, but . . . Whittlesey is equally true with yourself."[26] The Commissioner tried to get swift justice for Whittlesey. In July he complained that the trial was "suspended" because the two investigators were still on tour and not available to testify. Howard urged Stanton to order them back so that the trial could be completed.[27]

Howard himself was absent from the trial. In August he wrote Whittlesey a letter, designed to check the feeling among some of their friends in Maine that Howard had deserted his comrade. The Commissioner claimed that it would have been improper for him to appear as a character witness in a trial called by the Secretary of War or the President. Howard expected Whittlesey to be censured for neglecting to investigate the murder charge against James and acquitted on the other counts.[28]

On August 30, Howard again wrote to Whittlesey telling him that Stanton agreed to his appointment to a post outside North Carolina, to which he could move and then gracefully resign.[29] The new appointment, however, was delayed by the failure to make public the results of the trial acquitting Whittlesey. (The delay, Howard suspected, was caused by the President so that he could make maximum use of the Steedman-Fullerton charges in the election campaign.)[30] On January 1, 1867, Howard gave Whittlesey a new post, but he did not oblige him to resign. Whittlesey was appointed to Howard's staff in Washington, where he served until 1872.

25. O. O. Howard to E. M. Stanton, 22 May 1866, BRFAL.
26. O. O. Howard to Davis Tillson, 5 June 1866, OOH Papers.
27. O. O. Howard to E. M. Stanton, 17 July 1866, BRFAL.
28. O. O. Howard to Eliphalet Whittlesey, 21 Aug. 1866, OOH Papers.
29. Ibid., 30 Aug. 1866, BRFAL.
30. Ibid., OOH Papers.

Mistreatment of Negroes by bureau personnel was a grave charge. The only possible defense for what Boyden did, on James' orders, with Whittlesey's silent acquiescence, was that it was not typical of the acts of the hundreds of bureau members working in the South with the freedmen. In his response to the Whittlesey affair, Howard stressed the unusualness of the events in North Carolina: in that state (and in adjacent Virginia) with "over two hundred agents, accusations were brought against ten: seven officers and three civilians." And, to underscore his point, he added: "The majority of them have been honorably discharged." The Reverend Horace James was one of these; there is no record of a trial of David Boyden.

On August 23, 1865, Howard formally defended the Bureau to the President. He correctly emphasized that Steedman and Fullerton's purpose was to discredit the whole principle of having the bureau agents serve as exemplars of a new way of life for the freedmen. Howard knew that Johnson and Fullerton wanted the military commanders to assume the duties of the assistant commissioners to eliminate problems such as the agency's promotion either of all-Negro experiments like the one at Davis Bend or of Yankee-directed colonies, as Yankee Hall might have become. Howard sought to adopt the principle of combining the two administrative posts, but only if the "right kind of man" could be found."[31] He would not yield his resolution that the Bureau must protect and sustain the freedmen in a system of benevolent order. Even when the order went as badly awry as it did at Yankee Hall, he maintained his faith.

The Commissioner pointed out in his lucid and impressive reply to the investigators' charges that their "accusations" of the Bureau "keep the faults committed, and not the good done, prominently in view." He adroitly pointed out a major discrepancy. Fullerton and Steedman "had given unqualified praise to the Bureau in Georgia" and claimed that the new laws in that state "place the negro in all respects on a perfect equality with a white man." Howard then quoted Assistant Commissioner Till-

31. O. O. Howard to Andrew Johnson, 23 Aug. 1865, BRFAL.

son, whom the investigators had lauded for his "good judgment," as having said in a report that "the freedmen are denied the protection of the law, and . . . the interference of the Bureau is absolutely essential to secure justice."[32] In the Steedman-Fullerton report, agents who had at one time or another taken the freedmen's part in a quarrel were repeatedly singled out on conflict of interest charges or inefficiency, and the investigators skillfully made it look as if the bureau policies were the cause of all the freedmen's grief.[33] They attacked the contract system as "simply slavery in a new form."[34] The Negro press had been contending that this was true even before the Bureau was organized, but the free wage system, which the Negroes so much desired, depended on protection of the workers' right to move from job to job, and this was patently impossible under the Johnsonian governments in the South.[35] Fullerton himself had demonstrated this when he cooperated so closely with Mayor Kennedy in exploiting the vagrancy principle to discipline the labor force in Louisiana. The report concluded with an indictment of the Bureau and suggested that the freedmen would fare better if left to make their own way with their old masters.

The reporter for the *New York Herald,* along on the Steedman-Fullerton tour, gave the findings much publicity.[36] Opposition to the national government's continued involvement in freedmen's affairs, made respectable by Johnson's veto, was enhanced. The President had detailed Steedman and Fullerton to document the course of action to which he was fully committed. He was as determined to prove that the Negroes were safe only under the jurisdiction of the white Southerners as the Joint Committee on Reconstruction had been to prove the

32. Ibid.

33. C. W. Buckley to T. W. Conway, 18 June 1865, quoted in *Philadelphia Inquirer,* 17 July 1865; Report of James B. Steedman and J. S. Fullerton (Ala.), dated 20 July 1866, New Orleans, La., undated, unidentified news clipping, OOH Papers.

34. Ibid.

35. *New Orleans Tribune,* 12 Aug., 22 Oct. 1865.

36. Bentley, *Freedmen's Bureau,* pp. 128, 131.

opposite. While the generals were pursuing their investigation, Congress, interested in their findings already in the press, passed the bill enlarging and extending the Bureau despite Steedman and Fullerton's reports.

General Howard, notwithstanding the congressional vote of confidence, was afraid he might lose his job.[37] His response was a quiet, reasonable attempt to convince Johnson that the misdeeds were just exceptions to the Bureau's generally commendable conduct.[38] The freedmen were being badly served by Steedman, Fullerton, and Johnson; Howard chose not to expose that fact, but to try once more to convince the President to change his mind. In perhaps his strongest defense of his agency he wrote:

> Could the Freedmen's Bureau be now administered with your full and hearty coöperation of other branches of the Government it would fulfill the objects of its creation in a short time. . . . [I]f the Government would keep good faith with its new-made citizens, some sort of United States agency must be maintained in the Southern States.[39]

Samuel Thomas, who had allowed himself to be removed as assistant commissioner in Mississippi without a fuss and had joined the headquarters staff in Washington, urged Howard to make himself a martyr. Howard had contemplated that role: "Tell Mrs. Whittlesey I am not going to resign, until I am removed, and I probably shall not be removed until after the fall election," he wrote to his old companion.[40] Thomas thought Howard should not wait (and hope not to have to leave) but should resign to dramatize the injustice being done to the freedmen. Instead of endeavoring to placate Johnson, Howard should defy him for the sake of the freedmen: "Can't Howard do . . .

37. O. O. Howard to J. R. Sypher, 30 Aug. 1866, OOH Papers.
38. O. O. Howard to Andrew Johnson, 23 Aug. 1866, BRFAL.
39. Howard, *Autobiography*, 2, 308.
40. O. O. Howard to Eliphalet Whittlesey, 30 Aug. 1866, OOH Papers.

justice to his wards so vigorously that the President will remove him and shoulder the responsibilities of the hour?"[41]

Just a year after Howard had proclaimed, in Maine, his leadership in a great cause, things looked dark for his career and his cause. In August rumor was that the President would replace him with Davis Tillson.[42] The *New York Tribune,* speaking of the prospect of this change at the Bureau, said: "General Howard was called to do a certain work, Tillson will very likely be chosen *not* to do it."[43]

Almost as rankling to Howard as the move to unseat him was the rumor that General Fullerton was to become Andrew Johnson's private secretary. In two unworthy moments, Howard wrote to two of Fullerton's relatives in what appears to have been either an effort to force Fullerton to lessen his attacks on the Bureau or simply to get small-minded revenge.[44] Howard suggested piously that his old friend Fullerton was a good man gone wrong and mentioned reports of "drunkenness, debauchery, and gambling" by the Steedman-Fullerton party "from Washington to Texas." Unctuously, he suggested that it might be better for these reports to remain unpublished.[45] Presumably nothing came of this feeble effort at blackmail (although it might be noted that Fullerton got only the St. Louis postmastership for all his efforts in Johnson's behalf).

Fullerton toned down none of his stinging rebuke of the agency in which he had served when he attended the National Union Convention of Johnsonian supporters in Philadelphia later in the month. Howard had a cousin who lived in that city keep close watch on the meeting, which endorsed, with emo-

41. Samuel Thomas to O. O. Howard, 5 Sept. 1866, OOH Papers; quoted in Bentley, p. 133.

42. Washington *Evening Star,* 14 and 28 Aug. 1866; *New York Tribune,* 21 Aug. 1866.

43. *New York Tribune,* 21 Aug. 1866.

44. *Washington Daily Morning Chronicle,* 30 July 1866.

45. Copies of the two notes appear on the same (August 4) page of Howard's letter-press: O. O. Howard to G. H. Fullerton, 4 Aug. 1866, O. O. Howard to H. S. Fullerton, 10 Aug. 1866, OOH Papers.

tional demonstrations, the presidential policy of restoring governments in the South. Howard correctly predicted in his note to W. H. Merrick that Johnson would use the Steedman-Fullerton report in the fall elections, when he would try to discredit the radicals.[46]

Between sending the two letters to the Fullertons, General Howard wrote a far more characteristic letter to a rich friend in New York. He indicated to William E. Dodge his distress over the President's actions: "Would that our Father above would turn the heart and mind of Mr. Johnson to himself."[47] The quarrel between Congress and the President and between "sympathetic" and "apostate" officers of the Freedmen's Bureau was becoming farther and farther removed from the freedmen.

The real test of the Freedmen's Bureau was not whether Generals Howard or Fullerton had a distressing August, but whether the institution could use the power Congress had granted to it to meet the most pressing needs of the freedmen. The first of these was providing food for starving people. By midwinter Negroes in Alabama, were dying from lack of food, and the cause was not the war but the failure of crops planted the previous summer.[48] The realization that destitution to the point of starvation was a peacetime product may have been as dispiriting for those in the Bureau as the realization that race hatred did not diminish as the war receded in time. Food shortages were reported from Maryland south to Georgia and west to Louisiana, where floods had caused destitution in the lowlands. Droughts and invasions of insects caused similar crop failures in 1866 and starvation the following winter.[49] There was also starvation in the cities, and here it was more directly attributable to the war. Unemployed refugees crowded together in miserable shack

46. O. O. Howard to W. H. Merrick, 15 Aug. 1866, OOH Papers.

47. O. O. Howard to William E. Dodge, 6 Aug. 1866, OOH Papers.

48. Report of Wager Swayne, 27 May 1866, BRFAL.

49. *Facts About the Famine,* Pamphlet issued by Southern Famine Relief Commission, stamped 25 Jan. 1867, BRFAL.

villages on the outskirts of large towns and cities, and there was no one except the Freedmen's Bureau to care for them when their food ran out.[50]

Howard thought then that "for about a million and a half the worst starvation [could be alleviated] but as yet the one million bill has not passed and it looks as if it might not."[51] Radicals not wanting to encourage white pauperism and antinegro congressmen not wanting idle blacks to enjoy handouts made relief legislation hard to achieve.[52] Howard had been quoted in Congress as opposing the relief bill; he wrote John A. Bingham to correct this impression. "The present destitution calls loudly for the aid."[53] The bill passed in April.[54]

Appeals to alleviate extreme poverty were made to the private sector as well. A Connecticut man, C. P. Goodyear, serving as a bureau agent in Hampton, Virginia, wrote his minister that the Negroes there were "crowded into a narrow area" and lived in "hovels." He said there were "more women than men and more children than either." The men were "earning money oystering but the state legislature passed a tax to stop that." Goodyear hoped that Leonard Bacon would help him find "some of these people jobs as house servants in New Haven."[55]

Relief became a greater concern for the Bureau than it had ever been before.[56] Wager Swayne, hoping to move starving Alabamans, went to Texas to see whether Negroes could be exported to that state. In his enthusiasm for a solution to the

50. Max Woodhull to F. D. Sewall, 8 and 14 May 1866, BRFAL.

51. O. O. Howard to Richard Fuller, 15 Mar. 1867, OOH Papers.

52. R. M. Patton to O. O. Howard, 22 Aug. 1866, Stuart Eldridge Papers on loan to Yale University; O. O. Howard to J. A. Bingham, 18 Mar. 1867, OOH Papers.

53. Ibid.

54. O. O. Howard to R. D. Buck, 4 Apr. 1867, OOH Papers.

55. C. P. Goodyear to Leonard Bacon, 1 Apr. 1866, Bacon Family Papers, Yale University.

56. O. O. Howard to E. M. Stanton, 3 July 1866, BRFAL; A. P. Ketchum to Wager Swayne (copies to other assistant commissioners) asking for estimates of rations needed, 4 May 1866, BRFAL.

problem, Swayne may not have exaggerated when he spoke of "immense profits realized" there from the production of cotton and sugar, which had caused "a competition, or rather scramble for labor."[57] Swayne's idea was adopted for destitute Virginians as well as Alabamans.[58] In April, 400 Negroes in Alexandria were persuaded by the Bureau to contract to work in the "South and Southwest."[59] But by September, Howard was less enthusiastic about this solution. "I am very reluctant to encourage negroes to go to Texas so long as it is reported that they are killed and outraged, and have so little share of justice."[60] The destitute freedmen along the Atlantic coast expressed particular terror at the pospect of being exported to Texas and Mississippi.[61]

To urge Negroes to move from places where they were living in destitution to places where they could get jobs, the Bureau maintained employment agencies called "Intelligence Offices." Here bureau personnel made arrangements to supply their friends in the North with servants and to send workers needed in Texas, Louisiana, and Arkansas.[62] With great justification, this activity was viewed with considerable alarm.[63] The working conditions to which these deportees were being sent were open to considerable doubt. Shipments of freedmen (these Negroes volunteered for the jobs only because of destitution) were all too reminiscent of the sale of slaves. Only if there were a good agent in the county to which the workers were going could the Bureau truly relax about this procedure, and the Southwest was where the bureau men were most scarce; there were none at all in New

57. Report of Wager Swayne, 22 Feb. 1866, BRFAL.
58. O. O. Howard to S. C. Armstrong, 31 Aug. 1866, BRFAL.
59. Washington *Evening Star,* 14 Apr. 1866.
60. O. O. Howard to J. B. Kiddoo, 11 Sept. 1866, BRFAL.
61. Ibid.
62. Bureau men anxious to go north on leave often accompanied servants north so that their railroad fare would be paid by the Bureau. Saxton Diary, 28 June 1867; Washington *Evening Star,* 4 Jan. 1866.
63. The Washington *Evening Star* defended the practices of the Intelligence Offices as necessary because of the destitution (1 Mar. 1866); see also *Star* in reply to criticism in the *New York Herald* (Washington *Evening Star,* 22 Mar. 1866).

Jersey, New York, Massachusetts, and Maine, where house servants were sent.[64]

Funds for the relief of those unable to work were in short supply despite the congressional appropriation, and the Bureau received little help in providing for the destitute. General Fisk reported that Kentucky had just passed a bill making Negro taxes the only source of state relief for freedmen paupers. Fisk was "pained to say that the disposition is . . . to turn the poor, sick, infirm and children out . . . to starve and die, except they be cared for by the [federal] government."[65]

On April 27 a special relief commission was established in the District of Columbia under the direction of bureau officers and Dr. R. R. Reyburn, a Negro army surgeon.[66] Similar organizations existed in other southern cities. Clinton Fisk reported proudly that a private Negro organization in Nashville was providing wood, soup, and medical care to the needy without concern about color. Fisk added that more white people than black had been aided.[67]

The Governor of Kentucky, writing in support of Johnson's veto of Senate 60, had said: "We are willing and desirous to retain our negro population, to treat them kindly, employ them at fair wages, and secure them amply in life liberty and property: but we are not willing to take with them a Fredemen's Bureau, which places a Northern fanatic as overseer over white & black."[68] General Howard probably would have been more willing to give up his long struggle to keep Kentucky under bureau control if reports from there and elsewhere in the South had supported the Governor's claim that free labor concepts would be honored

64. The Bureau did try to follow up on some allegations of ill treatment, writing to the freedmen to ascertain if they were not paid wages, as alleged. F. S. Sewall to James Boyd of Glastonbury, Conn., 14 Jan. 1867, BRFAL. In 1866, 6,532 freedmen were sent north as servants from the District of Columbia; 387 were sent south. *Report of the Commissioner* (1866), p. 6.

65. C. B. Fisk Report, 5 Mar. 1866, BRFAL.

66. Washington *Evening Star,* 7 Jan. 1867.

67. C. B. Fisk to O. O. Howard, quoted in Washington *Evening Star,* 26 Feb. 1866.

68. T. E. Bramlette to Andrew Johnson, 12 Feb. 1866, AJ Papers.

in his state.[69] Theoretically, free labor was free to use its wages, buy land, or in any other way buy itself out of the need to labor for any given employer.

The executive agent of South Carolina, William Trescot, frankly flaunted such a concept in his relentless lobbying for the restoration of the sea-island lands. He told the President in March 1866 that "it will be utterly impossible for the owner to find labour that will work contentedly for wages along side . . . free colonies."[70] In Florida, the freedmen found that lumbering paid good wages, and the plantations there were short of farm workers as a result.[71] The *New Orleans Tribune* told about a novel move to block dispossession of the sea-island Negroes. Certain Florida planters did not want these able Negro farmers dispersed; instead they wanted them shipped as a group to work Florida plantations.[72] There was much evidence available to everyone in Washington that the white southern planters wanted tightly regulated labor and not free labor.[73]

The planters who told Steedman and Fullerton they preferred a free system had something other than the northern industrial system in mind.[74] They wanted to free themselves of the Bureau agents who, even while ensuring a labor supply, intruded concepts of an alien economy. The binding of the planter and worker to the crop was natural in a slave economy; after the war, the planters saw no reason to disturb this relationship. It was an exception when Thomas Osborn toured along the Suwannee River in Florida and found "a number of freedmen cultivating land for themselves, and occasionally doing a few days' work in the lumbering business. This appears . . . to be a nearer approach to the free labor system of the North than any other . . . met with."[75]

69. O. O. Howard to C. B. Fisk, 16 Mar. 1866, BRFAL.

70. W. H. Trescot to Andrew Johnson, 12 Mar. 1866, BRFAL.

71. T. W. Osborn Report, 13 Mar. 1866, BRFAL.

72. *New Orleans Times,* 25 Oct. 1865.

73. G. W. Kingsbury to J. S. Morrill, 18 June 1866, Justin Morrill Papers, LC.

74. Wharton, *The Negro in Mississippi,* p. 79.

75. T. W. Osborn Report, 17 Apr. 1866.

The bureau agents often enforced less than free labor conditions. J. E. Cornelius, an agent on Wadmalaw Island off the South Carolina coast, protesting the Fullerton-Steedman complaints and insisting that he was a competent man, explained that he had broken a "strike" of Negroes on a Bostonian's plantation at a crucial time in the crop year; he forced the Negroes to work under his surveillance, and he established a work-quota which the freedmen would have to meet if they were to get their wages.[76] On another plantation he sent troops to effect its restoration to its white owner. The planter accompanied the Union soldiers and, to Cornelius' satisfaction, offered "liberal" contracts to the dispossessed freedmen.[77]

At most, all the Freedmen's Bureau could claim rightly was that it introduced ameliorating factors into the regulation that was in effect over Negro farm workers. Commissioner Howard's proclamation in December 1866 of his advocacy of free labor as if it were an equal substitute for his efforts of a year earlier to make self-sufficient farmers of the freedmen shows how glibly the freedmen's hopes could be traded away.[78]

The Bureau struggled in nonagricultural areas too in order to serve free labor concepts. For over a year Howard contemplated the value to the freedmen and to his rich friends of establishing camps for destitute ex-agricultural workers, who would move west where their labor was needed to build the nation's growing railroad lines. He had discussed with Anson Blake, an associate of General John Adams Dix, the possibility of hiring the freedmen, paying half in wages, and giving them the balance in land—forty acres a year for four years—out of the government allotment to the railroad.[79] This did not materialize, but in December 1866, with no such provision for land, General Howard arranged for a crew of freedmen to be delivered as road gangs to his old friend, Confederate Colonel Samuel Tate, and

76. J. E. Cornelius to H. W. Smith, 1 July 1866, BRFAL.
77. Ibid.
78. O. O. Howard to E. O. C. Ord, 29 Dec. 1866, BRFAL.
79. O. O. Howard to Anson Blake, 15 July 1865, BRFAL; Anson Blake to O. O. Howard, 18 July 1865, OOH Papers.

other railroad men in Memphis, including Nathan Bedford
Forrest.[80] Howard felt nervous, as well he might, about the
arrangements and personally wrote to General Ord, Arkansas
assistant commissioner, asking him to provide a "capable discreet
officer," who could look after the freedmen who would be working on the Memphis and Little Rock line. Howard had interviewed Forrest, he told Ord, and was "of the opinion that he
[Forrest] is disposed to do everything that is fair and right for
the Negroes which might be employed."[81]

General Forrest, founder of the Ku Klux Klan, which was
organized in 1866, was the Confederate cavalryman who mas-
sacred Negro war prisoners at Fort Pillow. Now he was a businessman, and Howard judged him honorable. He entrusted the
freedmen to him. In Howard's defense, if one can be made for
this action, it might be said that the workers were destitute, and
the Commissioner did express anxiously to Ord his hope that
they could earn enough to buy permanent homes in Arkansas to
settle down. Howard's justification for dispatching crews from
the East was his "desire to do all in my power to facilitate free
labor in the South and at the same time to use the Bureau to its
utmost extent to protect the freedmen in all their rights and
interest."[82]

Some of the freedmen did not work on the railroad for long.
Trouble came from those who thought that Negroes should not
have even the pleasure of working under contract to General
Forrest. White workers wanted these jobs. In January 1867,
Howard reported to Stanton that "negroes who had been in the
Union army were shot down or driven off while employed along
the line of the Mississippi Central and Mobile and Ohio Railroads, so that it is unsafe to employ that class of hands."[83] The
freedmen were blocked from entry into even this unpromising
area of industrial labor.

80. F. D. Sewall to Samuel Tate, et al., 26 Dec. 1866, BRFAL.
81. O. O. Howard to N. B. Forrest, 15 Dec. 1866; O. O. Howard to
E. O. C. Ord, 29 Dec. 1866, BRFAL.
82. O. O. Howard to E. O. C. Ord, 29 Dec. 1866, BRFAL.
83. O. O. Howard to E. M. Stanton, 19 Jan. 1867, BRFAL.

The Negroes were never free from want. There was starvation to fight again the next winter and the winter after that. In February 1868, Commissioner Howard wrote to Orlando Brown in Richmond: "I fear that during this weather you have not so systematized your work as to relieve want extensively." He ordered Brown, the Connecticut doctor, to establish four soup houses, which should be placed "in retired position if you can get such, and have the most energetic, humane and able officer you have in charge of the work. Richmond is now inspected by the world . . . therefore policy as well as humanity urges upon you the most thorough and effective system." Howard told him that cheap meat could be gotten if "necessary to make the desiccated vegetable and potato soup 'good.'. . . Please [do] not spare any pains in caring for the poor in these terrible days," he continued.[84] Further, Howard stressed that the poor should not wait for their soup in the streets, where they would be seen. "It occasions remarks of every kind for and against the colored people. I have arranged it here [in Washington] so as to prevent that terrible spectacle."

The famine and the continuous hardship of many freedmen posed a constant dilemma for the Commissioner. Howard's concept of elevating the freedmen was forced to yield priority to the necessity of keeping them alive. And yet, to force the Negroes to put themselves at the mercy of their former owners without even a Freedmen's Bureau to protect them, as Fullerton wanted, was unsafe. As he entered the agency's last year of full operation, Howard summarized the problems his clients faced: "They [the planters] are trying to reduce the price of labor to board merely, to get control of those who are impoverished, and to check or hinder the exercise of the rights of the [workers] as citizens."[85]

Howard's solution to the dilemma was, by bending to all their demands, to buy the planters' commitment to some standard of fairness in their relations with their workers. He did not dare risk upsetting the economic apple cart, which the famines had

84. O. O. Howard to Orlando Brown, 7 Feb. 1868, BRFAL.
85. O. O. Howard to U. S. Grant, 2 Jan. 1868, BRFAL.

proved unsteady. But by serving the planters' interests as he continually did, he risked losing the support of the freedmen who wanted something much more out of freedom. The Negroes learned from bitter experience, when lands were denied them at Christmas 1865, that they could not count on promises. They would have to win the government to their cause by themselves; as Thomas Conway, who understood, said it:

> They have one idea which underlies every other, and that is, that notwithstanding the treatment they receive at the hands of the government . . . they believe it will yet secure them full protection, full liberty, and a full enjoyment of all their rights as citizens and men; and they are working very energetically in Louisiana for that purpose.[86]

86. *Report of the Joint Committee on Reconstruction,* pt. 4, p. 84.

13. Civil Rights and Riots

Senate 60 fell before a veto but its twin, Senate 61, the Civil Rights Act of 1866 survived.[1] The measures, as conceived by Lyman Trumbull, were designed to complement each other. Both were intended to enforce the Thirteenth Amendment, and the Freedmen's Bureau was expected to be the federal agency that would oversee the enforcement of the federally guaranteed rights in Senate 61. The full explication of the effect of the Thirteenth Amendment (which has been so overshadowed by the attention paid the Fourteenth) and the shifting definition of the Negroes' right to justice during Presidential Reconstruction lies outside the scope of this inquiry, but in order to understand the Freedmen's Bureau, General Howard's role in the implementation of the Civil Rights Bill must be explained.

The Bureau had been involved in adjudicating disputes between Negroes and whites since the agency was established.[2] The agents, informally, tried to negotiate a settlement, but if the matter was grave, they had recourse to the military provost courts. Howard's three-man courts were started in Virginia in September 1865 to handle minor legal disputes (as well as to settle contract quarrels).[3] The Commissioner counted heavily on the reopening of civil courts in the states to give the Negroes justice. In this, he was disappointed.

As soon as the states were reorganized and the courts reestablished, there was a systematic denial of the processes of justice to

1. Lyman Trumbull's brilliant speech in his bill's defense prior to the overriding of the veto temporarily made him the somewhat uneasy hero of America's freedmen and their equalitarian friends. Alfred H. Love to Lyman Trumbull, 5 Apr., L. F. Clark to Lyman Trumbull, 6 Apr., Emmet Hepburn to Lyman Trumbull, 7 Apr. 1866, Trumbull Papers, LC.
2. Bentley, *Freedmen's Bureau*, p. 152.
3. Howard, *Autobiography*, 2, 252.

the freedmen.[4] Congress sought to meet this problem with the Civil Rights Bill of 1866, which declared that the freedmen

> shall have the same right, in every State . . . to make and enforce contracts, to sue, to be parties and give evidence, to inherit, purchase, lease, sell, hold, and convey real and personal property, and to the full and equal benefit of all laws and proceedings for the security of person and property, as is enjoyed by white citizens.[5]

General Howard's Bureau, deprived of moral support by both the President's veto and Congress' failure to override the veto, borrowed some of the Civil Rights Bill's prestige. Since this legislation empowered the Bureau to enforce it, Howard eagerly put his agents to the task. The Commissioner directly concerned himself with the constitutionality and scope of the bill in July 1866, when he released to the press a statement approving a ruling by Chief Justice Bowie of the Maryland Court of Appeals, which held the bill constitutional and permitted the detention of a white man on the complaint of a Negro woman. The testimony of Negro witnesses was accepted in the case in which "Dr. A. H. Somers (white)" was accused of a "brutal and unprovoked assault on Hilliary Powell (colored)."[6] Howard followed the Civil Rights cases closely. From the *New York Tribune* he clipped the story of a Negro from Portland, Maine, who, while teaching in the South, brought legal action under the bill.[7] There were clippings too from the Negro newspapers, which he read regularly; he thought it essential that litigation of all sorts be brought to prove the bill of genuine worth to the freedmen. He had his agents distribute copies of the bill and urged Negroes to "wade through persecution and trial" to test the law.[8]

4. Bentley, p. 157.

5. John W. Burgess, *Reconstruction and the Constitution, 1866–1876* (New York, 1902), p. 68.

6. Washington *Evening Star,* 10 July 1866; *Washington Daily Morning Chronicle,* 11 July 1866; *Report of the Commissioner* (1866), p. 22.

7. *New York Tribune,* 18 July 1866, clipping in OOH Papers.

8. O. O. Howard to R. S. Turner, 29 June 1866, BRFAL.

The risk of the Civil Rights Act was that it could be used as an excuse for not giving the Negroes justice. Good laws could "render [the freedmen's] citizenship a mere abstraction," General Howard warned in November 1866.[9] Earlier that year, John C. Robinson, one of Whittlesey's successors as assistant commissioner for North Carolina, recommended that the state courts be given full jurisdiction over cases involving freedmen, because state laws forbidding Negro usage of the courts had been repealed and the federal Civil Rights Act had been enacted.[10] Neither state nor national legislative acts, on which Robinson was relying, insured, simply by their existence, that Bureau intervention was no longer needed. Robinson discovered this in the fall of 1866 and wrote to Howard in Washington asking what he should do about children who were being bound out by their parents. Such bonded servitude was involuntary for both parents and apprenticed children, if, as alleged, the parents were acting under intimidation. Howard, aware of that problem, answered Robinson:

> Even if the state-law makes no distinction of race or color, the practice or custom does. Please study the provisions of the Civil Rights Bill . . . and take such action as may be necessary to protect these poor people against the iniquitous practices. . . . Get the best legal advice you can in the country, if you yourself are at a loss what to do.[11]

Howard himself was at a loss. He was deeply concerned about impressment in the guise of legal apprenticing not only in North Carolina but elsewhere, particularly in Maryland. Howard was in closer contact than Robinson with lawyers of the sort he was recommending; he had just been staying with A. P. Ketchum's father, Edgar Ketchum, a powerful and able New York lawyer, and he had connections with others in Baltimore and Philadelphia. One of O. O. Howard's failings as Commissioner was his

9. *Report of the Commissioner* (1866), p. 14.
10. Washington *Evening Star*, 13 July 1866.
11. O. O. Howard to J. C. Robinson, 21 Nov. 1866, BRFAL.

inability to command these resources, which he clearly under-
stood were needed. Although Federal District Judges Hugh L.
Bond and John G. Underwood, Associate Justice Noah Swayne,
Wager Swayne's father, and Chief Justice Chase of the Supreme
Court were engaged in extending the scope of the Civil Rights
Bill to reach just such incidents as the one troubling Robinson,
other judges in southern courts were just as actively dismissing
suits brought under the Civil Rights Bill.[12]

Competent lawyers were essential if the bill was to be as
useful as it needed to be. It was asking the impossible for the
Freedmen's Bureau, with its nonlegal staff, to be both the
NAACP Legal Defense and Education Fund and the Department of Justice. And yet it tried. Later, when civil courts were
resumed in Virginia, bureau agents were available one day each
month when court was held in their county to serve as the
Negroes' advocates, or at least ensure that cases were heard.[13]

The Bureau did obtain regular legal service for some freedmen. Although Commissioner Howard told his friend Judge
Bond that the Bureau could not properly pay a privately engaged
lawyer, he did permit Edgar Gregory to hire a lawyer for the
freedmen in Maryland.[14] In the District of Columbia, in August
and September 1866, the firm of Browne and Smithers handled
115 civil cases and 88 criminal cases for freedmen, all presumably at government expense.[15] This was an important precedent for government assistance for disadvantaged defendants,
but it did not solve the problems of thousands of Negroes unable
to make effective use of the courts in the South.

The constitutionality of the Bureau's judicial activities had
been in jeopardy since April 3, 1866, when the Supreme Court

12. O. O. Howard to R. S. Turner, 29 June 1866, BRFAL; S. P. Chase
to J. C. Underwood, 10 June 1866, Underwood Papers, LC.; Charles Warren,
The Supreme Court in United States History (2 vols. Boston, 1926), 2,
600 n; O. O. Howard to E. M. Stanton, 21 Dec. 1866, BRFAL.

13. Alderson, "Influence of Military Rule and the Freedmen's Bureau in
Virginia," p. 92.

14. O. O. Howard to Hugh L. Bond, 11 Mar. 1867, BRFAL.

15. O. O. Howard, *Report of the Commissioner* (1866), p. 23.

ruled in a case having nothing to do with Negroes directly. As a result of *ex parte Milligan,* the trial of civilians before a military commission during wartime was held unconstitutional by the Supreme Court if the military court met at a point remote from where the war was being fought.[16] This libertarian decision imperiled the liberty of Negroes in the South. If conditions of war, rather than the freedmen's inability to get a fair trial in other courts, were to be requisite for bureau courts, then the bureau's judicial activities, like so many other services would be stopped.

The original bureau bill authorized bureau courts where no other courts existed or where local laws, such as proscription of Negro testimony, prevented freedmen from obtaining justice. The Act of July 16, 1866, taking cognizance of the Milligan decision, which made war a requisite for military trials for civilians, ordered bureau courts continued whenever conditions of "rebellion" existed.[17] Congress reinforced this provision in the Civil Rights Bill of 1866 and instructed the bureau agents to serve as marshals and justices of the peace. A week after Congress acted, Absalom Baird circulated an order from the War Department instructing his group in Louisiana to "arrest, detain & bring to trial without regard to color cases where civil law has, failed to administer justice."[18]

Bureau courts, which had been discontinued everywhere except Texas when civil courts reopened, were now brought back. In Virginia, in December 1866, General John M. Schofield, the assistant commissioner, remanded to one of these military tribunals the case of Dr. James Watson, a white man tried in a civil court for murder of a Negro and acquitted. Howard "rejoiced" at Schofield's move: "It is better to test the law [the Act of July 16, 1866] *now,* and if it is not sound Congress will make it so."[19] The President strongly disagreed and, under his proclamation of

16. *Ex parte Milligan,* 4 Wallace 2.
17. Burgess, p. 88.
18. Washington *Evening Star,* 23 July 1866; O. O. Howard, *Report of the Commissioner* (1866), p. 14.
19. O. O. Howard to John M. Schofield, 10 Dec. 1866, BRFAL.

April 2, 1866 restoring the writ of habeus corpus to the South, the bureau court, which was to retry Watson, was served with a writ, in the doctor's behalf. When Schofield refused to honor the writ, Johnson, by executive order, dismissed the military commission and freed Watson.[20]

Johnson's action was not challenged in the Supreme Court, and the status of federal courts (which might rule in favor of freedmen) did not end with the freeing of Watson. In January Howard complained to Stanton about the difficulty in getting Civil Rights Bill cases transferred from the local courts into the federal district courts, and he made another attempt to reestablish in all states the jurisdiction of the bureau courts in matters of local justice. [21] On January 30, 1867, the Commissioner sent a letter to all of his assistant commissioners asking them to test the Milligan decision to see if it reached far enough to invalidate the bureau courts recreated by the Act of July 16, 1866. The assistant commissioners were to find a local judge who would grant a writ of habeas corpus to a white defendant in a case heard in a bureau court. The Bureau would then contest the issuance of the writ before the Supreme Court. Howard told his men that he understood "the judges, or some of them . . . in Milligan . . . had no idea if it would apply in the states not yet represented in Congress. I should like to test Section 14 of the Bureau Law passed July 16, 1866."[22] This last was the clause instructing bureau agents to implement the Civil Rights' Bill.

The test was never effected. Congress, using the rejection of the Fourteenth Amendment by the Johnsonian legislatures in

20. Alderson, p. 132; Hamilton J. Eckenrode, *The Political History of Virginia Reconstruction* (Baltimore, 1904), pp. 50–51.

21. O. O. Howard to E. M. Stanton, 19 Jan. 1867, BRFAL.

22. O. O. Howard to Wager Swayne, et al., 30 Jan. 1867, BRFAL. These letters, possibly not written by a lawyer, but drawn in a hand other than that of a regular bureau clerk, suggest consultations by the Commissioner outside the Bureau. Stanton's, Townsend's, Chase's, and Underwood's letter books did not suggest an answer as to who helped Howard. Chief Justice Chase and Associate Justices Swayne, Miller, and Wayne dissented, and Justice Davis, who wrote the Milligan decision, was reported dismayed by the use Johnson made of it in the South. Warren, 2, 426, 444, 445 n.

the South as their justification, passed, beginning in March 1867, the Military Reconstruction Acts, assigning to army men the function of the Freedmen's Bureau, including the holding of military commissions if local laws did not afford the Negroes fair access to the courts. That law met the Milligan decision squarely and instructed the federal courts to sustain the use of army courts for civilians in the South.[23]

The Bureau neither ended the threat of starvation nor obtained punishment of individual men who murdered Negroes; in still another area of fundamental importance—in which the lives of freedmen were at stake—Howard's agency failed its clients. In the spring and summer of 1866 the Freedmen's Bureau proved itself unable to prevent or even to end swiftly, once they had started, major acts of lawlessness in which the safety of the whole Negro community was violated in two of the largest cities of the South. The Memphis Riot on the first three days of May 1866 and the New Orleans Riot of July 30 proved fatal to the basic concept of the Freedmen's Bureau's role in interracial relations in the South.

Street fighting between whites and blacks, which ended far more bloodily for the Negroes involved, was a Yankee contribution to racial conflict. Slavery had permitted of no events in the South like the brutal Draft Riots in New York City in 1863. Two weeks after the Grand Review, celebrating the Civil War's emancipation of the Negro slaves, Union troops of General Hancock's Fifteenth Corps clashed with black residents of Washington, D.C., in a nasty street fight.[24] In July 1865 in Charleston, South Carolina, a group of soldiers in the New York Zouave regiment stationed in the city got into a vicious quarrel with other Union Army soldiers, Negroes of the old Third South Carolina.[25] The white South Carolinians were not slow at learning; a year later, in June and July 1866, there were repeated

23. Burgess, pp. 112–13.
24. *Philadelphia Inquirer*, 12 June 1865.
25. Williamson, *After Slavery*, p. 258.

clashes in the streets of Charleston. Now the antagonists—black and white—were local citizens. Joel Williamson has suggested that the "political content" of black-white riots came only with "political elevation" of the Negro.[26] He is wrong if he refers only to the period after the Negro got the vote. The 1866 riots, which occurred because Negroes were asserting themselves and white men were determined that no elevation take place, were quite as political as any later clash. William Alderson, referring to a fight in Norfolk, Virginia, on April 16, 1866, in which three white men and two Negroes were killed, makes a direct connection between that clash and the fact that the Negroes involved were celebrating the passage of the Civil Rights Bill.[27]

On Saturday night, July 8, 1866, in the market area of Charleston, "swaggering" Negro soldiers were involved in a street fight and so were the police of the city. In this Charleston battle, in which a policeman and two Negroes were badly wounded, the Negroes were pursued to the Freedmen's Bureau headquarters, where they were protected.[28] The Bureau in Charleston was still a haven, but the participation of the police and the representatives of the civil government on the other side was reminiscent of a far bloodier event in Tennessee two months earlier.

On Tuesday afternoon May 1, 1866, a group of Negro soldiers just mustered out of service at Fort Pickering in Memphis, using their pay to celebrate, were drinking in a grocery store, which doubled as a saloon. A block away the police arrested a Negro and started back to the station house with him. The arrest troubled the neighborhood and word quickly reached the grocer's. The soldiers, joining the Negroes in the street, overtook the police and freed the prisoner.[29]

26. Ibid.

27. Alderson, p. 87.

28. *Washington Daily Morning Chronicle*, 10 July 1866.

29. *Memphis Riots and Massacres*, Report of the Select Committee, 39th Cong., 1st sess., House Report 101 (serial 1274); Paul D. Phillips, "A History of the Freedmen's Bureau in Tennessee," Unpublished Ph.D. dissertation (Vanderbilt University, 1964), pp. 280–91.

Heroes to the people on the block, the men then returned to their celebration. About an hour later a detachment of police arrived and arrested two of the more ambitious drinkers. As they were being escorted away, an even bigger crowd of Negroes pursued the police yelling at them in a menacing tone to release the men. One of the Negro soldiers fired his pistol; one of the policemen fired his. A hand-to-hand battle ensued, and the pistols were not neglected; a white policeman and a Negro soldier were killed.[30]

John C. Creighton, the city recorder, was riding through town in his buggy. He heard the noise of the riot and, in great excitement, stopped to pick up T. M. Winters, the sheriff, and told him that the Negroes had shot a policeman. They rode straight to the headquarters of General George Stoneman, the military commander, and requested that the general suppress the Negroes. Stoneman reminded the Sheriff and the Recorder that they were among those who opposed the army's interference in civil matters, and told Winters to get a posse.[31]

In the early evening the streets were full of people, many of whom called on the mayor, John Park, to do something about the unruly mob of Negroes. Park had been mayor both before the war and after the Union forces secured Memphis. He was an Irishman and a Unionist; with remarkable unanimity witnesses who testified about the events of Tuesday and the two bloody days that followed wrote him off as too drunk to be effective.[32]

Mayor Park did take one important step in the early evening of May 1. He wrote a short note to General Stoneman, whose forces consisted of 150 men and officers of the Sixteenth Regular Infantry, plus about 150 discharged Negro soldiers.[33] Park asked Stoneman to lend "cooperation with the civil police in suppressing all disturbances of the peace." He further requested 200 sol-

30. *Memphis Riots,* p. 104.

31. Ibid., p. 80.

32. See particularly testimony of City Registrar Lewis P. Richardson, ibid., p. 210.

33. Ibid., p. 50.

diers (he did not have to say that he had white soldiers in mind) "commanded by discreet officers to be held ready . . . in case of further continued lawlessness."[34] Stoneman, a "distinguished" soldier and "one of the most 'conservative' officers of the regular army," replied to the Mayor that he "should prefer that the troops be called upon only in the case of an extreme necessity, of which you must be the judge."[35] Stoneman had washed his hands; the Mayor and the Sheriff were on their own.

The head of the Freedmen's Bureau in Memphis was General Benjamin P. Runkle. He first encountered the riot as "I was coming out of my office" at the end of the day "talking with one of my officers about the success we had had in carrying out General Fisk's order relative to vagrants."[36] Runkle was referring to Clinton B. Fisk's Circular 9, which dealt with the persistent problem of refugee Negroes; people like those, whom John Eaton Jr. and Samuel Thomas had remembered, huddled so pathetically on street corners of the city during the war.[37] Runkle was proud of the Negroes for having whitewashed their huts, as the Circular required, and for having established their own Sanitary Commission. Their industriousness was commendable. They had raised $2,000 and had given it to the Bureau to pay for the care of "their own poor." Said Runkle, "I . . . had begun to congratulate myself that I could see day light in the city of Memphis."[38]

Having no men in his command, however, Runkle was unable to carry out conclusively the vagrancy clause in Fisk's Circular. Although many unemployed Negroes had "gone into the country,"[39] more of them still hoped for jobs in the city and freedom from plantation discipline. The vagrancy policy was designed to

34. John Park to George Stoneman, 1 May 1866, quoted in ibid., p. 51.

35. Elihu Washburne, chairman of the Select Committee, in his summary, ibid., p. 29; George Stoneman to John Park, 1 May 1866, quoted in ibid., p. 50.

36. Ibid., p. 275.

37. Ibid., p. 276.

38. Ibid., p. 275.

39. Ibid.

prevent the white citizens from feeling alarmed with unemployed Negroes loose in the city. As Runkle walked home that evening, he was troubled seeing white men riding on horseback into the city and crowds milling in the streets of the white part of town.

The cry of the night was: "The niggers . . . are going to take Memphis."[40] Judge Creighton, a member of the "conservative" Johnson Club, was quoted as rallying the forces of defense: "Boys . . . kill the last damned one of the nigger race, and burn the cradle."[41] White Memphis citizens invaded South Memphis, the black side of the town. They stole—"tell the Freedmen's Bureau in the morning," they yelled derisively when the owners protested—women were raped, and ninety-one of the ramshackle houses in which the Negroes lived were burned as were four of their churches and twelve of their schools.[42] Residents were killed, savagely. In case after case, survivors knew their attackers by name and were not at all surprised that many of them were on the city police force or in the fire department. One woman, Emma Lane, whose two-and-one-half-year-old child was shot (and "looked just as though she had been dipped in a tub of blood"), said of three of the assailants, "they belong to No. 7 engine"; a fourth "was a policeman."[43]

The morning did not bring calm. Attacks on the Negroes continued. Bureau Superintendent Runkle reported that "the freedmen began to come by dozens and by hundreds to my headquarters for protection. I could do nothing for them, for I had not a soldier at my command. I went down and asked General Stoneman if he would not give me troops under my personal command, to go down and protect these people." Stoneman had just sent out two patrols, but he told Runkle that "he had not

40. Ibid., p. 12.
41. Ibid., p. 355; Jack D. L. Holmes, "The Underlying Causes of the Memphis Race Riot of 1866," *Tennessee Historical Quarterly, 18* (1958), 195–221.
42. *Memphis Riots*, p. 22; Gerald M. Capers, Jr., *The Biography of a River Town* (Chapel Hill, 1939), p. 178.
43. Capers, p. 221.

many troops, and that he had a large amount of public property to guard; that a considerable part of the troops he had were not reliable; that they hated Negroes too."[44]

On Wednesday night Runkle and several freedmen barricaded themselves in the bureau headquarters expecting the mob in the streets to attack. They were threatened but the building was not destroyed. The Negro troops, who had returned to their army base, Fort Pickering, were also surrounded by a hostile crowd.[45] On Thursday, with South Memphis in a state of terror, the anti-negro forces focused on the center of the city. "Now let's clean out that damned Freedmen's Bureau"[46] was the cry, and there were also threats of burning the building of John Eaton's radical *Memphis Post*.[47] General Stoneman, surveying the carnage, finally decided that he should act. On Thursday, May 3, he sent troops into the city, their color unspecified in the press, declared martial law, and prohibited assemblies of either blacks or whites.[48] The Memphis riot was over. The Sheriff, anxious to minimize his responsibility, said "I never did see but one man killed and one wounded." The official record lists forty-six Negroes dead (including two children and three women), and two white men dead (one a policeman and the other a fireman).[49] Elihu Washburne, the chairman of the congressional committee that investigated, said that "a large number were killed whose names are not known" and likened the attack on the Negroes to the massacre of Negro prisoners at Fort Pillow during the war.[50]

The argument over who fired the first shot may never be settled; of much more consequence is to ask why, once started, it was not stopped. The dissenting member of the Congressional Investigating Committee, Congressman G. S. Shanklin of Ken-

44. Ibid., p. 275.
45. *Memphis Riots,* p. 275.
46. Ibid., p. 276.
47. Ibid.
48. George Stoneman's order of 3 May 1865, quoted in *Memphis Riots,* p. 52.
49. Ibid., p. 35.
50. Elihu Washburne, quoted in ibid.

tucky, recognized that the city officials did not end the attack and, not even attempting to refute the charges that city officials actively participated in the riots, he blamed the disfranchisement of rebels for the incumbency of city administrators of such low caliber.[51]

Shanklin did not mention that John Park had been mayor before the war, when no such disfranchisement existed. He claimed that the "governing class of a higher grade of society" did try to assert itself when the riot began. A group of "intelligent, cultivated . . . active and efficient businessmen" asked General Stoneman to put them in command of a detachment of his soldiers to suppress the mob. Shanklin reported that when Stoneman declined the gentlemen concluded that it would be "improper" for them to interfere further.[52] A modern scholar, Paul Phillips, reports that rather than trying to influence the Mayor or any other local officials to stop the killings, the governing class simply "remained in their homes."[53] Like Shanklin, Phillips implies but does not say that these leaders were not entirely unwilling to see the Negroes taught the painful lesson that they could expect to suffer if the "better classes of society" of the city were kept from political power.[54]

For the Johnsonian Congressman, Shanklin, the lesson was that "the most certain and quickest practicable mode to guard against a repetition of the Memphis tragedy" was to restore to political power those who had lost it because of participation in the rebellion. (Later in the summer of 1866, events in New Orleans were to prove that this was not necessarily a sure way to prevent a riot.) To restore "harmony," Shanklin wanted the military removed from the South and "above all, the Freedmen's Bureau, the manufacturer of paupers and vagabonds, the fruitful source of strife, vice, and crime, dispensed with."[55]

51. Ibid., pp. 37–44.
52. Ibid., p. 42.
53. Phillips, "Freedmen's Bureau in Tennessee," p. 287.
54. *Memphis Riots*, p. 42.
55. Ibid., p. 44.

Chairman Elihu Washburne in his majority report spent little time attacking the leadership group's involvement, or lack of it. Instead he focused his report on the savage quality of the killings of the freedmen.[56] If it was sensational, it was also well documented. The published journal containing the testimony of scores of witnesses to the events of the three days is eloquent in its simple, strong detail.[57]

The battle was between unequal forces. After the first fighting, the Negro residents who fought did so only in defense when they and their families were attacked. With great relief, Washburne reported that the Negro soldiers, so bold on the first day, remained in Fort Pickering in "the most complete subordination . . . although they had been in point of fact mustered out of the service."[58] As the Chairman put it, the "behavior of these colored men under the trying circumstances in which they were placed, seeing their families murdered and their dwellings burned, was such to extort admiration from all the officers of the fort."[59] However ugly the riot had been, it did not produce an armed uprising by the Negroes. General Stoneman, not using his white troops for fear they might join the attack on the Negroes, had been even more determined to avoid engaging black soldiers in any endeavor to stop the riot.

The villains of the riot in Washburne's report, as in most others, were the Irish immigrants, an alien strand of poor white trash.[60] It is clear from the testimony of witnesses that many of the killers were Irish although one Mary Grady made it plain that dislike of Negroes was not a congenital failing of her race.[61] To point out, as General Runkle did, the economic antagonism between the Irish and the other immigrants, the country Negroes who came into the city, is not to explain why it was expressed in wanton killings.[62] Neither group was new to Memphis in

56. Ibid., pp. 1–36.
57. Ibid., pp. 45–313.
58. Ibid., p. 32.
59. Ibid., p. 31.
60. For example, see Capers, p. 178.
61. *Memphis Riots,* pp. 186–88.
62. Ibid., p. 276.

1866, and other outside agitators—Bureau personnel, northern teachers in the Negro schools, and racial newspaper editors— did not by their abrasive presence make mass killings "almost inevitable."[63]

When a street brawl broke out, the city government, rather than controlling the outbreak, ceased to govern. Important to explaining the Memphis riot was not that John Park was Irish but that he was the mayor and, as the mayor, ineffective in curbing the riot in which members of his administration, including Judge Creighton, participated. As Congressman Washburne pointed out, the performance of these officials was a strong indictment of the governments to which President Johnson had entrusted the South.

Washburne felt that the events in Memphis were the result of Jefferson Davis' prophecy: "the principle for which we contended [in the war] is bound to reassert itself . . . at another time, and in another form."[64] As the *Memphis Avalanche,* expressed it: "The late riots in our city have satisfied all of one thing: that the southern men will not be ruled by the negro." The paper's editorial, three days after the riot, emphasized that "the negroes now know, to their sorrow, that it is best not to arouse the fury of the white man. . . . The negro population will now do their [sic] duty. Already we hear of many in South Memphis seeking houses in the country. . . . It is a good sign. . . . The country farmers need their labor"[65] The *Avalanche* concluded:

> Thank Heaven the white race are [sic] once more rulers in Memphis. In this connection let our people pay a just and merited respect to Major General Stoneman. . . . He has really had to fear that just here, under his immediate eye, would be commenced a war of races. Gradually he has been reducing the negro force here. . . . He knows the wants of the country, and sees the negro can do the country more good in the cotton fields than in the camp."[66]

63. Holmes, "Underlying Causes of the Race Riot," p. 221.
64. Davis quoted by Washburne, *Memphis Riots,* p. 32.
65. *Memphis Avalanche,* 5 May 1866, quoted in ibid., p. 334.
66. Ibid.

Memphis extremists had waited until all but a squad of Negro troops had been mustered out and, counting on the northern uneasiness over the danger of the black troops starting an armed uprising, they moved against South Memphis confident that the federal government would not use troops to stop them. Their gamble paid off.

The Freedmen's Bureau had proved its bankruptcy to both sides. Benjamin Runkle was heir to the post in which Davis Tillson had done so efficient a job in restoring a firm agricultural labor system.[67] Unluckily for the advocates of stability, the conditions on the cotton plantations were such that the Memphis Negroes resisted relocation, preferring to ignore available jobs in the country while competing for work in the city.[68] Fisk and Runkle's vagrancy policy had not submerged the urban Negroes to the satisfaction of white Memphis.[69] On the other side, the freedmen of Memphis "lost all confidence" in the Bureau after the riot. "They will not heed my counsel," reported General Runkle. He told of black men coming up to him and saying with great sadness, "you are the man we expected to protect us."[70]

In New Orleans at the end of July, there was another racial clash of great violence. Again it occurred when Negroes asserted themselves in their own cause. Here they sought political power and, as in Memphis, their white opponents were unrestricted in their efforts to halt them.

The politically active Negroes of New Orleans and their white allies were divided into two camps. The one led by Thomas Jefferson Durant and the leading Creoles de couleur, including the proprietors of the *New Orleans Tribune,* thought that Congress alone could effect the reforms that Negro Louisianans demanded.[71] They opposed as too dangerous the other party's

67. Taylor, *The Negro in Tennessee,* pp. 14–15.

68. Holmes, p. 222.

69. William Alderson, writing of Virginia, also found the cities to be the center of the Negro assertion of his rights ("Influence of Military Rule and the Freedmen's Bureau in Virginia," p. 124).

70. *Memphis Riots,* p. 276.

71. Rodolphe L. Desdunes, *Nos Hommes et Notre Histoire* (Montreal, 1911), p. 173.

attempt to bring about these radical reforms locally by recon-
vening the Convention of 1864 to amend the state's constitution.

The localists would not be dissuaded and, after rounds of ex-
traparliamentary maneuvers, which even the adroit ratifiers of
the federal Constitution might have envied, they succeeded in
calling the convention for the morning of July 30, 1866. A
parade of Negro workmen, demonstrating for the vote that they
hoped the convention would grant them, was stopped in front
of the Mechanics Institute, where the convention was being held,
by a crowd of white opponents. There was a fight in the street,
which was interrupted by the arrival of the city's police force
augmented by volunteers, who entered the Institute and forced
the door of the meeting room. Shots from the street below were
fired into the windows of the room and, as the delegates and
Negro spectators tried to escape through the door, they were
clubbed and shot. By official count, 48 men were killed and
166 wounded.[72]

The assistant commissioner of the Freedmen's Bureau, Absalom Baird, had feared just such violence.[73] The convention met
on Monday, and on the previous Saturday he heard about both
the Negro mass meetings of the night before, which the fiery
equalitarian Dr. Anthony Dostie addressed, and the street fight
that followed.[74] That Saturday morning Mayor John Monroe
of New Orleans and Lieutenant Governor Albert Voorhies of
Louisiana called on Baird and told him that they intended to send
the police to disperse the convention by arresting the delegates.
Troubled by the sound of this, Baird wired Secretary of War
Stanton to tell him that he would not permit this unless he received orders to the contrary from the President. He requested
an immediate reply.[75]

Stanton told Howard about the telegram but not the President, and for this reason Johnson always blamed Stanton for

72. *New Orleans Riots.* Report of the Select Committee, 39th Cong., 2nd
sess., House Report 16 (serial 1304).

73. *New Orleans Tribune,* 1 Aug 1866, clipping in OOH Papers.

74. New Orleans *Daily Picayune,* 28 July 1866.

75. *New Orleans Riots,* p. 547.

what transpired in New Orleans. The War Department's records are distressingly barren of evidence on the thinking and action of the Secretary and the Commissioner over the weekend preceding the riot.[76] But carelessness was uncharacteristic of both men; Edwin Stanton once stayed in his telegrapher's office until the early hours of the morning to be sure that his orders were received in an imperative situation.[77] Inability to realize the gravity of a situation was not impossible to imagine in Howard but harder to credit in Stanton. In view of what transpired in Memphis, which had been thoroughly investigated, Stanton's negligence in allowing Baird to repeat Stoneman's error is difficult to excuse. Stanton let Baird's request go unanswered; not even its receipt was ever acknowledged.[78] Probably expecting a brawl with a few injuries the result, the leading cabinet opponent of the President's plan of Reconstruction concluded that such would be worthwhile to prove that the orderly Johnsonian governments in the South, claiming to govern the freedmen better than the national government, were incapable of keeping even basic order when the freedmen asserted themselves. The dispersion of peaceful and loyal citizens would be the President's fault.

One alternative explanation is that Stanton expected Howard and Baird, within the Bureau, to devise some way to keep the peace without Stanton having to defy the President directly. If this were the case, Howard disappointed Stanton, because Baird never received any reply to his telegram.

On Monday morning, July 30, Munroe and Voorhies again called on Baird, and they did have a telegram. On Saturday Voorhies had informed Johnson of the previous night's violence; he also told the President that it was his and Munroe's intention to send the police to enforce a Grand Jury injunction against the convention.[79] Johnson had replied: The military will be expected

76. One specific item missing is a letter "marked personal" from Baird, referred to by Howard.

77. To read a dramatic story of a stay of execution for a Negro in South Carolina ordered by Stanton, see 9–11 July 1867, AJ Papers.

78. *New Orleans Riots,* Report of the Board of Investigation, 39th Cong., 2nd sess., House Executive Document 69 (serial 1292), p. 102.

79. Albert Voorhies to Andrew Johnson, 28 July 1866, AJ Papers.

to sustain and not obstruct or interfere with the proceeding of the Court.[80] Voorhies and Munroe showed Baird the telegram and asked about his intentions.

Absalom Baird faced a dilemma. He was not only the assistant commissioner but also the senior military officer in the city, because the department commander, Philip H. Sheridan, was out of the state. Was Baird to consider the telegram as the presidential instruction he required before allowing the delegates to be arrested or did he have an overriding responsibility to his freedmen clients?

The problem illustrates the importance of the character of a man acting as an assistant commissioner of the Freedmen's Bureau. Thomas Conway would probably have met the first policeman at the door of the building ready to block his passage to the upstairs meeting room. James Scott Fullerton might well have equipped the chief of police with an order sustaining the arrests. Absalom Baird, Louisiana's third assistant commissioner, merely closeted himself in his office. Only when the news that men were being killed reached the Freedmen's Bureau did Baird summon his troops. But the attackers knew the soldiers were an hour outside the city; they arrived to find the fight over.

When General Sheridan got back to the sobered city, his reaction was refreshingly direct. Although he had no sympathy for the purposes of the convention, which he had termed "revolutionary," he still opposed what happened on July 30. It had not been a riot, he said, it had been a "massacre."[81] His judgment was sustained by a thorough investigation: congressmen listened to scores of witnesses describe the bloody day. It was clear from their testimony that, at the very least, Mayor Munroe had not done all he could to prevent violence. Munroe owed his seat at city hall to a pardon obtained from President Johnson. Albert Voorhies represented the majority in the state legislature, which acknowledged Johnson's political leadership. The men whom the President had restored to political power proved incapable and even unwilling to protect loyal citizens.

80. Andrew Johnson to Albert Voorhies, 28 July 1866, AJ Papers.
81. P. H. Sheridan to U. S. Grant, 2 Aug. 1866, AJ Papers.

The day of the riot Commisioner Howard was in Washington at his desk dictating routine correspondence. His first reaction, upon receiving news of the riot, was to save the Freedmen's Bureau and his position. When the newspapers criticized the agency, he sent a telegram to Baird: "For our sake will not General Sheridan send me a refuting telegram."[82] Already under the attack of the Steedman-Fullerton report, Howard undertook once again to appease the President. Three weeks later, with his reasonable reply to the Steedman-Fullerton charges under his arm, he called on the President for a long uneasy conversation.[83]

Howard found the President restive because of the severe criticism directed at him for the riot; he was eager to pass the blame on to Stanton for not having shown him the Baird telegram with its warning of violence. Johnson did not admit that Voorhies had warned him of this directly and Howard found the President "fierce on the subject of Baird."[84]

Baird had to be sacrificed; he was transferred to the Department of the Great Lakes.[85] Seeking to replace him, Howard did not ask what his responsibilities to the freedmen of New Orleans were. He did not use the riot as a weapon to build a Freedmen's Bureau that was truly responsible to the freedmen. He did not try to find a man who would have worked with the Negro community the way Thomas Conway and Rufus Saxton did. Instead, he pleaded with General Sheridan to accept the post of assistant commissioner as an adjunct to his military duties on the grounds that "neither radical nor Johnson men claim you."[86] Reluctantly Sheridan took it. Since his days at West Point, General Howard had thought the army the wrong place to find solutions to problems involving human values. Now he yielded the freedmen to

82. O. O. Howard to Absalom Baird, 8 Aug. 1866, BRFAL.

83. Washington *Evening Star,* 24 Aug. 1866; O. O. Howard to Andrew Johnson, 23 Aug. 1866, BRFAL.

84. O. O. Howard to J. R. Sypher of *New York Tribune,* 30 Aug. 1866, OOH Papers.

85. Washington *Evening Star,* 19 Sept. 1866.

86. O. O. Howard to P. H. Sheridan, 22 and 23 Aug., 15 Sept. 1866, BRFAL.

a military man. The Memphis and New Orleans riots led directly to Military Reconstruction.

The New Orleans riot made clear that the Freedmen's Bureau had ceased to govern. The freedmen of New Orleans, independently, had tried to participate in governing themselves without waiting for guidance or leadership from Absalom Baird. They learned painfully that the Freedmen's Bureau would not support them in this enterprise: "Let the Freedmen's Bureau go down," declared the *New Orleans Tribune*.[87] The bureau men, on the other hand, learned no lessons from the riot. When General Howard sought someone new for Louisiana, he did not even consider what his constituents looked for in an assistant commissioner. The consent of the governed had been taken for granted for so long that the freedmen who gave it had been forgotten.

87. *New Orleans Tribune*, 12 Aug. 1866.

14. "Ce Bureau n'est déjà qu'une chimère."

In the Fall of 1865 the *New Orleans Tribune,* the Negro newspaper, wrote off the Freedmen's Bureau as only an illusion. From
the start that excellent paper doubted the reality of the Freedmen's Bureau as a giver of the substance of freedom to the ex-
slaves. It considered the agency the lineal descendant of the Bureau of Freed Labor to which General Banks gave the wartime
task of disciplining the black labor force.[1]

Perhaps the *Tribune* abandoned too quickly its hopes for the
Freedmen's Bureau. Senate 60 and a sustained appropriation
might have made something solid and lasting of the national
effort to bring the freedmen into the nation. The editors, writing
before the Bureau got its own budget and its full staff of officers,
may have foreseen that the Bureau would amount to nothing.
Certainly they were ahead of the historians. General Howard's
biographer spoke of the Bureau's growth: "From modest beginnings in 1865, under his direction it grew by 1868 into a large
and influential organization."[2] This is what the General wanted
his contemporaries to think as well.

After Congress passed the Act of July 16, 1866, extending the
life of the Freedmen's Bureau, Howard began to strengthen it
as an organization. Generals Steedman and Fullerton had called
the Bureau lax; new efficient procedures would make it taut. To
effect this reform, Howard brought to Washington the able engi-
neer John Wilson Sprague from Arkansas, conservative Davis
Tillson from Georgia, Edgar Gregory, the former assistant commissioner for Texas, and a surprising voice of the past, Chaplain Mansfield French, who served the Port Royal experiment
on the Sea Islands and still hoped that somewhere separate colo-

1. *New Orleans Tribune,* 28 Oct. 1865.
2. Carpenter, *Sword and Olive Branch,* p. 91.

nies could be established—where the Negroes could work alone toward their slow elevation.[3]

These men constituted a committee that was to revise bureau procedures; John William De Forest, the novelist and journalist, was its secretary.[4] Howard sought to institutionalize and perfect; the spirit of the great wartime commissions was being called to work again. Howard was committed to make his agency endure. And so it did, with money and men and countless reports. (De Forest as an agent in South Carolina wrote wittily of the problem of reports that he had helped create.)[5]

One of the aims of the reorganization was to achieve more complete coverage of the South. Since the start of the agency, Howard was aware of the concentration of bureau personnel in places long under Union control, like the Sea Islands. Yet in vast regions of the South, most notably Texas, there was a virtual absence of agents.[6] This imbalance was somewhat corrected, but even at its peak the number of agents was only 901.[7] The hope Howard held in 1865—that every county of the South have its own agent—was never realized.[8]

Even more impressive than the efficient development of manpower was the grant of an appropriation to the Bureau. In July 1866—for the year ending June 30, 1867—Howard as mentioned was given $6,940,450. Relief supplies and hospital costs took $4,773,250 of the total. The second largest item in the nearly $7,000,000 budget, $1,300,000 for transporation, largely paid for relocating 29,460 destitute freedmen to jobs in other parts of the country.[9] Bureau administrative costs absorbed

3. Washington *Evening Star*, 26 July 1866; Max Woodhull to O. O. Howard, 24 Oct. 1865, BRFAL.

4. E. D. Townsend's order of 18 July 1866, J. W. DeForest Papers, Yale University.

5. J. W. DeForest, *A Union Officer in the Reconstruction*, eds. J. H. Croushore and D. M. Potter (New Haven, 1948), pp. 1, 39–42.

6. Howard, *Autobiography, 2,* 343.

7. Bentley, *Freedmen's Bureau*, p. 136.

8. S. L. Taggart to T. W. Conway, 7 Aug. 1865, BRFAL.

9. *Report of the Commissioner* (1869), p. 515; Howard, *Autobiography, 2,* 321.

$326,000. Another $500,000 was designated for the repair and rental of schools with $21,000 more for school superintendent salaries. Other than this school allotment, there was no appropriation for any experiments to reform the social structure. There was no implementation of Howard's plan for the government to purchase farmlands and to sell them on time to black farmers. But Howard did not abandon the idea. He continued to try to interest Congress in it, and with no results he was reduced to pleading, unsuccessfully, with private holders of capital to effect such land redistribution in the South.[10]

The bureau agents in the field, rather than being able to add new programs to their old endeavors—distributing relief supplies, hearing complaints from planters as well as freedmen, negotiating contracts, and giving legal advice—were given, instead, a new chore. To Howard's dismay, in March of 1867 the Bureau was instructed to take on the burden of paying bounties due to Negro soldiers who had enlisted in the war.[11] To determine whether or not the rightful claimant was being paid was a most difficult task, made even more so by professional claim agents like Howard's own stepbrother, who, for a fee often as large as the claim, pressed the Bureau to effect payments.[12]

A more constructive enterprise, engaged in by the bureau agents in the transition from Presidential to Radical Reconstruction, was the registration of Negro voters, who were authorized to vote by the Reconstruction Acts of 1867. In counties all across the South, bureau agents registered black men and white men as voters in their radically reconstructed states. In October John T. Sprague, no admirer of the Negroes, nevertheless complimented

10. O. O. Howard to S. F. Jaquess, 15 Jan. 1868; O. O. Howard to S. C. Pomeroy, 24 Mar. 1868, BRFAL.

11. Howard, *Autobiography, 2,* 354; *Report of the Commissioner* (1867), p. 622.

12. Ironically the last official letter Howard signed as commissioner was a reluctant order authorizing a bounty payment of a claim he obviously believed false: "The legal officers have decided against me, I . . . will raise no further objections to payment." With those words he closed the books on the Freedmen's Bureau (O. O. Howard to the Secretary of War [Belknap], 30 June 1872, BRFAL).

his agents on having registered 15,441 Negro voters and 11,151 white and on having "taken measure for their quiet instruction . . . in their rights and duties under the reconstruction acts."[13]

The registration was an invaluable prelude to the experiments that were to follow during Radical Reconstruction. It was also a symbol, read in different ways by foe and friend of the freedmen, of the Bureau's sympathy for the black man's cause. But it must be remembered that while it drew on the careful organization of the agency throughout the South for its success, the enrolling of voters was administered not by the Commissioner of the Freedmen's Bureau but by the commanders of the five military districts of the South. Indeed, such registration implied a completion of a job which, it was soon learned, had not yet been done. Just as the Freedmen's Bureau began to work efficiently, it lost its real reason for existing: its authority to make decisions affecting the everyday lives of the freedmen.

On March 2, 1867, just a day short of two years after the bill creating the Freedmen's Bureau was passed, Congress enacted the first Military Reconstruction Act. In doing so, Congress reversed itself. In 1865 it sought to make the army function as a government for a disadvantaged group in the civilian society. Now it permitted this military organization, divided into five districts, to absorb an established agency of the national government much needed by the freedmen. The military was to reconstruct the South in a new way.

The military's ascendancy over the affairs of the Freedmen's Bureau began when General Grant, disputing the theory that no bureau at all was needed, suggested in December 1865 that the military officers in the South assume its duties.[14] Howard resisted this, and the congressional support for Senate 60 and later the Act of July 16, 1866 suggested that he was sustained in his position. In that legislation the Bureau pointedly was not subsumed into the army organization, but by the spring of 1866 that process was nonetheless well underway.

13. Bentley, p. 191.
14. Ibid., p. 109.

On May 26, 1866, Howard wrote T. D. Eliot, then engaged in getting a replacement for Senate 60 through Congress, telling him that seven of his assistant commissioners were now also commanders of the troops in their districts.[15] The implication was that now these bureau men could no longer have their programs thwarted by hostile military men as Saxton often had. At the year end, Howard's annual report stated his policy on personnel: "Whenever practicable military commanders of States have been appointed assistant commissioners."[16] Phrasing it as he did, the Commissioner conceded that the reverse of what Saxton sought was accomplished. The military was absorbing the Bureau.

Thomas W. Osborn, no champion of the freedmen himself, was replaced by John G. Foster, whose brutality in conscripting Negro troops had so troubled Saxton during the war.[17] To the comfort of the planters, Thomas J. Wood replaced Samuel Thomas in Mississippi, and J. B. Kiddoo took over in Texas, when Edgar Gregory was removed for being too radical.[18] Philip Sheridan, commander of the Department of the Gulf, assumed the Louisiana assistant commissionership after the riot, and Fisk's two replacements, John R. Lewis in Tennessee and Jeff C. Davis in Kentucky were also military commanders in their states.[19] (Davis, once flatly called antinegro by Howard, proved a fairer man to the freedmen than expected.)[20] Called "vindictive" by an admirer of Johnson's policies, Alfred H. Terry replaced Orlando Brown in Virginia and then was replaced himself by the "moderate-conservative mollifier," John M. Schofield, who was so skillful a leader of the conservatives in Virginia that that state

15. O. O. Howard to T. D. Elliot [sic], 26 May 1866, BRFAL.

16. *Report of the Commissioner* (1866), p. 1.

17. Davis, *Civil War and Reconstruction in Florida,* pp. 381–82; Bentley, p. 129; Saxton Diary, 3 Feb. 1865.

18. Wharton, *The Negro in Mississippi,* p. 78; Elliott, "The Freedmen's Bureau in Texas," p. 11.

19. Howard, *Autobiography,* 2, 287, 290.

20. Ibid., p. 290; O. O. Howard to E. M. Stanton, 30 Oct. 1865, BRFAL; Carpenter, p. 131.

escaped Radical Reconstruction altogether.[21] (Both Terry and Schofield kept Brown on to handle freedmen's affairs.) Three successive military men, Thomas A. Ruger, John C. Robinson, and James V. Bomford, directed the demoralized bureau work in North Carolina after Whittlesey left.[22] Only of Wager Swayne and possibly Saxton's replacement in South Carolina, Robert K. Scott (who turned out to be surprisingly helpful to the freedmen), could it be said that any assistant commissioners still gave the Bureau's concerns priority over their military command.[23]

By the time the Reconstruction Act of March 2, 1867 was passed, only three of Howard's men remained as assistant commissioners: Edgar Gregory in Maryland (which was not under military occupation), Charles Howard in the District of Columbia, and Wager Swayne in Alabama. And what was worse, the military men (whom Howard had no part in selecting) were by this date even more ill disposed to the freedmen than the first group, which had replaced the "sympathetic" bureau men. John T. Sprague, who regarded the Negro of "gross physique, degraded intellect, grovelling pursuits, habitual slothfulness, and licentious habits," replaced Foster in Florida. It was Sprague's judgment that "without stringent laws . . . the freedman will become a profligate barbarian."[24] Vernon Wharton quotes a Negro in Mississippi as preferring to have no bureau at all than one administered by Alvan C. Gillem, a Johnson follower who replaced General Wood as assistant commissioner.[25]

These military commanders, symbols of oppression for those who have hated Radical Reconstruction, executed Congress' assignments, some of which were favorable to the freedmen—most notably the registration of Negroes as voters—but in their daily

21. Alderson, "Influence of Military Rule and the Freedmen's Bureau in Virginia," pp. 246, 303.

22. Bentley, p. 216.

23. Abbott, "Freedmen's Bureau in South Carolina," pp. 123–24.

24. J. T. Sprague to O. O. Howard, 1 Oct. 1867, BRFAL, quoted in Joe M. Richardson, "An Evaluation of the Freedmen's Bureau in Florida," *Florida Historical Quarterly,* 41 (January 1963), p. 230.

25. Wharton, p. 78.

job of keeping order they acted as firm allies of the planters and provided a strict discipline over the laboring force of freedmen.[26]

Howard, who had long distrusted the army as an institution for guarding of personal liberty, now saw military men governing freedmen once governed by men like Conway, Thomas, and Saxton. Nor did the problem exist only on the command level. The reduction in the size of the army after the war gravely affected Howard. Controlling the Commissioners' source of personnel was always Johnson's most effective way of defeating progressive programs for the freedmen. Career men were threatened with denial of promotions, and volunteer officers always lay under the threat of being mustered out.[27] In August 1867, Johnson proposed that all the bureau officers be denied their (higher) brevet rank. But Grant would countenance no such insult to a wartime commander.[28] He intervened and succeeded in getting Johnson to agree that any such cut would not be confined to Howard's officers. The Act of July 16, 1866 empowered Howard to utilize the Veterans Reserve Corps by assigning to it officers whom he found valuable to retain as bureau agents.[29] At the end of 1867, however, this corps was mustered out and Howard had almost no men left who owed their place in the Bureau to him.[30]

The Commissioner had been discouraged with his staff for a long time. "A good many of my present officers lack zeal," he wrote W. D. Kelley to explain why few Negroes were being helped to establish homesteads.[31] In December 1866, after two bureau members from Pennsylvania were killed in Mississippi, Howard was deeply pessimistic.[32] He could get no friend of the freedmen to volunteer his services in that area of the state; with

26. Alderson, pp. 308–09; Bentley, pp. 48–49.
27. Saxton Diary, 13 Jan. 1865, 21 July 1866, 28 Aug. 1867.
28. Washington *Evening Star,* 29 Aug. 1867.
29. *14 U.S. Stat.* 173–76.
30. O. O. Howard to Edgar Ketchum, 30 Dec. 1867, OOH Papers.
31. O. O. Howard to W. D. Kelley, 11 Sept. 1866, OOH Papers.
32. O. O. Howard to Thaddeus Stevens, 30 Nov. 1866, OOH Papers.

resignation he wrote to General Wood, the assistant commissioner: "If the white Mississippians withhold from the Negroes the privileges that belong to them, they will have the pleasure of ruining the business prospects of their state and of depopulating their territory. . . . My conclusion is let us do what we can for the [freedmen] pressing the subject of education by every means in our power while the Bureau shall last."[33]

The records of the Commissioner's office best reveal how obsolete Howard's agency became in 1867. There was little authority left for the Commissioner to exercise. His official correspondence became routine; the intrusion of his outside activities relating indirectly (or not at all) to the freedmen grew.[34] The energetic sense of mission so prevalent in the correspondence of the early bureau days was lost.

Howard's annual reports also reflect this change. His first, in November 1865, was an appeal to Congress to act in the freedmen's behalf. In November 1866 he spoke of changes that were needed to enforce the Civil Rights Bill of that year, but the tone of the Report was set by its second sentence: "No material change has been made in the general organization of this bureau since the date of the last annual report."[35] Continuity was the long and thorough document's theme. A year later there had been a fundamental change "resulting from the appointment of district commanders, under the reconstruction act passed March 2, 1867. All officers and agents [of the Freedmen's Bureau] have been to some extent under the military supervision and control of these district commanders."[36]

An army person like General Alfred H. Terry in Virginia might have proved to be as concerned about the freedmen as the bureau man he replaced, but there was nothing to ensure this.[37]

33. O. O. Howard to T. J. Wood, 8 Dec. 1866, BRFAL.

34. Phrases like "divine favor" and "God's grace" began appearing in letters in Howard's adjutants' letter copybook. O. O. Howard to the Rev. J. A. Thorne, 20 Feb. 1867, O. O. Howard to Howard Potter, 3 Apr. 1867, BRFAL.

35. *Report of the Commissioner* (1866), p. 1.

36. Ibid.

37. Alderson, p. 71.

No qualification that someone involved in this work must have a "sympathy" for it existed. The army commander was under no obligation to consider that his responsibilities were established by the needs of the freedmen, whom he was governing in the way that Rufus Saxton and Thomas Conway and, to a lesser extent, their colleagues did.

Howard's authority had always been imperfectly established, and with the beginning of Military Reconstruction he lost it altogether. As Howard himself put it the "commanders of Individual States became *ex-officio* my assistant commissioners."[38] An observer other than the General might have said, more harshly but with greater accuracy, that the commanders had become their own assistant commissioners. They had taken the command of the Bureau at the state level away from the Commissioner in Washington. Individual agents could and did serve with distinction in the field, but when they reported to Howard now about workers being exploited or about a schoolhouse, which was burned down, he could only request that other far more powerful generals than he look into the matter. As a student of Reconstruction in Virginia has said: "The Bureau, which had been the most important function of the military during the first two years after the war, had been relegated to a position of secondary importance with the passage of the reconstruction acts."[39]

The work of the Bureau grew routine but this did not mean that the job was getting done. The needs of the freedmen were as great as ever. The crop failure of 1866 and the recession of 1867 had proved that their economic troubles were not a function of wartime conditions, and some of the hard-working bureau staff in the field began to wonder whether the agency was making any progress at all. Congressman Eliot, who was instrumental in the establishment of the Freedmen's Bureau and still chairman of the Select Committee on Freedmen asked the agents to support the conditions. On New Year's Day 1868, the superintendent of education in Tennessee, David Burt, wrote a long and

38. Howard, *Autobiography*, 2, 332.
39. Alderson, p. 279.

thoughtful reply, which was not encouraging: "As a whole, the Freedmen have made but little material progress in the last year."[40]

Burt's evaluation of the immediate situation in Tennessee was like a recount of the history of the Bureau and a prediction of the future for the freedmen. Just as Howard had done in the first days of the agency, Burt spoke of land first. To document the Bureau's failure to achieve its prime objective, land for the freedmen, he drew up a table for ten towns in which 133 Negroes owned their own farms, none of which were more than $800 in value. Elsewhere in West Tennessee, in "most of the towns [in which no land was owned by Negroes] a few men own teams worth an average of $150." The urge among the freedmen to acquire a capital asset to ensure the future was marked.[41] Burt continued:

> I do not know of over ten instances in which twenty five acres or more have been purchased by one man. . . . A planter in Hardinan [sic] County says, 'About a year ago, the negroes made inquiries for men who would sell them farming land, but they were soon frowned down.' If the negroes had the means with which to purchase, there is, in most localities, a determination that they shall not become free holders, and the few who have bought have done so of men who [were] obliged to sell, or who have sold at enormous prices. The intense desire of the colored people to acquire homes and lands has led some into bargains which bear hard on themselves and harder on the character of the seller.

The original goal of the Bureau to respond to Negroes' passion for the land, continued to be unsatisfactorily achieved.[42]

As the Bureau had when land ownership proved unobtainable, Burt then turned to the "masses [who] are dependent on labor for white landowners, or those who rent to them." From his ex-

40. D. Burt to T. D. Elliot [sic], 1 Jan. 1868, BRFAL.
41. Ibid.
42. Ibid.

perience in West Tennessee he learned the dangers of share-cropping. In the cotton region, a cropper's share was "averaged about $75," which he declared was inadequate to support a family "even with the corn that was raised" additionally. As the price for cotton fell, some planters refused to make even that payment "and attempted to make the transaction seem fair by presenting exorbitant or fictitious bills against the laborer." Burt complimented a large number of the freedmen for keeping accurate accounts, which made them as aware of this exploitation as he was. Despite this awareness, Burt doubted that the Negroes could escape the sharecropping bondage, which had replaced the contract system. He conjectured that a true crop failure "might be a blessing," if it "should change the present system of agriculture" in favor of crop diversification, but he sensed how unchanging the farming pattern of the South was to be: "When the season for cottonplanting comes round . . . the experiment will be tried again."[43] And it was the need for Negro labor to raise that cotton that kept the freedmen from being driven from the lands, as Burt feared they one day would be. For the present, he could only say that "the Government will have to feed many of the Freedmen in this state before another crop can be produced."[44]

The observant bureau man turned from the freedmen to their white neighbors in Tennessee, putting them in three categories. The first group of Tennesseans, "socially excommunicated from their churches," whom he saluted for their courage in the face of ostracism, which seemed particularly cruel to him, actively helped the freedmen to become independent citizens. These men "are satisfied with the freedom of the negroes and afford them sympathetic, valuable aid." Unluckily, he added, this group could best be characterized by its rarity.[45]

The third group (to discuss first those whom the Freedmen's Bureau could not hope to convert) "embraces nearly all the

43. Ibid.
44. Ibid.
45. Ibid.

illiterate and rough men in the state," claimed Burt, who then perceptively added: "It includes [as well] many of wealth and culture whose education or experience has taken in the notion that the negro was made for slavery, and, to this end, made an unprogressive and vile creature." Of the freedmen, this group thought "violence at the discretion of the white man . . . at any time, justifiable." Burt predicted that men who "deem the negro lawful game for 'the superior race' " and who think even "cruelty . . . is a laudable method of teaching him his place" would "create a feeling of servility" among the freedmen.[46] Because of this class of Tennesseans, it was imperative for the "General Government" to intervene and thus to protect the freedmen. They, and less obviously a second white group, made it essential that there be a federal agency to assist the freedmen.

The middle group of white Tennesseans "are those who propose to leave the negroes to themselves without advice or encouragement." Against this attitude, which had long bothered Commissioner Howard, the freedmen were responding in the most interesting way. Burt recounted his visit to one planter of this class, who was testing the sixty freedmen who worked for him. With the comment, "let us see," the planter handed Burt the Negroes' account books, which showed that "several had spent about one fourth of the amount stated in their letters of credit very foolishly; others, a portion less so—and a fair part had purchased only articles necessary to a plain subsistence."[47]

Burt knew that merchants tried to sell everything they could to the freedmen since the purchases were charged to the planter, who at the end of the year subtracted them from the share of the cotton profit due the workers. To Burt, the surprise was not the foolish purchases: "The wonder is, that a majority of them displayed a good sense and a degree of economy that would bear comparison with the financial management of many educated white men." But because many of the freedmen were frugal did not mean that the less wise should be left without guidance.

46. Ibid.
47. Ibid.

Burt felt that the "cold indifference" of the white men who would separate themselves from the freedmen and their problems "call[s] for some ubiquitous agency on the part of the General Government for their protection and help." Far from having finished its work, the Freedmen's Bureau must be reconstructed and made permanent. "If the Government is now to leave the Freedmen of Tenn. to . . . this class," the freedmen will not be able to "rise into . . . prosperity."[48]

Burt's specific recommendations were that the "infirm, the sick, the suffering should be reached and relieved where they are" and not lured to relief centers in the city: "To this end, the government should appoint movable, facile, kindly" men. Second, he proposed a method of preventing price exploitation by merchants who sold to the freedmen. The best solution to this problem was provided by the freedmen themselves, who "in some places have adopted the plan of protective Union Stores, furnishing the capital in shares of $10. In meeting their physical wants, the Government might take a hint from this plan." Turning to more general but no less pressing matters, Burt said: "The machinery for elevating the Freedmen should be simple, and capable of directly and speedily reaching all cases requiring material aid, or legal advice and defense."[49]

In the matter of who should direct the "ubiquitous agency" Burt did not mince words: "The Government should appoint Agents for discharging its duties to the Freedmen who will not be impatient or profane or abusive toward them. This is not the way to treat even such as are unworthy. The most deserving poor will shrink from such men. They destroy all the good moral influences that ought to accompany such charity." Burt was not only reflecting what troubled General Howard as he lost the power of appointment in the Freedmen's Bureau, but also he was underscoring the unhappy truth that many of the bureau agents from the start had not been, as Rufus Saxton put it, "sympathetic with the work." Said Burt: "If a man does not believe

48. Ibid.
49. Ibid.

that the negro has any possibilities for progress . . . he should not accept such a trust."[50]

The only important bureau operations still in existence in the Tennessee that Burt was describing was his own work with the schools. All the other agents had been withdrawn in 1867, but Burt, without ever mentioning the Freedmen's Bureau by name, argued strongly to Eliot that its work still needed to be done by a federal agency. (Burt's specific recommendation, with respect to the schools, was that a cabinet Department of Education be formed to administer a national school system.)[51] As he closed his letter, Burt reviewed the history of the freedmen: "on coming out of slavery, they naturally fled to the General Government for protection. Where else could they have found it? We recognized the claim. Where else can they find it now, and why should we not still recognize the claim."[52]

Howard knew that it was a mistake to let the Bureau become as weak as it did with the discharging of his staff at the end of 1867. Of the Military Reconstruction Act, which had been passed in March, he wrote: "I simply conformed to the new law, as I had to President Johnson's previous plans."[53] After a year, it was evident that the freedmen still needed the help of a federal agency; on March 26, 1868, Howard wrote to Henry Wilson advocating the continuance of the Bureau for another year. The freedmen and loyal whites "required its aid in the organization of labor, in the establishment and support of schools and for the relief of those who are actually destitute and unable to work."[54] Howard also cited another reason why the Bureau was still essential:

These [1868] elections will be the first of the kind in which the newly enfranchised freedmen have participated, and will be held at periods most vital to the gathering of the

50. Ibid.
51. Carpenter, *Sword and Olive Branch,* p. 144.
52. D. Burt to T. D. Elliott [sic], 1 Jan. 1868, BRFAL.
53. Howard, *Autobiography, 2,* 333.
54. O. O. Howard to Henry Wilson, 26 Mar. 1868, OOH Papers.

cotton and grain crops and hence the danger that the freedmen in their natural and proper zeal to exercise their rights
as electors may be led to neglect their duties as agricultural
laborers.[55]

Howard added: "Thus far the influence of Bureau officers has
been adequate to prevent or mitigate evils of this kind,"[56] and
the implication was clear, his agency should be given a new lease
on life.

Leaders of the freedmen affairs in Congress drafted a bill
which would allow the Bureau to continue in states in which
Howard, at his discretion, thought it needed. This provision,
however, was abandoned in favor of the bill, passed over the
President's veto on July 25, 1868, which conceived of the Bureau
as unnecessary in states reorganized under the congressional plan
of Reconstruction. (Ironically, removal of the Freedmen's Bureau was one of the rewards for being readmitted to the Union
under radical auspices.) After January 1, 1869, the Bureau was
to conduct only its educational work and the payment of bounties
to Negro soldiers, who had earned but had not collected a bonus
for enlisting in the war.[57]

Despite his misgivings expressed to Henry Wilson, Howard
complied with the law. The Bureau had ceased all but the educational and bounty work in the Union states of Maryland,
Kentucky, West Virginia, and in already-readmitted Tennessee at
the end of 1867. Rather than restoring the agents in those states,
as he acknowledged was necessary, Howard, instead, withdrew
them in six more states readmitted to the Union in 1868: Alabama, Arkansas, Florida, Louisiana, and the two Carolinas.[58]
By the end of 1868 the entire personnel of the Freedmen's Bureau—so large and efficiently displayed just a year before—had
dwindled to 159 men.[59]

55. Ibid.
56. Ibid.
57. *15 U.S. Stat.* 193.
58. Carpenter, pp. 144–46.
59. *Report of the Commissioner* (1869), p. 497.

As the Tennessee school superintendent, Burt, surveyed the unfinished work with the freedmen, he left Congressman Eliot with a final reminder: "As a nation we are under peculiar obligations to our ex-slaves."[60] Ironically, perhaps, Oliver Otis Howard identified himself more and more closely with the discharge of those obligations as his ability to use the Freedmen's Bureau for the freedmen's benefit diminished.[61] Yet stalwartly he maintained the dignity of one at the head of a powerful agency of the government, and he was even more insistent than ever that every effort in which he engaged was part of his great design for the freedmen:

> I have given to this enterprise [the fund raising for a building for the First Congregational Church in Washington in which were conducted Sunday School classes which he had organized for Negro children] with all my heart first and foremost for the Cause of Christ, to endeavor to put into operation here a working element untrammeled by the spirit of slavery and caste—an element avowedly assertive, warring upon prejudice as well as upon more flagrant sins.[62]

Publicly, Howard represented the nation's responsibility to the freedmen, but his power to execute that responsibility was gone. He made more speeches and engaged in many private activities, which he regarded as crucial to the discharge of a moral obligation to the Negroes. He was the connecting link for almost all the volunteer efforts that focused on the freedmen, and he hoped that the nation would one day return to that moral commitment he believed was at his disposal. "I believe it would narrow my means of serving the cause of Christ for me to leave the public service even if the [Sunday school] Union could give me a compensation as large as that I now receive," he wrote to

60. D. Burt to T. D. Elliott [sic], 1 Jan. 1868, BRFAL.

61. O. O. Howard to J. C. Underwood, 23 Mar. 1867, Underwood Papers, LC.

62. O. O. Howard to Theodore Tilton, 16 May 1867, OOH Papers.

George H. Stuart, who had once headed the Christian Commission. "I . . . must get bread for my large family. The public military service enables me to do this, and at the same time devote many hours to the promotion of the Master's work."[63]

As characteristic as it was for Oliver Otis Howard to describe his goals this way, the description does not obscure the fact that his prime job remained unaccomplished. The Freedmen's Bureau was not restaffed and made permanent as Burt advised, and it did not provide the Negroes of the nation with a satisfactory way of life. It is in this light that Howard's accomplishment as Commissioner of the Freedmen's Bureau must be judged.

In evaluating the General's performance, one of the most troubling matters to account for is the way he acted when he was surrounded with evidence that Johnson's administration was using the Freedmen's Bureau not to advance the cause of the freedmen but to impede it. To dramatize this fact, should Howard have resigned? The young radicals in the bureau headquarters in Washington in September 1866 felt that he should have; they wanted him to take the initiative. The right time for him to act, they said, was after the New Orleans riot, which Willard Saxton described as "rebels murdering freedmen. The war has not ended yet & Andrew Johnson is aiding it all he can."[64] Charles Howard discovered that, instead of the massacre's forcing Johnson to appoint pronegro agents, the opposite took place. The President was more adamant than ever that conservatives, who would appease the white enemies of the freedmen, were the key to peace. Charles was resigned to the loss of a promotion he had been expecting: the President ordered that it be given "to a 'my policy' man."[65]

Now, these members of the agency thought, was the time for Otis Howard to speak out. Johnson began his famous "swing around the circle" seeking support in the congressional elections.

63. O. O. Howard to G. H. Stewart [sic], 30 Dec. 1867, OOH Papers.

64. Saxton Diary, 3 Aug. 1866.

65. A. P. Ketchum to Willard Saxton, quoted in Saxton Diary, 8 Sept. 1866; C. H. Howard to Willard Saxton, cited in Saxton Diary, 9 Sept. 1866.

As A. P. Ketchum, another radical at bureau headquarters, described it: "The President is on his winding way to Chicago . . . killing his cause by contemptible speeches."[66] Could not General Howard be persuaded to attempt a flanking maneuver to save the freedmen's cause? The former assistant commissioner for Mississippi, Samuel Thomas, as has been noted, implored him to try. In September 1865, while serving in the Bureau in Washington, Thomas attended a convention of radicals in Philadelphia, which met to protest Andrew Johnson's National Union Convention of the previous month. The former Assistant Commissioner sought "to sound the popular heart on the Bureau question," and he reported to Howard that: "From Maine to Iowa the feeling is decided. They say, 'tell Howard to resign, or do better, take such decided grounds that the President will remove him.' The whole Country will make common cause with you and fight the battle of humanity, and equal justice & rights to all with your name as the rallying cry for the masses."[67]

Thomas, eager to force the convention to focus its attention on the plight of the freedmen, pressed Howard to understand the mood of the convention: *"This is the feeling.* The moment you are removed every gun in the Radical camp will be trained on the Bureau and its working under the President."[68] Thomas conceded that the "Southern delegations [white save for the integrated group from Louisiana] speak kindly of the Bureau . . . and seem to feel . . . it would increase their burdens greatly for you to leave," but he insisted that Howard owed it to the Negroes to oppose their exploitation and to expose their exploiters, including Andrew Johnson.[69] Thomas insisted that Howard would be supported in such an endeavor: "I have heard at least a hundred of the best men in the Convention [which was chaired by former Attorney General Speed, who once ruled in favor of

66. A. P. Ketchum to Willard Saxton, quoted in Saxton Diary, 8 Sept. 1866.

67. Samuel Thomas to O. O. Howard, 5 Sept. 1866, OOH Papers.

68. Ibid.

69. Ibid.

land grants to the freedmen, and was attended by prominent radicals from Congress and outside it] from all parts of the country say—'We'll take care of Howard. Tell him to fight vigorously and throw the responsibility of the failure of the Bureau to protect the Negro on the President.' "[70]

In reply, Howard reversed the line of the moral imperative as Thomas had posed it. It lay, he contended, with staying on the job. The radical's victory in the gubernatorial and congressional elections in his own state a week after Thomas's letter provided the opportunity not to resign: "Maine shows that this positive influence is not needed in the present contest, so I can afford to act according to the dictates of conscience and duty, if perchance expediency has tempted me to abandon my uncomfortable position."[71] With this rebuke to his plea for activism, Thomas resigned; he returned to his business career before the end of the year.

During the 1866 political campaign in which he felt the Bureau in jeopardy, Howard, protecting himself from the President's assault, remained in his office.[72] He wrote to Horace Greeley, whose *New York Tribune* covered the New Orleans events in detail, but he did not urge him to underscore further the plight of the freedmen; rather, he asked the editor, who was critical of Absalom Baird, to print the Assistant Commissioner's official report "so as to be fair to Baird."[73]

Howard, anxious to protect the Bureau's reputation, displayed no intention of breaking to the left. Instead, he sought neutrality. It was at this time that he pleaded with General Sheridan to accept the assistant commissionership in Louisiana on the grounds that "neither radicals nor Johnson can claim you."[74] Even with this strategy Howard feared he might be fired after the election if Johnson succeeded in getting his supporters into office, thus

70. Ibid.
71. O. O. Howard to Samuel Thomas, 12 Sept. 1866, OOH Papers.
72. A. P. Ketchum to Willard Saxton, quoted in Saxton Diary, 8 Sept. 1866.
73. O. O. Howard to Horace Greeley, 7 Sept. 1866, OOH Papers.
74. O. O. Howard to P. H. Sheridan, 19 Sept. 1866, OOH Papers.

gaining political strength. When the President's electoral effort failed, Howard's sit-tight policy succeeded.[75] The Bureau and his post in it were safe, because the President's antinegro uses of the Bureau remained unrevealed to the nation.

True, there is nothing to suggest that Howard's resignation would have forced Andrew Johnson to appoint someone who would have been able to do more for the freedmen.[76] The only two men known to have been considered by the President as a replacement would have been even more useful as a disguise for the subversion of the true purpose of the Bureau than was Otis Howard. (As a symbol of white beneficence, Howard could not have been excelled.) Only a Negro could have hidden it better, and it was Frederick Douglass, first, and John Mercer Langston, second, whom the President approached for the post. Both of these men, warned that they would be exploited, declined the offer. Howard stayed on.[77]

Is Howard rightly honored for his perseverance? He did not separate himself from the government as it made decisions affecting the freedmen (though many were detrimental to the Negro's cause). As long as he stayed and kept his Bureau in existence, a symbol of governmental concern for the freedmen remained. Perhaps his presence was valuable even if it only served as an embarrassing reminder to a government that was fast trying to forget the reason for the existence of a Freedmen's Bureau. His designation probably would not have converted the Bureau into an effective force for the betterment of the freedmen's condition, and he stayed on in a post most men considered undesirable. Certainly Howard would have had a more comfortable career in the 1870s if he had followed the advice of his friend General Sherman and accepted another assignment in the army rather than insisting on remaining in the Bureau.[78]

75. O. O. Howard to W. H. Merrick, 15 Aug. 1866, OOH Papers.

76. *New York Tribune,* 21 Aug. 1866.

77. Saxton Diary, 28 Aug. 1867; Washington *Evening Star,* 29 Aug. 1867; Bentley, *Freedmen's Bureau,* p. 196.

78. O. O. Howard to W. T. Sherman, 11 Nov. 1872, OOH Papers.

In his own day he was criticized for his perseverance. Trying to have him discharged, racists both in Congress and in the army converted his attempts to stretch his few available funds to maintain as many Negro schools, houses, and hospitals as possible into evidence of mismanagement and implications of fraud.[79] This was the only way they could expel from Washington this symbol of Negro intrusion into a white world.

Like the Negro legislators of the southern states during Radical Reconstruction, the Christian General was forced to face an American test of election more ancient than his own nineteenth-century requirement of kindness. If waste and unorthodoxy in the management of money could be proved, then the nation could abandon the Negro in good conscience. The charges were made and the freedmen were ostracized from the chosen people. Radical Reconstruction was discredited and the ex-slaves left in the care of their former masters. Similarly, disgraced for his unauthorized use of bounties due to Negro soldiers for building schools for the freedmen, Howard felt deserted: "Oh! that our loving Christian people all over the country would help us as they originally intended when they encouraged me to undertake this battle in their behalf."[80] When an army court of inquiry threatened him with official dishonor, the General at last allowed his old wartime comrades to help him.[81] At Sherman's insistence, Howard permitted Grant to send him West to command the Department of Columbia.

Modern admirers of the General praise him for facing a moral dilemma and making the right choice. Knowing that the Freed-

79. O. O. Howard to S. C. Pomeroy, 24 Mar. 1868, BRFAL; O. O. Howard to E. B. Washburne, 5 Jan. 1869, OOH Papers; Charges against General Howard, in *Report of the Committee on Education and Labor,* 41st Cong., 2nd sess., House Report 121 (serial 14380).

80. O. O. Howard to Edgar Ketchum, during the congressional investigation, 12 July 1870, OOH Papers.

81. O. O. Howard to W. T. Sherman, 11 Nov. 1872, O. O. Howard to U. S. Grant, 27 Nov. 1873, OOH Papers; "Proceedings, Findings and Opinions of Court of Inquiry . . . in the Case of Oliver Otis Howard" (1874), National Archives, War Department, Judge Advocate General's Department; Saxton Diary, 25 Feb. 1874; O. O. Howard to C. H. Howard, 6 Apr., 11 July 1874, OOH Papers.

men's Bureau was being used to exploit the freedmen, yet sure that the freedmen would be without a friend in the government if the Bureau were destroyed, he did not resign. Perhaps this is correct, but there are two matters that need consideration before we can accept the image of Howard as a man who virtuously persisted in his position when he could have resigned to accept one with far fewer difficulties.

First, Howard never really contemplated resigning. His position meant everything to him and he held tenaciously to it. Whenever it was threatened, he moved quickly to placate the White House. Though he wrote often of temptations resisted, he spoke of no other post with envy. In turning down the presidency of Union College in the summer of 1868, he wrote:

> I can-not help seeing that Providence has placed me in a peculiar position with an unusual array of forces and I trust the Divine blessing to give some positive early fruits and better some plants that will grow and produce abundantly. . . . After Congress adjourns Mr. Johnson may remove me. Yet we hope very strongly that General Grant will come in and that opportunities for extended usefulness will be reopened for all of us who love the Saviour and his children.[82]

In all of his correspondence with businessmen, politicians, churchmen, educators, and leaders of benevolent organizations, there is no hint that Howard sought to leave. Rather, he always requested contributions for one of his causes, and it is not necessary to impute selfishness to the man to see that any such contribution would enhance Howard's chances of holding on to a job he valued immensely.

Adversity, far from discouraging Howard, simply confirmed the rightness of his position. Even when Grant disappointed him and the Bureau was reduced both in significance and in size (the agency consisted of only the General and a few Howard University scholarship students working as clerks in a borrowed room at the school), he held to the illusion that the Bureau

82. O. O. Howard to J. T. Backus, 8 July 1868, OOH Papers.

would be made permanent.[83] He hoped that it would be absorbed into a new department of education, and he would move up to cabinet rank.[84]

Howard seems to have been remarkably unaware of the subtleties of the many dilemmas that the freedmen posed for him and for the nation. Having made his initial commitment to the former slaves and conceiving it as a moral crusade, he never doubted his course. If our chief concern was the moral measure of an exemplary nineteenth-century American, Howard's steadfastness might make him an outstanding man of his time.

But, if the range of measurement is widened to include the freedmen, how is Howard's performance to be evaluated? It was in their Bureau that he faced his dilemma of leadership. The freedmen are the ones who present the fundamental challenge to the judgment of Howard as a man who left the world a better place than he found it.

If Howard did not consider resigning and if he did nothing to strengthen the existing Freedmen's Bureau, what might he have done for the freedmen that he did not do? For one thing, he might have been more discriminating in his appraisal of the alternatives proposed for the Negroes. For example, entrusting the freedmen to Nathan Bedford Forrest is troubling even if the destitution of the time along with Howard's belief in the importance of capitalizing on every available labor-need of industry and commerce is taken into account. His agreeing to the recruitment of labor gangs contradicted the high goals he had set for himself when he became Commissioner at the end of the war.

Howard began work in the Bureau with a commitment to the radical aim of obtaining land for the freedmen. During the spring of 1865 he spoke at times as boldly as the southern aristocrat, Mary Boykin Chesnut, who, as noted, said in June, "The

83. Saxton Diary, 30 June, 22 Aug. 1869; O. O. Howard to Charles Sumner, 5 Feb. 1872, OOH Papers.

84. O. O. Howard recording conversation with U. S. Grant, 12 Jan. 1871, O. O. Howard Papers, Howard University.

Negroes must be taught to stand alone."[85] But like Mrs. Chesnut, he did not follow through on his boldness. By 1867, when Howard called himself a radical, he had long allowed his agency to be used to prevent the Negroes from becoming landowners and to keep them in their places as subservient agricultural laborers. Indeed, the whole contract system was a denial of the principal of individual farm ownership.

The bureau agents negotiated and enforced the contracts under which the freedmen worked. There can be no doubt that the contract system prevented many freedmen from having to work under more repressive conditions, but this does not alter the fact that the Freedmen's Bureau was engaged in the pacification of the freedmen. Much of the energy of Howard's Bureau was directed toward making the freedmen agree to work for their former masters. A student of the agency's work in Florida concluded that "the Bureau literally forced the Negroes to work for the planters."[86] Freedmen who experienced better conditions were discontented with the Freedmen's Bureau labor system. The Wadmalaw, Ossabow, and St. Catherines farmers demonstrated this when they departed for Savannah. They preferred to leave their houses, their furniture, and their crops, standing in the fields, rather than to sign contracts with their old masters as the Bureau urged them to do.[87] The Bureau hoped for good wages and compliance with the terms of the contracts, but this would not have permitted the freedmen to use pressure for bettering their position. Although many bureau agents individually rendered valuable service to the freedmen, it was far from the goal of advancement that Howard proclaimed when he became Commissioner.

Howard deplored keeping the Negroes at the "bare subsistence" level. Yet when freedmen struck to force a rise in their standard of living—and did so at the point in the crop year

85. Chesnut, *Diary From Dixie,* p. 539.

86. Joe M. Richardson, "The Freedmen's Bureau and Negro Labor in Florida," *Florida Historical Quarterly, 39* (October 1960), 170.

87. *New Orleans Times,* 20 Nov. 1865.

when their work stoppage most affected the planters and might have brought concessions—the Bureau sent in troops as strike-breakers.[88] Even though Howard was unhappy about the planters' organization that enforced maximum wages, he swiftly removed bureau agents who encouraged the freedmen to meet in bureau offices and resist the planters.[89]

The freedmen were deprived even when the Freedmen's Bureau, as their protector in their relations with the planter, protected them effectively. The Negroes did not learn how to protect themselves. When the bureau personnel in South Carolina during Saxton's regime assumed logically that a black man should be the third member of the boards to supervise contracts along with a planter and a bureau agent, they were soon over-ruled. Removing the Negro member from an already unbalanced board left the freedmen unrepresented in their own affairs. The white planters seem to have feared most giving a voice to the Negroes in labor matters. Their dislike of the Bureau was largely based on the belief that it would teach the freedmen to organize in their own behalf.[90] Those bureau agents who sought to teach the Negroes independence were quickly weeded out of the agency. When the Bureau, which they had come to depend upon, was gone, the freedmen, uninstructed, were on their own.

Another service that Howard might have rendered the freedmen called for a tactical change in lobbying for them. Instead of constantly playing down their demands to convince white audiences that there was nothing intrusive inherent in their quest for a new place in the society, he could have faced up to the fact that there was and called on white America to help make the change required. General Howard, a popular figure at the end of the war, could command audiences wherever he spoke in the North. Instead of repeatedly lecturing to raise money for

88. O. O. Howard to W. H. Trescot, 14 Jan. 1866, BRFAL; J. E. Cornelius to H. W. Smith, 1 July 1866, BRFAL; O. O. Howard to Davis Tillson, 8 Dec. 1865, AJ Papers.

89. O. O. Howard circular letter to assistant commissioner, 16 Jan. 1868, BRFAL; Williamson, *After Slavery,* p. 87.

90. Wharton, *The Negro in Mississippi,* p. 79.

the symbolic victory of building, against the opposition of his Abolitionist minister and much of his denomination, an integrated First Congregational Church of Washington, he could have used his influence in the North to make the nation face the realities in the South.[91] By citing the Negro farmers on the Sea Islands as evidence of success, he could have publicly stressed the wisdom of the congressional mandate to divide the abandoned lands on which some Negroes could start their own farms. Instead of endlessly praising the Emancipation Proclamation, he could also have borrowed from his friend Lyman Trumbull's fear that slavery was not yet a dead issue and admitted that some planters were distorting his contract system to continue the restraints of slavery in all but name. And, speaking as a major general, he might have used the courage of which he was capable and told the people of the North about the widespread antinegro incidents committed by the army men stationed in the South. Further, Howard might have revealed the President's subversion of the agency. That this would have caused Johnson to try to remove Howard is of course almost certain, but it is possible that Howard might have proved a difficult man to fire in 1865 or 1866.

The time for such action was neither at the congressional investigation in 1870 nor the military court of inquiry of 1874; neither was it in 1867 nor in 1868, when the Bureau was weakened to the point of impotence. It was even too late at the close of 1866, when Howard admitted to a friend: "I have been before New York audiences so much . . . that I feel reluctant [to lecture]. My name will not draw there."[92] The radicals in the Bureau said that the fall of 1866 was the time. Then, or perhaps even earlier. Immediately after the war

91. The time and effort spent by Howard on this project was immense and the correspondence involved equally enormous. Three full volumes of "Letters Received, 1866–68," devoted exclusively to the church building drive and integration controversy, stand in the OOH Papers as interesting response to Howard's vigorous letter-writing campaign, which is documented throughout his letter books.

92. O. O. Howard to Charles Gould, 19 Nov. 1866, OOH Papers.

Howard's prestige was enormous; in the late fall of 1865, when he returned disillusioned from his trip to the South, he took command of freedmen's affairs in a stronger way than he ever had before or would again. He enlisted the aid of powerful congressional allies—Trumbull, Wilson, Sumner, and others—and Senate 60 was the hopeful result.

But it was vetoed, and perhaps then, six months before the young radicals urged him to do so, was the time to go to the people. Immediately after the veto, as the Bureau continued under its original wartime grant of authority, Howard went back to business as usual and returned to the White House to negotiate with the President in the hope that Johnson's allies in the South, who regarded the veto as a great victory, would treat the Negroes kindly. Howard's failure to protest at this point limited his chances of effectively challenging the President later. By making no public objection, Howard had given Johnson a signal of acquiescence. Instead, he might have publicly challenged the wisdom of his Commander-in-Chief's philosophy, that the freedmen did not need a federal agency to help them, set forth in the veto message. Certainly this would have enraged the President (for this was the winter of Johnson's vivid discontent with Stevens and Sumner), but Howard might have proved an embarrassment to the President before he could have been dismissed. And the embarrassment would have been of some value to the freedmen.

At this time, the powerful businessmen, the main sources of funds for the freedmen's aid societies, felt that Howard's credentials were in excellent order. S. V. Merrick and John Wanamaker in Philadelphia and William E. Dodge, to mention one of Howard's richest friends in New York, were influential in their states. For reaching the public, Howard was so close to Horace Greeley that bureau dispatches in the *New York Tribune* were often Howard's own words. At this time the General was also in close alliance with Lyman Trumbull with whom he had written Senate 60 and who, in April called eloquently and successfully for the overturn of the veto of the Civil Rights Bill. Trumbull had much influence with the *Chicago Tribune.*

In addition to Trumbull and other members of Congress interested in the freedmen, such as Henry Wilson and T. D. Eliot, two powerful men from Maine, James G. Blaine and William Pitt Fessenden, though their interest in the freedmen was never marked, would not likely have stood by passively while a native son and war hero was dishonored. This last consideration would also have brought the two most powerful Union generals to Howard's side for neither Grant nor Sherman, despite irritation with his moralistic ways, ever wavered in their respect for their wartime lieutenant.

Had he spoken out, Howard would have been removed by the President, but not before the Commissioner had made it clear that the freedmen needed the help of a federal agency and that Johnson was the chief obstacle to their getting it. If the issue causing Howard's removal had been the treatment of the freedmen, emphasis would have been clearly focused on the Negro as the man crucial to all Reconstruction issues. Rather than being blurred in a morass of tenure of office and impeachment matters, the lines of Reconstruction dispute might have been clearly drawn and the deterioration of the freedmen's condition made brightly visible.

By not speaking up, Howard contributed immensely at a critical moment to the process—in the end it defeated Reconstruction—by which the nation pulled the wool over its eyes with respect to the freedmen. As long as the good General commanded the Freedmen's Bureau, many Americans felt free of the obligation to meet the plight of the ex-slaves. Perhaps the nation would not have met the obligation even if Howard defined it. Perhaps, but the test was never made. Because of his eternal hopefulness and his faith in the efficacy of his kind paternalism, Howard spared the nation the full force of the moral test that he had originally posed for it.

Finally, although Howard did not establish firm priorities in the programs he backed for the freedmen and although he neither resigned nor put himself in the position to be dismissed, there was yet a last way in which he might have better assisted the freedmen. He could have learned from the freedmen rather than insisting that they learn from him. He was one of few white leaders on whom the Negroes counted to recognize their need and truly reconstruct the land to give them an equal place in it. Howard, however, looked for guidance not in black aspirations but in the moral sureties of his business and church friends 'in his own white America. For a man devoted to education, he was remarkably unwilling to learn the exciting lessons which were uniquely available to him.

It was not Howard but the Thomas Conways and Rufus Saxtons among the bureau members who learned from the freedmen. Even they were suspect to their clients but they paid the freedmen the compliment of responding to their aspirations. On occasion Howard seemed to also. During his visit to the Sea Islands in January 1865, he was deeply impressed by the Negroes' demonstration of their quest for a new way of life. This was again true when he talked with black men in the towns of northern Florida and on his voyage up the Mississippi in the fall of 1865, but these confrontations were contradicted by encounters in Edisto and New Orleans, where he deeply disappointed the Negroes. Rarely did he pursue an education among the freedmen learning from them and working with them to achieve their goals.

Howard sought to "befriend" the freedmen—to protect them and show them the loving kindness of a father. By summoning the nation to a restoration of kindness, Howard hoped to keep the freedmen from harm. In April 1866, in the nation's capital, he enjoined a mass meeting of politically conscious Negroes to take as their gospel: " 'God is love,' . . . and carry it into yonder cottage. There you will find it will make the different parts of the same family agree; it will make the children kind to their parents and kind to each other. It will create a scene beautiful in itself; a picture lovely to look upon."[93] But to achieve this, the child must not be rebellious—neither must he grow up and demand all that is due a free man come into his majority.

The Negroes who had not known a way of life better than working as the white men told them to work were remarkably

93. O. O. Howard speech, 27 Apr. 1866, *Autobiography*, 2, 324.

willing to accept the Freedmen's Bureau's advice. True, the Negroes of Union Springs were restless when they thought that by proclaiming amnesty, President Johnson revoked the Emancipation Proclamation; the Negroes of Augusta mocked Davis Tillson in front of Generals Fullerton and Steedman; some Sea Islanders left rather than submit; the Louisiana Negroes pressed their cause in the most sophisticated of political maneuvering. Yet, why was there not more restlessness—why no rebellion?

To white America, the Freedmen's Bureau's basic job was to prevent rebellion. For both the most fervent of the freedmen's friends and cruelest of their enemies, the aim was to ensure that, in the aftermath of the war, Negro violence, similar to that which had attended the end of slavery in the Caribbean, did not erupt. When Rufus Saxton was asked what would result from "the withdrawing of the military and the Freedmen's Bureau, and leaving the freedmen of the South to the legislation and rule of the white population," he replied: "I think the result of such a policy . . . would be fearful to contemplate. I fear it would lead to insurrection, and to a war of races."[94]

Thomas Conway, convinced that under Johnson's policies slavery would be reintroduced, stated that "The negroes . . . will struggle manfully against such a result." For him, there were two means of preventing the "anarchy, violence and bloodshed," which he feared would "end in extermination for the blacks" of Louisiana.[95] One was the maintenance of a strong military establishment"; the other was to give the Negroes political rights.[96] He advocated the latter: "The extension of equal rights for all our citizens will save us."[97] In Alabama Wager Swayne reported that "before Christmas apprehensions were quite generally expressed that the disappointment of the Negroes at not getting land would produce outbreaks and perhaps a general insurrection." The Assistant Commissioner knew that local militia groups were disarming the Negroes in Alabama, a state where

---

94. *Report of the Joint Committee on Reconstruction,* pt. 3, p. 102.
95. Ibid., pt. 4, pp. 82–83.
96. Ibid., p. 84.
97. Ibid., p. 85.

"nearly every man . . . carries arms." The local white forces were
seeing to it that the freedmen had no lethal ways to express their
unhappiness when the holiday did not bring them their forty
acres. Swayne was disposed to stop the vigilantes but "not being
able to say or to feel quite sure that insurrections might not
occur, and, aware that if they did occur, interference, from whatever motive, . . . to prevent or suppress them, would appear
inexcusable, I forebore to interfere."[98]

Orlando Brown volunteered his opinion of the Negro troops
in Virginia: "I think that in the case of an insurrection they
would fight desperately." Asked how they would fight "if Union
troops were brought against them to put down an insurrection,"
he replied: "They were examined on that subject when there
was talk of an insurrection at the holiday, fearing that they
might have such ideas." Brown had concluded from his interro-
gation that Yankee troops would create more "demoralization"
among the Negroes than the rebel soldiers would.[99]

The old specter of slave insurrection, long a residence of
southern plantation houses, now stalked the halls of Congress.
Grave congressional Northerners of the Joint Committee on
Reconstruction now responded to the same fear, which had so
long troubled white men who lived among Negroes in the
South. Some might have dismissed the restrained testimony of
Rufus Saxton and the long learned discussion of the Louisiana
Negroes given by Thomas Conway as the exaggerations of
repudiated men. But conservatives who did so would still have
had to contend with the remarks of Wager Swayne and Orlando
Brown. Clearly the insurrection theme dominated the line of
questioning in this select committee of senators and representatives, chaired by a model of senatorial respectability, Pitt Fessenden, as it inquired into the gravest of national problems.

In the end it was the judgment of this committee—and of the
majority of Congress—that the only way to prevent repression
of the Negro so severe that "it would eventually end in insurrec-

98. Ibid., pt. 3, p. 140.
99. Ibid., pt. 2, p. 128.

tion" was to give the Negroes in the South the vote.[100] The
strategy of those who thought fear of Negro violence would
guarantee the retension of southern dominion over the local
blacks produced, temporarily, the opposite result.[101] With Negro
ballots the Republican party, the victorious war party, could
ensure that peace would continue in the postwar period. As the
Memphis and New Orleans killings proved, the Freedmen's
Bureau had not succeeded in that task.

That congressmen and bureau men feared insurrection does
not mean that it was imminent.[102] Clinton Fisk, quickly investigating a rumor that an uprising had begun, found the only
armed Negro in the area to be a farmer hunting squirrel.[103]
Modern scholars, also curious about the absence of insurrection
and the reported docility of the slaves, have suggested that the
explanation lies in the psychological conditioning of the American Negroes by slavery. Samuel Thomas shared with Stanley
Elkins a view that the former slaves were stunted and stunned
as they became free men, and he suggested an interesting
variant explanation of the Negroes' psychic damage.[104] During
the war Thomas was in charge of a camp for destitute homeless
freedmen who had been cruelly caught between two fierce
armies, which were crisscrossing Tennessee.

Working in the camp was grim. "I hope I may never be
called on again to witness the horrible scenes I saw in those
first days," wrote Thomas. "Our efforts to do anything for these

100. Ibid., p. 127.

101. Samuel Thomas to O. O. Howard, 12 Nov. 1865, BRFAL.

102. A white settler in the South was still, in 1872, worried about "a
worse war than our last one . . . unless measures are speedily taken to
rectify the wrongs heaped upon the black laborer" (Stearns, *Black Man of the
South,* p. 344).

103. *Report of the Joint Committee on Reconstruction,* pt. 3, p. 30: General George Thomas found no evidence of insurrectionary feeling among the
Negroes in Tennessee. He was more troubled by the antagonism between the
white Union soldiers and the black ones, G. H. Thomas to Andrew Johnson,
9 Sept. 1865, AJ Papers.

104. Stanley Elkins, *Slavery: A Problem in American Institutional and
Intellectual Life* (New York, 1963), pp. 81–139.

people, as they herded together in masses, when founded on any expectation that they would help themselves, often failed; they had become so broken down in spirit, through suffering, that it was almost impossible to arouse them."[105] The experience of war had proved to be a new middle passage—a way out of slavery perhaps as demoralizing as the trip from Africa, which had introduced their ancestors to the peculiar institution.

To endure in silence, to accept without protest, may have been a legacy of slavery to the freedmen—or, for some, of the war which ended it. But the freedmen had other teachers of the doctrine of acquiescence. They were Northerners. The Freedmen's Bureau, failing its primary assignment, the establishment of a new way of life for the southern Negroes, may have succeeded in its secondary pursuit. It undertook to make the freedmen accept the terms that the white society imposed. Those terms, marriage, thrift, industriousness, were coupled with similar goals: one's own farm, the use of the profits of one's labor, and a voice in the governing of the communities of which they were a part. Later when such rights and opportunities were denied, bureau men of a different stripe worked to make the freedmen accept limitations and endure the disappointment of a freedom they had come to mistrust.

In April 1867 General Howard sent a supply of tracts written by Clinton B. Fisk to General A. G. Gillem, then the assistant commissioner in Mississippi, and asked that they be circulated and "read to the plantation Negroes." Fisk had arranged with the Boston Tract Society for the publication of a talk, which he had found useful in quieting discontentment among the freedmen in Tennessee and Kentucky. Titled *Plain Counsel for Freedmen,* it began with this dedication:

> To the Freedmen of the United States: Now happily released from the house of bondage, and fairly set forward in the path of progress, these Plain Counsels are respect-

105. Samuel Thomas to John Eaton, Jr., quoted in Eaton, *Grant, Lincoln, and the Freedmen,* p. 19.

fully and affectionately dedicated by one who has marched
with them through the Red Sea of strife, sympathized with
them in all their sufferings, labored incessantly for their
well-being, rejoiced in their prosperity, and who believes
that, guided by the pillar of cloud by day, and of fire by
night, they will reach the Promised Land,
                    Signed: "Clinton B. Fisk."[106]

In his pamphlet Fisk told the freedmen that every "man is born
into the world with a right to his own life, to personal liberty,
and to inherit, earn, own, and hold property. These rights are
given to him by the great God; not because he is a white man,
a red man, or a black man, but because he is a MAN."[107] In the
wake of this bold rhetoric, Fisk urged the freedmen to be sympathetic to the "old master," who had lost so much during the
war: "Do not fall out now, but join your interests [with the
planters] if you can and live and die together." The onus of
preventing acts of racial prejudice was put on the freedmen:
"Prejudices are like tender toes. Do not step on them."[108] The
freedmen were warned by the future presidential candidate of
the Prohibition Party that the money that might buy a farm
must be squandered neither on whiskey nor women. The Negroes were also told that they should "be sorry for the past," in
which as slaves they had broken "God's law of marriage," and
should marry and settle down.[109] As if he were Benjamin
Franklin, Fisk, in his do-it-yourself freedom book, promised the
freedmen success. "White men are very much influenced by a
man's success in making a good living, and if you are thrifty and
get on well in the world, they cannot help respecting you."[110]

Within this context the Freedmen's Bureau's contribution to
Negro education needs to be reexamined. The importance of

106. Hopkins, *Clinton Bowen Fisk,* p. 104.
107. Ibid.
108. Ibid., p. 105.
109. Ibid., p. 106.
110. Ibid., p. 105.

the role that graduates of Howard University, Fisk University, Atlanta University, and many other schools, which started with bureau help, have played in the Negro's advancement is past question. There is no denying either the courage or resourcefulness of the northern teachers such as Rebecca Bacon, who went South to teach and ended up founding an integrated church as well when she discovered that Hampton Institute's chapel was for the white faculty only. Her reason: "I'll be whipped if I'll go where my scholars can't & I said so."[111] If lessons of protest of great significance to black America in the latter third of the twentieth century were learned in these schools, it should be remembered too that it was at Hampton that Booker T. Washington learned the lessons he taught so persuasively at the close of the nineteenth.

Howard and the Bureau actively sponsored these schools and there was an attractive energy to this enterprise; the picture of Negroes, old and young, getting their first lessons is a moving one. But the harsh fact remains that much of the purpose of these schools was to channel the energy of the Negroes into waiting for freedom rather than fighting for it.

The schools were the only evidence to which Howard could point when late in his life he sought to prove that his agency had been a success. Once land reform had priority but redistribution of the southern farmlands had not come about. The labor system, which Howard had sponsored, had not produced a prosperous, resourceful class of agricultural workers. Nothing had been accomplished to give the Negroes an economic base on which to grow. Even the Freedman's Savings Bank, an institution in which the freedmen were encouraged to lay aside money toward their own advancement, was allowed to fail.

The Freedman's Savings Bank was started during the war in the northern outposts of the South. Ex-slaves were encouraged to put aside as much of their wages and their proceeds from their farming ventures as was possible. Cutting across state lines to

111. Rebecca Bacon to Leonard Bacon, 7 Nov. 1869, Bacon Family Papers, Yale University.

create a branch banking system, Congress chartered the bank on March 3, 1865.[112] This was also the day the Freedmen's Bureau was established, and the bank's work was directly in line with the theme of thrift preached by the bureau agents.

The bank was never large but it grew steadily. Just prior to its collapse in 1874 it had thirty-four branches with deposits totaling $3,299,201.[113] When the bank's doors were closed, 61,131 persons—most but not all of them freedmen—were unable to withdraw the money they had deposited.[114] Approximately half of them were depositors whose savings had mounted to not more than $50. The losers were poor men; only 3,000 of the accounts were larger than a few hundred dollars.

General Howard regarded the bank as part of the cluster of enterprises—schools, hospitals, freemen's aid associations—which, with the Bureau, made up the whole of the mission to the freedmen. To a business man who had contributed to freedmen's aid, he wrote often: "Will you not become a trustee. We need your clear head and firmness to help a good work."[115] Howard's endorsement was printed on the passbooks: "I consider the Freedman's Savings and Trust Company to be greatly needed by the colored people, and have welcomed it as an auxiliary to the Freedmen's Bureau. signed Maj. Gen'l O. O. Howard."[116] John W. Alvord, the Congregational minister who organized the bank, served first as its corresponding secretary and then as its president at the same time that he was superintendent of education in the Freedmen's Bureau. It is not surprising that freedmen depositors considered the bank to be an official function of a government that could be counted on to ensure the safety of their money.

In line with the charter, the bank's trustees invested its assets for the first four years in government bonds. These men, close

112. "An Act to Incorporate the Freedman's Savings and Trust Company," *13 U.S. Stat.*, 510–13 (3 Mar. 1865).

113. Walter L. Fleming, *The Freedmen's Savings Bank* (Chapel Hill, 1927), p. 99.

114. Ibid., p. 141.

115. O. O. Howard to R. P. Buck, 14 Oct. 1871, OOH Papers.

116. Fleming, p. 146.

associates of Howard's through their service on the boards of
charitable freedmen's aid associations, were New Yorkers of a
conservative stripe. Unfortunately, in 1870 the charter of the
bank was amended allowing for the investment of half of the
bank's assets in real estate mortgages. This change in policy
accompanied the move of the head office to Washington, where
a sumptuous building was constructed across from the Treasury
building on Pennsylvania Avenue.[117] The dapper middle-class
Negro clerks bustling about its walnut-paneled interior suggested to the gilded age that the progress of the freedmen in the
nation's capital was great.

As the power of the Freedmen's Bureau waned, Otis Howard
attempted to keep functioning his many freedmen enterprises
by working all of the private activities, including the bank, as
interrelated parts of a whole. For example, if the Freedmen's
Bureau, as was entirely correct for it to do, granted money to
a northern church group, which was sponsoring the building of
a school in the South, and if the churchmen did not yet have
enough money to equip the school or provide for a teacher,
Howard would convince them to invest the grant in another of
his projects. The Reverend J. Brinton Smith, an Episcopalian
who sought to establish a school in Raleigh, North Carolina,
invested the funds granted him in mortgages on houses sold to
Negroes in Washington, D.C.[118] Other groups made loans to the
First Congregational Church of Washington taking pledges of
contributions as collateral.[119] Such unorthodox complex financial
arrangements kept many freedmen activities aloft on a kite string
of credit.

Howard never doubted that a project like the financing of the
church was in the interest of the freedmen as a whole. He was
determined that his church, with Negro Sunday school classes
and Negro members, have a splendid new building as an

117. Washington *Evening Star*, 15 Oct. 1869.
118. O. O. Howard to J. B. Smith, 22 Sept., 2 Oct. 1868, OOH Papers.
119. Both the financing of the church building and the schism over Negro
participation in the church is exhaustively documented in the . Howard
Papers.

example for the whole nation. By insisting on integration, Howard split not only his own congregation but also his whole denomination. Those he embarrassed over this issue were not all sorry when, as a result of having personally overextended himself in the 1870s, he had to withdraw from such activities. Many projects beneficial to the freedmen would not have been started if Howard had not been bold in his use of bureau money and zealous in obtaining funds from private contributors. So sure was he of the goodness of his cause that he involved the Freedman's Bank in these endeavors as well.

As early as 1871 Howard's able lawyer, Edgar Ketchum, warned him about the bank's affairs: "We *must* as just men get our affairs upon a right basis and we must banish . . . all loans without security (as at Jacksonville) and we must have no friendships *in the bank* but only the hard rules of business."[120] The branches did need watching as Howard and the trustees had been repeatedly warned by alert bureau members like Samuel Thomas, later a most able banker himself.[121] But it was not in the branches that the critical trouble came. After moving to Washington and changing its investment policy, the bank came under the domination of Henry D. Cooke, who, in addition to being his brother Jay Cooke's agent in the capital, was the district's territorial governor. The Freedman's Savings and Trust Company along with Henry Cooke's other bank, the First National Bank of Washington, became the vehicle for substantial underwriting of the building boom, which took place in Reconstruction Washington.

Renowned for their Christian piety, the Cookes had the confidence of General Howard. For him to engage their cooperation in his ventures for the progress of the freedmen, as well as in other causes in which he was interested, was to risk much. In August 1871 Howard wrote to two close associates in the freedmen movement, Eliphalet Whittlesey and A. P. Ketchum: "If

120. Washington *Evening Star,* 22 Jan. 1869; Edgar Ketchum to O. O. Howard, 10 June 1871, OOH Papers.

121. Samuel Thomas to O. O. Howard, 27 Mar. 1866, BRFAL; T. J. Wood to M. H. Hewitt, 4 May 1866, BRFAL.

you see anybody who would like to invest in Northern Pacific Bonds please let come through me. J. Cook & Co. [sic] have promised to subscribe to our Y-M-C-A's debt $5000 in case I sell 50,000 of their bonds."[122] Quid pro quo with the Cookes proved costly to the depositors of the Freedman's Bank.

With the crash of 1873, precipitated by the failure of Jay Cooke & Co., which overextended itself speculating in Northern Pacific bonds, the Freedman's bank was in grave danger of failing. Frederick Douglass was brought in as President to shore the confidence of Negro depositors, but his incumbency did nothing to restore the worth of the bank's assets. Walter L. Fleming in his study of the bank concludes that the trustees appointed Douglass so that "colored officials [would] be in charge when the bank failed as they were sure it would."[123]

Before, the failure associates of the Cookes found temporary financial refuge at the bank's loan window. When the Freedman's Bank's doors finally had to close, its books were riddled with loans like the one made to R. L. Fleming, who, with the Cookes, owned the Seneca Sandstone Company and, like them, had been a contributor to Howard University and other freedmen activities.[124] On January 8, 1874, Fleming borrowed $26,300 putting up as security 130 shares of YMCA stock— evidence that $22,011.92 was owed him by a builder of "colored schools," and other collateral declared to be worth $4,055. When the bank closed, Fleming still owed it $16,286 on this note. His collateral was sold for $12,388 and suit was brought to collect the rest, but too late as Fleming too was bankrupt.[125] After decades of attempts to settle the affairs of the Freedman's Savings and Trust Company, the Negro depositors were awarded less than fifty cents on each dollar they had deposited,

122. O. O. Howard to Eliphalet Whittlesey (also to A. P. Ketchum), 17 Aug. 1871, OOH Papers.

123. Fleming, p. 85.

124. James H. Whyte, *The Uncivil War: Washington During the Reconstruction: 1865–1878* (New York, 1958), p. 255.

125. Report of the Select Committee to investigate the Freedman's Savings Bank and Trust Company (Bruce Report), 46th Cong., 2nd sess., Senate Report 440 (serial 1895).

and most of the owners of smaller accounts were never located.[126]

Enemies of any effort to aid the advancement of the freedmen or any attempt to discredit the doctrine that the Negroes were better off under the dominion of white Southerners made excellent use of the death of the Freedman's Bank. One congressional investigating committee explained the situation: "Missionaries, of whom the chief was Alvord, perambulated the South, invoking religion, politics, education, and *teaching* the blacks how 'to toil and save,' and then trust their hard-earned savings to Alvord and his associates to invest for them."[127] As in the case of the vehement attacks on Howard for his investment in a building block company, which supplied bricks to Howard University (where a wall collapsed killing a workman), castigation of Alvord provided an opportunity to vilify all efforts encouraging the freedmen to advance. The congressmen were relentless: "The wolves literally became the pastors of the flock, and without compunction or remorse, devoured the younglings committed to their care."[128]

The legislators failed to realize that damning the missionaries was no substitute for reimbursement of the freedmen depositors. Well into the twentieth century, individuals in Congress vainly argued that the government had a moral obligation to pay the depositors in full. Filed in the National Archives are thousands of worthless records of deposits of the first few dollars the nation's Negroes earned as free men and put aside to buy farms.[129] Like the matter of the Freedmen's Bureau's forty-acre grants, another promise was cruelly withdrawn.

Most of the Freedmen's Bureau work ended on December 31, 1868. But the agency, with a total staff of 158 men in 1869 and

126. Fleming, pp. 120–21.

127. Report of the Select Committee on the Freedman's Bank (Douglas Report), 44th Cong., 1st sess., House Report 502 (serial 1710).

128. Ibid., p. IV.

129. Records of the Freedman's Saving Bank and Trust Company, Records of the Comptroller of the Currency, National Archives, Diplomatic, Legal and Fiscal Branch (Record Group 101).

87 in 1870, continued on until June 30, 1872, when it closed its books.[130] It continued to pay bounties due the Negro army volunteers and to operate the few remaining hospitals for the freedmen until they were closed and the last most pathetic survivors of the war—"1 is blind and insane; 3 are deaf and dumb; 13 are maimed"—were boarded out or moved to the Freedmen's Hospital in Washington.[131]

There is still much to be learned about the attempts of the Negroes in the nation's capital to establish and secure their equality by examining the ambiguous role played by Howard and the shadow of the Freedmen's Bureau after 1868. It bears telling, but it is another story. The national institution that had begun with such bright promise was long since dead. The rebuilding plans of Rufus Saxton, J. B. Roudanez, and the Edisto farmers needed the whole nation's support. The Freedmen's Bureau could have been the builder but it was not, and a radical Congress gave that job to southern legislatures. Radical Reconstruction, with its achievements and failures in the states of the South, took the place of national responsibility. It introduced the freedmen to American politics; but as the nation's Negroes were given the chance to fend for themselves as southern voters, they lost an institution that might have made permanent their claim to be represented in the nation as a whole.

When that claim was entered again, it was made by the Negroes themselves. The Freedmen's Bureau had been theirs, but it failed them by substituting paternal supervision for man to man respect. As one of the Negroes, who most importantly entered the claim in behalf of his people, said of the Freedmen's Bureau: "The passing of a great human institution before its work is done, like the untimely passing of a single soul, but leaves a legacy of striving for other men. The legacy of the Freedmen's Bureau," wrote W. E. B. DuBois, "is the heavy heritage of this generation."[132]

130. O. O. Howard to the Secretary of War, 29 June 1872, BRFAL.
131. *Report of the Commissioner* (1870), p. 6.
132. DuBois, *Souls of Black Folk,* p. 39.

Bibliographical Note

Manuscripts

The two major manuscript collections on which this study was based are the Records of the Bureau of Refugees, Freedmen and Abandoned Lands (BRFAL), Record Group 105 in the National Archives, and the O. O. Howard Papers (OOH Papers) in the Bowdoin College Library. Record Group 105 is a large collection, and until it is microfilmed the guide to its use is Elizabeth Bethel, Sara Dunlap, and Lucille Pendell, *Preliminary Check List of the Records of the Bureau of Refugees, Freedmen and Abandoned Lands, 1865–1872* (Washington, D.C., National Archives, 1946).

Essential to a comprehension of the directions in which the Bureau did (and did not) move was a reading in its entirety of the series of letters sent by the Commissioner from May 1865 through June 1872 (BRFAL 1). There is an eighteen-volume registry of letters received (BRFAL 20), which gives a brief abstract of each letter and an index of these letters (BRFAL 21) which enables the researcher to find the actual letter (BRFAL 19) with relative ease. The extraordinarily able and helpful staff of the bureau section of the Archives, under the direction of Mrs. Sara Dunlap Jackson, make this material swiftly available.

Several important series of volumes are BRFAL 25, synopses of reports of the assistant commissioners; BRFAL 155, an indexed registry of reports received from the bureau superintendents of Education in the various states; BRFAL 158, which gives these reports in full; BRFAL 23, T. D. Eliot Papers, materials supplied to the congressman who sponsored bureau legislation; BRFAL 249, which gives an engrossing and appalling picture of life in the displaced persons camp, Freedmen's Village, in Arlington; and BRFAL 319, records relating to riots, murders, and outrages.

General Howard's Papers in 234 volumes (many now boxed) are rich in social history for the period 1833–1908 as well as indispensable to an understanding of what the Commissioner sought to accomplish during the bureau years. Although the collection has not yet been cataloged, the General's bent for record keeping makes the papers convenient to work with. The flyleaf indexes to each volume of letters sent and general indexes of letters received (supplemented with rear-page indexes in those volumes omitted from the general indexes) have been preserved.

General Howard by no means confined his interest in the freedmen to his work in the Bureau as those O. O. Howard Papers that are at Howard University and the Records of the First Congregational Church of Washington, D.C., show. Of particular interest at Howard University is a manuscript diary kept by the General in the 1870s.

Of the great usefulness in gaining the perspective of the Freedmen's Bureau held by one of its minor officials who served as a clerk in the important agency offices of Beaufort and Charleston, South Carolina, and then at headquarters in Washington was the diary of S. Willard Saxton. This personal journal is in the private possession of W. Saxton Seward and Paul S. Seward. In all, the diary spans eighty years and the volumes for the bureau period tell much of the efforts of the diarist's brother, Rufus Saxton, in the freedmen's behalf. Also helpful in this connection are the Saxton Papers in Mr. Saxton Seward's possession and those in the Yale University Library. The Papers of John Mercer Langston, an important official of the Freedmen's Bureau in its latter days, were read from the microfilm in the Schomburg Collection at the 135th Street Branch of the New York Public Library. The Papers of the New Orleans radical, Thomas Jefferson Durant, are at the New York Historical Society.

The Andrew Johnson Papers, microfilmed by the Library of Congress, were indispensable to an understanding of the Freedmen's Bureau's place in Presidential Reconstruction. The Lyman Trumbull Papers in the Library of Congress revealed observations on the freedmen's needs that reached the congressional sponsor of the continuation of the Bureau. Other Library of Congress papers of particular help were those of Justin L. Morrill, for information on bureau witnesses before the hearings of the Joint Committee on Reconstruction; Salmon P. Chase, Elihu B. Washburne, Nathaniel P. Banks, William Eaton Chandler, and Alexander R. Shepherd, for the Bureau's operations in Washington, D.C.; Lewis Tappan, for the participation of one of the most admirable of the philanthropists who aided the freedmen; John C. Underwood, the radical Unionist federal judge in Virginia (there is also an interesting correspondence between Alice Underwood Hunt and Harriet Beecher Stowe included in this collection); and William Pitt Fessenden.

The Fessenden Papers at Bowdoin were also helpful (but they do not suggest that General Howard's gentlemanly senator was a very likely candidate for strenuously leading a hypothetical middle route between President Johnson and the radicals, as some historians have proposed). The Charles H. Howard Papers are an important new collection at Bowdoin. These letters contribute much to an understanding of the work of the two Howard brothers in the army and in the Bureau. Of much interest at Bowdoin is the diary kept by Thomas W. Osborn while he served on General Howard's staff during the war.

A search for other personal papers of the assistant commissioners was disappointing. In most instances, the assistant commissioners' letters and reports in the bureau records were the only sources for determining their attitudes toward their clients. Several collections in the Yale University Library yielded surprisingly rich supplementary detail on work with the freedmen. The Alexander Stewart Webb Collection documents clearly the active participation of the occupying Union army in the frustration of bureau programs. The Papers of Charles B. Wilder and of his nephew John Augustus Wilder in the Todd Family Papers tell much of pre-bureau work with freed Negroes in Virginia. In the Bacon Family Papers are the letters of Rebecca Bacon, who, as a school teacher at Hampton Institute, practiced the equality her father Leonard preached at the Center Church. The former minister of the leading Negro Congregational Church in New Haven, Amos G. Beman, worked for the American Missionary Association in Tennessee, and his papers tell of Negro attitudes toward freedom in that state. The John W. DeForest Papers yield some information on the novelist's work in the Bureau, and the Stuart Eldridge Papers, on loan to the Yale Library, contribute the acid comments of a radical bureau member often highly critical of his agency's treatment of the freedmen.

Public Documents

General Howard's *Autobiography* published in 1908 probably ought to be considered as much a public document as his Annual Reports as commissioner of the Freedmen's Bureau. In his memoirs, as in his yearly reports, he sought to explain what his agency's work was and, more guardedly, what it should have been. Howard worked hard on those reports. They reveal much about the quality of the work with the freedmen as well as the quantity and are available as House Executive Documents, *Report of the Commissioner of the Bureau of Refugees, Freedmen and Abandoned Lands,* 1 Nov. 1865, 39th Cong., 1st sess. (serial 1255); 1 Nov. 1866, 39th Cong., 2nd sess. (serial 1285); 2 Dec. 1867, 40th Cong., 2nd sess. (serial 1324); 14 Oct. 1868, 40th Cong., 3rd sess. (serial 1367); 20 Oct. 1869, 41st Cong., 2nd sess. (serial 1412); 20 Oct. 1870, 41st Cong., 3rd sess. (serial 1446); 20 Oct. 1871, 42nd Cong., 2nd sess. (serial 1503).

The "blueprint" for the Freedmen's Bureau was the *Report of the Freedmen's Inquiry Commission,* 22 June 1864, 38th Cong., 1st sess., Senate Executive Document 53 (serial 1176). Important in the history of the Bureau are *Report of the Joint Committee on Reconstruction,* 30 April 1866, 39th Cong., 1st sess., House Report 30 (serial 1273); *Memphis Riots and Massacres,* Report of the Select Committee, 39th Cong., 1st sess., House Report 101 (serial 1274); *New Orleans Riots,* Report of the Board of Investigation, 39th Cong., 2nd sess., House Executive Document 69 (serial 1292); and *New Orleans Riots,* Report of the Select Committee, 39th Cong., 2nd sess., House Report 16 (serial 1304). Charges against General Howard are in *Report of the Committee on Education and Labor,* 13 July 1870, 41st Cong., 2nd sess., House Report 121 (serial 1438). Also consulted were the *Official Records of the Rebellion,* the *United States Statutes at Large,* and the *Congressional Globe.*

Published Reports

Information on predecessor organizations of the Bureau was in *Report of the Board of Education for the Freedmen, Department of the Gulf for the Year 1864* (New Orleans, 1865); T. W. Conway, *Report on the Condition of the Freedmen of the Department of the Gulf,* dated 9 Sept. 1864 (New Orleans, 1864), and Thomas W. Conway, *Final Report of the Bureau of Free Labor, Department of the Gulf,* dated 1 July 1865 (New Orleans, 1865). J. W. Alvord's much cited *Letters from the South Relating to the Condition of Freedmen* (Washington, D. C., 1870) gave an appraisal of the Negroes by the Bureau's General Superintendent of Education.

Alvord's several semiannual reports on Freedmen's schools published by the Government Printing Office were also helpful.

General Howard and his lawyer replied to charges against the Commissioner's conduct as head of the Bureau in *Statement of Br. Maj. Gen. O. O. Howard Before the Committee on Education and Labor . . . and Argument of Edgar Ketchum Esq.* (New York, 1870). Included are remarks praising Howard made in the House of Representatives by Congressmen G. F. Hoar, W. Townsend, John A. Peters, and J. P. C. Shanks.

Periodicals and Pamphlets

The journals of several of the freedmen's aid societies revealed more of their approach to the freedmen than secondary works consulted. *The National Freedmen,* the journal of the New York Freedman's Relief Association (running from March 1865 to September 1866), *The American Freedman,* the organ of the merged American Freedman's Union Commission, and the American Missionary Association's *The American Missionary* were of particular value. The pamphlet by James McKaye, *The Mastership and Its Fruits: The Emancipated Slave Face to Face with His Old Master* (New York, 1864) told of the distressed conditions of the Negroes in the Mississippi Valley. R. S. Rust, *The Freedmen's Aid Society of the Methodist Episcopal Church* (New York, 1880) reveals an attitude of responsibility to prepare "five million of freedmen for the duties of Christian citizenship." The removal of Negro students from the "demoralizing influences" of their homes was considered desirable. One goal was the preparation of Negro missionaries for Africa. An interesting early call for the distribution of land to the Negroes is Elizur Wright, Jr.'s *The Programme of Peace by a Democrat of the Old School* (Boston, 1862).

Newspapers

The *New Orleans Tribune* (*La Tribune de la N. Orleans*), a most impressive newspaper, voiced the Negro position eloquently. The Augusta, Georgia, *Loyal Georgian* was also helpful. The Washington *Evening Star,* sympathetic to the Bureau, was the best news source of information on its activities. The deterioration of the *Star's* attitude toward the freedmen is revealing. Its rivals, the Washington *Daily Intelligencer* and the *Washington Daily Morning Chronicle,* were also helpful.

The *Philadelphia Inquirer* was particularly useful for General Howard's appeal for support in the city in which he had perhaps his greatest backing. Henry Boynton's Abolitionist Cincinnati *Daily Gazette* led a vendetta against the General's integration efforts.

The Bureau used the *New York Tribune* as an outlet for its position on controversial issues. The *New York Times* was a major source of information.

The London *Pall Mall Gazette,* which Henry Wilson and Lyman Trumbull followed, favored Presidential Reconstruction. James G. Blaine's Augusta, Maine, *Kennebec Journal* provided a background on Howard's state. In New Orleans, where there was a rich range of papers, the New Orleans *True Delta* and the *New Orleans Times* were helpful.

In the Howard Papers is a scrapbook of news clippings. Clearly many are from Negro newspapers in the South, although the name of the paper is often missing. These were helpful not only because they revealed the freedmen's attitudes, but also because they disclosed how well posted the Commissioner was on his clients' affairs.

Theodore Tilton's *The Independent* in New York and *The Commonwealth* in Boston voiced pronegro opinion in the North.

Collected Letters and Contemporary Accounts

The following works added to the understanding of Howard as a wartime leader: M. A. DeWolfe Howe, ed., *Home Letters of General Sherman* (New York, 1909); David P. Conyngham, *Sherman's March Through the South* (New York, 1865); George W. Pepper, *Personal Recollections of Sherman's Campaign in Georgia and the Carolinas* (Zanesville, 1866); John G. Barrett, *Sherman's March Through the Carolinas* (Chapel Hill, 1956); Katherine M. Jones, ed., *When Sherman Came: Southern Women and the "Great March"* (Indianapolis, 1964); Rachel Sherman Thorndike, ed., *The Sherman Letters* (Boston, 1894); and Mark DeWolfe Howe, ed., *Touched With Fire: Civil War Letters and Diary of Oliver Wendell Holmes, Jr., 1861–1864* (Cambridge, 1946).

Ward Thoron, ed., *The Letters of Mrs. Henry Adams, 1865–1883* (Boston, 1936) contains a colorful description of the Grand Review. The following provided rich information on conditions in the

South: J. T. Trowbridge, *The South: A Tour of Its Battlefields and Ruined Cities, A Journey Through the Desolated States and Talks with the People* (Hartford, 1866); Whitelaw Reid, *After the War: A Southern Tour, May 1, 1865 to May 1, 1866,* ed. C. Vann Woodward (New York, 1965); Henrietta Stratton Jaquette, ed., *South After Gettysburg: Letters of Cornelia Hancock 1863–1868* (New York, 1956); Eliza Frances Andrews, *The War-Time Journal of a Georgia Girl, 1864–1865,* ed. Spencer Bidwell King, Jr. (Macon, 1960); Charles Stearns, *The Man of the South, and the Rebels* (New York, 1872); and Edward King, *The Great South* (London, 1875).

One of the other excursions in Henry Edwin Tremain's *Two Days of War: A Gettysburg Narrative and Other Excursions* (New York, 1905) was to the Sea Islands, and there is much valuable information on the land question here. Joseph Schafer, ed., *Intimate Letters of Carl Schurz* (Madison, 1928) and Frederic Bancroft, ed., *Speeches, Correspondence, and Political Papers of Carl Schurz* (6 vols. New York, 1913) are particularly valuable on the development of an organized resistance to President Johnson in the late fall of 1865. In his *The New South* (New York, 1885), Carl Schurz offers an interesting contrast to his views in the year the war ended.

John William DeForest, *A Union Officer in the Reconstruction,* eds. James H. Croushore and David M. Potter (New Haven, 1948) is a collection of the novelist's account of his work for the Bureau in South Carolina. Isabel C. Barrows, ed., *First Mohonk Conference on the Negro Question* (Boston, 1890) is a fascinating compendium of comments on the Negro at a conference attended by General Howard, ex-President Hayes, Albion Tourgee, Elizabeth Hyde Botume, and others.

*Special Studies Relating to the Freedmen
and the Freedmen's Bureau*

Prior to George R. Bentley's *A History of the Freedmen's Bureau* (Philadelphia, 1955), there was only one study on the agency as a whole—Paul S. Peirce, *The Freedmen's Bureau: A Chapter in the History of Reconstruction* (Iowa City, 1904). Bentley was the first scholar to explore deeply the records of the Bureau in the National Archives, and the present inquiry, which does not attempt to duplicate his explanation of the working of the agency, owes much to

Bentley's detailed study. Differences in interpretation are discussed in the introduction.

Bentley's book, together with the Cox articles, John and LaWanda Cox, "General O. O. Howard and the 'Misrepresented Bureau,'" *JSH*, 19 (1953), 427–56, and LaWanda Cox, "The Promise of Land for the Freedmen," *MVHR*, 45 (1958), 413–40, also discussed in the introduction, are part of a whole new season of writing on the Freedmen's Bureau. Careful reevaluations of the agency in the various states have been undertaken and proved of great usefulness in analyzing the goals and achievements of the men who led the Bureau. Unfortunately, in seeking to update the work of the Dunning School, many of the new state studies, while eschewing white racial superiority, neither achieve a firm new viewpoint nor exhibit the richness of detail of the best of the famous turn-of-the-century books on Reconstruction. In the better work on the period, scholars are at last remembering to ask how the freedmen felt about the Freedmen's Bureau and other matters of importance to them.

South Carolina has received far and away the best attention from Reconstruction scholars. Francis B. Simkins and Robert H. Woody's *South Carolina During Reconstruction* (Chapel Hill, 1932), which replaced John S. Reynolds' *Reconstruction in South Carolina, 1865–1877* (Columbia, 1905), is still useful, but a very different picture is emerging from the excellent scholarly treatment of this state. Willie Lee Rose's *Rehearsal for Reconstruction: The Port Royal Experiment* (Indianapolis, 1964) is a superb account of the freedmen's life on the Sea Islands during and after the war. When the planters left, Northerners sought to define a new way of life for the ex-slaves and optimistically expected the nation to adopt for the postwar South those programs that could be demonstrated to work. Another important book, Joel Williamson, *After Slavery: The Negro in South Carolina During Reconstruction, 1861–1877* (Chapel Hill, 1965), is based on a close reading of plantation manuscripts. The Sea Islands were unique because they provided the Negroes with a wartime divorce from their old masters, but Williamson tells us much about the planters and the ex-slaves on the mainland, where there was never a break in their day-by-day relationship with one another. The best of the new state studies, just published, is Martin L. Abbott's *The Freedmen's Bureau in South Carolina, 1865–1872* (Chapel Hill, 1967). Also helpful are Abbott's "Free Land, Free Labor and the Freedmen's Bureau," *Agricultural History, 30* (1956), 150–57, and "The Freedmen's Bureau and Negro Schooling in South Carolina," *South Carolina Historical Magazine, 57* (1956), 65–81; Alrutheus A. Taylor's *The Negro in South Carolina During Reconstruction* (Washington, D.C., 1924); Luther P. Jackson's "The Educational Efforts of the Freedmen's Bureau and Freedmen's Aid Societies in South Carolina, 1862–1872," *Journal of Negro History, 8* (1923), 1–40; and Laura J. Webster's *The Operation of the Freedmen's Bureau in South Carolina* (Northampton, 1916).

Mississippi has long been distinguished by Vernon L. Wharton's clear-sighted study, happily now available in paperback, *The Negro in Mississippi: 1865–1890* (New York, 1965). Unfortunately, the book has little on the Freedmen's Bureau, and there is no published study to update James W. Garner, *Reconstruction in Mississippi* (New York, 1901).

Louisiana holds fascinating stories to be told, which might give us information on the interesting contrasts between urban and rural Negro society during and after the Civil War. The Banks administration, which, unfortunately, probably yielded as many precedents for bureau policy as the Port Royal experiment, badly needs study. See Gerald M. Capers' *Occupied City: New Orleans Under the Federals, 1862–1865* (Lexington, 1965); T. Harry Williams, "General Banks and the Radical Republicans in the Civil War," *New England Quarterly, 12* (1939), 268–80; and Charles Kassel, "The Labor System of General Banks: A Lost Episode of Civil War History," *The Open Court, 42* (1928), 35–50. A most interesting group of biographical sketches of Negro leaders in Reconstruction New Orleans is Rodolphe L. Desdunes' *Nos Hommes et Notre Histoire* (Montreal, 1911).

Still highly reliable, although wrongheaded, and a model of careful scholarship is John R. Ficklen's *History of Reconstruction in Louisiana* (Baltimore, 1910). Unluckily, Roger W. Shugg chose to regard the Negroes as a separate caste and did not treat them as another laboring group in his discerning *Origins of Class Struggle in Louisiana* (Baton Rouge, 1939). His "Survival of the Plantation System in Louisiana," *JSH, 3* (1937), 311–25, is an important earlier statement of his theme, revealing how much of the freedmen's economic subservience remained after slavery ended.

Louis R. Harlan's "Desegregation in New Orleans Public Schools During Reconstruction," *AHR* 67 (1962), 663–75, is a critical article suggesting how wide Negroes' hopes for freedom were and how great their disappointment was to be. Of Howard A. White's two useful studies, "The Freedmen's Bureau in New Orleans," Unpublished M.A. thesis (Tulane University, 1950), is more sharply focused than "The Freedmen's Bureau in Louisiana," Unpublished Ph.D. dissertation (Tulane University, 1955). Willie M. Caskey's *Secession and Restoration of Louisiana* (Baton Rouge, 1938) is as useful, particularly on political matters, as Donald E. Everett's "Demands of the New Orleans Free Colored Population for Political Equality, 1862–1865," *Louisiana Historical Quarterly*, 38 (1955), 43–64. John C. Engelsman, "The Freedmen's Bureau in Louisiana," *Louisiana Historical Quarterly*, 32 (1949), 145–224, has useful data on the home colonies.

Wager Swayne, who held his assistant commissionership longer than any other man in the Bureau, deserves closer attention than he has been paid by students of Reconstruction in Alabama. Walter L. Fleming's old study, *Civil War and Reconstruction in Alabama* (New York, 1905), has been partly updated by Elizabeth Bethel in "The Freedmen's Bureau in Alabama," *JSH, 14* (1948), 49–92. Also see Horace Mann Bond's *Negro Education in Alabama: A Study in Cotton and Steel* (Washington, D.C., 1939) and "Social and Economic Forces in Alabama Reconstruction," *Journal of Negro History*, 23 (1938), 290–348. Thomas B. Alexander's essay, "Persistent Whiggery in Alabama and the Lower South, 1860–1867," *Alabama Review, 12* (1959), 35–52, is a perceptive study of the group with which, it appears, Swayne got on well.

Arkansas too has been neglected; see Thomas S. Staples, *Reconstruction in Arkansas, 1862–1874* (New York, 1923). Alan Conway's *The Reconstruction of Georgia* (Minneapolis, 1966) updates C. Mildred Thompson's *Reconstruction in Georgia: Economic, Social, Political, 1865–1872* (New York, 1915), but a study that would contrast the Saxton and Tillson administrations is still needed. E. Merton Coulter's *Civil War and Readjustment in Kentucky* (Chapel Hill, 1962) treats half of Clinton Fisk's bureau domain. Tennessee has had more attention: T. B. Alexander, *Political Reconstruction in Tennessee* (Nashville, 1950); A. A. Taylor, *The Negro in Tennessee, 1865–1880* (Washington, D.C., 1941); Weymouth T. Jordan, "The Freedmen's Bureau in Tennessee," *East Tennessee Historical Society Publications, 11* (1939), 47–61; and Paul D. Phillips, "A History of the Freedmen's Bureau in Tennessee," Unpublished Ph.D. dissertation (Vanderbilt University, 1964), a helpful study. Gerald M. Capers, *The Biography of a River Town* (Chapel Hill, 1939), describes Reconstruction. Memphis and the riot is discussed in Jack D. L. Holmes' "The Underlying Causes of the Memphis Race Riot of 1866," *Tennessee Historical Quarterly, 18* (1958), 195–221.

Another work by A. A. Taylor is *The Negro in the Reconstruction of Virginia* (Washington, D.C., 1926); to the outdated Hamilton J. Eckenrode, *The Political History of Virginia During Reconstruction* (Baltimore, 1904) has been added the important work by William T. Alderson, "The Influence of Military Rule and the Freedmen's Bureau on Reconstruction in Virginia, 1865–1870, Unpublished Ph.D. dissertation (Vanderbilt University, 1952). Alderson, an admirer of Johnsonian Reconstruction (or at least of the moderation which he thought characterized it), has made the important contribution of documenting that the agents of Radical Reconstruction, the military commanders, did more than the radicals' archenemy Johnson had been able to do to frustrate radical social programs. Unlike James E. Sefton's recently published *The United States Army and Reconstruction, 1865–1877* (Baton Rouge, 1967), Alderson is under no illusion that the army men were nonpolitical during Reconstruction. He credits General Schofield with doing more than any Virginian in determining Virginia's unique political adjustment to Radical Reconstruction. Also helpful was Alderson's more conventional study, "The Freedmen's Bureau and Negro Education in Virginia," *North Carolina Historical Review, 29* (1962), 64–90.

Florida was not densely populated, and much of the attention paid to that state has been speculation about colonization of Negroes in its then empty southern region. Unfortunately the only full-length treatment of colonization in this period is Willis D. Boyd's "Negro Colonization in the National Crisis, 1860–1870," Unpublished Ph.D. dissertation (University of California, Los Angeles, 1953), which deals almost entirely with the rather feeble efforts of the American Colonization Society to send freedmen to Africa. See also Boyd's "Negro Colonization in the Reconstruction Era, 1865–1870,"

Georgia Historical Quarterly, 40 (1956), 360–82. A study of domestic Negro colonies and of the freedmen as homesteaders is still
needed. The best recent studies of the freedmen in Florida are by
Joe M. Richardson: "The Negro in the Reconstruction of Florida,"
Unpublished Ph.D. dissertation (Florida State University, 1963);
"The Freedmen's Bureau and Negro Labor in Florida," *Florida
Historical Quarterly,* 39 (1960), 167–74; and "An Evaluation of
the Freedmen's Bureau in Florida," *Florida Historical Quarterly,* 41
(1963), 223–38. These importantly replace William W. Davis. *The
Civil War and Reconstruction in Florida* (New York, 1913). Also
see George F. Bentley, "The Political Activity of the Freedmen's
Bureau in Florida," *Florida Historical Quarterly,* 28 (1949–50),
28–37.

The only helpful study of the Bureau in Texas is Claude Elliott's
"The Freedmen's Bureau in Texas," *Southwestern Historical Quarterly,* 56 (1962), 1–24. Charles W. Ramsdell, *Reconstruction in
Texas* (New York, 1910), and W. C. Nunn, *Texas Under the Car-
petbaggers* (Austin, 1962) were also consulted. Another state badly
in need of a close study is Eliphalet Whittlesey's North Carolina.
J. G. de Roulhac Hamilton's *Reconstruction in North Carolina*
(Raleigh, 1906) is understandably out of date. The rich manuscript
collections in that state, together with Whittlesey's personality, almost guarantee a colorful story.

The story of the Bureau in Washington, D.C., has also been neglected. James H. Whyte, *The Uncivil War: Washington During
Reconstruction, 1865–1878* (New York, 1958), an important book
which exposes the tragedy of the end of home rule in the capital,
has important information on the bankruptcy of the Freedman's
Savings Bank in which O. O. Howard and his friends Henry D. and
Jay Cooke played an important role. Constance McLaughlin Green's
fascinating *Washington: Village and Capital, 1800–1878* (Prince-
ton, 1962) was also helpful, and even more relevant is her *The
Secret City: A History of Race Relations in the Nation's Capital*
(Princeton, 1967). Useful too was Lillian G. Dabney's *The History
of Schools for Negroes in the District of Columbia, 1807–1947*
(Washington, D.C., 1949). W. A. Lowe, "The Freedmen's Bureau
and Civil Rights in Maryland," *Journal of Negro History,* 37
(1952), 221–76, and "The Freedmen's Bureau and Education in
Maryland," *Maryland Historical Magazine,* 47 (1952), 29–39, treats
the agency in that border state.

Land for the freedmen has not yet been fully treated. Paul W. Gates' *Agriculture and the Civil War* (New York, 1965) is helpful, as is his "Federal Land Policy in the South, 1866–1888," *JSH, 6* (1940), 303–30; C. Vann Woodward's *Origins of the New South, 1877–1913* (Baton Rouge, 1951) tells of the agricultural patterns immediately after Reconstruction. See also James S. Allen, "The Struggle for Land During the Reconstruction Period," *Science and Society, 1* (1937), 378–401; Manuel Gottleib, "The Land Question in Georga During Reconstruction," *Science and Society, 3* (1939), 356–88; and the Cox article, "The Promise of Land for the Freedmen," mentioned above. Needed are a work in intellectual history dealing with the meaning of land to the freedmen (and indeed, to all Americans in the nineteenth century) and an economic historian's study of the bridge from slavery to sharecropping.

Biographies and Memoirs

In pursuit of both major and minor assistance, the biographies and memoirs following were consulted. Blanche Ames Ames' *Adelbert Ames, 1835–1933* (New York, 1964) adds little to explain Howard's political ties to his distant cousin. Samuel Chapman Armstrong, who founded Hampton Institute with bureau help, is the subject of several uncritical studies. Edith Armstrong Talbot's *Samuel Chapman Armstrong* (New York, 1904) is the most valuable, particularly in revealing bureau attitudes toward the freedmen. Francis Greenwood Peabody, in *Samuel Chapman Armstrong* (Boston, 1898), suggests that Armstrong viewed his scholars as his missionary family in Hawaii viewed the Polynesians. Armstrong's own *Education for Life* (Hampton, 1914) is also revealing.

Harold Francis Williamson, in *Edward Atkinson: The Biography of an American Liberal* (Boston, 1934), tells of a man of the sort Howard looked to for aiding the freedmen. Both James G. Blaine, *Twenty Years of Congress* (2 vols. Norwich, Conn., 1884–86), and Harriet S. Blaine Beale, ed., *Letters of Mrs. James G. Blaine* (2 vols., New York, 1908), were useful. Mrs. Blaine had a nephew in the Bureau, and both she and her husband saw a good deal of the Howards. Frank A. Rollin, in *Life and Public Services of Martin R. Delany, Sub-Assistant Commissioner, Bureau Relief of Refugees, Freedmen, and of Abandoned Lands, and Late Major 104th U.S. Colored Troops* (Boston, 1883), tells of one influential Negro leader, and Philip S. Foner's *The Life and Writings of Frederick*

Douglass (4 vols., New York, 1950–55) is the chief source for information on the great Negro leader of the nineteenth century. Philip Wade Alexander, in "John Eaton, Jr., Preacher, Soldier and Educator," Unpublished Ph.D. dissertation (George Peabody College for Teachers, 1939), adds little to Eaton's own very valuable memoirs, John Eaton, *Grant, Lincoln and the Freedmen* (New York, 1907). Awaited is Helen C. Walker's study of Eaton and the freedmen in Tennessee.

Charles A. Jellison, *Fessenden of Maine* (Syracuse, 1962) updates Francis Fessenden, *Life and Public Services of William Pitt Fessenden, Senator from Maine* (2 vols. Boston, 1907). Alphonso A. Hopkins' *The Life of Clinton Bowen Fisk* (New York, 1890) would be merely quaint if it did not often quote the Assistant Commissioner. Also consulted were the following: Walter Merrill, *Against Wind and Tide: A Biography of William Lloyd Garrison* (Cambridge, 1963); Russel B. Nye, *William Lloyd Garrison and the Humanitarian Reformers* (Boston, 1955); John L. Thomas, *The Liberator: William Lloyd Garrison* (Boston, 1963). The last work is a probing study of Abolitionism as well as one of its leaders. Ulysses S. Grant, *Personal Memoirs,* ed. E. B. Long (Cleveland, 1952) tells something of the beginnings of the work with the freedmen under the armies of the West.

General Howard, for whom so much failed, succeeded with his memoirs. Oliver Otis Howard's *Autobiography of Oliver Otis Howard* (2 vols. New York, 1908) is a distinguished work. John A. Carpenter's *Sword and Olive Branch: Oliver Otis Howard* (Pittsburgh, 1964) is a scholarly, laudatory book. Robert W. Winston's *Andrew Johnson Plebeian and Patriot* (New York, 1928), George Fort Milton's *The Age of Hate: Andrew Johnson and the Radicals* (New York, 1930), and Lloyd P. Stryker's *Andrew Johnson: A Study in Courage* (New York, 1929) all prove how much a point of view can change within a generation. With the needs of the Negroes front and center, Johnson is a different man, and even Eric L. McKitrick in his most perceptive study, *Andrew Johnson and Reconstruction* (Chicago, 1960), which does not purport to be a biography, does not get to the bottom of racial matters in the seventeenth President's administration.

Another Reconstruction figure who needs sober reassessment is John Mercer Langston. His job in the Freedmen's Bureau was more important than is sometimes realized, while his contribution to equality may have been less so. Langston's own memoirs are *Autobiography: Intellectual, Moral, Spiritual* (London, 1882) and *From the Virginia Plantation to the National Capitol* (Hartford, 1894).

George Francis Dawson's *Life and Services of Gen. John A. Logan* (Chicago, 1887) was helpful on the general with whom Howard did not get along. Virginia W. Johnson, *The Unregimented General: A Biography of Nelson A. Miles* (Boston, 1962) tells little of the bureau service of the Indian fighter. Benjamin F. Perry, *Reminiscences of Public Men with Speeches and Addresses* (Greenville, S.C., 1889) and Lillian Adele Kibler, *Benjamin Franklin Perry, South Carolina Unionist* (Durham, 1946) were helpful on the Governor with whom Rufus Saxton found it hard to work. Robert F. Durden, *James Shepherd Pike: Republicanism and the American Negro, 1850–1882* (Durham, 1957) treats the man who contributed much to the distortion of the nation's picture of Reconstruction. John M. Schofield, *Forty-Six Years in the Army* (New York, 1897) is a valuable memoir of a conservative commander. The most interesting and loyal friend General Howard had was William Tecumseh Sherman, and his *Memoirs of General William T. Sherman* (2 vols. New York, 1886), like his letters to the Commissioner, reveal much about both men. Unlike Sherman, his antagonist Edwin M. Stanton did not show his hand—eloquently or otherwise. The sympathetic Benjamin P. Thomas and Harold W. Hyman's *Stanton: The Life and Times of Lincoln's Secretary of War* (New York, 1962) tells relatively little of the Secretary of War's views on the Freedmen's Bureau, which was in his department.

Willard Saxton spoke of the freedmen's affection for Thaddeus Stevens and viewed his death as an important turning point in their fortunes. Ralph Korngold, *Thaddeus Stevens: A Being Darkly Wise and Rudely Great* (New York, 1955), and Fawn M. Brodie, *Thaddeus Stevens: Scourge of the South* (New York, 1959), treat this extraordinary man. The Reconstruction views of a less colorful congressional leader, Lyman Trumbull, are still not fully explained. Helpful were Horace White's *The Life of Lyman Trumbull* (New York, 1913) and Mark M. Krug's *Lyman Trumbull: Conservative Radical* (New York, 1965). There is a job for a legal scholar on Trumbull's Thirteenth Amendment and its enforcement prior to Radical Reconstruction. Alexander M. Bickel, "The Original Understanding and the Segregation Decision," *Harvard Law Review*, 69 (1955), 1–65, and Laurent B. Frantz, "Congressional Power To Enforce the Fourteenth Amendment Against Private Acts," *Yale Law Journal*, 73 (1964), 1353–85 are two articles that have made the start. See also Charles Warren, *The Supreme Court in United States History* (2 vols. Boston, 1926). Everette Swinney, "Enforcing the Fifteenth Amendment, 1870–1877," *JSH*, 28 (1962), 202–12, suggests that many of the difficulties that the Freedmen's Bureau had in enforcing the earlier amendment were repeated.

Another important senator is the subject of H. L. Trefousse, *Benjamin Franklin Wade: Radical Republican from Ohio* (New York, 1963). Henry Clay Warmoth, *War, Politics, and Reconstruction: Stormy Days in Louisiana* (New York, 1930), although the autobiography of a scoundrel of a carpetbagger, tells little of how the Negroes gave him his start with their votes in 1865. Compiled by Gaillard Hunt, *Israel, Elihu and Cadwallader Washburn* [sic] (New York, 1925), contains some helpful information on Elihu Washburne, the congressman who investigated the Memphis riot. No longer taken as the gospel, Gideon Welles' *The Diary of Gideon Welles* (3 vols. Boston, 1911) is still valuable to an understanding of Presidential Reconstruction. Henry Wilson's historical works are as rich as his biography, Elias Nason, *The Life and Public Services of Henry Wilson* (Boston, 1876), is useless. Wilson deserves a good modern biographer.

General Works

The Second Reconstruction inspired a good deal of scholarly attention to the First. Trying to convince ourselves that the nation's new and much more successful effort to grant its Negroes equality has accomplished more than it has, there has been a tendency to be overly sanguine in applauding, as allies, those who seemed to side with the freedmen last time. Kenneth M. Stampp's *The Era of Reconstruction, 1865–1877* (New York, 1965) has this failing, but in other respects it is an important corrective and very ably gives "general currency to the findings of scholars during the past few decades." Two other valuable syntheses are John Hope Franklin, *Reconstruction: After the Civil War* (Chicago, 1961), and Rembert W. Patrick, *The Reconstruction of the Nation* (New York, 1967). Stampp's bibliographical note updates the well-known bibliography in J. G. Randall and David Donald's *The Civil War and Recon-struction* (Boston, 1961). No attempt is made in this note to dis-cuss comprehensively the historical literature of the period.

The following were helpful in seeking to appraise the problems of the freedmen's adjustment to the end of slavery: Frank Tannen-baum, *Slave and Citizen: The Negro in The Americas* (New York, 1946); Abram Kardiner and Lionel Ovesey, *The Mark of Oppres-sion: Explorations in the Personality of the American Negro* (Cleve-land, 1964); Leon F. Litwack, *North of Slavery: The Negro in the Free States, 1790–1860* (Chicago, 1961); Charles W. Wesley, *Negro Labor in the United States, 1850–1925* (New York, 1927); Nathan Glazer and Daniel Patrick Moynihan, *Beyond the Melting Pot: The Negroes, Puerto Ricans, Jews, Italians, and Irish of New York City* (Cambridge, 1963); Stanley M. Elkins, *Slavery: A Prob-lem in American Institutional and Intellectual Life* (New York, 1963); Eugene D. Genovese, *The Political Economy of Slavery* (New York, 1964); W. Kloosterboer, *Involuntary Labor Since the Abolition of Slavery Throughout the World* (Leiden, 1960); Bell Irvin Wiley, *Southern Negroes, 1861–1865* (New Haven, 1938); Benjamin Quarles, *The Negro in the Civil War* (Boston, 1953); James M. McPherson, *The Negro's Civil War* (New York, 1965). Henderson H. Donald uncritically accepts the stereotype of the im-provident ex-slave in *The Negro Freedman* (New York, 1952).

The brilliant study by George M. Frederickson, *The Inner Civil War: Northern Intellectuals and the Crisis of the Union* (New York, 1965), does much to break up fuzzy myths of leaders of the white North. James M. McPherson's *The Struggle for Equality: Aboli-tionists and the Negro in the Civil War and Reconstruction* (Prince-ton, 1954) was helpful although few bureau men were Abolition-ists. John G. Sproat's "Blueprint for Radical Reconstruction," *JSH,* 23 (1957), 25–44, is the best study of the agency's origins. Henry L. Swint's *The Northern Teacher in the South, 1862–1870* (Nash-ville, 1941) has valuable information on the teachers in the bureau-assisted schools.

Timothy L. Smith's *Revivalism and Social Reform in Mid-Nine-teenth-Century America* (New York, 1957) suggests that America was ready in 1865 for a wide attack on social injustice by all of the major Protestant denominations. General Howard, appealing to exactly the group Smith describes, made the same miscalculation.

Ira V. Brown's *Lyman Abbott: Christian Evolutionist: A Study in Religious Liberalism* (Cambridge, 1953) and "Lyman Abbott and Freedmen's Aid, 1865–1869," *JSH*, 15 (1949), 22–38, suggest the essentially conservative nature of those who were expected to assist the freedmen. Richard Bryant Drake in "The American Missionary Association and the Southern Negro, 1861–1888," Unpublished Ph.D. dissertation (Emory University, 1957), tends to overpraise the American Missionary Association at the expense of the secular friends of the freedmen. Ralph E. Morrow's *Northern Methodism and Reconstruction* (East Lansing, 1956) is an important study of one major denomination.

Three old studies, out of date but curiously provocative, are John W. Burgess, *Reconstruction and the Constitution, 1866–1876* (New York, 1902); Walter L. Fleming, *The Freedmen's Savings Bank: A Chapter in the Economic History of the Negro Race* (Chapel Hill, 1927); and James S. Allen, *Reconstruction: The Battle for Democracy, 1865–1876* (New York, 1937).

Georges Clemenceau's *American Reconstruction, 1865–1870* (New York, 1928) is a stimulating look at Reconstruction by a European; W. R. Brock's *An American Crisis: Congress and Reconstruction, 1865–1867* (London, 1963) is another. Like McKitrick's *Andrew Johnson and Reconstruction,* mentioned above, LaWanda and John Cox's *Politics, Principle, and Prejudice, 1865–1866* (New York 1963) is an important reappraisal of the administration of the seventeenth President. George R. Woolfolk's *The Cotton Regency: The Northern Merchants and Reconstruction, 1865–1880* (New York, 1958) and Robert P. Sharkey's *Money, Class, and Party: An Economic Study of Civil War and Reconstruction* (Baltimore, 1959) are two books, which, although very unlike, prohibit quick generalizations about businessmen with whom the Bureau dealt. Edmund Wilson's *Patriotic Gore: Studies in the Literature of the American Civil War* (New York, 1962), provocative in many ways, was informative on Howard's teacher, Calvin Stowe, and his loyal commander, William Tecumseh Sherman. W. E. B. DuBois' *The Souls of Black Folk* (London, 1905), discussed in the introduction, and his *Black Reconstruction in America* (New York, 1935) long ago focused attention where it belonged—on the freedmen in Reconstruction.

Index

AMERICAN HISTORY TITLES IN THE NORTON LIBRARY

Samuel Flagg Bemis *The Latin American Policy of the United States* N412

Ray Allen Billington, Ed. *The Reinterpretation of Early American History* N446

Fawn Brodie *Thaddeus Stevens* N331

Robert E. Brown *Charles Beard and the Constitution* N296

Edmund Cody Burnett *The Continental Congress* N278

Richard L. Bushman *From Puritan to Yankee: Character and the Social Order in Connecticut, 1690-1765* N532

George W. Cable *The Negro Question: A Selection of Writings on Civil Rights in the South* N420

Mark Lincoln Chadwin *The Warhawks: American Interventionists Before Pearl Harbor* N546

Dudley T. Cornish *The Sable Arm: Negro Troops in the Union Army, 1861-1865* N334

John Paton Davies, Jr. *Foreign and Other Affairs* N330

Dwight Lowell Dumond *Antislavery* N370

Herbert Feis *Contest Over Japan* N466

Herbert Feis *The Diplomacy of the Dollar* N333

Herbert Feis *The Spanish Story* N339

Herbert Feis *Three International Episodes: Seen from E. A.* N351

Robert H. Ferrell *American Diplomacy in the Great Depression: Hoover-Stimson Foreign Policy, 1929-1933* N511

Robert H. Ferrell *Peace in Their Time: The Origins of the Kellogg-Briand Pact* N491

Dewey W. Grantham *The Democratic South* N299

Fletcher Green *Constitutional Development in the South Atlantic States, 1776-1860* N348

Michael Garibaldi Hall *Edward Randolph and the American Colonies, 1676-1703* N480

Holman Hamilton *Prologue to Conflict: The Crisis and Compromise of 1850* N345

Pendleton Herring *The Politics of Democracy* N306

Preston J. Hubbard *Origins of the TVA: The Muscle Shoals Controversy, 1920-1932* N467

Rufus Jones *The Quakers in the American Colonies* N356

George F. Kennan *Realities of American Foreign Policy* N320

Gabriel Kolko *Railroads and Regulation, 1877-1916* N531